Social Situations

to Rom Harré

Social Situations

MICHAEL ARGYLE
*Reader in Social Psychology in the University of Oxford
and Fellow of Wolfson College*

ADRIAN FURNHAM
Department of Experimental Psychology, University of Oxford

JEAN ANN GRAHAM
Department of Experimental Psychology, University of Oxford

CAMBRIDGE UNIVERSITY PRESS
CAMBRIDGE
LONDON   NEW YORK   NEW ROCHELLE
MELBOURNE   SYDNEY

Published by the Press Syndicate of the University of Cambridge
The Pitt Building, Trumpington Street, Cambridge CB2 1RP
32 East 57th Street, New York, NY 10022, USA
296 Beaconsfield Parade, Middle Park, Melbourne 3206, Australia

First published 1981

Phototypeset in V.I.P. Plantin by
Western Printing Services Ltd, Bristol
Printed in Great Britain at the
University Press, Cambridge

British Library Cataloguing in Publication Data
Argyle, Michael
Social situations.
1. Social psychology
I. Title II. Furnham, Adrian
III. Graham, Jean Ann
301.1   HM251   80-40882

ISBN 0 521 23260 0 hard covers
ISBN 0 521 29881 4 paperback

Contents

v

Contents

Contents

Preface

It is now familiar from many lines of research that social situations have a great impact on all aspects of behaviour, but little is known about how to describe or analyse situations. In social-skills training, for example, it is common to find clients who have difficulties with particular situations, but it is not always clear how they should be instructed to cope with these situations.

This book reports a new approach to the analysis of social situations, a related programme of research which was financed by the SSRC, and it reviews other research on situations. Our own main studies are described in the form of research reports at the ends of chapters.

As well as contributing to the understanding of social behaviour, situational analysis is important for the analysis of personality. In addition it has widespread practical applications, to social-skills training, mental health and deviance, intergroup behaviour, personnel selection and consumer research.

We are most grateful to Michael Brenner, Anne Campbell, Peter Collett, David Clarke, Jerry Ginsburg, Peter Hancock, Rom Harré, Miles Hewstone, Jos Jaspars, Marga Kreckel, Peter Marsh, David Pendleton and Greg Young for their ideas, collaboration with research and comments on the manuscript. Our thanks also go to Ann McKendry for making sense of and typing innumerable redrafts of assorted scraps of paper.

Oxford, November 1979   M.A.
                                                            A.F.
                                                            J.A.G.

1

Introduction

A number of recent studies by Milgram, Zimbardo and others have demonstrated the extraordinary extent to which behaviour is affected by situations. If we want to explain and understand social behaviour we must explain how situations influence it.

The experiment by Milgram (1974) showed that normal members of the public would give what they thought were near-fatal electric shocks to another person in 65 per cent of cases, if ordered to do so by the experimenter. In the experiment by Zimbardo (1973) normal university students, who were asked to play the role of prison guards, did so in such a tyrannical way that others, students ordered to be convicts, became emotionally distressed, and the experiment had to be terminated. Studies of religious sects show that people who are quite normal on week-days can speak with tongues, handle snakes and have near-psychotic experiences on Sundays (Argyle and Beit-Hallahmi, 1975).

An account of experimental studies of the effects of situations on behaviour is given in Chapter 3.

Why we need to analyse situations

There are several reasons why it would be useful to understand situations better. In our work on social-skills training we frequently came across people who could not cope with particular social situations – for example, parties, committee meetings, 'dates' (Trower, Bryant and Argyle, 1978). Sometimes they were mistaken about the purpose of these situations, or about the rules. We found that we had to explain situations to them, as best we could, as well as teach the skills involved. It was like teaching someone to play squash by first explaining the principles of the game and then teaching him how to hit the ball. Our scheme for analysing situations arose partly out of the need to explain situations to such social-skills trainees.

A second reason for our concern with situations was our interest in personality–situation interaction. Recent research in this area has produced important findings, for example that behaviour is at least as much determined by situation and personality–situation interaction as by general traits of personality. Functional relationships of the form $B = f(P,S)$ have been found, showing, for example, how anxiety is a joint function of trait anxiety

I

and the stressfulness of situations (Endler and Magnusson, 1976*b*). However, in order to take this approach any further we need to know the main situational variables, and the ways in which they combine with personality characteristics to produce behaviour. What exactly is it about 'dates' and the persons concerned which results in A avoiding them, B having rows in them and C enjoying himself enormously?

Traditional social psychology would also profit from the study of situations. It has often been assumed that general principles of social behaviour could be found, which would apply to all situations. Small-group research, based on laboratory experiments, did find some rather general principles, such as conformity and the formation of leadership hierarchies; on the other hand the study of work groups, families, groups of friends and therapy groups showed that further processes operated in each of these settings (Argyle, 1969). In the study of sequences of interaction in dyads it has been hoped similarly that some kind of universal grammar might be found. In Chapter 8 we discuss how far sequences of interaction are universal and how far they are dependent on the situation. One of the main questions we shall examine is whether features of social behaviour are universal and if so how far they vary between situations. Obviously some rules are different in different situations, but which ones exactly? Are there also any universal rules which apply to all situations? Language is used in nearly all situations, but how much does it vary in vocabulary, in grammar or other features? How does the situation in which we assess somebody's personality affect that assessment?

Lastly situational analysis would help with the solution of a number of practical problems. Environmental psychologists have succeeded in improving a number of situations, for example in prisons and hospitals, by changes in the physical environment. This could be taken a lot further by understanding how to control other aspects of situations. A number of areas of applied psychology can be helped by situational analysis – for example, personnel selection and consumer psychology. The treatment of mental patients and criminals has traditionally been carried out from an exclusively trait approach to personality. If situations and personality–situation interaction are just as important as traits in predicting behaviour, then we should be trying to modify situations that upset people or tempt them to break the law, and we should be trying to fit people or prepare them to deal with certain situations. We shall discuss developments of this kind in Chapter 13.

A note on the term 'situation'

There has recently been an unprecedented abuse and overuse of the term 'situation' in popular language and writing. In fact the word, alone or in conjunction with others such as 'ongoing', 'stable', etc., is used so often and so incorrectly that satirical magazines and newspapers regularly point to particularly amusing or meaningless examples of its use. It is used to signify any set of circumstances, and is often used as a shorthand or substitute for a better description. Etymologically the word means 'a place with its surroundings that is occupied by something', although according to the *Oxford English Dictionary* it may be used to describe any state of affairs in which one finds oneself.

Social psychologists have unfortunately also used the word to mean any naturally occurring and culturally understood behaviour sequence. As a result the term situation has become what Hardin (1956) called a 'panchreston' – an overgeneralised, vague word which is attempting to explain all, but essentially explains nothing. Certain definitions of the term 'social situation' have been made, for example:

1. Eysenck, Arnold and Meili (1972): 'A general term for the field of reference (stimuli, objects, fellow men, groups, values, etc.). . . of a person acting in society . . . the social situation may be defined by three categories of the data and the manner in which they are linked: (*a*) the actual data which influences the acting person, (*b*) the attitudes which are brought into play at the time of the act, and (*c*) the degree of ego involvement or awareness of the actual data and attitudes on the part of acting person' (p. 1008).

2. Goffman (1961*a*): 'By the term social situation I shall refer to the full spatial environment anywhere within which an entering person becomes a member of the gathering that is (or does then become) present. Situations begin when mutual monitoring occurs and lapse when the next to last person has left' (p. 144).

One possible way to overcome confusion, ambiguity, even ridicule, is to adopt another related term – scene, setting, episode, encounter, environmental condition – which may be associated with a particular theoretical or methodological position. However, because of the historical use of the term situation in social and personality psychology we shall continue to use it here.

A situation could be described as the sum of the features of a social occasion that impinge on an individual person. We shall consider some of these features in Chapter 2. However this description does not allow for the fact that a person contributes to the situation himself, so a better description might be the sum of the features of the behaviour system, for the duration of a social encounter. Some psychologists want to emphasise the perception of situations, so they might describe a situation in terms of an individual's perception of the features of a social encounter. Our emphasis is somewhat different. When social-skills trainees complain of social difficulties they refer to common social occasions such as 'going to the pub', 'meals at home', 'seeing the doctor', 'interviews', 'shopping', 'committee meetings', and other socially defined events. We shall be primarily concerned with common situations in the subculture, with which most people are familiar, and in which most social encounters take place. We shall see later that there is considerable agreement on the properties of such situations.

By situation we shall mean a type of social encounter with which members of a culture or subculture are familiar. There may be other kinds of encounter, with which most people are not familiar, which will be enigmatic situations for such people, though there is some evidence that they try to treat such encounters as instances of more familiar situations.

Previous approaches to situational analysis

There have been a number of previous approaches to the analysis of situations, which will be discussed in Chapter 2. The most widely used method of analysing situations hitherto has been multidimensional scaling, as used by Wish and Kaplan (1977) and others. Valuable as the dimensions are that emerge from these studies, we have not found them very useful in social-skills training, for example. Describing situations in terms of dimensions might lead to a description of a 'date' as social, cooperative and informal; this would not be of much help to someone who wanted to know how to handle this situation, any more than it would be a help to someone who wanted to know how to play squash to be told it was social, competitive and formal. And we foresaw a danger of 'trait' approaches to situations ending up with hundreds of alternative dimensions, as in trait approaches to personality.

A further problem with the dimensional approach to situations is that it seems possible that situations are discontinuous – like the elements of chemistry and unlike the dimensions of physics. Are there any games intermediate between chess and water-polo, or any social situations intermediate between a wedding and an auction sale?

Symbolic interactionists maintain that people *construct* situations, and negotiate a shared definition of the situation. We agree that participants do alter the nature of situations along dimensions like friendly – hostile, or tense – relaxed, within a given situational framework, for example a tennis lesson or a visit to the dentist. They may be able to modify the rules; for example a series of seminars, or family meals, may develop a local modification. In many conversations there is the gradual establishment of a shared vocabulary, and a body of information which can be taken for granted. We also agree that participants sometimes change the nature of the situation entirely, as when a philosophy tutorial turns into psychotherapy, or a tennis lesson into a love affair. However, when this happens there is a transition to another socially defined situational structure, rather like a change from tennis to squash; in each case there is a discontinuity. It is true that new situations gradually evolve in the culture, as in the case of 'brainstorming',

T-groups and encounter groups. The same is true of the gradual development of games, like rugby football. This and other previous approaches to situations are discussed in Chapter 2.

Mention should be made of two previous lines of work which are similar to ours. Barker and Wright (1954) and Barker (1968) developed a well-known method of surveying behaviour settings in a community. Our idea of a situation is similar to their behaviour setting, in being a culturally defined occasion with its special setting and rules. The Barker and Wright behaviour setting, however, appears to be a combination of typical behaviour and physical setting; we think that properties of the situation, like physical setting, should be used to explain and predict behaviour. And we want to include a number of other features in the analysis of situations, such as goals, rules and repertoire.

Schank and Abelson (1977) have been developing an artificial-intelligence approach to situations, to discover the precise information a person would need to eat a meal at a restaurant, for example. These authors use some of the same features as we do – plans and goals, and scripts. However their scheme does not deal with skills, difficulties or individual differences, or the inter-personal dynamics dealt with by our goal structure, and does not present a standardised method for analysing situations.

The main features of situations

There are a large number of possible features in a situation. Clearly we have to walk a knife-edge between partisan zealotry regarding one or two elements (roles, rules, etc.) and benevolent eclecticism which sees every minor variable as having a possibly important effect on behaviour. Some elements will always be more important in certain situations than in others, but if we neglect some elements in favour of one or two major ones we run the danger of having a biased view, and studying trivial variables.

It is important to decide, as Ginsburg (1980) has pointed out, whether the situation can be characterised independently of the people participating in it, because the features of situations may seem as if they are desires, traits or states of people. We can illustrate the problem with one central situational feature: 'goal'. People have goals in the form of needs, drives and wants which they bring to situations, which in turn provide the means for satisfying certain wants and stimulating others. We propose to consider situational goals as the description and specification of the social goals that the situation affords. These goals are constrained and are related to other factors such as situational rules, roles and sequential structure, and thus have to be considered in relation to these other features. Thus goals are features within the social situation and empirically measurable. Individual wants and needs are not strictly necessary for the analysis of specific social situations, though they are important for predicting and explaining how particular people enter or behave in social situations. Therefore although the terms we use to describe the features of situations are commonly found in the personality or social interaction literature they are not to be seen as properties of persons.

Finally, we have deliberately chosen not to invent or use other less ambiguous descriptors to outline the features of situations, because we believe that as our final goal is to understand the behaviour of individuals in situations, it is important to have a similar notation for person and situation in which to describe and explain that behaviour (cf. Murray, 1938).

We have taken games as models for social situations. In each case the participants agree to follow certain rules; they pursue certain goals and only certain moves are recognised as relevant acts. In his analysis of games Avedon (1971) proposed the following features:

1. purpose (i.e. how to win)
2. procedure for action (i.e. moves)
3. rules
4. number of participants
5. roles of participants
6. results, or pay-off
7. abilities and skills required
8. interactive patterns, e.g. competition between teams
9. physical environment
10. equipment required

In adopting the game analogy we are using 'game' in a rather general sense; we want to underplay the element of competition, which is often absent from social situations, and do not want to emphasise the physical activities involved. 'Game' can, therefore, include the kinds of situation that Harré and Secord (1972) call 'rituals' and 'entertainments'.

For the analysis of social situations we have selected nine main features, which turn out to be quite similar to those listed by Avedon and others independently for the analysis of games. These are:

Goals and goal structure. Most social behaviour is goal-directed, and cannot be understood until the goal or goals are known. The goals may be in a certain order, with a number of subgoals on the way to the end-goal. Situational goals are related to individual forms of motivation, e.g. making friends and affiliative motivation. Situations provide occasions for attaining goals, and probably exist for this purpose. People enter situations because they anticipate being able to attain certain goals. These goals can be regarded as a feature of the situation, and the main goals attainable in a situation can be assessed. However, an individual may be motivated to pursue more than one goal, and these goals may help, interfere with, or be independent of each other. The same applies to the goals of different

6

people. These interrelations between goals will be called the goal structure (see Chapter 4).

Rules. Rules are shared beliefs which dictate which behaviour is permitted, not permitted or required. Rules are generated in social situations in order to regulate behaviour so that the goals can be attained. The importance of social rules to social behaviour was emphasised by Harré and Secord (1972) in their analysis of the structure of formal episodes as an example of their role–rule model for social behaviour. They maintained that rules generate actions through the actor's use of them in monitoring and controlling his performance. We shall accept a weaker definition: that a rule exists if most people note and disapprove of its being broken. Rules are also part of the social construction of reality, and make possible complex games and routines of many kinds (see Chapter 5).

Roles. Nearly every situation has a number of specified roles which provide the individual with a fairly clear model for interaction – a cricket match, for example, has people taking the roles of umpires, fielders, batsmen and spectators. Roles can change within situations (supervisor to counsellor), while some people hold many roles at the same time (father, doctor, host). Roles can be seen as encompassing the duties or obligations or rights of the social position. Roles are interdependent and involve a great number of expectations about the actions, beliefs, feelings, attitudes and values of the person holding that role. Situations generate role-systems in order that situational goals can be attained. These include the formation of a leadership hierarchy and the division of labour (see Chapter 6).

Repertoire of elements. Games all have a limited repertoire of acts that are permitted and count as meaningful moves. Some situations, such as auction sales, have very restricted repertoires. We shall discuss methods for establishing what the repertoire is in a given situation, and then investigate the extent to which repertoires vary with situation, and how far there is a universal repertoire, in a number of areas of social behaviour (verbal, nonverbal, etc.). We expect that: repertoires will vary with situations; elements provide the steps needed to attain goals; and repertoires will be organised into contrasted subgroups relevant to these goals (see Chapter 7).

Sequences of behaviour. The elements of behaviour in a situation may come in a distinctive sequence. There are a number of sequences that occur in many situations, such as adjacency pairs, social-skill sequences and repeated cycles of interaction, though the contents may vary between situations. The same applies to the episodic structure of situations; often the

7

main task is subdivided into subtasks which have to be done in a special order. There are clear differences between situations in which one person (e.g. an interviewer) is in charge, rambling conversations, and true discussion or negotiation. Rituals and formal situations have a strictly ordered sequence of events (see Chapter 8).

Concepts. Characteristic shared concepts are developed for handling many situations, and we expect that these will be the concepts needed to deal with the group tasks and to attain situational goals. Constructs for persons are partly universal, partly situation-specific. Situations of intergroup conflict produce constructs derogatory of the out-group. The forms of attribution and explanation vary with the situation. Sometimes there is an elaborate conceptual build-up, connected for example with games, healing or religion, which must be mastered in order to cope with the situation (see Chapter 9).

Environmental setting. A number of variables within the setting are important. *Boundaries* are enclosures within which social interaction takes place. It is the immediate, often clearly perceptible, boundary of action that we are considering – that is, the room in which behaviour occurs, rather than the entire building, suburb or town. All boundaries contain *props* that are necessary within that boundary – a bar contains a counter, chairs, tables, alcohol, etc., while a lecture room contains chairs, desks, blackboard, chalk, etc. Each prop has a particular social function, and there is often a special social meaning and symbolic significance attached to it. *Modifiers* are physical aspects of the environment – e.g. colour, noise, light, odour and humidity – that affect the emotional tone of the behaviour being enacted. They seem to be particularly important elements in a situation when they are at extremes, though these extremes are determined by the situation itself (extremes of noise in a library are different from those in a playground, as are those of heat in a sauna and heat in an office). *Spaces* refers to the distances between people and objects. Spatial behaviour has been investigated in relation to four basic phenomena: privacy, personal space, territoriality and crowding (see Chapter 10).

Language and speech. Just as every scientific discipline, every sport, every job has its own language and jargon, and every geographic area an accent and speech pattern, so every situation has linguistic features associated with it. The various aspects of language and communication, such as vocabulary, grammar, codes and voice tone, are partly situation-specific. That is, there are certain features of language that are situation-specific while others are applicable to all or many situations. Some situations are much more restricted and constrained than others with regard to language use, while others call for a modification in just one aspect of speech (see Chapter 11).

Difficulties and skills. Some situations present unique social difficulties for the people in them because of the stress that results. Social situations, like jobs, often require certain skills or talents in order to be successfully executed. Indeed difficulty in social situations may be seen as a direct function of social skill – the more a person has the relevant skill in dealing with the situation, the less the difficulty experienced. Some situations, however, require other skills, such as perceptual and motor skills, memory skills or linguistic skills. Thus, just as one might specify job requirements so one might specify situational requirements. Furthermore, investigation into the commonly experienced difficulties that people have in social situations often provides unique insight into the processes underlying these situations (see Chapter 12).

The interpretation and explanation of situations

Although we are thinking primarily of set-piece, culturally defined situations, we are not thinking only, or primarily, of formal situations, although we are in a sense taking games and formal situations as models for informal situations. In the research reported in this book we have studied both formal and informal situations, and found that informal situations have rules, roles, and all the other features listed.

Any particular situation will be a special case of, say, a party, interview, etc. There is a wide range of parties, and their properties vary between cultures and subcultures. It is important to specify the subculture in research on situations. But within a given subculture there is still considerable variation between possible parties: they can vary along dimensions of size, noisiness, etc., and may fall into distinctive types. It is a matter for research to find out the extent to which there are common features in all these parties, and the extent to which different types of party need to be distinguished.

Psychologists have long distinguished between the objective, publicly measurable situation and the subjective interpretation of situations. Sociologists have often emphasised the subjective 'definition of the situation'. Our emphasis is on the objective situation; environmental setting, repertoire of elements, sequences of behaviour, language and roles can be assessed by objective methods, although they can also be assessed by analysis of ratings by participants. Goals, rules, concepts and difficulties are subjective entities and are most readily obtained from reports by participants, but here we can use the consensus of such reports, and only accept that the situation has a rule or other feature when there *is* sufficient agreement among participants drawn from a particular subculture. An individual may have a deviant perception of the rules. We would want to say that he is mistaken, and that he may even be a suitable candidate for social-skills training. There are other possibilities however: he may persuade the others to agree with him, as in the case of industrial consultants, and he may be able to act as an innovator.

We want to put forward a particular theoretical model to explain the existence of classes of situations and to explain why they have the properties that they do have. It is proposed that situations emerge within a culture because they have the function of enabling people to attain goals, which in turn are linked to needs and other drives. Sometimes those present are seeking the same goals, as on a 'date', sometimes different ones, as in a selling situation. All the other features of situations can be explained in terms of facilitating the attainment of these drive-related goals. The elements of the repertoire are the steps needed to attain the goals; sequences specify the necessary order of these steps; rules coordinate and restrain behaviour; roles create the necessary division of labour and social control, and so on. In a sense we see the first feature, goals, as the independent variable, and all the other features as dependent variables. However, rules, for example, are only partly determined by drives, because the same goals can be attained in more than one way; different cultures have worked out different sets of rules for buying and selling – barter, bargaining, fixed price with personal service, supermarkets, auction sales. Other aspects of situations can be explained in terms of 'latent functions' (which may be system needs, e.g. to maintain social cohesion) or in terms of displaced drives (e.g. the ritualised expression of aggression).

Indeed all common situations have a long history, and we can see the alternative systems which have been tried out. For example, the situation of a supervisor directing a group of workers has taken very different forms (1) in the Roman Empire and other ancient civilisations, when the workers were often slaves, (2) under feudalism, (3) in the mediaeval craft guilds, (4) in the early Industrial Revolution, and (5) under later industrial conditions, complete with automation, trade unions, industrial democracy, etc. (Argyle, 1972). These changes are partly due to broader changes in society, to the spread of ideas and beliefs, and to technology.

We can look at situations as social systems, with interdependent parts; if one feature is altered, other features will have to change as well. So any of the features can be considered as a possible independent variable, though some of them, especially sequences, skills and difficulties, are more naturally dependent variables.

For each of the features listed we have examined previous research. In some cases there is research in which aspects of the situation have been manipulated as the independent variable; in other cases, such as the repertoire of elements, we have studied the repertoires in a number of different and well-studied situations.

Research methods

At the end of a number of chapters we have added short accounts of some of our own studies of situations. Some of these are shorter versions of published papers. The design of most of these experiments is the same: the situation has been taken as the independent variable and one feature as the dependent variable. Sometimes we have selected situations that are contrasted in some way, e.g. task versus social; in other cases we have taken a wide sample of situations and used cluster or factor analysis to find the groupings of situations in terms of the particular feature being studied. We have preferred to use cluster analysis for situations, following our belief that situations fall into types rather than along dimensions. In most cases we have made predictions about the variation of features between classes of situations. Sometimes this has involved factor analysis or other statistical treatment of the features to discover their structure. In all of these studies we have made extensive use of statistical analysis of the data.

Some of our other studies have been simply exploratory, to find out whether a particular feature, such as goal structure, can be measured and to look at some analyses of real situations. Sometimes situations have been the *dependent* variable, as in our studies of the choice and avoidance of situations.

Most of these studies have worked with reported behaviour and subjective assessment of rules, etc. In all cases we have looked for, and found, a high degree of consensus between members of a subculture. We have worked with real-life settings, and often with samples of the most common real-life settings.

2

The analysis of social situations

Introduction

Perhaps one of the most confused, ambiguous and least researched branches of modern psychology is the social and physical context in which behaviour occurs, and its effects on behaviour. The sterility and unrepresentativeness of the psychology laboratory for research into social behaviour has been well documented (Rosenthal, 1966; Rosenthal and Rosnow, 1969), and the necessity of field work emphasised. Many psychological processes have been studied in situations so far removed from the natural situations in which these behaviours occur that different psychological processes altogether may be operating – hence the poor laboratory studies. Experiments like the Prisoners' Dilemma Game exclude verbal and non verbal communication; there are no obvious rules or other features of the situation and there is no established relationship between the interactors (Argyle, 1969). It has been demonstrated that laboratory experiments can obtain misleading results: Argyle and McHenry (1971) found that wearing spectacles added to perceived IQ *only* if the person in question did not speak. Psychologists have selected and manipulated one or two elements in the social setting they are studying, and which they expect to influence certain aspects of behaviour (the dependent variable), while attempting to 'control' all other relevant variables (Fraisse, 1968). These 'situational' variables have ranged from task conditions and mood states to confederator interaction and furniture arrangement, yet the subjects have rarely been consulted afterwards as to how they perceived the 'situation' as defined by the experimenter, or to see whether they perceived it in the same way as he did.

No attempt has been made to begin to define what the elements in a natural everyday social situation are, how they are related and how they affect the behaviour of people in them. Experimenters from a number of different backgrounds have stressed the effect of the immediate social situation on individual and group behaviour though they have used different names for the situation: episode, setting, scene, context, environment. Frederickson (1972), in an often-cited paper, has called for a classification of situations based on elicited behaviour, though he never defines the elements in, or parameters of, situations. Sells (1963) does, providing over

200 dimensions of a stimulus situation, a list which is unwieldy and impractical, with a large number of irrelevant variables and with no way of categorising them conceptually.

Recently researchers with different interests in social psychology have called for a renewed look at social situations. Bromley (1977), whose interest is person perception, has written: 'Human action takes place within a set of overlapping and interlocking situations and a proper account of the stimulus person's behaviour requires some understanding of the "total situation" in which behaviour is embedded' (p. 257). Duncan and Fiske (1977), in their metatheory for face-to-face interaction, also stress the role of the situation, the result of an individual's actively perceiving and classifying one or more entities (social phenomena) in terms of one or more categorisation used in his culture. They write: 'Consideration of situations is essential, not only for a participant's choosing appropriate conventions to perform in a given interaction but also for others' interpretation of that participant's performance. It is impossible to evaluate or to assign significance to a conventional act apart from knowledge of the situation in which the act occurred' (p. 260). Milgram (1974), whose laboratory work on obedience dramatically revealed the importance of the situational factor, wrote prophetically: 'For social psychology of this century reveals a major lesson: often, it is not so much the kind of person a man is as the kind of situation in which he finds himself that determines how he will act' (p. 205).

But how can situations affect behaviour? Consider the number of psychological and physical situations of various types and duration that one passes through every day. Take, for instance, the case of an average businessman. He wakes up in bed with his wife, with whom he interacts as protector, spouse and lover, before leaving the bedroom for early-morning ablutions in the bathroom. After dressing he goes to breakfast, in a different room, with his three children aged six, eleven and sixteen, where assuming the role of father and teacher he checks his youngest child's homework while chastising the sixteen-year-old's dress. Thereafter he goes to his car, beside which is waiting his neighbour's wife, to whom he gives a lift every morning and with whom he enjoys chatting during the twenty-minute drive. At work he greets his secretary who comes into his office to take down letters. Later on in the morning he goes down to the workshop with an errand and speaks to a number of his employees, including a shop-floor representative and the newest employee. Thereafter he walks with a business neighbour two blocks to a Rotary Club luncheon at a local hotel, where he is president with numerous duties. His afternoon includes entertaining a travelling salesman, completing some of his own work and interviewing another employee who wants special leave. After work he picks up his eleven-year-old daughter from ballet lessons in a church hall, where he chats to her teacher for a while, then drives home, only to change and leave with his wife for dinner at the home of an old bachelor friend, popping in on the way to the local general hospital to visit a neighbour who has recently undergone a major operation. After dinner he comes home and watches the TV for half an hour before going to bed at 11.45 p.m.

Consider the number of different physical environments our businessman has passed through – the home environment, a factory floor, a hospital ward, an hotel dining room, a church hall – each with its specific physical and behavioural constraints and demands. Consider the amount of time he has spent with a wide range of people, with whom he has a different role relationship – father, spouse, partner, employer, president, visitor, friend. Each episode has had different goals, rules, concepts, and lasted for different amounts of time; all of these factors have influenced the way he has behaved. Further, he has had expectations about how to behave in each situation and he carries from one situation to the next the emotional residue from the last.

But how did physical and interpersonal factors affect his behaviour in each different situation? Indeed what do we mean by a situation? What are the components of a situation and what is an adequate description of a situation? How can we tell when situations are functionally equivalent and when different? When does one situation begin and another end? When are situations negotiated and when are they imposed? Will a taxonomy of situations be useful and if so how do we go about constructing it?

All of these questions are important and must be answered if we are to talk about situational determinants of behaviour. Firstly, let us consider how the concept of social situation has been dealt with in overlapping areas of psychology, noting different emphases, inadequacies and theoretical standpoints. Thereafter a list of the major elements in a social situation will be offered and a tentative model suggested whereby they interact.

The concept of situation in different branches of psychology

Personality theory. Traditionally personality theorists have studied intrapersonal and interpersonal variables, often mentioning the importance of situational variables though rarely studying them directly (Allport, 1961; Cattell, 1965). The dichotomy between internal (personality) and external determinants can be traced back to Aristotle and Plato (Pervin, 1978a), though by definition personality theorists have concentrated primarily on internal determinants. However, since the 1950s, when learning theorists attempted to use their principles and methods to study personality (Dollard and Miller, 1950; Mischel, 1968), a debate has ensued regarding the primary determinants of behaviour (Endler and Magnusson, 1976a; Krauskopf, 1978). The person–situation debate has covered such issues as the cross-situational consistency of behaviour (Bem and Allen, 1974), the stability of behaviour over time (Block, 1971), the attribution of causes to personal or situational determinants (Jones and Nisbett, 1971) and the prediction of behaviour (Epstein, 1979).

As a result of research on the variance due to persons, situations and person by situation ($P \times S$) interaction, an interactional view has become popular in the personality field, described by Ekehammar (1974) as the *Zeitgeist* of today's personality psychology. According to interactionism all behaviour is the result of a continuous, indispensable interaction between the person and the social and physical situation he finds himself in. Not only do the social and physical aspects of situations influence an individual's behaviour but people also choose, avoid and change situations while acting in them (Argyle, 1976; Endler and Magnusson, 1976*b*). Interactional psychology has made a forceful and important criticism of trait theory and social learning theory, and has redirected the attention of personality theorists. However, as Buss (1977) has pointed out, the concept of interaction has been used in different ways – statistical and psychological – and the relationship between person and situation is codeterminal or bidirectional.

Despite this valuable and timely critique, the analysis of situations in personality theory has been fairly superficial. Endler and Magnusson write: 'Since behaviors occur in situations, then logically much interest and effort should be devoted to empirical studies of situations' (p. 15); and they make two main distinctions as regards situations – objective/subjective and macro/micro – though they also mention weak/strong, relevant/irrelevant, facilitating/inhibitory. These distinctions are often ambiguous and not clearly spelt out, glossing over difficult points.

In an important sense interactional psychology has not practised what it preached. The way in which social situations are considered experimentally is grossly inadequate. Consider the way in which situations are described in some of the most quoted papers: 'Getting ready to go to bed', 'Failing exams' (Endler and Hunt, 1969); 'Caught pilfering', 'Having an injection' (Magnusson and Ekehammar, 1975); 'When alone', 'Smoking after dinner' (Sandell, 1968); 'Going to bed at night' (Moos, 1968). Others have tried to use fuller descriptions – 'Today you got up full of energy and never really wanted to go to class. As a result, the long hours of sitting and lectures has made you very restless. It is now afternoon and you are finished your last class' (Bishop and Witt, 1970) – but rarely are the social, physical and temporal parameters of the situation considered. However nowhere have interactionists begun to answer what appear to be fundamental questions: What are the elements in a situation? When are situations similar and when different? When does one begin and another end?

When interactional theorists talk about situations (or their synonyms) they are often talking about general activity types or institutionalised settings. To use a two-word description such as 'failing exams' gives one no idea at all of the different circumstances under which one hears or reacts to this news; the details of where, when or with whom one hears the news are ignored. It seems that interactional psychology has been satisfied merely with demonstrating that behaviour is a function of more than personality traits alone, but has not gone on to specify how situations affect behaviour or indeed what a situation is. Even Frederickson (1972), who suggests numerous ways of creating situation taxonomies, never confronts the problem of defining social situations. Personality theorists have become skilled over the past fifty years at making conceptual distinctions between people and have enhanced an already rich vocabulary which deals with person concepts – it is now up to interactional psychology to do the same with situations.

Ekehammar (1974) has suggested five possible ways to begin the description and classification in psychology: *a priori* physical and social characteristics, need concepts, single reactions, individual reaction patterns and individual perceptions. The majority of the work of the leading interactionists, such as Endler and Magnusson, has used perceptual or reaction data, seeking to determine the underlying dimensions of various classes of situations. Further, they have always been concerned with between, rather than within, situation analysis. Much of their work has been concerned with stressful situations (see Chapter 12), though other studies have been concerned with more general situations. Magnusson (1971) found five factors underlying thirty-six situations, variously described and chosen from a domain common for Swedish students. The factors were labelled 'positive and rewarding', 'negative', 'passive', 'social interaction' and 'activity'. Using a different method but the same situations Magnusson and Ekehammar (1973) found similar factors, with one addition which they labelled 'ambiguous'.

Thus, though personality theorists in general, and interactional psychologists in particular, are now paying considerably more attention to the interaction of person and situation in determining behaviour, their attempts at defining or describing situations have been rather poor. During the course of this century personality theorists have made great headway in conceptual distinctions between personalities, yet the equivalent attempts to describe or understand the situations in which these personalities act are still in their formative stages.

Symbolic interactionism and ethnomethodology. The work of these microsociologists on the situation is quite different to that of the environmental psychologists and very sophisticated, concentrating on the process of interaction. The basic assumption of these theorists is that people create a symbolic social environment where even physical objects assume importance because of their social meaning, and that the social meaning of objects in the symbolic environment must be described in subjective value terms from the standpoint of the perceiver. For them, a description of the physical or objective situation is improper and impossible because it is the perceived situation of the actor (the environment he construes) that is important and worthy of investigation, and it is this subjective and symbolic construal of the situation with which the actor interacts. This approach concentrates on the dynamic process of social interaction, looking at the individual, the situation and the social system as a whole.

Symbolic interactionists look upon the concept of the situation as Thomas and Thomas (1928) did when they wrote: 'Preliminary to any self-determined act of behaviour there is always a stage of examination and deliberation which we may call the definition of the situation. Situations defined as real are real in their consequence'. Ball (1970*a*) reiterated:

Thus, to define a situation is to engage in the *social construction of reality*; since this process involves knowledge, it is the *construction of social reality*; and because definitions become shared, external to the individual actor, they become Durkheimian *reality of social construction*, with consequences, as Thomas cautioned us, which are very real – as real as their existential causes. (p. 31)

As Ryan (1970) pointed out, Thomas and other sociologists became interested in the definition of the situation through studying how immigrants and other subgroups perceived situations. They argued that what a person or group will do in any situation depends on how they define it, and that any group will be better able to control a situation when it can make its definition *the* definition. The idea of the culturally determined or defined nature of social situations runs through much of the symbolic interactionist literature (Wolff, 1964).

For symbolic interactionists who draw upon the work of Mead (1934), Berger and Luckman (1966) and McHugh (1968), definitions of the situation emerge out of interaction and communication. Situations are not passively there; they are actively perceived and negotiated. Definitions are neither purely mentalistic nor subcultural; they are dynamic, the one person defining the situation for the other and vice versa. Stone and Farberman (1970) best sum up this approach:

There has always been the problem in the study of human conduct in locating the source of symbolic transformation. We have already seen that man responds not to some objectively given environment but instead to a symbolic transformation of that environment. This transformation can only be accomplished by man's use of symbols, for most of which he is not responsible, but which he must implement in his definition of situations. Symbols are nothing without man. Man is nothing without symbols. The very fact that man must use symbols to define the situations in which he conducts himself implies communication, since those very definitions require the meaningful response of others. . . . Situations in other words are staged. By this we mean that the elements of a situation are typically assembled,

17

arranged, manipulated and controlled by human beings so that the vast range of possibilities of human conduct is circumscribed once other humans enter the constructed situational scene . . . the definition of the situation is a process. (pp. 148–50)

By far the most prolific and interesting symbolic interactionist approach is that of Goffman, who in 1961 (*c*) coined the term 'the neglected situation', maintaining that situations had not been studied sufficiently. For Goffman (1967) a 'situation' or face-to-face interaction occurs when two or more people come into the range of one another's senses and ends when there are no longer two people within this range. Lauer and Handel (1977) point out that to define the analytic boundary of the study of social situations is to distinguish between the determinants and consequences of situated conduct that are concretely within and without the situation. Determinants include 'structural properties', the physical characteristics of the setting, and the focus of the interaction. Consequences include stable social relationships, normative systems excluding those of the situational properties, and lasting effects of events in the situation. Goffman's approach has been to find the norms governing co-presence, such as involvement and openness, and to look at the processes employed in maintaining the focus of attention. He has made a particular study of ritualised exchanges (Goffman, 1969, 1971).

Both symbolic interactionists and ethnomethodologists have put heavy stress on language and meaning, using Whorfian examples of how the very names of situations affect the behaviour in those situations. However the two groups do not differ so much in their conceptual analysis of situations as in their methodology for investigating actors' perceptions and definitions of situations. As Billig (1977) has shown, ethnomethodologists advocate philosophic detachment and disassociation, believing that one must step outside the normal social world in order to investigate it without assumptions, while interactionists and ethnologists advocate sympathetic *rapprochement* and understanding.

Denzin (1974) states the basic concern of ethnomethodologists as the 'penetration' or disruption of normal social situations to uncover the rules and rituals which the participants take for granted. Ethnomethodologists hold that once a situation is defined, this definition holds for the duration of the encounter, and that meanings given to persons, or objects, hold for future occasions. Because people label and symbolise objects and people in the same way when identifying and attaching meaning to them, they bring to any situation a common vocabulary and lexicon of terms which facilitates interaction. The methodology used by ethnomethodologists is that of quasi-experimental field studies where normal social situations are disrupted in order to challenge and hence reveal the normal rules (Garfinkel, 1967). Other techniques involve extremely detailed

18

analysis of transcripts of conversation, unobtrusively recorded in real-life settings.

Perhaps because of what is seen to be their methodological weakness, symbolic interactionism and ethnomethodology have not made the impact they deserved on social psychology. Otherwise the concept of the situation might have received greater attention than it has in experimental social psychology.

'Ethogenics'. Harré and Secord (1972) object to ethnomethodological approaches because they believe that social action cannot be explained in terms only of rules and conventions, dramaturgical self-monitoring being an essential component of all social action. Ethogenists maintain that all social behaviour is monitored rule-following, and that people present suitable personas for the social situations/episodes. The concept of an episode is central to this approach. It is defined as any natural division of social life and contains not only overt behaviour but also the thoughts, feelings, intentions and plans, etc., of the participants. Harré and Secord (1972) distinguished between formal episodes, where reference is made to explicit rules in accounting for the sequence and type of the actions performed, and casual episodes, in which reference is made to physiological, chemical or physical mechanisms. The overt and covert structures of episodes are distinguished, the former describable in terms of acts and actions, the latter as the waxing and waning of powers and emotions. They wrote:

In general social behaviour is the result of conscious self-monitoring of performance by the person himself, in the course of which he continues to assess the meaning of the social situation in which he finds himself and to choose, amongst various rules and conventions, and to act in accordance with his choice, correcting this choice as further aspects of the situations make themselves clear to him. . . . To an ethogenist, everything of interest that occurs in human life happens in the course of, or as a culmination of, or as the initiating of an episode. (pp. 151–3)

The method whereby these episodes are understood is that of gathering accounts from the participants through open-ended, free-response interviews. Ethogenists hope in this way 'to discover the rules, plus conventions, images and so on that people use to guide their behaviour' (p. 151). They are concerned primarily not with the accuracy of measurement or the quantifiability of data but rather with the representativeness and richness of the accounts collected. There seem, however, to be no guidelines as to the informants from whom accounts should be obtained, or how the accounts should be selected or interpreted.

Later De Waele and Harré (1976) set out a microsystematic and rigorous methodology for studying personality that involves the assessment of situations. Four approaches are to be used together: collection of a detailed autobiography, observation in social settings, a social enquiry into the person's global life-situation and the use of deliberately contrived problem and conflict situations. They wrote:

On the ethogenic view, situation definitions being an integral part of the cognitive matrix through which interaction performance and problem-solving express themselves, the study of situations, their possible requirement and meanings, are inseparable from the study of an individual personality. This is not only a theoretical principle but also a methodological one, which means that in the assessment of an individual personality generalizations of social performances over situations and their storing in the individual's cognitive matrix as a standardized solution can never be taken for granted, but have to be proved and investigated inductively in each case. (pp. 232–3)

Harré and Secord (1972) make a number of distinctions in the structure of 'formal' episodes, which they argue serve as models for the inventory of a set of rules and a homeomorph for the analysis of the overt structure of an 'enigmatic' episode. Their taxonomy has three levels: simulated/ genuine, ceremonial/casual, cooperative/competitive. In another paper Harré (1972) makes the distinction between situations that have specific rules and those that have general rules, and between those where the end-state is determined and those where it is not. These two distinctions permit categories of situations that have a different role–rule structure: ritual (specific rules, consummatory), routine (specific rules, non-consummatory), games (general rules, consummatory) and entertainment (general rules, non-consummatory). He maintains that most episodes in everyday life are neither casual nor formal, but enigmatic; and he draws heavily on symbolic interactionist ideas and methods for analysis.

An example of ethogenic analysis has been provided by Marsh, Rosser and Harré (1978), who made a detailed study of two situations – school classrooms and football terraces – in an attempt to reveal the rules and constraints that underlie seeming disorders. Through extensive quoting of the accounts of informants they try to recreate these situations and discover their structure. This detailed, in-depth approach seems an excellent point at which to begin an analysis of specific social situations, though it is debatable as to whether it is sufficient.

Environmental and ecological psychology. For the most part environmental psychologists concern themselves with man's perception of and reaction to his physical environment, built and natural (Lee, 1976). Environmental psychology, with its multidisciplinary and pragmatic approach, usually measures the cognitive and behavioural responses of people to physical features in physical environments. However, the ghost of architectural determinism lurks in most environmental thinking and experimentation.

20

Stokols (1978) noted that

the environment is constructed in multidimensional molar terms, and the focus of analyses generally is on the interrelations among people and their sociophysical milieu rather than on the linkages between discrete stimuli and behavioral responses. It should be noted, though, that much of the research in this field has attempted to isolate physical dimensions (e.g. noise, temperature, space) of the broader milieu in order to assess their specific effects on behaviour. (p. 207)

As Stokols points out, environmentalists are rarely interested in everyday social situations, but rather in certain aspects of behaviour (sitting, littering) in certain very specific surroundings (supermarkets, hospitals) at one extreme, and gross measures of satisfaction and contentment with large environmental areas at the other. The very neglect of the term social situation in environmental psychological writings in favour of environment, setting or place emphasises the 'objective' and larger boundary interests of environmental psychologists. In that it is closely allied to human ecology, urban sociology, architecture, planning, natural resources management and behavioural geography, environmental psychology is extremely eclectic and is often racked by two major debates which directly affect the way the social situation is conceptualised and investigated:

1. Should the environment be construed in objective (physical) or subjective (psychological) terms? This is closely allied to, but not synonymous with, taking behavioural and perceptual measures.
2. Should people be conceived as active or passive modifiers of environmental forces?

Naturally if one believes in people actively choosing, defining and changing their environments, which they perceive and respond to subjectively, the conceptualisation of and methodology for investigating social situations will differ widely from those of the behaviourist, who sees his subjects as passively responding to the objective environment. The latter approach is still very common and to some extent reflects much environmental psychological research, though there is a movement to a more transactional psychology.

Stokols (1978) uses the above two alternative approaches to give four modes of human–environment transaction (Table 2.1).

These dimensions yield four *modes* of human–environment transaction: 1. *interpretive* (active–cognitive); 2. *evaluative* (reactive–cognitive); 3. *operative* (active–behavioral); and 4. *responsive* (reactive–behavioral). The first mode involves the individual's cognitive representation or construction of the environment; the second, his evaluation of the situation against predefined standards of quality; the third, his movement through or direct impact on the environment; and fourth, the environment's effects on the individual's behavior and well being. (p. 259)

21

TABLE 2.1. *Modes of human–environment transaction and related areas of research*

Phase of transaction	Form of transaction	
	Cognitive*	Behavioural
Active	*Interpretive* Cognitive representation of the spatial environment Personality and the environment	*Operative* Experimental analysis of ecologically relevant behaviour Human spatial behaviour (Proxemics)
Reactive	*Evaluative* Environmental attitudes Environmental assessment	*Responsive* Impact of the physical environment Ecological psychology

From Stockols (1978).
* In the present schema, the term 'cognitive' refers to both informational and affective processes.

Though mental maps have become a popular area of research (Gould and White, 1974), as has the relationship of personality to specific environmental behaviours (Craik and McKechnie, 1978), environmental psychologists have not concentrated on social situations but rather on physical objects or stimuli in these situations. Various research areas, such as proxemics (Lundberg, Bratfisch and Ekman, 1972) and crowding (Stokols, 1972), have noted how subjective perceptions and objective measurement do not match, yet despite this regular finding laboratory experiments in environmental psychology have often ignored the subjects' experience, perception and definition of the experimental situation. Although there is evidence of a transactional or interactional approach in environmental psychology, the most popular approach is still to consider how the physical environment affects behaviour and not vice versa.

Ecological psychology, for a long time ignored by mainstream psychology, has recently excited new interest. Barker (1968), the major proponent of ecological psychology, maintains that the psychologist can proceed in either of two ways in understanding human behaviour:

1. As transducer – docile receiver of psychological phenomena which he categorises or interprets as they occur (T data).
2. As operator – creating situations in which he asks his subjects to act (O data).

The message of ecological psychology is that to understand behaviour as it occurs we must stop looking at the level of detail which is so characteristic of the experimental (O data) methods, or for specific stimulus – response (S–R) relationships between aspects of the environment and behaviour; rather we must consider complete behavioural units and study them in relation to environmental inputs. Behaviour itself cannot even be defined outside an environmental context – indeed the unit of enquiry of necessity becomes the behaviour setting – both behaviour and the setting in which it occurs being part of the same whole. Barker has provided a language for identifying, describing and analysing behaviour settings and dynamic processes within them. Although environmental and ecological psychology have slightly different approaches to the social situation, they both share a fairly similar molar view of the situation and a behaviouristic approach to experimentation. They are closely aligned to the pure social learning theory position, which holds that individual difference variables are a function of the environment (environmental contingencies shaping relatively enduring psychological structure). Essentially they underplay the role of the subject, both in selecting, avoiding, negotiating or defining social situations, and in recognising the social psychological aspects of any situation (rules, goals, roles, concepts) (see p. 5).

Experimental social psychology. The term social situation is often found in experimental social psychology literature (Cottrell, 1942; Krause, 1970; Pervin, 1978*b*), but there seems to be no coherent or consistent way in which it is used. The term situation is primarily used to refer to interpersonal conditions in the laboratory – usually independent variables such as task conditions (confederate behaviour, difficulty), role-playing scenarios or vignettes, induced mood states or imagined activities. For some psychologists any aspect of the experiment that does not involve intrapersonal variables is termed situational, as a shorthand term. Inevitably this leads to confusion, as the dimensions of the situation are never spelt out and the artificiality of the laboratory never considered: hence poor validity, replication difficulties and problems in generalisation to other situations. The effect of different aspects of the situations on the dependent variable is never fully considered.

Pervin (1978*b*) has reviewed the various definitions, measurement techniques and attempts at classifications of stimuli, situations and environments. He found that the definitions were blurred and inadequate, the three major conceptual problems being the level of analysis (molar or molecular), whether the definition should be in objective or subjective terms, and the relationship to behaviour. Pervin (1976) suggested that for experimental purposes a situation can be adequately described in terms of *who* is there, *what* is going on and *where* it is taking place.

To illustrate, consider the diverse ways in which the term situation is used in two currently popular areas of research in social psychology: locus of control and attribution theory. Rotter (1955) wrote that 'In the half a century or more that psychologists have been interested in predicting the behavior of human beings in complex social situations, they have persistently avoided the incontrovertible importance of the specific situation on behavior' (p. 247). He maintained that situations, like behaviours and reinforcements, could be objectively defined, and the relationships between them spelt out. Out of this work grew the locus of control of reinforcement concept, which distinguished between people who believe their actions can and do affect the course of their life ('internals') and those who believe their life is controlled by luck, fate, chance and situational factors beyond their control ('externals'). Despite the origin of the locus of control concept as one of a situation-specific expectancy, and the stress on the importance of such situational variables as predictable and unpredictable, controllable and uncontrollable, skill and chance (Phares, 1976), many studies have used the internal–external control (I–E) scale as a personality measure, without taking account of situational constraints.

Endler and Edwards (1978) reviewed the work on person-by-situation interactions that is to be found in the locus of control literature. Such factors as the success or failure of the situational outcome, the difference in task versus social demands, and intrinsic versus extrinsic reinforcement, differentially affect 'internal' and 'external' subjects. They concluded that although the I–E concept has been treated primarily as a person variable, with little attention being given to situation constraints, a number of studies have shown the importance of the interaction between the two.

One of the most researched areas at the moment is that of attribution, which attempts to specify processes within a perceiver that are invoked in the explanation and prediction of the behaviour of others. A number of theories exist to explain the attribution process, and experimenters have studied the attribution of causality, responsibility, etc., to both self and others, and the interpersonal and social consequences of attribution. The theory grew out of work on social perception, and attempts to show how both situational factors and personal motives may influence attribution; there is constant reference to the role played by the situation.

One of the most consistent findings is that people tend to perceive their own behaviour as occurring largely in response to various situational factors, but that the behaviour of others is seen as stemming mainly from their personality. There are two possible explanations of this consistent finding. The first is that actors and observers have different foci of attention: actors do not observe their own behaviour but focus on situational cues and so tend to perceive these as a major cause of actions, whereas observers concentrate on the actor's behaviour itself, overlooking situational determinants. The second is that actors and observers have different types of information available: actors have private information as to how they behaved in different situations whereas observers have information only from the actor's behaviour in the one particular situation and hence assume that present behaviour is typical of past actions, and attribute it to a stable disposition.

A number of studies have demonstrated the above phenomena. Nisbett *et al.* (1973) asked subjects to indicate which trait (of twenty) best described themselves and four other persons; they were given the option of 'depends on the situation'. They found, as predicted, that subjects chose the option 'depends on the situation' significantly more frequently in describing their own behaviour than in describing that of others. Storms (1973) used video-tapes to demonstrate that when actors were induced to focus upon their own behaviour rather than the situation in which they were acting, and the observers on the situation in which the actor behaved rather than the actor alone, there were marked changes in their pattern of causal attribution. However, despite the central role of the concept of the situation in the attribution literature it has not been explored and the various aspects of the situation that affect the attributional process have not been stipulated. Heider (1958), in his theory, considered only such things as task difficulty, environmental coercion and luck to be environmental/situational forces, while Jones and Davis (1965) added to these three variables that of situational pressures.

Kelley (1972) proposed that people consider three types of information in the attribution process:

1. Consensus: the extent to which other persons act in the same manner as the individual in question.
2. Consistency: the extent to which this person acts in the same manner on other different occasions.
3. Distinctiveness: the extent to which this person acts in the same manner in other situations or only in this situation.

Kelley suggested that an observer is likely to make an internal attribution (about him or herself) under conditions of low consensus, high consistency and low distinctiveness, and more likely to make external attributions (about the situation in which they find themselves) under conditions of high consensus, high consistency and high distinctiveness.

Attribution theories, in studying the explanation of behaviour and perception of causality, have not fully considered the role of different aspects of the situation in this process. They rarely make the distinction between physical and psychological aspects of the situation and have totally neglected the various subtle situational determinants of attribution. Also there is an important distinction between the situation in which and about which attribution and explanations are offered. Often in experimentation subjects have been presented with only brief stimulus material (films, or more often vignettes) and an inadequate, rather arbitrary description of an episode to which they are supposed to respond. It is not at all certain that the aspects of the episodes that social psychologists describe in stimulus vignettes are those that people perceive, recognise or respond to, or conceive of as important in everyday life. It is particularly the more subtle and often powerful situational determinants of behaviour that are ignored.

It should not be forgotten that in much of their experimental work experimental social psychologists actually create social situations, often highly unusual ones, such as in the Asch conformity experiment. Many have criticised the laboratory experiment (Mixon, 1972; Silverman, 1977), not least because of the experimenter's neglect of the subject's perception of this unusual circumstance. Although 'situational' variables are often manipulated, an insufficient number of experimenters bother to check afterwards as to whether the subjects 'defined' the situation in the way the experimenters had hoped. In fact critics of the experimental laboratory approach have revealed a consistent 'subculture' of the situation with its implicit rules, roles, concepts and goals.

A functional theory of situations

Why do certain regular situations exist in a society, and why do they have the features they do have? We suggest a functional explanation, based on functional theories that have been put forward to account for social institutions in general. We are aware of the various criticisms that have been made of functionalism, but we think that it is possible to formulate a functional theory of situations that is not open to these criticisms. Previous theories have been about aspects of societies as a whole. We shall be concerned with situations.

People often explain their own behaviour in terms of their purposes, so it is not surprising that social scientists have had ideas about the purposes served by social institutions (Ryan, 1970). Some institutions have fairly obvious functions: there is no mystery about the existence of shops or manufacturing industry. It is much less obvious, however, why in some societies there are churches, a royal family, complicated kinship systems or witchcraft.

Functional explanations are similar to ecological ones: it is possible to explain at least some features of primitive societies in terms of the way they survive (by hunting and gathering, by agriculture, herding and food storage) in their particular environments (Berry and Annis, 1974). The social institutions are then sustained by socialisation practices, which train children in appropriate forms of behaviour (Barry, Child and Bacon, 1959).

A distinction is often made between manifest and latent functions (Merton, 1949). For example the incest taboo is found in nearly all human societies; its functions are, however, obscure. It may be for the prevention of genetic inbreeding, or the avoidance of sexual rivalry inside the family, but since most people do not know about this its functions must be regarded as latent. Social institutions may have dysfunctions as well as functions: for example the practice of giving tenure to senior officials in bureaucratic organisations means that younger people are held back. It has usually been supposed that there are a number of functional equivalents, i.e. different institutions, each of which could serve the same function. If one is abolished, it can be predicted that one or more of the others will be strengthened.

Functionalists emphasise that functions cannot be equated with individual purposes or motivations; the functions are the objective consequences, which may be quite different from the motivation (Merton, 1949). However, latency is a matter of degree, and often functions and purposes are closely linked. This can be illustrated by the case of matrilineal cross-cousin marriage, as analysed by Homans and Schneider (1955). A young man marries a daughter of one of his mother's brothers. The *function* is thought to be the integration of kinship groups. The *motivation* is probably not very different, since boys have a warm relation with their mother's brothers in these societies and may well be attracted to one of their daughters; the girl will like this because when she has to leave her home her new home will be with someone whom her father likes, and where her father can intercede on her behalf (Johnson, 1961). It is likely that many 'latent' functions are partly manifest to some of those involved.

An example of functions that were latent, at least to outside observers of a society, is provided by the stone axes used by Australian aboriginals. When missionaries tried to be helpful by providing free steel axes, social life was seriously disturbed, because only older males possessed stone axes, which were therefore part of the status system, and they were obtained by a form of trading which integrated different groups (Sharp, 1952).

A regular pattern of behaviour, or other social institution, is explained by showing how it enables the needs of individuals or society to be met. Society is seen as a system of parts, in a state of equilibrium, i.e. it returns to a steady state after a disturbance. Durkheim (1895) took as evidence for this stability the relatively unchanging crime and suicide rates in countries. Malinowski's version of functionalism (1944) related elements of culture firstly to individual biological needs. In addition he postulated instrumental needs, which are derived from the activities needed to satisfy biological needs, and the social institutions required by them; the areas of instrumental need are economics, law and social control, education and politics. Thirdly he postulated integrative needs of society, to regulate cooperative activity.

Parsons *et al*. (1953) proposed four fundamental social or system needs:

1. Pattern maintenance and tension management: the need to socialise members of the group and help them manage anxiety.

2. Adaptation to the environment: requiring division of labour and other role differentiation.
3. Goal attainment: cooperating to attain joint group goals, such as security and economic productivity.
4. Integration of individuals and subgroups: arranging for decision-making procedures, a hierarchy of authority, processes for dealing with friction created by cooperative activity, and dealing with deviance.

One difficulty is that while individuals have purposes, it is not clear in what sense groups or societies do. Groups and organisations often do formulate their aims and lay down rules, and in the course of government and administration alter the rules or other arrangements in order to pursue their goals (Ryan, 1970). But what about goals of which the members are not aware? The society might fall apart if a need, for example for social integration, was not met, but we would require evidence that social institutions had appeared in order to meet this function.

The main attraction of functional explanations, for us at least, lies in the possibility of explaining aspects of society that are not easy to account for in terms of common-sense, or are contrary to common-sense – in other words where there are latent functions. There appear to be two main kinds of latent function: system needs of the kind listed above, and cases of displaced or transformed motivation, such as have been found to be part of the basis of religious phenomena.

Functional theories are sometimes presented in an entirely speculative way, with no attempt at verification. Functions have been suggested for all kinds of things, including ignorance and doing nothing. A number of methods of verification are possible, however, such as the 'mental experiment' (imagining what would happen if the feature to be explained were absent: Merton, 1949) and the analysis of deviance (deviance should have serious consequences if the postulated needs are not met: Johnson, 1961). By far the most convincing way of testing functional theories, however, is by comparing groups which do and do not possess a particular social institution. Whyte (1948) found that the use of an order spike, or other means of preventing waitresses giving orders directly to cooks in restaurants, had the effect of reducing tensions between them. Theories of the motivational basis of religious institutions have been tested in a similar way, by making predictions from theories. For example if religious beliefs are substitute forms of gratification, deprived people should be more religious, and their beliefs should reflect the nature of the deprivation (Argyle and Beit-Hallahmi, 1975).

It has been objected that functional theories are teleological, and thus incur the logical error of placing the cause of an event after it in time. However, this takes place in any self-regulating system with a negative feedback loop. For example in a thermostat the behaviour of the system leads to the goal of a certain temperature being attained, though the goal was actually set *before* this temperature was reached. There is no mystery here once the mechanism has been described. Homeostatic processes, whereby the body maintains the constancy of its internal environment, operate in a similar way. Teleological explanations are also given in biology to explain the existence of parts of the body in terms of their contribution to the working and survival of the organism. The process behind such functional relationships is natural selection acting on spontaneous mutations in the genes. It seems unlikely that there is much natural selection of whole societies (Cohen, 1968), but there could well be natural selection of situations. The emergence of a number of new kinds of group meetings shows this happening. 'Brainstorming' was popular in the 1950s, but has now disappeared. T-groups were popular in the 1960s, but are now rarely seen except in a highly modified form.

It has been objected that functionalism encourages or reflects a conservative bias by emphasising the positive functions of every aspect of the *status quo*, from the class system to the royal family. Like Cohen (1968) and others we do not think that this need be so. Advocates of social change can try to bring about alternative institutions to meet the same needs, or to meet them better, and to avoid areas of dysfunction in society (e.g. groups of people whose needs are not being met). Functionalism does, however, contain a warning for reformers – that existing institutions may be serving hidden functions, like the aboriginals' stone axes, and it is important to understand these hidden functions before changing things too much. Our approach to situations includes analysing those situations that are found difficult or stressful. A possibly 'conservative' solution to this problem is to train people to deal with these situations better; a more radical solution is to attempt to redesign the situations.

Coser (1964) objected that functionalists see conflict as dysfunctional, and argued that conflict can have positive functions: for example duelling can allow the free expression of pent-up hostile feelings, and thus preserve the group. Groups can define themselves through struggling with other groups; and conflict can bring about what may be beneficial social changes. We are interested in situations involving conflict, of which duelling is an example, and see no difficulty in their functional analysis.

All of the varieties of functionalism so far considered have been put forward to explain society-wide institutions, rather than situations. We propose to use the theory to explain the features of different situations. There are a large number of different situations within a culture which can be compared and contrasted, so the testing of functional theories should be possible. However a particular situation does not have to satisfy all the needs listed above; it might be relevant to only one or two. We propose in the first instance to try to relate situations to the goals that members of a subculture think they are pursuing there; certain elements and rules and so on are clearly necessary for these goals to be realised. We shall then consider whether there are aspects of situations that have latent functions, either in terms of system needs or of displaced motivation, and try to test such theories in a predictive manner. We shall take up the question of system needs first in connection with rules (p. 134f.).

Methods for analysing social situations

There appear to be a number of different methods available for analysing social situations. Each comes from a different theoretical tradition, addresses itself to different questions, and has different strengths and weaknesses. Although we have argued in this chapter for one approach, we do not seek to deny the usefulness or relevance of other approaches in studying social situations. There seem to be at least six approaches, three from experimental social psychology, two from the environmental psychology tradition and one from microsociology.

Dimensional approach. A number of different statistical methods are able to 'reduce' a data set to a small number of underlying dimensions – that is, show how various stimuli (situations) load on a set number of factors, which can be variously labelled. A subject's perceptions of, or reactions to, situations along certain bipolar scales, or the similarity between situations, may serve as input for factor analysis, cluster analysis and multidimensional scaling, which may all serve the same end. These methods have the advantages that they are descriptive yet allow for hypothesis testing, and can manage large amounts of raw data. They are problematic, however, in that factors have to be intuitively labelled, and considerable pilot work is necessary in selecting the best of the stimuli and rating scales. This method does allow for cross-situation comparisons and categorisation of situations along a number of dimensions.

The dimensional approach has been used successfully to reveal factors of perception or reaction to various situations. The method is usually questionnaire-based and involves four stages. These are: firstly, the selection and description of a number of stimulus situations, which may be done in terms of *a priori* classification or theory or in terms of the self-reported experiences of the sample population; secondly, the selection of rating scales or the specification of a rating task such as similarity ratings or groupings, the statistical technique to be employed determining this phase of the study; thirdly, the data analysis in terms of the preferred statistical technique; and, finally, interpretation of the factors, dimensions or clusters. This last stage may be done intuitively or empirically. Various decisions have to be made at each stage in the research strategy which have consequences for data interpretation.

The most commonly used approaches are those of factor analysis and multidimensional scaling, the latter gaining in popularity because of its flexibility and power. Ekehammar and Magnusson (1973) advocated factor analysis of similarity ratings, a technique they used a lot in later papers (Magnusson and Ekehammar, 1973, 1975; Ekehammar, Schalling and Magnusson, 1975). They maintained that this technique has six advantages: situations as a whole, rather than some limited detail, are used as stimuli; individual and group data can be used; the method is not reactive; faking is reduced; the method is simple for raters; and it is fast. On the other hand Forgas (1976, 1979) advocated the use of multidimensional scaling (MDS), as a more adaptable technique and one that allows for the empirical labelling of factors. The many different types of MDS analysis available (INDSCAL, TORSCA, ALSCAL, etc.), the range of possible judgemental tasks and the sophistication of the statistical techniques make this a very powerful and useful tool. Although hypothesis testing is done within this approach it is primarily descriptive.

Componential approach. This strategy, sometimes called the structuralist or categorical approach, argues that social situations are discrete, not continuous entities – a structured system of interdependent parts. The approach seeks to determine the components and elements in each unique situation type, and to understand the relationship of these elements. It is argued that some elements are common to all situations – rules, roles, concepts, props, etc. – but that they take many different forms. That is, although rules are to be found in each situation they might be very different rules: for example, the rules for silence in a library or at a football match, the props necessary for a lecture or a dinner party. The analogy most often quoted is that of the morpheme in linguistics. Once the list of elements is established, it is necessary to see how the elements are applied to each situation. This method allows one to build up a detailed and complex picture of a situation, and to get some idea of the interrelationship and sequence of actions. It also allows for cross-situational comparison though at an elemental level. The major weakness of the approach is that it fails to produce a comprehensive and exhaustive list of salient situational and personality elements and to explain their interaction.

The nature of the component under consideration usually suggests which experimental method is most applicable. Thus observation may be most applicable to investigating repertoire and sequences while questionnaires are more applicable to the investigation of concepts and rules. The componential approach has been useful in the analysis of games (Avedon, 1971). Various methods are applicable in this approach: questionnaire, observation, interview, experimental manipulation, role-playing, etc. Although cross-situational comparisons are possible, this approach is primarily concerned with describing how various components of situations (e.g. rules, roles) vary across situations, and how they are related to one another. Once the components have been established on 'theoretical and empirical bases', the way they operate in specific types of situation is considered. This can be done from the point of view of both the person in the situation (the subjective view) and the people observing the situation (the objective view). This approach also pays attention to various person variables such as the personality, age, sex, etc., of the people in the situation. It is primarily aimed at the establishment of models for the relationship of components to one another, such as the equilibrium model for gaze and other associated nonverbal behaviours (Argyle and Dean, 1965) or social skill (Argyle, 1969).

Because of the theoretical position of the componential approach, cluster analysis is favoured as the main descriptive statistical technique, as well as other nonparametric techniques to test specific hypotheses. To a large extent the componential approach uses techniques that best analyse the data as it is collected, rather than letting the statistical analysis dictate the type of data gathering. Thus it is more concerned with the structuring of elements within different situations than the dimensions of similarity between them.

Study of particular kinds of social behaviour. This approach is more limited than the above two in that it seeks exclusively to investigate the influence of salient situational variables on a particular kind of behaviour. Experimental psychologists soon became aware of the fact that altruism, gaze, accidents, etc., are partly determined by a number of external (as well as inter- and intrapersonal) variables, which they set about investigating. These external variables may be those in the laboratory or in the real setting. However, as most researchers have no theoretical model to guide them, the variables they list and test are often seemingly arbitrarily chosen. As a result some important variables may be omitted, while others of limited importance are overemphasised. Further, the behavioural process nearly always becomes the dependent variable and the situational factor the independent variable, and never vice versa, implying misleading unicausality. This has led to the anomaly of 'situational factors' in one area of study being unrelated to and uninterpretable in another. The approach can, however, produce a detailed pattern of the relationship between a number of salient situational variables and an important behavioural process.

Several methods are used by this approach, but especially laboratory or natural-setting experiments in the case of behaviour such as conformity and altruism, and observation in the case of doctor–patient communications, etc. Laboratory and natural-setting experiments are usually devised to test the relationship of a number of salient independent variables – such as the number of people present, or the significance of certain props – with the dependent variable. Thus any commonly occurring situation in which the psychological process under investigation occurs, is considered worthy of investigation.

These observational studies are primarily descriptive, at least in the initial stages, although hypothesis testing does often occur at later stages. Studies on the spatial use of certain buildings, children's play behaviour in a particular setting, and institutionalised client–professional interactions fall into this category. The level of observation and the sort of behaviours observed have important implications for the number and type of situational variables considered. Obviously the representativeness of the special situation(s) in which these behaviours are observed restricts or facilitates generalisability to other similar situation types.

Environmental approach. Environmental psychologists have for some time been investigating various aspects of social situations. They have concentrated mainly on the physical aspects of situations – rooms, public places, noise, heat, light conditions – but not exclusively, seeking to understand how certain parts of the built environment are perceived or related to behaviour. The dimensional approach to analysis is most often used, though there is now some interest in facet theory. Environmental psychologists are not as interested in social situations – and social behaviour – as social psychologists are, and seem happier with the concept of place. Although aware of the symbolic and social significance of props and rooms in the built environment, and of the difference between objective measurement and subjective experience, this approach has concentrated on physical features often to the exclusion of their social relevance.

As Lee (1976) has pointed out, there are three principal methods used in environmental psychology: building appraisal, observation and experiment. Building appraisal can take many forms, for example comparing various forms of behaviour with established norms, measuring behaviour before and after people have occupied the building, and comparing rehoused occupants' behaviour with that of equivalent samples who have not yet moved. Observation techniques may be used on naturally occurring or controlled phenomena. It is important that observations are representative of the phenomena that occur in the situation, and are done unobtrusively. The sophistication and availability of recording techniques can lead to very accurate observation. Environmental psychologists have used time, space and event recording observations in their studies. Finally experimental methods are also used to test specific hypotheses.

Ittelson *et al.* (1974) have argued that there are a number of methodological techniques available to the environmental psychologist – experimental, 'holistic' survey, 'exploratory research' and the field study – though the nature of the problem studied and the theoretical approach of the researcher will determine which method is most appropriate. They quote Craik's (1970) basic research paradigm of environmental psychology: 'When an environmental psychologist sets out to study the comprehension of any environmental display, he must deal with four issues. How shall he present the environmental display to the observer (media of presentation)? What behavioural reactions of the observer is he going to elicit and record (response format)? What are the pertinent characteristics of the environmental display (environmental dimensions)? And whose comprehensions is he to study (observers)?' (p. 66).

Ecological approach. This approach, linked closely to microsociology and anthropology, is most similar to the componential method. It uses mainly detailed observation, and unstructured self-report, to describe in physical, temporal and social terms naturally occurring behavioural units, called settings, often in a small community. Subcultural factors, neglected in other studies, are considered important as aspects of social situations. The aim of this approach is to develop a detailed taxonomy of the common settings of a community. The strength of the approach is in its detail and comprehensiveness, and the fact that it stresses the importance of looking at naturally occurring settings. However it is limited in that it only looks at behaviour and so cannot investigate the cognitive processes of the people in the behaviour settings. Also observation alone seems insufficient to understand fully the relationship between situational elements.

The method advocated by the ecological approach is simple, though very detailed and time-consuming, and similar to those used in microsociology and anthropology. The first stage is to establish the range of salient settings to be investigated, and then the representativeness of the locales to the population and area of study. Laboratory, role-play or field experiments are not done as a rule. Only natural phenomena are considered and observed. Next, trained observers position themselves, ideally unobtrusively but sometimes openly or as equal participants, in various settings and write extended observations and commentaries on what is happening in the behavioural setting. The observers are trained to note the behavioural episodes within the stream of behaviour and to describe them as fully as possible. Numerous observations of similar settings are made over time and the results collated to establish 'standing patterns of behaviour' for that setting. This includes the overt behaviour (verbal, nonverbal, movements, signs) and inferred moods, motivations and cognitions of the persons in the setting. It may be qualitative or quantitative, though usually a mixture of both. Barker (1968) advocated the analyses of action patterns in terms of five behaviour mechanisms: affective behaviour, gross motor activity, manipulation, talking and thinking.

There is a minimal amount of measurement and hence of data analysis. No specific data-gathering or observational techniques such as the Bales scheme are used, the emphasis being on the richness and fullness of the observation rather than on simplistic tabulation or the counting of various responses. Although observers inevitably have contact with the population they are observing, the statements and explanations of the inhabitants are not considered to be relevant data.

Ethogenic approach. This approach, also described as the roles–rules approach, is particularly concerned with the analysis of social episodes; the concepts of social rules, and social roles, are central to the analysis. What distinguishes this from the categorical, or ecological approach, however, is the proposed method of analysis, which relies exclusively on actors' testimonies or accounts of past events. Subjects are encouraged to generate their own accounts of the event, in their own terms, so providing a rich data source from which the experimenters re-create the scene, much as one might do in a court of law. However, this method does not take into consideration such factors as memory deficits, social desirability factors or language abuse, and cannot be used for hypothesis testing validation. Further it seems unclear as to how accounts are selected or integrated.

The ethogenic approach is diametrically opposed to the ecological approach in its data gathering, yet similar in its neglect of systematic data analysis or computation of the results. Marsh *et al.* (1978) note that the ethogenic approach adopts the intensive design, that is a detailed study of a few cases selected as typical, following unspecified prior observations. The interpretation of actions is done by the analysis of accounts: 'Since the basic hypothesis of the ethogenic approach to the understanding of social action is that the very same social knowledge and skill is involved in the geneses of action and of accounts, by recording and analysing each separately, we have two mutually supporting and reciprocally checking ways of discovering the underlying system of social knowledge and belief' (p. 21).

Thus the method is twofold. Firstly there is some form of detailed recording of behaviour, usually by sound or videotape. Secondly the accounts of the participants are collected by skilled interviewers who presumably have some knowledge of the event. It is rather unclear as to how the recordings of the event are analysed except to check the truth or validity of the accounts. Similarly there seems no rigorous way of analysing the form and content of accounts. Marsh *et al.* advocate the identification of social situations distinct in the culture of the population they are observing and then the sorting of the accounts into these situational categories. Within these categories the rules of interpretation and action are sought. Once again no computation or statistical analysis is done as the data are not numerical.

Thus there is a wide range of techniques available for the study of social situations. They differ in their methods of data collection (which include accounts, observation, questionnaires, judgement tasks, laboratory experiments, role-playing), data analysis (multivariate statistical designs, simple frequency data, taxonomic reconstruction, restructuring the nature of the situation into a script) and data interpretation. Some techniques have been borrowed from other well-established research traditions, while others have been devised specifically for research in this area. Each has specific strengths but resultant drawbacks. Hence an eclectic approach may be most useful.

Methodological and conceptual problems

There remain a number of difficulties and points for debate regarding research into the analysis of social situations. Some are fundamental to the very nature of the discipline – such as the advantage of verbal reports over observed behaviour, or dimensional versus componential analysis – while others are very specific to this area – such as the size and definition of the unit under scrutiny. Debates in this area, such as the cross-situational consistency of behaviour, have generated a lively and interesting discussion in the past between psychologists from varied backgrounds (Mischel, 1968; Alker, 1972; Bem, 1972; Endler, 1973). There appear to be at least six areas of controversy.

Should situations be objectively or subjectively defined and measured? The implications of the answer to this question to a large extent dictate how the other controversies should be resolved. This is at the heart of what Pervin and Lewis (1978) call the 'internal–external issue' – the tendency of psychologists from virtually all fields to focus exclusive attention on one or other sets of determinants. Murray (1938) distinguished between the alpha press of the observer (actual environment) and the private beta press of the individual which is to a large extent consensually shared by members of a group or culture (p. 69), and he considered both worthy of study. Researchers into situational determinants of behaviour divide into two camps on this issue, though some acknowledge the usefulness of a *rapprochement* between these approaches. Environmental psychologists and social learning theorists characteristically attempt to classify situational effects in objective terms (Sells, 1963; Lazarus, 1971b), while personality and social psychologists stress the importance of the subject's perception and definition of the situation (Lewin, 1935; Rotter, 1954; Argyle, 1976).

36

Symbolic interactionists (Stone and Farberman, 1970), on the other hand, insist on the exclusive use of the latter approach.

The distinction is particularly apparent when some experimentalists consider exclusively physical features in the environment, such as furniture, light or spatial layout, while others consider social rules, roles, norms, etc. The distinction between physical and social elements in a situation is, however, very vague, if not misleading, as nearly all physical features have a symbolic and hence a social meaning. To argue for a subjective definition of situations implies the actor's definition, while the objective definition of situations implies the observer's definition. Whereas the former approach stresses the cognitive conceptualisation and emotional reactions of the actor in the situation, the latter stresses behavioural responses to clearly measurable differences. Nearly all researchers take some cognizance of both factors, though they do so at different points along a continuum.

Should verbal reports, questionnaires or behavioural measures be used? It has been extensively documented that self-report measures have low correlations with overt behaviour (Argyle, 1976), yet despite much investigation into reasons for this phenomenon (Nisbett and Wilson, 1977) psychologists working in that area have continued to use predominantly self-report questionnaires. Wicker (1971) suggested refocusing investigations from the outcome and purpose of behaviour to the behaviour itself, assessing variables other than attitudes and cognition. The few studies in this area that have used behavioural measures (Moos, 1969, 1970; Mariotto and Paul, 1975; Mellstrom, Zuckerman and Cicala, 1978) have obtained results different from those of self-report studies of the same type of behaviour in the same population. Behavioural measures usually find higher situational and lower personality variance than self-report measures, as one would expect, because each measure is differentially sensitive. Self-reports can be open-ended and collected as accounts (Harré and Secord, 1972) or structured in controlled questionnaires (Endler, Hunt and Rosenstein, 1962); they are easy to obtain and score but open to biases in terms of memory deficit, rationalisation, lies, etc., and are inapplicable to several groups. Behavioural measures, on the other hand, do not suffer to the same extent from self-conscious manipulation by the subjects and can provide clear objective measures. However they do not provide clear evidence of the subject's cognitions and are difficult to collect. Obviously a combination of both techniques seems an ideal approach: behaviour and self-report as De Waele and Harré (1976) suggest.

Are global evaluative scales more useful than specific measures? In evaluating either one's own or another's behaviour or reaction to certain situations, one must do so along certain dimensions or on certain scales.

Many interactionist studies have made use of extremely vague global behavioural rating scales which have been shown in other studies to give poor inter-rater reliability. On the one hand, studies that have considered such minor effects as scratching and foot movements have high inter-rater reliability, though possibly low relevance. It has been demonstrated that the highest interaction component in a $P \times S$ study has been between ratings on general evaluative factors, but not on behaviour-specific measures. Further, some studies provide subjects with a very restricted response set which does not allow them to report their actual feelings. Pilot studies would ensure that salient measures are provided at an appropriate level of description and that inter-rater reliability is acceptable.

Are situations discrete or continuous? The approach one takes to this problem necessitates the use of either dimensional or categorical statistical analyses. Essentially the 'discrete' school holds that each situation has a number of specific elements that do not lie on dimensions. The alternative view holds that situations can usefully be characterised by abstract descriptive dimensions, with the help of factor analysis and multidimensional scaling. The difficulties of the former idiographic approach, which draws inspiration from symbolic interactionists and psycholinguists, is that although it may make a useful and insightful analysis of certain categories of situations it makes comparison between situations very difficult. The nomothetic approach characteristic of multivariate methods of studying personality theory (Cattell, 1965; Eysenck, 1973) has three limitations: factors are not always easy to interpret or label, they are not very useful for understanding or predicting behavioural processes, and they ignore many aspects of the situation. Once again this debate is by no means new, and concerns the level of analysis one wishes to use; the two approaches may be profitably used in conjunction.

What stimuli should be used? There are at least three related problems here: Who generates the stimulus situations? How are they presented to the subjects? Are we considering potential or actual situations? Recently studies have made sure that the situations people are asked to judge are relevant and meaningful to them by getting subjects to generate them themselves by the use of diaries (Forgas, 1976; Pervin, 1976). This method seems more useful than if an experimenter chose *a priori* a set of situations out of an unspecified universe. However there are two possible disadvantages: firstly, if the subject population is very heterogeneous then certain situation labels may have quite different associations, meanings or requirements for certain subgroups; and secondly they may restrict and censor a set to only socially acceptable situations. There is also the problem of presenting the stimuli. This can be done in terms of short, five to ten word descriptions

(Endler *et al.*, 1962), paragraphs (Bishop and Witt, 1970) or slides (Forgas and Brown, 1977). Short descriptions may call up stereotypic cognitive representations of certain situation types, while photographs or video allow subjects to attend to specific details. Visual, vocal and verbal reports could be usefully combined, and congruently or incongruently presented. Finally there is the important theoretical distinction between potential situations, i.e. cognitive stereotypes capable of affecting behaviour, and actual situations that are affecting behaviour. Nearly all research has concentrated on the former – symbolic representations of stereotypical social situations – while neglecting the latter, which are more difficult to assess. It would be beneficial for situational assessment if this overbalance were redressed.

Should the psychological or sociological tradition be adhered to? Because the study of social situations is at the interface between social psychology and microsociology, we have the choice between two distinct traditions. The psychological tradition has focused primarily on the behaviour of individuals and has not been as concerned with wider social or group forces that affect the individual in each or every situation. The sociological tradition is not as concerned with the personality or demo-graphic variables of the subject as how societal forces come to influ-ence social behaviour in a given situation. Psychology favours a quantitative empirical approach and is popular in North America, while sociology favours a qualitative rationalist approach. Israel and Tajfel (1972) and Tajfel and Fraser (1978), in an attack on individualistic social psychology, have offered an alternative methodology, whereby the two approaches can be usefully combined. Curiously, reviewers in the psychological tradition have criticised experimentalists for not taking sufficient interest in individual differences: 'The expansion of inquiry to include a broader sample of adults in a variety of community settings is a heartening develop-ment. However, with few exceptions community adults were studied in such a limited and trivial fashion as to contribute very little to the knowledge of personality' (Carlson, 1971, p. 205). One of the reasons for the divergence between these two traditions has been the difference between the processes under inspection: whereas researchers in the psychological tradition have investigated in depth such things as individual differences and nonverbal behaviour, researchers in the sociological tradition have been more interested in such things as group affiliation, the development of norms, deviancy, etc. However, the study of social situations provides a unique opportunity for these approaches to be usefully integrated.

Clearly these six controversies are neither exhaustive nor unique. A strong stance on one controversial issue often implies where a person will stand on all the others. Nor are these the only controversial issues in this area; others include the appropriateness of statistical techniques, the generalisability of data, etc. However, it is apparent that there are two main approaches to the study of social situations. Although this distinction is rather crude, there being many researchers who fall into both, or neither camps, it may be useful in conclusion to highlight these differences; this is done in Table 2.2.

TABLE 2.2. *Approaches to the study of social situations*

General approach:	Psychological	Sociological
Definition of the situation:	Objective	Subjective
Stimulus presentation:	Potential	Actual
Stimulus evaluation:	Specific	General
Data collection:	Behaviour, Questionnaire	Accounts, reports
Analysis:	Dimensional	Categorical

Despite the difficulties and controversies in the ways of approaching the analysis of social situations, work does progress on many fronts. Whereas some other areas of investigation have caused a sharpening of the distinction between different research traditions and counterproductive argumentation, it is hoped that the study of social situations will lead to cooperation and productive research.

3

The effect of the situation on behaviour

Introduction

Social psychological research and theorising has investigated a wide range of behavioural processes, such as anxiety, aggression and altruism, in terms of the personality structure and dynamics of the individual or within the confines of limited experimental paradigms. Historically there seem to have been phases where either the traitist or the situationalist viewpoint and method has been more popular. Also, within certain research areas one has seen the predominance of one or other approach at different times (Hollander, 1978).

It seems, however, that despite the situationalist approach, which is often very behaviouristic in its definition of, and experimentation with, situational variables, the concept of the social situation has been neglected in social psychology. This has led to two anomalies. Firstly, some areas of social psychological research, such as conformity or anxiety research, have consistently paid attention to social situational variables and often the process has been conceived of in interactional terms, while other areas, such as impression formation, have often ignored situational variables. This means that the study of some psychological processes has taken cognizance of the role of the social situation in that process, while in the study of others it has been completely ignored. There are many reasons for this – theoretical, experimental and historical. Further, it is possible to conceive of the processes as being on a continuum, much the same as the environment–genetic continuum, from purely situationally determined to purely personality determined; hence the patterns of emphasis and the neglect of situational variables. For instance, personality factors may be the most important in determining altruistic behaviour but situational factors more important in determining conformity behaviour. That is, the weight of person or situation factors in determining various behavioural processes may be quite different. There have, however, until recently been few studies that have considered the nature of the interaction between personality and situational variables. Recent studies on such diverse behaviours as dominance (Dworkin and Kihlstrom, 1978), drinking (Sandell, 1968), eating (Belk, 1975), self-disclosure (McCloskey, 1978) and cinema-going (Belk, 1974) have demonstrated that an interactional approach is useful, indeed necessary, in the study of many psychological phenomena.

41

The second anomaly is that there seems no consistent or exhaustive way of dealing with the social situation and its effects on social behaviour. For some researchers the social situation consists entirely of laboratory demands, for others it might be only isolated physical determinants, and for yet others it may be a random selection of social and psychological variables. The selection of salient situational variables seems amazingly arbitrary both within and across different areas of psychological investigation. This problem no doubt arises because there seems to be no theoretical model or list of possibly salient elements available to social psychologists for investigating the various aspects of the social situation (Goffman, 1967; Frederickson, 1972). As Sherif (1976) wrote:

A social situation is a complicated affair. . . . The participants define the situation, themselves and each other in terms that reflect their cultural backgrounds, their roles and positions . . . each participant is affected by the physical and social character of the location where the encounter occurs including that of other people who happen to also be there. The activity under way or the problem posed by the situation to the participants also affects the actions of each individual. His or her actions in turn become part of the situation for other participants. Such interaction among persons in activities in socio-physical locations is the earmark of any social situation. (pp. 26–7)

For each psychological process different situational variables might be salient, though there are likely to be some that are always important. The only area that has received considerable attention from a social situational or interactional viewpoint is anxiety, though Endler and Edwards (1978) have also reviewed person-by-situation interactions in locus of control and conformity research. In the remainder of this chapter we shall consider social situational variables that have been found to be important in determining eight widely different psychological processes. These have fallen into different areas of psychological experimentation and theorising, varying from industrial to clinical psychology; they have been investigated by different techniques, which range from self-report inventories to role-playing and natural observation; and they have been influenced by different disciplines, from psychiatry to sociology. This is not to argue for a situational psychology that ignores structural or intrapersonal differences, but to point out the paucity of organised research into situational determinants of behaviour.

Aggression

One of the most investigated areas in social psychology is that of aggression and violence. Psychologists have looked at the biological basis of aggression, its social and survival function, the legitimate and illegitimate aggressive outlets in society, the nature of interracial, interreligious and subcultural aggression, as well as the influence of environmental factors on aggression. Individual determinants of aggression, such as certain personality correlates, demographic variables and genetic structure, have all been investigated. Toch (1969) has studied extensively the structure of violent individuals, providing a thorough typology of the violence-prone person – such as self-image compensators, bullies, sadists, self-defenders and immature people – and concludes that the pre-disposition towards repeated aggression stems from many different sources.

Recently, more attention has been drawn to the situational determinants of aggression, and both laboratory and field experiments and observation have become more concerned with the relations of personal and situational variables and also of different types and degrees of situational variables that lead to a manifestation of aggression. Untangling the relationship between the various salient situational variables that lead to aggression is difficult and complicated. However it has been shown that the occurrence, ferocity, direction and form of the aggression are strongly determined by a combination of situational variables.

Environmental stressors. Various environmental stressors have been shown to lead to aggression: this occurs most often when social rules are broken or subjects are exposed to stressors such as extremes of heat or noise for long or unpredictable periods of time.

Crowding and invasions of personal space. Consistent invasions of a comfortable personal space, working under crowded conditions or living in a densely inhabited area often, though not always, lead immediately to aggression. Man has learnt, however, to tolerate and adjust to certain crowded conditions such as lifts or underground trains. Efran and Cheyne (1974) found that the act of invading the personal space has affective consequences – subjects in invasion conditions indicated more negative feelings and displayed more unpleasant facial expressions than non-invaded control subjects. As regards density and crowding it seems that under some conditions density appears to lead to aggressive behaviours, while under others it leads to withdrawal as a coping strategy. Baum and Roman (1974) argued that aggression occurs under conditions of high spatial density while withdrawal is chosen under conditions of high social density (p. 276). Rohe and Patterson (1974) found that the incidence of destructiveness and aggressive behaviour increased significantly as a function of increasing the spatial density in a children's day-care centre.

Noise. Studies have shown that the effects of steady and of unpredictable noise are different. Usually, unpredictable erratic noise is likely to elicit more aggression than steady constant noise. Geen and O'Neal (1969) exposed subjects to either an aggressive or a non-aggressive film under noisy or non-noisy conditions. They found that subsequent aggression was increased by exposure to an aggressive movie and by exposure to an environmental noise.

Heat. Various researchers have proposed that high temperatures lead to aggressive behaviour (Goranson and King, 1970; Griffitt, 1970). Baron and Bell (1975) proposed a curvilinear relationship between negative affect and aggression, high temperature leading to an increase in willingness to aggress against others, very high temperature leading to other responses, such as escaping, being more dominant.

It has been suggested that other stressors such as odour and light may, in extremes and combined with other factors, influence people to aggress against other people, themselves or inanimate objects.

Goal blocking and frustration. The frustration–aggression hypothesis, widely held but rather simplistic and overgeneralised, states that the blocking of goal-directed behaviour leads to aggression. However, experimental results show that only when goal blocking is severe and arbitrary or unjustifiably enacted does it lead to aggression. These experimental results contradict the hypothesis perhaps because the nature of the frustration – i.e. the subject's perception of how and why his goal was blocked – was different. Clearly some situationally induced frustration does not lead to aggression. However certain types of frustration, combined with other variables, do facilitate aggression.

Attack. A number of studies have demonstrated the effect of various forms of attack (especially of physical attack and insults) upon the occurrence of aggression. Borden, Bowen and Taylor (1971) demonstrated in the laboratory that most individuals will strongly counterattack any physical provocation. Greenwell and Dengerink (1973) showed that subjects respond aggressively to apparent intentions of attack. Verbal attacks have also been shown to produce an aggressive response (Geen, 1968) but the magnitude of frustration and the content of the attack have neither been equated nor controlled in these studies.

Models. A great deal of experimentation has dealt with the effects of social models of aggression, especially aggression in films and on TV (Bandura and Walters, 1963). Although the studies have been criticised on methodological and theoretical grounds, most of them reveal that exposure to scenes of violence does increase the tendency of observers to behave in a similarly aggressive manner to the model, because of the learning of new ways of aggressing, the reduction of social constraints and the desensitisation of feeling for the victim. Laboratory studies with aggressive confederates have led to similar results, especially with children (Baron, 1972; Grusec, 1972). Anecdotal evidence has also shown that one aggressive act in a tense situation is enough to spark off an aggressive episode. Eysenck and Nias (1978) in their extensive review of the literature conclude that exposure to media violence leads to a mild degree of imitation, especially in children.

Arousal. It has been proposed that situational conditions that lead to heightened arousal facilitate overt aggression under specific circumstances. These arousal conditions can be manifold: task conditions of competitiveness, loud noise, social conditions with exercise (dancing), etc. However it seems that arousal leads to aggression only where aggression is a relatively strong or dominant response for the individuals in question, and they must label or interpret their feelings of arousal as anger or annoyance. Konečni (1975) demonstrated that increased arousal stemming from loud sounds affected later aggression only when subjects had previously been provoked. Similar studies using various drugs which act as depressants rather than stimulants have been carried out. Taylor, Gammon, and Capasso (1976) showed that small doses of alcohol inhibit aggression, while larger doses increase it; however marijuana in small doses has no effect and in large doses acts as an inhibitory factor.

Props symbolising aggression. Berkowitz (1974) proposed that certain cues (people or objects) associated with aggressive acts (culturally, subculturally or personally) are important situational determinants of aggression in that they elicit aggressive responses from people ready to aggress. Berkowitz and Le Page (1967) demonstrated that angry subjects delivered more electric shocks to a victim in the presence of weapons than in their absence; however, this and other similar studies have been criticised for their possibly artefactual results. But as Baron and Byrne (1977) noted:

Regardless of the validity of the controversial 'weapons effect', however, there can be little doubt that Berkowitz's more general proposal that aggression is 'pulled' from without, rather than merely 'pushed' from within has attained widespread acceptance. In fact, it seems safer to say that his views in this respect have been extremely influential in causing social psychologists to shift their search for the determinants of aggression largely from internal conflict and motives, to external, environmental factors. (pp. 429–30)

Cultural norms. Anthropologists have studied both under-and over-aggressive societies. Gorer (1968) reviewed anthropological investigations of societies whose goal is one of peaceful isolation. Three characteristics are particularly noticeable in these societies: they live in rather inaccessible places; they are oriented to concrete pleasures and necessities of life and do not emphasise power or achievement; and they make little distinction between male and female roles, responsibilities or stereotypes. Other observers have pointed out that cultural norms inhibit or encourage various forms of aggression.

Restraints on aggression. Some situations have inbuilt social or physical restraints upon the expression of aggressive behaviour. These restraints may be in the recognised forms of reprisal, effects of surveillance, the concern of others for the victim, etc. Fox (1977) described some of the inherent rules, roles and sequences that control aggression and fighting in rural Ireland: 'There was always this stereotyped sequence of events, the insults, the rushes. There were certain conditions under which the fight would start. There had to be enough close kin of each principal on the one hand and enough related to both on the other. The close kin of each were the "holders-back", whilst the kin of both were the negotiators' (p.143). Marsh *et al.* (1978) have demonstrated some of the norms that develop in various groups – schoolchildren and football fans – to restrain and control aggression, including its ritualisation (see below, p. 131).

It seems clear then that there are a number of important situational determinants of aggression which when occurring alone or together lead directly to manifestations of aggression.

Altruism

Since the late sixties there has been growing interest and research into altruism (prosocial behaviour, bystander reactions, helping behaviour). A number of theories have been developed (psychoanalytic, cognitive, learning theory) to account for altruism, and the developmental aspects of altruism have been studied (Rushton, 1976).

In this area, unlike most others, social psychologists have paid equal attention to the personality variables of the people concerned, and the situational conditions under which people engage in altruistic behaviour. Most importantly many of the experiments have taken place in natural field settings and the interaction between the helper and the helped has been particularly studied. As Darley and Batson (1973) pointed out:

Although personality variables that one expects to correlate with helping behaviour have been measured, these were not predictive of helping. Nor was this due to a generalised lack of predictability in the helping situation examined, since variations in the experimental situations, such as the availability of other people who might help, produced marked changes in rates of helping behaviour. (p. 107)

Darley and Batson (1973) concluded, in their celebrated Good Samaritan study of situational and dispositional variables in helping behaviour, that whereas personality variables may help to predict the dimensions of kinds of helping that take place, *whether* a person helps or not is more situationally controlled. Rushton (1976) maintains that numerous studies have revealed a correlation of only about 0.30 between altruistic behaviour in different situations.

A number of environmental or situational variables that affect altruistic behaviour have been isolated, though these are by no means exhaustive. Experimenters have been most interested in the social influence process by which bystanders inhibit or facilitate helping behaviour.

Number and actions of bystanders. Studies have revealed that altruistic or prosocial tendencies are inhibited by the presence of others for a number of reasons. Latané and Darley (1968) found that a subject alone is much more likely to respond to cries of help than when in the company of others. Similarly they showed that not only the presence but also the activity of others in the situation influences behaviour. Subjects nearly always conformed to the inactivity of bystanders in an 'emergency' situation. Latané and Rodin (1969) showed that subjects were more likely to go to the aid of an 'injured' experimenter as a function of their relationship to the person they were with in the situation – they helped most when alone (about 70 per cent of the time), about 40 per cent of the time when with a friend, about 20 per cent when with a stranger, and less than 10 per cent when with an unresponsive stranger. Ross (1971), investigating the effects of children as bystanders, concluded that they inhibit an adult's altruistic response less than other adults because a grown person feels some responsibility for taking charge, but adults are still more inhibited than when alone because children are also witnesses to any potential blunders.

The effect of models. Bryan and Test (1967) showed that simply observing others helping (changing a tyre, donating money) makes one more likely to help. Macaulay (1970), however, found a 'boomerang' effect in modelling, in that people who donated money or made a fuss about not giving, both increased the donating of subjects: they broke the ice as it were, or lowered constraints about acting toward others. A number of studies have found that exposing a child to an altruistic model can enhance the amount and direction of that child's subsequent altruistic behaviour. It seems that relatively brief exposure to salient models can produce durable and generalisable behaviour changes in child observers, though this depends on the salient characteristics of the model (nurturance, power).

Reinforcement. Moss and Page (1972) found that reinforcement in one situation led directly to helpfulness in a second situation occurrring shortly thereafter, whereas negative reinforcement led to less helping in the second situation. Thus reinforcement principles can clearly be useful in increasing helpfulness, but this is only one process amongst others.

Ambiguity of the situation. It seems that any reasons for creating ambiguity in the minds of the observers and hence not allowing them to define the situation as that necessitating a helping response inhibit that response from taking place. Clark and Word (1974) proposed that any factor that creates ambiguity in understanding the situation inhibits altruistic responses; in their experiment, whenever ambiguity was low, subjects went to the aid of the victim every time. Yakimovich and Saltz (1971) found that a cry for help clarified a situation for a bystander to the extent that altruistic response tripled – with no cry for help on the part of the experimental confederate only 29 per cent of subjects did anything to help, but with the cry over 80 per cent helped. Similarly Ellsworth and Langer (1976) found that more help was elicited in non-ambiguous conditions than in ambiguous conditions, but that the differences between the two conditions was significant only when the victim stared at the subject.

Familiarity with the situation. Because it seems a common experience that people are slightly anxious, confused and overwhelmed on first encountering a novel situation, experimenters (Latané and Darley, 1970) have proposed that these feelings of uncertainty of the social rules interfere with altruistic behaviour. They reported that New Yorkers were more likely to help a victim in a familiar (subway) setting than in one that was not so familiar (airport). Sherrod and Downs (1974), in a more experimentally based laboratory study, showed that subjects who had been exposed to confusing auditory messages in a stimulus overload situation were less likely to grant a confederate a favour than were subjects who had not previously experienced the stimulus overload.

Cultural rules. Collett (1977) has pointed out the importance of social rules in social behaviour. Clearly our culture has developed certain rules for behaving in emergency and non-emergency situations – don't stare, do nothing unless one owes responsibility, follow the example of others. Abstract norms like social responsibility and reciprocity guide actions in various situations: for instance it has been found that people reciprocate less when help is seen as accidental or required than when it is intentional or voluntary. The way these rules operate can be seen with children who have not fully internalised these cultural or subcultural norms and rules. Staub (1970) found that younger children were more likely to help peers than older children were; the latter reported certain social constraints and inhibitions. And they found that children were much more likely to help if previously given permission to enter a room in which a staged accident had happened (Staub, 1971).

Characteristics of the victim. The sex of the victim as a variable in altruism has been extensively studied. Pomazal and Clore (1973) found that cars stopped much more often for stranded female motorists than for males,

48

and also that female hitch-hikers were offered lifts sooner than males – a fairly well substantiated result. Latané and Dabbs (1975), however, showed that the sex effect depended on the traditional sex roles of the area: males were more likely to help females in the Southern USA cities than in Northern ones. Fisher and Nadler (1976) found that the resources of the donor and the victim are important in determining whether help results. Aid which represented a high cost to the donor in terms of resources resulted in positive self-feelings in the recipient, but low cost (in this case the lack of donation of chips in a game) led to a relatively negative self-image in the recipient. Emswiller, Deaux and Willits (1971) found that people from the same group tended to help each other more than people from other groups ('hippies' versus 'straights'). Finally Gaertner and Bickman (1971), looking at black–white helping differences in the USA, found that blacks helped blacks and whites equally, while whites were more likely to help members of their own race.

Accident parameters and bystander calculus. It seems that if the situation requiring the subject to help is difficult or expensive in terms of money, time or self-esteem, a subject is less likely to help. Walster and Piliavin (1972) showed that with two levels of arousal held constant, the probability that the observer will provide direct help to a victim depends on a bystander calculus, which refers to the relative costs of providing direct help and the rewards for providing such help. Piliavin and Piliavin (1972) showed that people were more likely to help a non-bleeding than a bleeding victim. Piliavin, Piliavin and Rodin (1975) found that subjects were less likely to help a birthmarked person in an underground than the same subject without a birthmark.

Latané and Darley (1970) have provided a five-stage model for the analysis of behaviour in emergencies, a model that is situation-specific and interactional, applying to emergency and non-emergency situations alike. The critical steps are: notice that something is happening; interpret the situation as one in which help is needed; assume personal responsibility; choose a form of assistance; and implement the assistance.

Assertiveness

Over the last ten years the concept of assertiveness has become popular in both academic and popularist circles, especially in North America. Assertiveness training, developed originally to treat individuals with passive inhibited life-styles, has been successfully used in the treatment of social inadequacy, depression, marriage breakdown and delinquency. A number of tests have been developed to measure assertiveness, by self-report inventories (Wolpe and Lazarus, 1966; Galassi *et al.*, 1974) or behavioural tasks

(McFall and Twentyman, 1973; Young, Rimm and Kennedy, 1973). They have been used mainly on psychiatric populations and students. The reliability and validity of these tests has not been determined sufficiently and is unsatisfactory, but the major problem in the area of assertiveness and assertiveness training is the generalisation of training across situations. Where the objective of assessment is to provide an accurate estimate of an individual's capability, performance and deficiency across a wide range of situations, a representative sampling of situations in the domain of study is vital. Alas, this aspect of assessment has largely been neglected. Hersen, Eisler and Miller (1973) found that some training methods led to more generalisation across different situations than others, and stress that 'the client must be taught to discriminate in which situations his newly acquired assertiveness will be appropriate' (p. 520).

The problem with the concept of assertiveness is that it is both complex and situation-specific. It seems that several constructs are usually included under the general heading of assertion, such as defence of one's own rights and the restriction and rejection of unjust demands, social competency, independence, capacity to take control of various situations, skills of initiating, communication of positive feelings and personal expressiveness. Assertiveness may be either positive or negative – the expression of positive emotions such as affection, empathy, admiration and appreciation, or of negative emotions such as hostility and defiance. Behaviours that are assertive in one circumstance may not be so in another. Some people may be perfectly socially skilled in a wide range of social situations but inadequate and unassertive in a special group of situations, or unable to distinguish situational constraints or requirements in certain 'phobic situations'. Assertive behaviour involves a complex pattern of combined verbal and nonverbal responses to specific situations, and it seems impossible to talk of a trait of assertiveness or to train people to become more assertive without paying close attention to the situational determinants of assertive behaviour. Surprisingly little research has, however, been done in this area.

Power and status of interactors. The most important determinant of assertiveness is an individual's power or status. This may be based on his position in an organisational hierarchy or in an informal group, his social class, or his age. In general it seems that it is more difficult to be assertive (rather than passive or aggressive) with people of greater power, more dominant role and higher status than with people of lower power, etc. This is probably more true of negative assertion – refusing requests, disagreeing, responding to criticism – than of positive assertion, though this too may be difficult. Clinical psychologists have in fact developed programmes to teach assertive skills needed at job interviews and in employer–employee interactions (McGovern *et al.*, 1975).

Competence at group task. People are more assertive and assume positions of leadership when they are more competent at the task in hand, or know more about the topic under discussion than the others present. Carter and Nixon (1949) found that leadership in a group changed when the task was changed.

Sex of the other person. A great number of studies have demonstrated sex effects, though results have been contradictory, depending on the scale used and the population sampled. In general it seems that females are less assertive than males in responding to members of the opposite sex (Eisler *et al.*, 1975). However a number of studies have shown that there is no sex difference in overall scores of assertiveness (Chandler, Cook and Dugovics, 1978; Crassini, Law and Wilson, 1979).

Situational rules and complexity. The more complex the situation, and the more unfamiliar a person is with the rituals and routines in such situations, the more difficult it is for him to be assertive. Where the rules are unclear to a person, such as in arranging for future contacts, asking favours, complimenting others, etc., he is likely to have difficulty in being assertive (Gambrill, 1977). Galassi and Galassi (1979) found that situations in which an individual is annoyed or angry because his rights have been ignored or violated cause most difficulty.

Cultural norms. Different cultures have different norms of assertiveness, especially among women (Furnham, 1979). Hall and Beil-Warner (1978) demonstrated that Anglo-Americans were more assertive than Mexican-Americans, and interpreted their findings in terms of the needs and cultural experience of Mexican-Americans. The stress on assertiveness in North America is not found in many other societies.

Zeichner, Wright and Herman (1977) concluded:

Clearly, the interaction between some situational variables and social skill seems to determine which behaviour will be emitted by the socially interacting individual. The low homogeneity in performance observed across situationally variant areas of social skill suggests perhaps the need to reconsider the concept of the 'good dater' or the 'assertive' person. This lack of homogeneity may support the notion that different situations require different frequencies of the same social behaviour and perhaps indicates that individuals who are socially competent in one situation may not be competent in other situations. (p. 380)

Thus it seems that trainers and experimenters in assertiveness recognise that it is not a unified concept and is largely determined by situational constraints and demands, though experimentation on situational determinants of assertiveness is still rather limited (Gambrill and Richey, 1975).

Attraction

The study of interpersonal attraction has been around in psychology for at least sixty years, though most work was done in the 1950s and 1960s. There seem to be a number of problems with the conceptualisation and operationalisation of attraction, which is a multifaceted attitude made up of evaluative, cognitive and behavioural components. A number of different approaches to attraction have been formulated – reinforcement–affect model, exchange theory, stimulus–value–role theory – and the process of interpersonal attraction has been interpreted in terms of existing approaches in social psychology such as the social-skills model, personal construct systems and the ethogenic approach.

Duck (1977) in his review of the studies in this area concluded:

First, that research on interpersonal attraction has perhaps overstressed the static phenomena such as are visible and operative in short term encounters; and helps to make subjects assume that all observed acts reflect 'disposition' rather than 'episodes'. Second, it alerts one to the possibility that getting to understand inter-personal attraction and actually getting to know a person are similar procedures – both built up by consideration of many different features. At present, explanations of the roots of attraction tend to be global, static and dispositional (e.g. 'personality similarity causes friendship') and not sufficiently embedded in the awareness of episodic fluctuations, differences or changes (e.g. 'personality similarity causes friendship to deepen, but it doesn't start it off or finally cement it'). (p. 19)

As Duck has pointed out, most of the work on interpersonal attraction has taken the process of attraction *in vacuo*, with very little cognizance of the social context in which it occurs; in a very real way the context influences the perception of, and reaction to, others and the development of and changes in attraction. As La Gaipa (1977) stated:

No adequate system has been developed for classifying the variables essential for defining the social context in which exchange occurs, even though one major role assigned to situational variables is that of regulating the exchange processes. . . . Parameters include the 'temporal' dimension, such as prior history and future expectations, and the 'spatial', e.g. physical distance. A second role assigned to situational variables is an interpretative function since the meaning of a social act depends on the context in which it occurs. (p. 162)

Similarly Levinger (1974) has pointed out that the social situations that psychologists create for the experimental study of attraction between pairs usually involve brief contacts, and that a variable that particularly affects attraction in short meetings (e.g. physical attractiveness) will not necess-arily have the same impact in deeper relationships.

Some studies have considered situational influences on the process of attraction. By far the most common studies are those on proximity and environmental stressors.

Proximity. It has long been known and established that the probability of friendship and attraction developing is determined in part by the structure of the environment – the physical distances between people at work, in housing or at recreation, and the temporal distances between periods of interaction. One of the earliest studies was that of Festinger, Schachter and Back (1950) who showed that friendship groups in a housing estate were most often made up of next-door neighbours; and that inside residences the most popular persons were those who lived in rooms on stairways and hence were more likely to meet people. A later study by Warr (1965) showed that physical proximity is a factor in determining both positive and negative sociometric choices and that positive choice leads to stable interaction patterns over time even when people have been physically separated. Byrne and Buehler (1955) demonstrated that students were more likely to become friendly if they were assigned an adjacent seat in a classroom, while Nahemow and Lawton (1975) found that old people became friendly simply as a function of living on the same floor of high-rise buildings. Segal (1974) found that the first letter of the surname is an important factor in establishing friendship in certain institutions, as the alphabet often determines seating and living arrangements. However, this is not true under all conditions. Subjects must be of equal status and the situations socially rewarding, rather than the reverse. It seems, therefore, that environmental planning can have a significant effect on friendship formation and interpersonal attraction merely by altering the proximity of people's living space and thus encouraging more or less interaction. However it is not always clear why interaction should lead to attraction. Zajonc (1968) has argued that repeated exposure to any stimulus results in an increasing positive evaluation, irrespective of the nature of the first response. It is possible that repeated rewarding experiences avail people of the opportunity to work out a synchronised interaction pattern, and to develop shared constructs. It seems that if people are not initially attracted to one another they can and will reduce their contact and proximity or simply ignore one another. However, very few studies have considered other salient parameters of the propinquity situation, such as the role relationships, the duration of contacts, the physical environment in which contact takes place – all of which might further our understanding of the attraction process.

Environmental stressors. According to the reinforcement–affect model, environmental conditions have a direct influence on our emotions which in turn affects our attraction to others. Gouaux (1971) found experimentally that subjects in an elated mood tended to be more attracted to a stranger than subjects in a depressed mood, irrespective of the fact that the stranger was not responsible for the mood state of the subjects. Such environmental stressors as light, heat and sound have been demonstrated to affect psychological stability and reactions.

Griffitt and Veitch (1971) found that under conditions of high temperature and high population density, measures of liking or disliking were more negative than under more comfortable conditions. Veitch and Griffitt (1976) found that the hearing of broadcasts of good news led a subject to like a stranger, while after hearing bad news, subjects showed dislike of a stranger. It seems, then, that any situational variable that can affect the mood or emotional state of an individual acts as a mediating variable in his attraction to others in that situation.

Role relationships. A number of theorists have maintained that role expectation may determine the circumstances under which certain behaviours lead to attraction. Schultz (1960) found that different patterns of compatibility characterise different role relationships. For the role of room-mate, affective compatibility was the most important area of compatibility, while for the role of travelling companion compatibility in the sphere of dominance appeared more important. Hendrick and Brown (1971) found that extroverts perceived extroverts as more attractive than introverts in their role relationship as reliable friend, partygoer and leader. It is possible that a person becomes attractive because of the role that he holds (Hurwitz, Zander and Hymovitch, 1960) and that this initial attraction may generalise to an overall impression of him. There are various kinds of rewarding roles, such as that of nurse, which often lead to initial attraction. Yet as Kerckhoff (1974) points out: 'With such varying definitions of the "same" roles current within the society, any attempt to generalise a theory of interpersonal attraction that ignores the "normative framework" within which the attraction occurs is doomed to failure' (p. 72).

Rituals/conventions. Harré (1977) has proposed that action sequences are different for friends and acquaintances. He maintains that we go through a *Bruderschaft* (friendship) ritual in order to keep our friends and cement our friendship, but argues that in order to understand *Bruderschaft* we must understand its opposite – *Feindschaft* (enmity). He is particularly interested in how friendships work, after initial attraction, and concentrates on a microsociological analysis of the rituals, formal and informal, which maintain a state of friendship or enmity. He believes that we have to keep up certain rituals of meetings and partings in order to express stability of friendship. He quotes Douglas (1972), who argues that the structuredness of entertainments is a measure of the degree of intimacy that the entertainment expresses – the more unstructured the entertainment the greater the distance from real intimacy of the social relation it expresses. This as yet very little investigated area of research seems most promising.

Thus experimental work on the process of attraction has begun to give more consideration to the role of situational factors and to reformulate ideas about attraction. As yet, however, little work has been done.

Conformity

Although the impetus of research into conformity and persuasibility has slackened, a great deal of experimental work has been done in this area. Recent reviews (Furnham, 1978; Wiesenthal *et al.*, 1978) have pointed to the neglect of interactional studies considering personality and situational variables in the conformity process. This is also true of work done on traits designed to measure conformity, such as social desirability.

Most of the experimental work has been based on certain paradigms: the Asch (1952) group perception experiment, the Crutchfield (1955) booth judgement experiment, and the work of Festinger (1957) and Schachter (1959) on verbal behaviour towards deviates. Although there have been a few studies in natural settings, little is known of the generality or dynamics of conformity across situations outside the laboratory.

Early researchers in this field (Gordon, 1952; Crutchfield, 1959; McDavid, 1959; Vaughan, 1964) recognised that conformity is the result of the interaction between person and situation variables, though the vast amount of empirical research has focused on the effect of either of these two variables on conformity, rather than on the interaction between them (Allen, 1965; Endler and Edwards, 1978). Those studies that have considered the interaction between person and situational variables (Becker, Lerner and Carroll, 1966; Sistrunk and McDavid, 1971) have usually focused on one personality variable, e.g. achievement motivation or authoritarianism, and tested the interaction with one situational variable, e.g. task difficulty or group status on conformity behaviour. However recent reviewers (Endler and Edwards, 1978; Furnham, 1978) have stressed the need for studies investigating the dynamic interaction between these independent variables. Wiesenthal *et al.* (1978) found the fewer than 15 per cent of over 320 articles they reviewed included both personality and situational variables.

The empirical laboratory studies have isolated a large number of salient situational variables that might affect conforming behaviour:

1. *Task difficulty and ambiguity*. The more difficult the task, or ambiguous the stimuli, the more subjects look to others as sources of information, especially in opinions and abilities that have reference to social reality.
2. *The nature of the stimulus*. Conformity behaviour varies considerably as a function of what type of judgement people are asked to make (count metronome clicks, give opinions, solve arithmetic

problems); the more factual and clear the problem the less the conformity that results.

3. *Source certainty*. The more certain a person is of the reliability and correctness of his influence source, the more likely he is to conform to it.

4. *Group size*. Researchers have disagreed as to whether the relationship between group size and conformity is linear or curvilinear, though there does appear to be an optimal conformity-inducing group size (Rosenberg, 1961).

5. *Unanimity of group judgement*. The more unanimous the group judgement, the more conformity is elicited; quite small amounts of deviation within the majority lead to a large reduction in conformity responses.

6. *Group composition and attraction*. Cohesive groups of high status, and prestigious males, tend to elicit most conformity; the more attractive the group, the more a person is likely to be influenced by it.

7. *Group acceptance*. High-status people have idiosyncrasy credit and can deviate, as do very low-status or rejected group members; people of middle status usually conform most.

8. *Private or public behaviour*. People tend to conform more when asked to give their judgement or to behave publicly rather than privately.

9. *Previous success or failure of the group*. Numerous experiments have demonstrated that a person will conform more to a group that has a past history of success than to one that has consistently failed.

10. *Consistency of the minority*. Moscovici and Lage (1976) have shown that a convinced, coherent minority forming a representative sub-group of individuals can greatly influence majority opinion. It is most important that the minority is consistent in its position if it is to have any effect on the majority.

These salient situational variables stem largely from laboratory work and are as a result rather restricted. Field studies on conformity might well reveal a wider and perhaps less obvious range of situational variables.

McGuire (1968) in his work on personality and susceptibility to social influence set out six principles that account for the sometimes significant but generally low intercorrelations between a wide range of tests of social influence. He maintained that conformity is the result of two mediating processes – reception and yielding (i.e. the reception and comprehension of certain messages, and secondly willingness actually to yield to the persuasive influence) – but that salient personality variables (e.g. intelligence) might affect these processes in opposite ways. His third principle is the situation weighting principle: 'The weights of the mediators will tend to vary from situation to situation in predictable ways: different social situations vary greatly in the absolute and relative strains they put on reception and yielding' (p. 1148). As regards receptivity and conformity, if situations are extremely hard or easy in terms of their strain on the subject's capacity for attention and comprehension (ambiguous, subtle, complex) a salient personality variable (self-esteem) will tend to affect influenceability mainly via its relation to yielding. In situations of intermediate difficulty, where there will be a wide range of individual differences in attention and comprehension, the salient personality variables' effect on influenceability will be considerably determined by its relation to receptivity as well as to yielding. As regards situational demands on yielding, if the situation compels yielding so that virtually everyone is at the asymptote of complete yielding, then the person's individual proclivities toward yielding will be unimportant in determining the outcome; but if there is an intermediate level of social pressure then the personality variable effects on the yielding mediator will be of considerable importance (see Fig. 3.1).

McGuire states as the first methodological requirement for personality–influenceability research the analysis of social influence situations, suggesting the drawing up of an *a priori* classification scheme in which situations differ in attention, comprehension, yielding, retention and action. 'It should provide us with a set of social influence situations of known characteristics from which we can, in designing an experiment to test a specific personality–influenceability hypothesis, choose the situations that provide the most appropriate test' (p. 1173).

Conformity behaviour is thus a complex interaction between personality and situational variables. It is possible that the two sets of variables act in quite different ways and that the psychological processes are quite different. As regards personality variables it seems that people on the extremes of a salient personality variable (e.g. self-esteem) may act in the same way in most social influence situations, whereas a person intermediate between the two extremes may be more variable in his responses. However, regarding salient situational variables it seems that extreme situations, as defined on a salient dimension – that is at either end of the extremes – may lead to similar susceptibility in conformity, whereas moderate, middle-range situations lead to the opposite effect.

This implies not only that the interaction is very complex, as there seem to be a large number of potentially salient situational and personality variables already identified that directly affect conformity, but also that the psychological processes involved in the interaction might be operating quite differently for the two types of variable.

Finally it is important to note that people choose or avoid getting involved in social influence and other situations, and that while in them they try to change them (see p. 79f.).

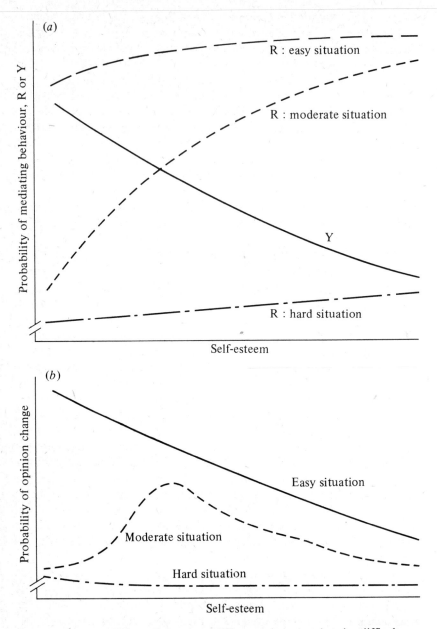

Fig. 3.1. Effects of situational differences in comprehension difficulty on the resultant personality–influenceability relationship. (*a*) Three levels of reception difficulty as they affect the mediators. (R, reception; Y, yielding.) (*b*) The three levels as they affect the resultant influenceability measure (opinion change). (After McGuire, 1968, p. 1151.)

Nonverbal behaviour: gaze

Nearly all the elements of nonverbal behaviour are situation-specific. Bodily contact, for instance, is a function not only of the age and sex of people (Henley, 1973), and the nature of the message they are giving (Argyle, 1975), but also, and most importantly, the social event that is being enacted. Bodily contact is differentially appropriate and meaningful at an encounter group, spiritual healing service, wedding ceremony or parting, etc. Similarly spatial behaviour (proximity, orientation) is a function of seating arrangements, special significance of certain prescribed areas, private territories, age, status and height of interactor, etc. Gestures and bodily movements too are to a certain extent situation-specific (Morris *et al.*, 1979) in both their sending and their receiving. In fact elaborate gestural codes have been established to communicate in certain specific situations, such as cricket (the umpire's signals), auction sales (bidding), conducting (baton movements) and horse-racing (tick-tack).

We shall illustrate the nature of situational determinants of nonverbal behaviour by looking at gaze, which is of central importance in social behaviour and which has received considerable experimental attention over the past fifteen to twenty years. Gaze has been studied by developmental psychologists, psychiatrists, anthropologists and sociologists, but has been primarily the concern of social psychologists. A number of important situational determinants have been established.

Cooperation and competition. Harré and Secord (1972) have maintained that one of the most important distinctions between social episodes is whether people in the episode are competing or cooperating. Exline (1971) studied the effect of need for affiliation, sex and cooperative versus competitive situations on gaze. He found that females with a high need for affiliation looked much more in situations where competition was subdued, while females with low need for affiliation looked a lot more in competitive situations, though this was not true of males.

Attractiveness of the other person. People tend to look at others more when they like them, find them attractive or have similar attitudes, than when they do not (Exline and Winters, 1965; Efran, 1968; Kleck and Rubenstein, 1975). This result has been confirmed by different experimental methods – manipulating attraction, pre-selecting subjects, role-playing, etc. But as Argyle and Cook (1976) have pointed out, the reasons for the like–look effect are not clear.

Cultural rules and meaning. There are wide cultural norms about the use of gaze during social interaction which are explicitly taught in the culture and socialised in young children (Tomkins, 1963). Morsbach (1973) reported that people in Japan do not look each other in the eye, preferring the neck, while Watson (1972) showed that in Nigeria a higher-status and/or older person must not be looked directly in the eye during conversation. Watson (1972) demonstrated that too much gaze was considered threatening, insulting and disrespectful by Africans, Asians and Indians, whereas too little gaze was seen by Arabs and South Americans as impolite and insincere. The wearing of dark glasses, and of particular types of eye make-up, is often culture-specific, and also situation-specific. In our culture Goffman (1963) has asserted that gaze, like other forms of social behaviour, is rule-governed – for instance we should not gaze at strangers in public places. Most rules seem to govern too much of the particular behaviour rather than too little of it. Greetings and farewells have been closely studied (Goffman, 1971; Kendon and Ferber, 1973; Collett, 1980) and seem to have common patterns of gaze.

Distance. Following from the Argyle and Dean (1965) equilibrium model, a great deal of work has been done on the relationship between gaze and interpersonal distance, though there is some controversy in this field as to when the model works and what variables are involved. It is well known that in crowded places (lifts, tubes) there is aversion of gaze, and that when people who are conversing are quite a long way from one another they gaze more regularly than when close to one another. Coutts and Schneider (1975) studied gaze and mutual gaze in a naturalistic setting (waiting-rooms) using pairs of subjects different distances apart. The results strongly confirmed the inverse relationship between proximity and gaze. Patterson (1973) found that the inverse relationship holds best when subjects are allowed to choose their own distance for interaction, and when the distances are within certain zones. Recently Patterson (1976) has proposed that movements towards greater intimacy lead to increased arousal in the target person; if this movement is perceived positively it will lead to reciprocity, but if negative it will lead to withdrawal and equilibrium maintenance.

Content of conversation. Another prediction from the equilibrium model is that gaze is a function of the intimacy of the topic of conversation. Exline, Gray and Schuette (1965) showed that subjects looked less when being interviewed about personal matters than about preferences for films, sports, books, etc. Schulz and Barefoot (1974), also using interview situations, found that increased intimacy of gaze caused decreases in the subject's gaze while speaking but not while listening. The nature of this relationship presumably accounts for the institutionalisation of the Catholic confessional and the psychoanalyst's couch, both places where intimate topics of conversation occur, and where the speaker cannot see the listener, and vice versa. However when the conversation concerns aggression, dominance, ingratiation (Lefebvre, 1975) or persuasion (Mehrabian, 1972), there is more gaze on the part of the speaker.

Status. Research from many sources has demonstrated that gaze is related to the social status of people within a group. Both experimental (Efran, 1968; Exline, 1971) and role-playing methods have shown that people of higher status are gazed at more by those of lower status than vice versa, though there are a number of possible intervening variables such as the direction the higher-status person is facing or who is talking most. Burroughs, Schultz and Aubrey (1973) demonstrated that gaze and leadership are fairly highly correlated ($r = 0.69$), i.e. that people look more at those they regard as leaders. Sissons (1971) showed that there are differences in the amount of gaze, head-nodding and smiling that middle-class subjects give to working- and middle-class subjects respectively. She found that working-class subjects do less 'ritual work' than middle-class people.

Environmental setting and props. When certain props are present which are of mutual interest to the interactors mutual gaze is reduced, and staring at the props occurs. In an observational study between customers and assistants in a department-store, Argyle, Lalljee and Lydall (Argyle, 1978b) found very little gaze in this situation. Similarly Argyle and Graham (1976) demonstrated that mutual gaze drops very greatly when a detailed object salient to the interaction is present (map for planning a holiday) or when it is possible to look out of a window. Further, the absence of a relevant object produces increased gaze both at the person and the background.

Interaction sequence. A great deal of work has been done on the relationship of gaze and ongoing sequence of social behaviour. People gaze at one another at discrete and salient points in the interaction where certain information or reinforcement is needed or given. The coordination between speech, gaze and other non-verbal signals has received a great amount of experimental attention, though the results are highly debated (Beattie, (1979). Kendon (1967) found that people gazed at the endings of long utterances, although this finding has been challenged by Levine and Sutton-Smith (1973) and by others. Steer and Lake (1972) found that the amount of gaze between two people significantly increased when there was a change of task.

Leadership

We are not concerned here with situational variables that lead to the emergence of a particular person as leader, but rather with styles of leadership adopted in different situations, and the optimum style of leadership.

Like the person/situation debate in personality theory, the different approaches of experimenters on leadership outlined by Hollander (1978) are by no means exclusive. The situational approach to leadership has failed to distinguish adequately between task demands, which play a major part, and the structure, size, history and resources of a group and its physical setting. As Hollander (1978) pointed out, leaders may create or redefine situations in which they are effective. Further, personality traits are important relative to the situation in which they are displayed. Finally a leader's qualities in a given situation vary with the group.

The situational approach, popular in the 1950s, held essentially that different situations require different leadership functions to be performed (Gouldner, 1950). Each situation requires of the leader that he should exercise influence, but the functions and styles differ widely. Thus an individual who served effectively as a leader in one group or context might well be pushed into the background in some other situation or group. The most important feature of the situation is the task to be done, and this defines the group situation. Other salient elements are the group's structure and size, the organisational rules, and the group's past history of success and failure.

Fiedler's three dimensions of leadership situations. Leadership, or supervision, of groups is an important area of professional social skills. It is now known that different kinds of leaders and different styles of leadership are most effective in different situations. Fiedler (1964) put forward a theory of situational variability which has led to a great deal of research. He worked with a single dimension of leadership, the LPC or least-preferred co-worker score: a high score indicates acceptance of least-preferred co-workers, and this indicates concern with people; a low score indicates rejection of such co-workers and hence more concern with the task. Fiedler used three dichotomies of situations: good versus bad relations with the group, high versus low power of the leader, and high versus low structure of task. He predicted that high-LPC (person-centred) leaders would be most effective over moderately favourable or unfavourable situations, while low-LPC (task-centred) leaders would do better under very favourable or very unfavourable conditions.

Comparisons of high- and low-LPC leaders under generally favourable and unfavourable conditions have mostly confirmed the theory (e.g. Chemers *et al.*, 1975). However some studies have not obtained the predicted results; sometimes the correlations are low and non-significant, and there is doubt over the meaning of the LPC scores – perhaps it reflects characteristics of least-preferred co-workers (Wrightsman, 1977). It was found by Mitchell, Larson and Green (1977) that knowledge of how well a group had done affected ratings of situational dimensions, and also affected assessment of leaders on LPC – though this is usually measured by questionnaire.

Fiedler maintains that any one leader will be effective only in a certain range of situations, and cannot be effective in all. We dispute this conclusion; it should be possible to learn a range of different leadership skills, appropriate to different situations.

There are other aspects of situations that affect the optimum leadership style. (*a*) In a large group there is more need for centralised control. Hemphill (1950) found that there was greater tolerance of leader-centred direction in groups of over thirty members. (*b*) When decisions have to be taken quickly, and in times of crisis, more authoritarian leadership is needed. (*c*) When the group members have authoritarian personalities they get on better with an authoritarian leader (Haythorn *et al.*, 1956). It is quite possible for a leader to shift his leadership style up and down the authoritarian–democratic scale, as the situation requires. (*d*) Thurley and Wirdenius (1973) and others have found that the optimum style of supervision of industrial work groups depends on details of technology, e.g. assembly-line versus machine-minding, the incentive scheme, and so on.

Social structure and rules. The structure of a group both leads to and is dependent on, the style of leadership that emerges in that group. A segmented group structure with a minimum of intercommunication and maximal status differences between group members favours autocratic leadership, while integrated groups with maximum involvement and participation favour democratic leadership. Certain agreed social rules might prevent a certain type of leadership – such as authoritarian or *laissez-faire* – from occurring.

History of the group. Both internal and external factors can cause self-stabilising changes in the structure of a group: different sub-groupings, dissident elements being forced out, scape-goating, problematic members, ideological shifts can lead to dramatic changes in leadership. External changes such as threat or conflict, or dramatic changes in conditions, can greatly affect the leadership. New members or loss of members can grossly change the tone of a group and affect leadership.

Crises. In crisis situations, where the group goal is blocked or the group's existence is threatened, the emergence and skill of leaders are most apparent. Hamblin (1958) found firstly that leaders have more influence in times of crisis than in times of non-crisis, and secondly that members of a group accept leadership when faced with a crisis. In situations of group instability conditions ideal for the emergence of leaders are likely to occur. Crockett (1955) demonstrated that divided groups provide excellent conditions for the usurpation of leaders.

Self-disclosure

The amount, type and timing of self-disclosure to others have recently received much attention in the social and clinical literature (Chaikin and Derlega, 1976). It is the contention of many clinical psychologists that self-disclosure is related to mental health (Maslow, 1954; Rogers, 1961). Jourard (1971) has pointed out that the non-disclosing person is cut off from the insight and feedback that others give him, and he is not given self-disclosure in return. The non-discloser is thus a lonely, isolated and uninsightful person.

However for self-disclosure to be successful, useful or even meaningful, it must be carried out at the right time, in the right situation and to the right people. Indeed, inappropriate self-disclosure may lead to ridicule, rejection and humiliation. 'Appropriate' implies norms and rules about self-disclosure in a culture or subculture. Further, the appropriateness of any instance of self-disclosure is a function of a number of situational variables – the context of the disclosure, its recipient, its intimacy level, etc. – which have been empirically investigated. Both Himelstein and Kimbrough (1963) and Highlen and Gillis (1978) concluded that there is a need for stricter experimental control of situational variables. One of the major problems in self-disclosure research, however, is that most studies have relied on pencil and paper questionnaires or laboratory encounters rather than on observational data in natural settings. This has led to possible experimental artefacts, epiphenomenal results and the neglect of certain important factors such as nonverbal communication, alcohol consumption, the length of interaction, etc. However one of the most promising approaches to self-disclosure using a traditional method is the interactionist model of McCloskey (1978), who followed the S–R technique of Endler *et al.* (1962). A variety of studies have consistently thrown up a number of important situational variables.

The context of disclosure. A great number of contextual factors have been shown to affect self-disclosure (Goodstein and Reinecker, 1974), including such nonverbal variables as physical distance. Jourard and Friedman (1970) showed that physical closeness to the experimenter increased disclosure time for both male and female subjects. Robbins (1965) found that subjects would reveal more to others in a highly cohesive group. Drag (1971) found that the number of persons in a group affected the amount of self-disclosure. Most self-disclosure occurred in groups of four, rather than in those of two or eight people. Olberz and Steiner (1969) found that sequential and reinforcement variables affected self-disclosure. People are less likely to divulge information about themselves when they are aware that they are being observed, i.e. in public rather than in private situations. Much work has been done on disclosure during group therapy sessions

(Cozby, 1973). Highlen (1976) showed that subjects matched their self-disclosure with the tone of the situation, for example expressing anxiety in negative situations.

The status and target of self-disclosure. Goffman (1967) noted that it is more appropriate for a person of low status to disclose personal information to one of higher status than vice versa. Chaikin and Derlega (1976) confirmed this hypothesis experimentally and noted that most forms of peer self-disclosure are seen as highly appropriate. Slobin, Miller and Porter (1968) found that workers disclosed more to their bosses than to their subordinates, but most to fellow workers on the same level. Simonson (1973) found that high self-disclosure was reciprocated among people of fairly equal status, but led to a reduction of self-disclosure on the part of the low-status people (students) when the disclosure was seen as coming from someone of high status (psychotherapist). Furthermore, intimate disclosure on the part of the high-status person was seen as unusual and upsetting. Perhaps self-disclosure places one symbolically on the same level as the target of disclosure.

There is more self-disclosure to those who are liked as opposed to those the discloser dislikes or is indifferent to (Certier, 1970). Students disclose most to same-sex friends; older people disclose more to opposite-sex friends, who are presumably spouses or the equivalent (Jourard, 1971). On the other hand there can be extensive disclosure to strangers, under certain conditions, since the stranger poses no threat and is not in a position to pass the information on to relevant others (Simmel, 1950).

Students reveal much more – nearly as much as to same-sex friends – to mothers than to fathers. However, disclosure to parents falls rapidly with age over the period 17 to 40. In general there is more disclosure to females (Jourard, 1971).

Roles. To a large extent the appropriateness of different types of self-disclosure is a function of the particular role that one is playing at the time. Institutionalised role relationships such as doctor–patient or confessor–confessee demand deep self-disclosure, while others quite clearly prohibit it. Goffman (1959) pointed out that unless such information is directly related to the outcome of the transaction, it is highly inappropriate for a salesperson to disclose personal information to a customer. Young (1969), who had subjects role-play therapists with peers, found a sex-by-role interaction: males were more responsive to role differences than females were. Goodstein and Reinecker (1974) concluded:

In summary it appears that a number of situational factors, especially the opportunity for mutuality of disclosure, but also group or experimenter expectations, instruction, directness and order of the disclosure, reinforcement for self-disclosure, the role and status of the target of the disclosure, size and relevance of the group, and a variety of yet unexplored variables affect the self-disclosure process. (p. 64)

Rules and norms. There appear to be a number of rules and norms in self-disclosure. Altman (1972) has noted that there is an obligation to reciprocate disclosure, and that this is stronger in the early stage of the relationship than in later years. However, Jones and Gordon (1972) showed that one should not be hasty in revealing good fortune as this is evaluated negatively, whereas modesty in early stages is more positively evaluated. Numerous authors (e.g. Chaikin and Derlega, 1976) have pointed to the reciprocity norm, which is related to the equity theory of social relationships. The essential implication is that the recipient of high disclosure who fails to reciprocate with information about himself puts himself and the discloser into an inequitable relationship, with the discloser providing more inputs than the recipient. There are also rules against disclosing 'deviant' information. Derlega, Harris and Chaikin (1973) showed that people dislike and distrust deviant high disclosures more than conventional high disclosures. This supports the notion that it is the content rather than the intimacy of disclosure that is weighted more heavily in evaluating others.

Conclusions

This review of how eight important areas of research in social psychology have approached the situational determinants of each kind of behaviour has revealed three facts. Firstly, that whereas researchers in aggression, altruism and attraction have studied numerous, and often similar, situational determinants of behaviour, researchers on assertiveness and leadership style have done much less to investigate the immediate physical and psychological situation in which these processes occur, and its possible effect on them. Secondly, that in those areas of research – aggression, altruism and attraction – that have dealt with the situational determinants of behaviour situational variables have not been selected in any consistent way. Obvious variables such as situational stressors or social norms have been looked at by most researchers in this area, while others such as social rules or temporal sequences have been ignored, there being no useful model to use. Thirdly, that very few interactional studies or approaches have taken cognizance of the interaction of person and situation factors as they relate to behavioural processes under investigation.

Because of the nature of laboratory-based experimental work that looks at psychological processes in controlled, highly unrealistic situations, and the emphasis in social psychology on intra- and interpersonal aspects of behaviour, ignoring the person–environment interaction, social psychology has not yet developed a clearly defined or consistent way of looking at situational determinants of behaviour.

Conclusions

If one is to have a truly interactional (or transactional) social psychology one must be able to investigate adequately and thoroughly the situational determinants of behaviour. We suggest that the balance should be temporarily redressed from a study of intra- and interpersonal factors to one of situational factors, and thence to a relationship between the person and the situation. It is apparent in this review that some researchers have begun to do this by manipulating both personal and situational variables and seeing how they affect the dependent behaviour. However the relationship between the personal and situational variables that are isolated is not always clear, and often moderating variables have to be postulated.

4

Drives and goals

Introduction

Our central hypothesis is that situations enable people to attain goals, which in turn satisfy drives; all the other features of situations can be explained functionally in terms of their contribution to the attainment of goals and the satisfaction of drives. Our main theoretical antecedent is Lewin, and we shall use ideas from Murray, from the McClelland–Atkinson group and from exchange theory. However we shall be concerned with drives and goals as properties of situations rather than of individuals.

Animals and people have biological *needs*, for food and water etc., which energise and direct behaviour and whose satisfaction is necessary for survival. There are a number of other motivational systems which can be regarded as *drives*; like needs they direct and energise behaviour, but they are not based on any biological deficit and the survival of the individual does not depend immediately on their satisfaction, though the survival of group and species may do. Drive-related behaviour results in satiation of the drive in some cases, but not in all.

In groups of monkeys it can be seen how each drive contributes to the survival of the individual or group. Sexual and maternal drives need no explanation; aggression enables groups to defend themselves and their territory; dominance produces a stable leadership hierarchy, which makes it possible to keep order internally and to defend the group in an organised way (DeVore, 1965). Biological drives are innate, though in higher mammals – especially in man – the means of satisfying them are learnt. Social drives, including sex in man, are mainly acquired through socialisation, and reflect the culture and the needs of society. There are great variations between cultures in the typical strength of these drives. Some cultures are very aggressive, some are greatly concerned about status and loss of face. These variations can sometimes be traced to the environmental setting – tribes which are constantly having to defend themselves against enemies need to have aggressive members, and so aggression is encouraged in children (Zigler and Child, 1969).

Social situations allow the attainment of *goals*, which in turn satisfy needs and other drives. We define a goal as a state of affairs, whether a bodily state, behaviour of self or others, or condition of the physical world, which

68

is consciously desired, or is pursued without awareness, and gives satisfaction when attained and frustration when not attained. We maintain that in every culture a pattern of social situations develops which will satisfy needs and other drives by provision of appropriate goals.

Murray (1938) developed an account of the motivational properties of situations, using the same list of drives that he used to describe individuals. These include what he called the 'needs' for achievement, affiliation, aggression, dominance, autonomy, harm-avoidance, sex, understanding, nurturance and many others. Murray proposed that a situation to which an organism reacts or attends may be classified according to the kind of effect – facilitating or obstructing – it exerts or could exert upon that organism. This tendency or 'potency' in the environment is referred to as a 'press'. Thus, a press may be thought of as a temporary gestalt of stimuli which usually appears in the guise of a threat of harm or a promise of benefit to the organism. So objects in the environment may be classified, by the organism, as hurting, nourishing, befriending, coercing, comforting, etc.

Why do people enter social situations or engage in social behaviour at all? A functional account would suppose that they are motivated to do so, i.e. they expect that certain needs will be satisfied or certain goals attained. Although different people seek different things, social behaviour seems to be the product of several different drives. Also people learn that certain needs will be satisfied in certain situations, and some situations have developed as cultural institutions because they satisfy needs. Thus, having a meal is a situation for satisfying the hunger drive, and the classroom situation is one for satisfying the desires to teach and to learn. People may seek a number of specific goals in social situations, such as help with work or other activities, friendship, guidance, power, admiration. Situations develop gradually and continue to change, during long historical periods, as a result of other changes in society, and through processes of leadership and social influence. During living memory we have seen the emergence of a number of new situations – discos, encounter groups, pop concerts, TV panel games, radio phone-in programmes – and we have seen the emergence and disappearance of sit-ins and teach-ins. Earlier in this book we developed the analogy between situations and games. In recent times we have seen the emergence of new games, such as Monopoly, Scrabble and paddle-ball, an increase in the popularity of squash, extensive modifications to cricket and rugby football, and the near-disappearance of fives and real tennis.

Lewin (1935) offered a conceptual model of the way goals affect behaviour. He represented the person in a situation by that person's 'life-space', which shows all the features of the person and the setting which affect his behaviour at a given moment. Since the characteristics of the life-space were deduced from observed behaviour it could not be used to predict behaviour; it could not be elicited by interview or related methods because people were not aware of all the relevant features. The parts of the situation in which Lewin was particularly interested were goals, positive and negative, routes to goals, and barriers (Deutsch, 1968).

Lewin recognised positive and negative regions of the life-space, corresponding to states to be sought and avoided, for example on account of previous rewards and punishments, shown as C and D in Fig. 4.1. Alternate routes to goals are shown, as in A and B, and the presence of barriers, in our example blocking route B. Points *en route* may be, or become, sub-goals themselves.

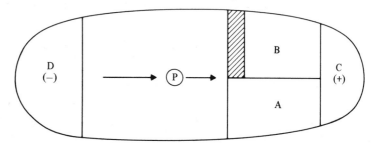

Fig. 4.1 Lewin's representation of goals in the life-space. C, positive goal; D, negative goal; A, route to C; B, route to C blocked by barrier.

Lewin did not explain how goals acquired their positive and negative valences, apart from suggesting that these can be derived from rewards and punishments. We want to go further, and suggest that they are based on the satisfaction and deprivation of drives. Negative valences are not necessarily the opposite of positive ones, as has been found in the case of achievement motivation (p. 83).

The idea that there are routes to goals and that goals may have to be attained in a certain order was developed by Schank and Abelson (1977). For example, a professor has the goal of settling in a certain town; this can be done only if one of a number of other goals can be met (e.g. buying a house or renting a flat); these may in turn involve yet other goals, such as borrowing money. When a house has been bought, additional goals become possible – 'goal embellishment' – such as sending for his housekeeper and dog, which help with the main goal of 'settling'. New goals may emerge because of the events occurring during a situation. For example, in the course of a committee meeting certain issues not on the original agenda may emerge so that there are additional goals in the situation.

The concept of barriers is important in the analysis of situations with negative valences. Where there is double-avoidance conflict, for example, it may be possible to avoid both negative valences unless there is a barrier (see

Fig. 4.2). For example a child might want to avoid eating both cabbage and turnips; this is no problem unless he has to eat one of them.

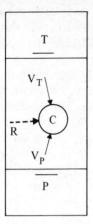

Fig. 4.2. Lewin's (1935) representation of double-avoidance conflict. This type of conflict occurs when, for example, a child stands between two negative valences (V); he is being sought by threat of punishment (P) to do a task (T) he does not want to do. R is the resultant.

A social situation, by definition, requires at least two participants. For two or more people to enter a situation voluntarily each must expect to be able to satisfy one or more drive. Sometimes they can satisfy the same drive, as in sexual or affiliative situations. This also applies to the cooperative performance of a task, a goal which may be linked to various drives. Sometimes complementary goals and needs are involved, as in parent–child, teacher–pupil, buyer–seller and other encounters. Sometimes the goal on one side is simply money, which can be exchanged for almost anything. In 'exchange theory' as formulated by Thibaut and Kelley (1959) and Homans (1961) – and as derived from economics – social behaviour is explained in terms of the future rewards or satisfactions each participant hopes to receive from the other. In this formulation, for a relationship to be sustained each party must get enough out of it and each will produce acts which are calculated to benefit him. In research using the exchange theory approach, one goal per person is usually considered (Chadwick-Jones, 1976). From the theory it follows that people seek and remain in social situations because of the rewards they receive. Social situations contain a cooperative element; each person depends on rewards mediated by the other.

Thibaut and Kelley (1959) were the first to analyse social situations in terms of pay-off matrices. This approach assumes that a person's behaviour will be determined by his subjective pay-off matrix. Within this framework, a social encounter is viewed as a choice for each person between several possible social acts, each combination having a pay-off for each of them. Outcomes are compared with a person's 'comparison level' (what a person thinks he deserves or considers normal); an outcome less than this level is felt to be unsatisfying. Although there is an exchange of rewards, one person may receive more than the other.

However not all behaviour is goal-directed. In our repertoire study (experiment 7.1), we found that subjects listed as typical events not only goals and events leading to goals but also non-goals. For the situation 'an evening at home', for example, they mentioned 'feeling exhausted' and 'feeling irritable'. This also applied to the most clearly structured situation, 'a visit to the doctor', where feelings of 'worry', and 'anxiety' were important elements in the situation, though they would not be considered as a necessary route to the goals of the participants in the situation.

The goals of situations

Motivation has been studied primarily as a property of individuals rather than of situations. We shall discuss in a later section the effect of situational variations in *arousing* drives. Our concern here is with the goals and the drives which are satisfied in different settings. Most people know the situations which will enable different goals to be attained; in a sense research is rather superfluous. It also follows that we can study this matter by a rather easy kind of research – asking people. It is not quite so straightforward as this, however, since there are individual differences in motivation; furthermore it is not always obvious how two goals are related to each other.

We have found that while there is a fairly high degree of consensus about what goals can be attained in each situation, there are also individual variations (experiment 4.1). It is likely, though this has not yet been tested, that there is a lot more variation in some situations than others. For example there is quite a wide range of possible goals at a party, and a much smaller range at a job selection interview.

Two general factors of social behaviour and motivation have often been obtained: 'task' and 'socio-emotional' (Bales, 1950; Foa, 1961). However there is another, a whole area of motivation: biological needs. In experiment 4.1 we factor-analysed the reported goals for each role position in a number of situations, and in most cases obtained three independent factors: (*a*) own well-being (i.e. bodily needs); (*b*) acceptance and other social needs; (*c*) specific task goals. Maslow (1954) proposed that there is a hierarchy of needs, with bodily needs at the bottom, followed by social needs, and self-actualisation at the top. He maintained that the higher needs become activated only after lower needs have been satiated, though the evidence for this is weak. The main supporting evidence for the theory comes from the lowest needs in the hierarchy – when people are very hungry, thirsty, cold or afraid they are not much concerned about higher needs, as a number of studies have shown (Cofer and Appley, 1964). There is not such clear evidence about the upper part of the hierarchy. However, studies of the motivational concerns of workers at different levels of seniority are certainly consistent with Maslow's hypothesis. At lower levels people are most concerned about pay and security; at higher levels (where they are paid more) they are more concerned about achievement and success. (Pay is not included in the Maslow scheme since it is thought to be related to a number of needs.) It has also been found that higher-level managers attach more importance to autonomy and self-actualisation (Vroom, 1964; Cumming and El Salmi, 1968). However, these results could be due to more ambitious men rising higher in the hierarchy. So the studies do not test the central Maslow hypothesis that the satisfaction of a lower need results in greater concern with a higher one. This hypothesis was tested in a study of forty-nine young managers over an interval of five years. Only very weak connections were found between greater lower-need satisfaction and increases in higher-need strength (Hall and Nougaim, 1968). Certainly in experiment 4.1 it appeared that several different kinds of goal were sought simultaneously in common social situations.

Biological needs include hunger and thirst, breathing, and keeping at the right temperature. In several social situations eating and drinking are common goals, together with some concern for bodily comfort. For some reason social psychologists have, in the past, often overlooked biological needs as motivators of social behaviour. Interaction with doctors and nurses, and between parents and children, allows pursuit of further biological goals, health and bodily fitness. Sex may be classified as a biological drive, though it is not a need; it is one goal amongst others in many social situations when members of both sexes are present. The goal of sexual motivation which is sought is often no more than some degree of social response, such as mutual gaze, proximity and other nonverbal signals.

Social needs include a number of separate drives, which are satisfied in different situations. The social needs most widely recognised by psychologists are:

1. dependency
2. affiliation, acceptance, approval
3. dominance
4. status, recognition and self-esteem

Again there is widely shared common-sense knowledge about which situations will satisfy these drives. Affiliation, for example, is likely to be satisfied in small social groups, especially in groups of friends, when they are engaged in primarily 'social' activities such as parties, dances and meals together. For some people, especially the socially inadequate, affiliation is mainly a negative drive – avoidance of rejection.

The basic social need may be self-esteem; recognition and status awarded by others are subgoals which produce self-esteem. Status and recognition can be obtained by winning things, or by visibly succeeding in other ways, being a successful performer, holding a higher rank, dressing up in impressive uniforms or academic dress, etc.

We have found that most situations contain specific tasks, and these define one of the main goals for a situation. Sometimes there is what is usually called *intrinsic motivation* to perform a task which is satisfying in its own right, because it is interesting, uses the person's abilities and produces a sense of well-being and satisfaction. Sport and most leisure activities come into this category, as does work for many people. Task goals may be instrumental to other goals or motivations. Do social occasions have task goals? For the hosts or organisers there are clearly task goals; for the others there are the central activities of talking, dancing, eating, etc., which perhaps function as tasks here.

Money is a goal when a person is selling something, working for a living or negotiating wages or other settlements. Industrial managers can manipulate the work situation so that money is a goal which can be reached via subsidiary goals of greater productivity etc. Individual incentive schemes have been found to produce a 39 per cent increase in rate of work; group bonus schemes create more cooperation, but a much smaller increase in output (Argyle, 1972). Task performance is also motivated by *achievement needs*, especially when performance can be assessed against some standard of excellence. This will be discussed in a later section.

Goal structure

When a person is influenced by two goals, or when there are two people present with at least one goal each, the two or more goals may be related in a variety of ways. They may interfere with or facilitate the other, or they may be independent. The main goals and their relationships we shall call the 'goal structure'. We start with Lewin's conceptual analysis of life-space, with its barriers and routes to goals but we shall modify it in several ways.

1. We have already said that we want to relate goals to drives.
2. We want to find methods of analysing the goal structure of situations independently of behaviour, so that behaviour can be predicted.
3. We shall analyse separately inter- and intrapersonal goal relationships.

4. We shall make further distinctions about the ways in which two goals may be related.
5. We shall show the relations between goal conflict, difficulty in dealing with situations and social skill.

If a person is influenced by two goals, these may be related in several ways:

1. Independence: the pursuit of one goal neither helps nor hinders the other.
2. Instrumentality: the pursuit of goal A helps, or is a step towards, goal B (e.g. P is hungry and also wants to know what a certain restaurant is like).
3. Double instrumentality: each goal helps the other (e.g. teaching and research).
4. Being part of a larger goal (e.g. dressing and getting washed).
5. One-way interference: one goal interferes with the other (e.g. getting someone to go away and keeping on good terms with him).
6. Two-way interference (e.g. working and playing football). There are also cases of logical incompatibility (e.g. having a cake and eating it).

In fact people are usually motivated by a number of different goals. In the study of job satisfaction, for example, it is found that there are a number of separate areas in which workers may be satisfied, including money, job content, status, working conditions, co-workers and supervision (Argyle, 1972).

Lewin showed that there can be several different kinds of conflict between two goals: pursuit of two positive goals, avoidance of two negative regions of behaviour, and simultaneous approach and avoidance. Approach–avoidance conflict occurs when the same goal has been associated with both reward and punishment, or in other ways leads to both positive and negative goals. Miller (1944) showed how the avoidance component declined faster with distance, creating an equilibrium position; this model was used by Argyle and Dean (1965) to explain the adoption of a particular level of gaze and proximity, and the way one intimacy signal can compensate for another. Approach–avoidance conflicts are also behind restraints in aggression and sexual behaviour. When aggression is aroused by another's annoying or insulting behaviour, avoidance forces such as anticipation of the other's retaliation, other social disapproval, or internalised anxiety are also aroused. The result is a reduced, modified or displaced form of aggression – mild verbal protest, being rude to someone else, watching wrestling on TV.

However, restraints on behaviour are not only due to fear of punishment. There is also altruistic concern for others. It is now believed by many biologists that although animals are basically selfish, some aspects of altruistic behaviour have emerged in the course of evolution because they result in improved chances of the survival of genes. Animals look after their own immediate relations because they share a proportion of genes (50 per cent for children, brothers and sisters, 25 per cent for cousins and grandchildren, etc.: Dawkins, 1976), which are thus helped to survive. the most familiar example of this is the concern of parents for young children.

Consider now two persons with one goal each. Our set of six relationships is possible between these goals also.

1. Independence.
2. Instrumentality corresponds to *helping behaviour*, e.g. a nurse wanting to look after a patient's health.
3, 4. Double instrumentality corresponds to *cooperation*, towards the same goal, as in affiliative behaviour, or towards different goals, as between doctor and patient. Cooperation may involve elements of conflict. In situations devoted to affiliative or sexual activity, for example, one person may want to go faster or further than the other. There are more complex cases, such as the Prisoner's Dilemma Game, where each party is tempted by the possibility of larger gains to shift from cooperative action (Jones and Gerard, 1967).
5. One-way interference corresponds to one person *frustrating* another, as in the case of a punitive parent, boss or custodian.
6. Two-way interference corresponds to *conflict* and *competition*. Competition exists if when A attains his goal, B does not. Examples are competing for food, in races or for jobs. This can be represented in game theory terms as a zero-sum game: whatever one wins, the other loses. In real life, competition need not be a zero-sum game, since one may gain without the other losing anything, or losing very much, as when two people hope to win a raffle. Conflict exists when the interests of two parties are opposed, as in competition, or when two parties are pursuing different and incompatible goals, and when relations between the two have become hostile as a result.

We now come to goal structures where there are two people and two (or more) goals each. Take assertiveness as an example. P wants to persuade Q to do something Q does not want to do; for example, a husband wants to persuade his wife to go to a certain place for their summer holiday. Each has the second goal of sustaining good relations with the other. If P wins he loses some of Q's goodwill and damages the relationship, and vice versa. This can be represented as:

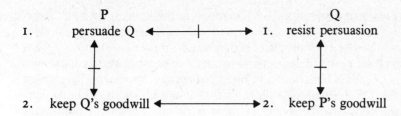

According to this somewhat speculative analysis there is one interpersonal conflict, two similar intrapersonal conflicts and one cooperative linkage of goals. In experiment 4.2 we report some actual cases of the analysis of goal structure.

Most social situations contain two or more goals for each person, so that both inter- and intrapersonal conflicts may be present. We suggest that this is one of the main sources of difficulty, anxiety and avoidance of situations. We further suggest that this form of difficulty can often be overcome by the use of relevant social skills. Here are some examples.

Supervision. A leader wants to look after and keep on good terms with members of his group. These goals are partly incompatible, since if he is on more equal terms with them he loses his authority. The solution lies in the democratic-persuasive style of supervision, whereby he consults and persuades, as well as performing his task-leadership role and looking after the group members (Argyle, 1972).

Assertiveness/persuasion. If our analysis above is correct, there are both internal and external goal conflicts. In order to influence the other person without damaging the relationship the appropriate skill is to be rewarding and to use forms of persuasion which appeal to his interests.

Making friends. This is a problem for those who want to make friends but are afraid of being rejected – an approach–avoidance conflict. The avoidance component may prevent the positive goal from being attained. Training may consist in reducing the anxiety by behaviour therapy, or in teaching new social skills so that rejection is less likely.

Avoidance of negative consequences. When barriers prevent escape from the situation, a problem is created when all the options are negative. Facing the boss when one's work has been unsatisfactory is an example. These situations can be alleviated by appropriate skills – in this case apology, recognition of failure, offering explanations, and showing determination to do better, are possible approaches.

A very important aspect of situations is the amount of *surveillance*, especially by parents and teachers (in the case of children) or by policemen, people in authority or people of higher status (in the case of adults). What matters is the power of these people to punish or produce negative outcomes if certain kinds of behaviour take place. Numerous experiments have shown that children cheat more if they think that no-one is looking, and that there is more aggressive behaviour if there is no-one present to punish the aggressor. The likelihood of cheating is a joint product of the reward to be gained by success and the lack of surveillance. The likelihood of aggression is a joint product of the level of instigation, e.g. by insults, and the probable absence of sanctions. In Chapter 13 (p. 359) we discuss the effects of closed-circuit TV and other forms of surveillance in reducing shop-lifting, vandalism and other forms of crime. The goal structure is like this:

1. to engage in aggression, or other forbidden behaviour

2. to avoid external punishment

3. to avoid internal disapproval

There are two forces which normally keep the forbidden behaviour in check: external sanctions and internalised standards. In situations of little or no surveillance only internal controls, if any, are left to restrain the forbidden behaviour, and these controls may not be sufficient. Internal controls can also be weakened, for example by alcohol.

'Temptation' can be interpreted as the prospect of entering a situation where it is known in advance that certain goals can be attained and that surveillance is weak. An alcoholic about to enter a pub is an example.

Appearing in front of an audience is an extreme of surveillance and includes a variety of situations in which attention is focused on the self, such as public performances, being in front of TV cameras, evaluation by an interviewer and being the only person of a certain type (e.g. male, white) present. Many people are positively attracted towards these situations, as opportunities for self-display, or anticipated rewards of other kinds. However many people are also made anxious by appearing in front of an audience, presumably through fear of failure and disapproval, and may avoid it. Appearing in front of an audience affects the galvanic skin response (GSR). Paivio (1965) developed questionnaire scales for measuring both forms of motivation, which he called Exhibitionism and Audience Anxiety. He discovered that the scales were independent of each other, so that some people score high on both forms of motivation; they made shorter speeches in an experimental situation and had a higher rate of speech errors than others.

The selection of situations

Situations are not straightforward determinants of behaviour, because people can choose which situations to enter. Individuals also avoid situations, either because they are not interested in the goals offered or because they feel that they cannot cope with these situations.

One area in which selection of situations has been studied is choice of occupation. Differences in motivation affect occupational choice. Those high in achievement motivation choose high-status and risky occupations. In the USA, at least, they choose finance and business in preference to other professions. They want to take risks in the hope of making a lot of money; they want to build up large enterprises and make their mark on the world (Atkinson, 1958). There is also evidence that they play a crucial role in initiating economic growth.

The effect of other kinds of motivation is shown by questionnaire studies of values. For example, Rosenberg (1957) found that students high on his people-oriented scale chose social work, medicine, teaching and social sciences; students scoring high on his self-expression scale chose architecture, journalism and art; students scoring high on intrinsic-reward orientation chose sales, hotel management, estate agency and finance. Finer discriminations can be made from the Strong Vocational Interest Blank or from the ten dimensions of the Kuder Preference Record, which measures preference for outdoor, mechanical, computational, scientific, persuasive, artistic, literary, musical, social service and clerical work. This scale is widely used in the USA for vocational guidance for school-leavers.

A person's self-image affects his choice of occupation, though the two develop side by side. If he chooses his occupation fairly late, e.g. at the end of college, he will already have a fairly well-developed self-image; the choice of job is a further crystallisation of this. While the self-image partly reflects abilities or other objective properties of the person, these may be perceived inaccurately; in addition the self-image is a somewhat complex product of past experience, and is not always very closely related to objective qualities of personality – as, for example, in people who feel 'inferior'. A study was carried out in which students scored themselves for fifteen attributes such as creativity, leadership and intelligence and the extent to which various occupations required them. There was an average correlation of 0.54 between the two sortings for the occupation that they had chosen for themselves, and lower correlations for other occupations (Vroom, 1964). This shows that people choose occupations which they think require the qualities which they think they possess. The self-image may also include elements of the job chosen. A student may come to see himself as an embryo-scientist as the result of playing the role of scientist, and through close association with and admiration of scientists. Similarly he may come to see himself as a future businessman, journalist, clergyman, etc., as a result of vacation jobs or university club activities. People's understanding of different jobs includes a good deal of mythology. Hudson (1968) found that British schoolboys thought that the typical arts graduate would probably wear fashionable clothes, flirt with his secretary, like expensive restaurants, and run into debt; the novelist was seen as 'imaginative, warm, exciting and smooth'; the psychologist was similar to the novelist, but intelligent and lazy.

Holland (1966) suggested that because people in vocational groups have similar personalities, they will respond to many situations in similar ways and they will create characteristic interpersonal environments. He found six occupational types: conventional, artistic, realistic, investigative, enterprising and social, each of which sought out and created specific interpersonal environments. For instance conventional environments encourage people to engage in conventional activities such as keeping records, and organising material, whereas investigative environments encourage people to engage in activities such as research and scholarly work.

People also choose educational settings that will suit them. They take courses which will lead to the right careers, and universities that have a congenial social atmosphere. Stern, Stein and Bloom (1956) found that authoritarians in the USA often join military academies rather than universities. This group used the Murray (1938) approach whereby individual needs and environmental 'press' are measured in a similar way. Individual needs were assessed from expressed perferences for each of 400 activities comprising the Activities Index (Stern, 1969). By 'press' is meant 'the situational climate, the permissible roles and relationships, the sanctions', etc. Press includes the explicit goals of an organisation, which can be stated by key people, but also implicit objectives, which can be detected from the actual practices, the behaviour which is in fact rewarded or encouraged. Press consists of the individual goals which are commonly pursued, and whose pursuit is generally approved of. A number of studies reviewed by Pervin 1968 have shown that there is lower satisfaction and higher drop-out rates when there is a mis-match between student and college.

It has also been found that the choice of institutional setting is a function of personality and psychopathology. Eddy and Sinnett (1973) used detailed activity records, clinical assessments and personality measures to ascertain how emotionally disturbed college students spent their time in a university institution. They found, as predicted, that extroverted action-oriented people appeared to spend more time in socialisation areas (lobby at the weekend, and the park and bars during weekdays) which provide opportunities for social interaction. There was also a relationship betweeen sex and setting – females were associated with activities such as spending time shopping, visiting and grooming while males were associated with socialising in the lounge.

Another area of selection of situations is leisure activity. There are twenty-four hours in a day, of which people spend about eight sleeping and, for five or five and a half days a week excluding holidays, eight working, which leaves an average of about eleven hours per day free. Some of this is spent dressing, eating, travelling, etc., but quite a lot of time is left, in which people can do more or less what they like. What do they do with it? The main types of leisure activity are:

1. constructive leisure (gardening, community work, etc.)
2. cultural pursuits (music, further education, etc.)
3. sport
4. family-centred leisure
5. social activity
6. relaxation (TV, light reading)

Everyone has his or her preference for leisure activities, presumably reflecting motivations, and to some extent abilities. Bishop and Witt (1970) found that choice of leisure activity was partly a characteristic of persons and partly a function of recent activities and experiences, e.g. 'a period of frustration and tension, a period of satisfying work, a day of feeling full of energy'.

Within the category of 'social activity' people exercise preferences to seek or avoid such settings as pubs, restaurants, discos, prayer meetings, encounter groups, 'dates', etc. We have been particularly interested in the extent to which situations are avoided because people feel anxious in them, or feel that they cannot cope with them. Young people in particular find many common situations, like parties and discos, very difficult, and avoid them (Bryant and Trower, 1974). (The types of situations which cause most difficulty are discussed in Chapter 12.) This finding, together with the idea that situations provide for the satisfaction of common drives, suggest that many people are in an approach–avoidance conflict about certain situations. The solution may be to find a less frightening alternative situation in which the same needs can be met.

Mehrabian and Russell (1974) found that there is a general factor of approaching and avoiding situations. Approaching includes physical movement towards, degree of exploration and looking, length of stay and like–dislike. They found that arousal-seekers showed more approach to places with varied stimuli; Mehrabian (1978) found that high-arousal-seekers approached preferred settings more. Zuckerman (1974) found that sensation-seekers entered certain situations more than those low on this dimension (p. 84f.).

We have carried out three new studies on the factors affecting choice of situations. In experiment 4.3 Furnham reports an investigation of the effect of personality variables in choice of leisure activity. He found for example, that extroverts spend more time at social events and in physical pursuits. In experiment 4.5 Argyle and Furnham report a study of role relationships as a factor in choice of situation. The relationship which affected situational choice most was that of spouse (or equivalent), while colleagues, friends and family were associated with different situations. In experiment 4.4 Furnham reports a study which showed that the nature of the intended communication (e.g. giving bad news) influenced the situation and the medium (e.g. telephone) selected for the purpose.

The situational arousal and satiation of drives

We saw earlier that people seek out situations which they expect will enable them to satisfy needs. Approaching and entering the situation may arouse the need further, and goal-directed activity may then satiate the drive. Level of arousal is a joint product of the initial state of the organism – e.g. hungry – and of the properties of the situation. If a person has not eaten for several days, it does not require a very enticing meal to make him want to eat. His initial state is the effect of experience in a number of recent situations. Sometimes people seek general arousal, for example at fairs or noisy parties. When people approach any situation they are probably anticipating both the arousal and the later satisfaction of drives. Here are some examples of the arousal and satiation process.

Hunger. The hunger drive is aroused in the first instance by deprivation, and to a lesser extent by the approach of a habitual feeding time. The individual then seeks out a situation where the need can be satisfied – the kitchen, a restaurant, etc. Entering this situation then arouses the hunger drive further by the sight or smell of food, other people eating it, and imagining items described on the menu. Eating progressively reduces the hunger drive until satiation sets in, apart from the paradoxical effect that eating foods such as salted peanuts increases the desire to eat.

Aggression. This has a biological basis, but is not a need that has to be satisfied. Aggression is aroused in one situation, and discharged (sometimes resulting in satiation) in that or a second situation. The situational factors that arouse aggression (insults, attack, etc.) have been discussed already (p. 43f.). The aggressive behaviour which follows may consist of a physical attack on the person who was the cause of insult or frustration, or less direct forms of aggression. Aggression is cathartic, i.e. satiates the drive, only under fairly specific conditions – if the subject attacks the other physically (e.g. by giving electric shocks) or sees him harmed physically, but not by verbal aggression, attacking physical objects or watching other aggressive activities on film or TV (Baron and Byrne, 1977).

Achievement motivation. There are persistent individual differences in n.Ach, so that some people seek and others avoid occasions for meeting standards of excellence. It is possible that a period of deprivation, i.e. failure, can increase need for achievement, though over a longer period it would have the reverse effect. There are certain features of situations which arouse n.Ach; these include emphasising the 'importance' of performance, encouraging subjects to do their best, making it clear that they will be evaluated, competition with others, and testers looking poor performers in the eye. When achievement motivation is measured by the projective method it is found that some people have images primarily about successful outcomes while others have more failure imagery. This corresponds to Lewin's positive and negative valences, and is the basis for a distinction between achievement-oriented and failure-oriented personalities. Achievement-oriented personalities are motivated primarily by hope of success; they prefer situations in which success depends on skill rather than on chance, and where there is about a 50 per cent probability of success. Failure-threatened personalities are concerned to avoid failure rather than to seek success, prefer situations in which success depends on luck rather than on skill, and where the probability of success is very high or very low (Atkinson, 1977).

Women have special problems; they are sometimes found to have a fear of success, consisting of fear of social rejection, or concern for their femininity or 'normality' (Horner, 1970). Since many forms of achievement are felt to be incompatible with the female role, they may seek achievement in feminine domains, which often involves competence in social skills. However later studies have shown that these results may be due to stereotypes; women only fear success for themselves if they anticipate negative consequences of success in a particular situation. This can equally well apply to men, e.g. if a male is about to be top of the nursing-school class (Cherry and Deaux, 1975).

Achievement does not necessarily result in satiation; indeed individuals are likely to be encouraged to seek more success as a result. A high-jumper does not retire when he has jumped 5 feet 6 inches: he revises his target upwards.

Affiliative motivation. Under what conditions is affiliative motivation aroused? If affiliation is to be regarded as a drive similar to hunger and thirst, it should be aroused by deprivation – in this case by isolation. A number of experiments have been conducted in which subjects have been isolated for periods of up to four days. It has been found that periods of

83

isolation as short as twenty minutes make children more responsive afterwards to social rewards. However, other experiments suggest that isolation does not arouse affiliative motivation unless it creates anxiety (Walters and Parkes, 1964). Schachter's experiments (1959) showed that anxiety can arouse it alone. Probably affiliative motivation is also aroused by anticipation, of parties and other social events. Affiliative behaviour may bring a number of benefits, such as reducing anxiety, providing a means of checking opinions against those of others, inhibiting aggression and making cooperation easier. However, affiliation appears to act as an autonomous drive, quite apart from such consequences. Schachter (1959) measured the arousal of affiliative motivation by means of the percentage of subjects who chose to wait in a room with other subjects rather than by themselves. He found that most subjects preferred to wait in a room with other anxious subjects rather than in a room full of students waiting for something quite different. He found that affiliation was aroused by the prospect of receiving large electric shocks, especially in first-born and only children. This is because first-born and only children have a stronger attachment to their parents, are made anxious by separation, and learn that social contact reduces anxiety (Sutton-Smith and Rosenberg, 1970).

Anxiety. This can be regarded as a drive state – a negative one – since it energises and directs behaviour and, when reduced, provides satisfaction and can act as a powerful reinforcer for learning. Why do people enter anxiety situations at all? One possibility is that they are seeking the satisfaction of reducing the anxiety, e.g. in parachute-jumping or other dangerous sports. Or they may enjoy the anxiety, through being able to label it as 'excitement' or 'exhilaration'.

People are not seeking a state of quiescent stupor all the time; often they are seeking higher levels of arousal. The anxious situation may be part of the route to an important positive goal, as in the case of nervous academics reading papers at conferences. The rise and fall of anxiety over time in parachutists has been traced by Epstein and Fenz (1965). Thirty-three experienced and thirty-three inexperienced parachutists estimated their degree of fear at different points before, during and after a jump. For the novices fear increased continuously until the 'ready' signal and then decreased; for the experienced jumpers fear decreased from first thing in the morning, presumably because they had learnt how to control their anxiety (Fig. 4.3). Physiological measures of anxiety on ten of each group showed a similar sequence.

Zuckerman (1974) established a personality dimension of 'sensation seeking'. This dimension has several correlated components, of which the main ones are 'thrill-and-adventure seeking' ('a desire to engage in outdoor sports or other activities involving elements of speed and

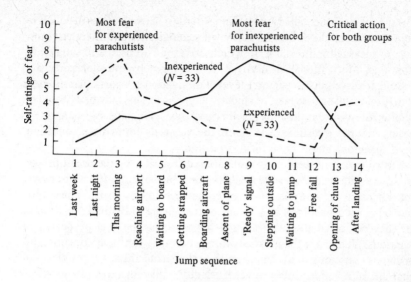

Fig. 4.3. Parachutists' self-ratings of fear experienced before, during and after a jump. (Adapted from Epstein and Fenz, 1965, by Weiner, 1980.)

danger') and 'disinhibition' ('positive attitudes towards variety in sexual partners, social drinking, wild parties and gambling'). The scale correlates with extroversion and with various physiological measures. Those who score high on the sensation-seeking dimension are found to engage more in all these risky and noisy activities; either they seek them out or low-sensation-seekers avoid them, or both.

Research methods

How can we discover the goal structure of a situation? Lewin's method would be to observe behaviour and infer the properties of the life-space of an individual; if most people behaved in the same way the properties of the situation could presumably be deduced. In the study of animals, which cannot be interviewed, ethologists deduce the goals being sought by observing whether there is persistence with varied effort towards some goal, which ceases when the goal has been achieved. We could study people at a restaurant, and observe that they make efforts to obtain and eat food, after which they relax and go home; they also talk to each other a great deal, so perhaps that is a goal too.

Another possible method is to measure the motivational state of people before and after they are in some situation. Those who go to a restaurant would have a higher level of blood-sugar afterwards; those who go to a pub would have more alcohol. However most of the goals and drives in which we are interested could not be measured physiologically, and there are other ways of measuring the extent to which drives are aroused and satiated by situations. Motivational arousal can be measured by questionnaire; it is possible to distinguish a person's level of motivation at a particular moment from his normal or base level of anxiety, anger, etc. This may be assessed by suitable questions, as those of Spielberger (1966), for state anxiety and trait anxiety. 'State' questions ask about the subject's immediate condition, 'trait' questions about his typical condition.

A third means of measuring motivational arousal is by the use of projective tests; suitable pictures are available for achievement, affiliation, power and other drives, as well as for aggression (Atkinson, 1958). These tests have been used primarily as a means of measuring individual motivation, but they could equally well be used for assessing the goal properties of situations. They have the great advantage that they can assess unconscious as well as conscious motivation: on the other hand there are problems of reliability and validity. Part of the difficulty with projective methods as a means of measuring stable individual differences is their great sensitivity to the nature of the situation, and to the subjects' recent experiences (Carney, 1966). However this makes projective tests very suitable for the purpose we have in mind.

There is another way of finding the goals which are operating in a given situation, and that is to ask people. One objection is that the subjects may be affected by social-desirability biases, and reveal only acceptable motivations. This should be minimised if subjects are anonymous and suitably motivated by instructions. A more serious problem is that the subjects may simply be unaware of some goals, as psychoanalysts have emphasised. It would be possible to use indirect questions such as 'What would give you most satisfaction (or make you most disappointed) in situation X?' Or the matter could be pursued by in-depth interview. In experiment 4.1 we found that subjects were able and willing to indicate the extent to which 'sexual activity' and 'making a favourable impression', amongst other goals, were relevant to different situations. More difficult perhaps are the 'system needs' emphasised by functionalist sociologists, which give rise to latent functions such as integrating the group (p. 26f.). We argued earlier that such needs are usually reflected in social needs of individuals, and we found in experiment 4.1 that people were able to rate the relevance to different situations of such goals as 'making new friends', 'getting to know people better' and 'being accepted by other(s)'.

In experiment 4.1 we describe the methods we have developed. We used pilot studies to obtain provisional lists of goals for each role in each situation; further subjects rated each goal for its importance in each situation and role. Principal-components analysis for each situational role was used to reveal whatever structure or organisation is present in the way goals are rated for importance and how the goals form higher-order goals or categories. There are therefore two criteria for deciding whether a goal is relevant to a particular role in a situation: a sample of members of a subculture must rate the goal as important, and it must form a definite factor in a principal-components analysis or similar method.

How can the goal structure, the relation between goals, be discovered? Again the best method may be to ask people. In experiment 4.2 we describe a set of procedures for establishing the instrumental and conflict relationships between goals, both intrapersonal and interpersonal.

4.1.   The main goals of social situations
J. A. GRAHAM, M. ARGYLE AND A. FURNHAM
[A fuller version of this study is given in Graham *et al.* (in press).]

The experiment to be described here was designed first to find out what the main goals are in eight different social situations. One role in each situation was considered. This was followed by an analysis of a different set of four situations with both the roles in each situation being considered. A list of goals was drawn up based, to a large extent, on a preliminary study.

Preliminary study

A list of eight common social situations (each involving two people) was presented to three female student subjects in their early twenties. They were asked to write down all the goals/aims they thought the person in each of the roles in each situation would usually have (i.e. what they were trying to do or achieve). These goals were collected together and to this list of goals were added some of the basic motivations of social behaviour as described by other research workers, and some goals thought by the authors to be relevant.

These goals (approximately 120) were mostly fairly specific and so were reduced to a smaller number (eighteen) of higher-order, more general categories. For example, 'appearing physically attractive', 'appearing interested', 'appearing clever', 'appearing witty', were all grouped together to form a higher-order, more general goal category of 'making favourable impression, appearing attractive, interested'.

Main experiment

The aim of the main experiment, which consisted of two studies, was to find out which of the eighteen goals in the list were thought to be important in the more familiar role of each of eight social situations. By 'more familiar' is meant the role most people are likely to have experienced.

Drives and goals

Method

Subjects. Subjects for the first study were sixty female students in their early twenties from a college for occupational therapy. Subjects for the second study were thirty-seven female student nurses.

Procedure: first study. Subjects were presented with eight lists (one for each of the eight situations) of the eighteen goals, and asked to indicate how important they considered each goal to be in the more familiar role (e.g. the role of interviewee in the interview situation, the role of patient in the visit to the doctor situation). The response categories used to rate each goal were 1 for no, 2 for perhaps and 3 for yes. The order of presentation of situations and goals was varied and counterbalanced. The goals and situations are listed in Table 4.1.

Procedure: second study. The list of goals was revised slightly for the second study so that it would be relevant to the new set of four situations – a small party or gathering, complaining to a neighbour about noise, nursing someone who is physically unwell, and a friendly chat with a neighbour – and so that it would take account of both situational roles where appropriate (e.g. the goal 'being looked after' was complemented with the goal 'looking after other').

The procedure was similar to that used in the first study except that twenty-one goals were now used instead of eighteen. Three of the situations involved two different roles and one situation involved one role (i.e. each person adopts a similar role). The goals, situations and respective roles are listed in Table 4.2.

The subjects were asked to rate the importance of each goal in each situational role, using a five-point scale from 1 (not at all important) to 5 (very important). The order of presentation of goals, situations and roles was varied and counterbalanced.

Results: first study

Frequency counts were taken of the responses in each of the three categories of importance (yes, no and perhaps) for each of the eighteen goals in each situational role. The goals in each situational role which at least 60 per cent of the subjects agreed were important (yes rating) or could be important (perhaps rating) were selected. These are shown in Table 4.1.

Results: second study

The frequencies of ratings of 3 (fairly important), 4 (important) or 5 (very important) given to each goal in each situational role were tabulated.

The two studies produced very similar results as to which goals were most important in the various situational roles.

TABLE 4.1. *Percentages of subjects checking goals in eight situations (first study)*

Goals	Friendly chat	Interview	Doctor's	'Date'	Wedding	Complaining	Hostess	Class
1. Being accepted by others	80	78	—	81	85	—	93	—
2. Conveying information to others	—	80	71	—	—	85	(65 perhaps)	80
3. Helping look after other person(s)	—	—	—	—	—	—	76	—
4. Dominating others, being in control of the situation	—	—	—	—	—	—	—	—
5. Having fun, enjoying yourself	92	—	—	100	92	—	97	73
6. Reducing own anxiety	—	—	80	—	—	—	—	—
7. Maintaining a satisfactory level of self-esteem, self-respect	65	85	—	80	—	81	88	—
8. Financial prospects	—	—	—	—	—	—	—	—
9. Physical well-being	—	—	95	—	—	—	—	—
10. Eating, drinking	$(58)^a$	—	—	70 $(59)^a$	68	—	87	—
11. Sexual activity	—	—	—	—	—	—	—	—
12. Doing well, answering questions correctly	—	97	—	—	—	—	—	77
13. Making favourable impression, appearing attractive, interested	—	100	—	95	95	—	83	—
14. Seeking help, advice, reassurance	63	—	95	—	—	—	—	—
15. Persuading the other to do something, influencing his/her behaviour	80	—	—	—	—	90	—	—
16. Obtaining information, learning something new, solving problems	—	—	—	—	—	—	—	—
17. Pleasant social activity	92	—	—	93	83	—	92	—
18. Making new friends, getting to know people better	68	—	—	93	83	—	90	—

Values shown are rounded off.
^{a} With these two exceptions, only scores of 60 and above are included in the table.

A principal-components analysis was carried out for each role using all of the ratings on the five-point scale. The loading of individual goals on to a factor, considered in addition to the mean importance rating of individual goals would, in turn, indicate which goals behaved in a similar way when rated for importance, and hence how the goals grouped together to form higher-order goals and how they should be labelled.

The following criteria were used for inclusion of goals contributing to a factor and, in addition, contributing substantially to a higher-order goal which could be considered 'important' in the situational role: eigenvalues $\geq$ 2.0, factor loadings $\geq$ 0.4 and a mean importance rating $\geq$ 3.0 with more than 65 per cent (a frequency of at least twenty-three out of thirty-five) of the subjects rating the goal at least fairly important. From the varimax rotated factor matrix for each situational role no more than three of the possible factors had eigenvalues $\geq$ 2.0. For all situational roles the two or three factors which had eigenvalues $\geq$ 2.0 accounted for between 47 and 55 per cent of the total variance. Those goals which met the above criteria for each situation were labelled; they were now of a higher order and were also of substantial importance for their particular situational role. The original goals (and their factor loadings and mean importance ratings) which contributed to the higher-order goals are listed in Table 4.2.

The relative importance of the main goals, with respect to one another in a situational role, may also be considered. For the nursing situation the most important goal of the nurse should be 'taking care of the other', and indeed this has the highest mean importance ratings for the components making up the factors (see Table 4.2). 'Looking after self' and 'mutual acceptance' are less important, which might be expected since they are only really important in facilitating the patient's being taken care of. Similarly for the patient, 'own well-being' has the highest mean importance ratings for the components making up the goal factors for this role. The fact that 'obtaining information' and 'mutual acceptance' are given lower mean importance ratings for their components makes sense in that these are subgoals to the goal of the patient's well-being.

For the party situation it is less obvious how the goals should be expected to interrelate in terms of relative importance. For the complaint situation it is at least clear that the most important of the goals would be 'persuasion' on the part of the complainer. This indeed is supported by the fact that the persuasion goal factor's one component, 'persuading the other to do something', received the highest mean importance rating (4.51) within that situation.

TABLE 4.2. *Factor loadings and mean importance ratings of goals in four situations (second study)*

Situation 1: a small party or gathering

Situational role 1: hostess

Goal	Factor loading	Mean
'Own physical well-being'		
Own physical well-being	0.71	3.03
'Looking after others'		
Conveying information	0.36	3.97
Physical well-being of others	0.68	3.91
Obtaining information	0.87	3.14
Reducing other's anxiety	0.73	3.82
'Developing relationships'		
Being accepted	0.85	4.6
Conveying information	0.51	3.97
Looking after other	0.67	4.62
Making favourable impression	0.75	4.31
Being accepting	0.53	4.77

Situational role 2: guest

Goal	Factor loading	Mean
'Developing relationships'		
Being accepted	0.79	4.49
Conveying information	0.42	3.06
Pleasant/enjoyable social activity	0.43	4.31
Making favourable impression	0.47	4.31
Being accepting	0.55	3.74
Making new friends	0.84	4.34
'Exchanging information/making favourable impression'		
Conveying information	0.59	3.05
Making favourable impression	−0.41	4.31
Obtaining information	0.46	3.11
Being accepting	0.52	3.74
'Own well-being'		
Reducing own anxiety	0.54	3.14
Own physical well-being	0.77	3.11

TABLE 4.2 (*cont.*)

Situation 2: complaining to a neighbour about a constant noisy disturbance

Situational role 3: complainer

Goal	Factor loading 'Dominance/persuasion'	Mean
Conveying information	0.77	4.22
Taking charge	0.64	4.40
Persuading the other	0.73	4.51
'Being accepted'		
Being accepted	0.45	3.31

Situational role 4: complainee

Goal	Factor loading 'Dominance'	Mean
Being accepted	0.54	3.20
Taking charge	-0.76	3.85
'Own physical well-being'		
Own physical well-being	0.50	3.17
'Self-esteem/being accepted'		
Being accepted	0.65	3.20
Self-esteem	0.71	4.37
Making favourable impression	0.72	3.11
Own physical well-being	0.46	3.17

Situation 3: nursing someone who is unwell

Situational role 5: nurse

Goal	Factor loading	Mean
'Mutual acceptance/self-esteem'		
Being accepted	0.87	4.11
Reducing own anxiety	0.40	3.34
Self-esteem	0.78	4.20
Eating/drinking	−0.48	3.14
Being accepting	0.81	4.02
Making new friends	0.65	3.40
'Taking care of other'		
Conveying information	0.60	4.25
Looking after other	0.79	4.60
Physical well-being of other	0.81	4.65
Reducing other's anxiety	0.89	4.80
'Looking after self'		
Eating/drinking	0.65	3.14
Seeking help	0.77	3.28
Obtaining information	0.62	4.05
Own physical well-being	0.69	3.4

Situational role 6: patient

Goal	Factor loading	Mean
'Mutual acceptance'		
Being accepted	0.60	3.60
Obtaining information	0.42	3.22
Being accepting	0.80	3.11
'Obtaining information'		
Obtaining information	0.47	3.22
'Own well-being'		
Reducing own anxiety	0.71	4.54
Self-esteem	0.43	4.28
Being looked after	0.61	4.48
Seeking help	0.85	4.48
Own physical well-being	0.75	4.57

TABLE 4.2 (cont.)

Situation 4: a friendly chat with a friend of the same sex, in the evening
Situational role 7: friend

Goal	Factor loading	Mean
	'Friendship exchange'	
Looking after other	0.76	3.22
Reducing own anxiety	0.52	3.0
Own physical well-being	0.71	3.08
Seeking help	0.60	3.37
Reducing other's anxiety	0.81	3.62
Making new friends	0.74	4.17
	'Social'	
Pleasant/enjoyable social activity	0.76	4.31
Reducing own anxiety	0.63	3.0
Self-esteem	0.83	3.97
Sustaining social relationships	0.44	4.48

4.2. Goal structure

J. A. GRAHAM, M. ARGYLE AND A. FURNHAM

[A fuller version of this study is given in Graham *et al.* (in press).]

In this experiment the main goals of three of the situations studied in experiment 4.1 were used to look at the interrelations between the goals for each situational role. Pairs of goals were studied both within the same individual or role and between the two roles of each situation. Interrelations were considered in terms of compatibility, conflict or independence of achieving different goals within a pair. The type and direction of compatibility or conflict were investigated in the second part of the experiment.

It was expected that for situations involving persuasion, assertiveness and complaints each person would be influenced by social needs (to be accepted, liked, etc.) and by the goal of changing the other's behaviour in some other way. This would be likely to generate inter- and intrapersonal conflict (76f.). Our complaint situation was expected to have the most conflict. For situations involving differences of status, dominance, supervision, leadership, nursing, etc., it was expected that at least two goals would be operative for each person, but here the goal of establishing good relationships would be instrumental to influencing the other's behaviour. For social events like making friends, parties, etc., there is no real task, so it was expected that there would be very little conflict of any kind. The party situation was expected to contain the least conflict, as the point of this situation is presumably to have a pleasant social occasion.

Preliminary work

Most of the higher-order goals listed in Table 4.2 were used here. The labels remained the same. It can be seen that there is some consistency of goals across roles and situations – e.g. 'own well-being' occurs several times. Three goals were used for each situational role. In the case of situational role 2, guest at a small party, one of the higher-order goals was derived from a bipolar factor 'exchanging information/making favourable impression'. The negative end was suppressed in this case (as only one goal loaded negatively on the factor) and the higher-order goal was thus considered to be 'exchanging information'. In the case of the complaint situation, the two poles of the bipolar factor were used as separate higher-order goals ('dominance' and 'persuasion'), because in addition to the fact that they both seemed to capture important aspects of the situation, it seemed that this polarity might in itself contain the essence of the conflict inherent in this situation.

Method

Subjects. The subjects for the first study were nineteen males and females who were third-year occupational therapy students attending a

95

course on social-skills training. Subjects for the second study were seventeen females who were third-year occupational therapy students attending the same course (these were a different group from those used in experiment 4.1).

Procedure: first study. The following three situations, with the respective roles of the two people in them, were used:

Situation	Roles
A small party or gathering	Hostess/guest
Complaining to a neighbour about constant noisy disturbance	Person complaining/person being complained to
Nursing someone who is physically unwell (could be at home in bed)	Nurse/patient

For each situation three main goals of each of the two persons in that situation were listed. They were then listed in pairs for each situation: firstly the three possible paired combinations of the three important goals for role 1, followed by the three possible pairs for role 2, followed by the nine possible paired combinations for both roles combined (i.e. each goal of one of the roles paired with each goal of the other role).

Subjects were asked to rate each pair of goals listed for each situation according to how much they were compatible or in conflict with one another, using a five-point scale (see Table 4.3).

Procedure: second study. Subjects were asked to indicate the direction rather than the amount of interference or facilitation between pairs of goals. A set of nine categories was used as shown in Table 4.4. These nine categories seemed to cover the types of interrelationship between goals which would be likely to occur.

Results

Frequency counts were taken of the responses in each of the five categories (for the first study) of compatibility and conflict, for each pair of goals within and across situational roles. The mean and modal response for each pair of goals is shown in Table 4.3, along with the proportion of subjects selecting each of the modal response categories. Frequency counts were also taken of the responses in each of the nine categories for types of compatibility and conflict for each pair of goals within and across situational roles. The modal responses for the pairs of goals are shown in Table 4.4, along with the number of subjects selecting each of the modal response categories. It can be seen that the results for the two methods are largely in agreement. Those cases in which there is not complete agreement appear to be those where different possible interpretations of the specific nature of the goals are likely.

4.2. Goal structure

The results for the three situations were represented diagrammatically. Fig. 4.4 represents the modal responses for goal pairs in these situations. In this figure the results of the first and second study are combined, the values representing the mean conflict values (if the five-point scale is conceived of as a unidimensional scale representing increasing degrees of conflict). Only those values at the extremes of the scale are shown (i.e. between points 1 and 2 and between points 4 and 5) in order to highlight the points of likely difficulty. The solid lines represent the compatibility end of the scale and the broken lines the conflict end of the scale. The type/direction of compatibility or conflict (second study) is also shown on the figure. The double lines represent those instances in which the conflict or compatibility works both ways, as indicated by the modal response category for type or direction of compatibility or conflict. Single lines represent those instances in which the conflict or compatibility works one way only (the arrow indicating which way). The mean conflict values shown on the figure represent the mean values for all of the goal pairs within each role and across roles.

Discussion

The value of the method used can be partly assessed by an examination of the results obtained. The fact that there is a substantial amount of agreement in the findings obtained by use of the different methods (1) for the main goals and (2) for interrelations between goals, provides some validation for the methods.

Three main goals were obtained for each situational role (via the above methods). It is interesting that these formed a fairly similar pattern for each situational role in five cases out of six. The three were (1) social acceptance, developing relationships, (2) own well-being, (3) achieving a specific situational task goal. In the case of the complainer in the complaint situation, goals (1) and (3) were present and goal (2) was implicit, since the point of the complaint ('persuasion') was to remove an unwelcome noise. Dominance and persuasion were separate goals. There is, however, considerable variation between situations in the specific nature of the goals sought. In the first place the task goals are very different in each case. Secondly, the type of social relationship sought at a party, when making a complaint and when nursing is, apart from 'acceptance', quite different.

'Dominance' emerged as a goal factor for both sides in the complaint situation, but not in the other situations. From other studies it would be expected that two dimensions of social motivation might be commonly found – dominance as well as affiliation. However we did not include many scales in the dominance area, which would therefore make such a factor less likely to appear. From the frequency data of experiment 4.1 it was found that 'taking charge' was rated as important as a goal, by most subjects, for the hostess and nurse roles, but not for guests or patients.

97

TABLE 4.3. *Mean conflict, modal responses and number of subjects agreeing in first study*

	Small party			Complaining			Nursing		
Goals	Mean	Modal response	No. of subjects agreeing[a]	Mean	Modal response	No. of subjects agreeing[a]	Mean	Modal response	No. of subjects agreeing[a]
A and B	3.42	4	8	2.63	2	8	1.58	1	12
A and C	2.11	2	8	4.26	4	9	1.79	2	10
B and C	1.63	1	14	2.0	1	9	3.42	4	7
D and E	1.42	1	14	2.32	1	7	2.11	2	8
D and F	2.32	2	9	3.11	4	9	1.74	1	11
E and F	2.36	3	8	1.95	1	8	2.05	2	8
A and D	2.95	4	6	4.89	5	18	1.26	1	16
B and E	2.26	2	8	3.37	4	7	2.58	2/4	6
C and F	2.79	2	8	2.84	2	7	4.16	4	14
A and E	3.05	3	8	4.0	4	8	2.84	2	8
A and F	3.58	5	9	4.58	5	12	2.37	2	9
B and D	1.42	1	13	4.05	4	9	1.58	2	11
B and F	2.0	1	9	2.79	4	7	1.89	1	11
C and D	1.21	1	15	3.84	4	8	3.26	4	8
C and E	1.89	2	9	2.47	2	9	3.95	4	10

TABLE 4.3 (*cont.*)

Goals:

	Hostess	*Complainer*	*Nurse*
A =	Own physical well-being	Dominance	Mutual acceptance/self-esteem
B =	Looking after others	Persuasion	Taking care of other
C =	Developing relationships	Being accepted	Looking after self

	Guest	*Complainee*	*Patient*
D =	Developing relationships	Dominance	Mutual acceptance
E =	Exchanging information	Own physical well-being	Obtaining information
F =	Own well-being	Self-esteem/being accepted	Own well-being

Scores:
1 Likely to be compatible
2 Might be compatible
3 Do not relate
4 Might interfere
5 Might be in conflict

a Out of a total of nineteen.

TABLE 4.4. *Modal response categories and number of subjects agreeing in second study*

Goals	Small party		Complaining		Nursing	
	Modal response	No. of subjects agreeing[a]	Modal response	No. of subjects agreeing[a]	Modal response	No. of subjects agreeing[a]
A and B	3/8	4	2/3	4	3	7
A and C	1/3/7	3	6	9	3	7
B and C	3	7	2	7	8	4
D and E	2	8	1	11	1	5
D and F	1	5	6	6	1	8
E and F	5	5	2	7	1	10
A and D	3	5	9	10	3	15
B and E	3	6	6	5	5	6
C and F	1/3	7	3	11	5	5
A and E	5	9	6	10	2	4
A and F	5	7	6	9	1	7
B and D	3	8	7	7	1/3	6
B and F	1	14	1/2/3	3	1	12
C and D	3	12	1	5	5	4
C and E	3	8	3	7	5	8

Goals: A–F as in first study (see Table 4.3).
Modal response categories:
1   Achieving first goal could help with achieving second goal
2   Achieving second goal could help with achieving first goal
3   Achieving each goal could help with achieving the other
4   Both goals are part of a larger goal
5   Both goals are independent – they have not much to do with one another
6   Achieving the first goal could interfere with achieving the second goal
7   Achieving the second goal could interfere with achieving the first goal
8   Achieving each goal could interfere with achieving the other
9   Achieving both goals is impossible

[a] Out of a total of nineteen.

We conclude that dominance is a goal that is relevant to some roles but not others.

From the diagrammatic representation of the results (as in Fig. 4.4) it was seen that in the case of the party situation there was, as expected, no conflict: there was mostly two-way interpersonal compatibility and one-way and two-way intrapersonal compatibility. The hostess's goal of 'looking after others' appeared to be one of the most central goals in that it had three two-way links with other goals; the guest's goal of 'developing relationships' also had three links. The goal of the hostess's 'own well-being' seemed to be the most independent goal, without strong interrelations with the other goals.

The complaint situation was quite different from both of the other situations in that all of the interpersonal links were negative (average 3.64); this situation was expected to have the most conflict. The central goal appeared to be 'dominance' on the part of the complainer, which had four links. If this goal was absent, the situation would be greatly improved. It seemed to have more conflicting relations with other goals than did the goal of 'persuasion', which was the real point of this situation (and most important as assessed by the importance ratings in experiment 4.1); persuasion was seen as leading from or being helped by the goal 'being accepted'. Presumably the complainer is more likely to be successful in his persuasion if he is accepted first. The dominance of the complainee may still, however, interfere with the 'persuasion' goal of the complainer. This is more complex than the goal structure we had predicted for assertiveness situations, and three goals, not two, are involved on each side.

The nursing situation was different again. A key goal appeared to be the nurse looking after the patient ('taking care of other'), which had three links; 'own well-being' of the patient, and 'mutual acceptance' on the part of both roles also had three links. The only conflict was between the nurse looking after herself and the well-being of the patient. As predicted, there were clear instrumental links in which the nurse's taking care of the patient led to mutual acceptance (acceptance by the patient, at least, would be expected) which in turn was instrumental in the patient's well-being. This is in keeping with the general expectation for situations involving a status/dominance type of role differentiation: that the establishment of good relationships is instrumental in influencing the behaviour of the other (the person being dominated).

In further studies it would be useful to include dominance as a possible factor in the goal structure; no dominance factor appeared with the scales we were using.

What use can be made of this kind of goal structure analysis? It is likely that some of the situations that are found difficult have conflicts between goals, though this has yet to be established; we now have a measuring instrument that will enable us to test this hypothesis. However, knowledge of the goal structure, especially of the main points of conflict, would help in handling these situations by providing a map for steering through these conflicts. How could the difficulty in making a complaint be reduced, for example? From our results the most important step would seem to be to abandon dominance (on the part of the complainer) as a goal: the remaining goals would be 'being accepted' and 'persuasion', and the first is instrumental to the second. Could the conflict in nurse–patient encounters be avoided? In terms of goal conflict one of the problems seems to lie in the nurse's concern for her own well-being; the solution to this may lie in steps such as greater medical precautions to protect nurses, which would remove this source of anxiety.

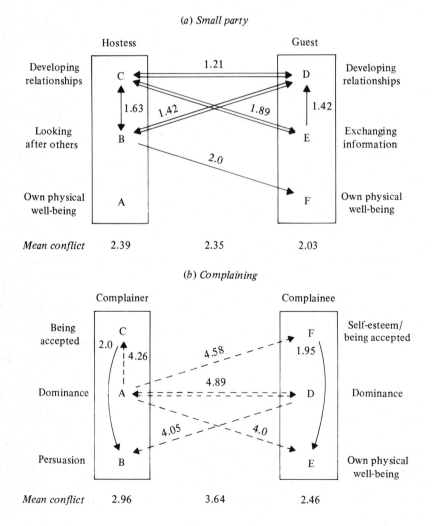

(a) Small party

Hostess | Guest

Developing relationships — C ⇄ D — Developing relationships
1.21
1.63 | 1.42 | 1.89 | 1.42
Looking after others — B — E — Exchanging information
2.0
Own physical well-being — A | F — Own physical well-being

Mean conflict   2.39   2.35   2.03

(b) Complaining

Complainer | Complainee

Being accepted — C | F — Self-esteem/ being accepted
2.0 | 4.26 | 4.58 | 1.95
4.89
Dominance — A ⇄ D — Dominance
4.05 | 4.0
Persuasion — B | E — Own physical well-being

Mean conflict   2.96   3.64   2.46

(c) Nursing

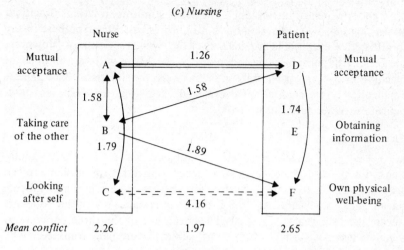

Fig. 4.4. The goal structure of three situations.

4.3. Personality and the choice and avoidance of social situations

A. FURNHAM

[A fuller version of this study is given in Furnham (in press).]

One of the most important criticisms of the apportioning of variance in the P × S debate is the fact that person and situation cannot be separated as independent factors, because people choose to interact in and seek out specific situations, these choices reflecting their personalities. The very fact that people spend their time in certain situations is a function of their personality. A corollary of this is that we should be able to predict certain personality traits if we know the situations that people choose.

Researchers in each of the areas concerned with person–situation 'fit' have looked at the problem slightly differently. The work on personality and job match has been concerned with very abstract dimensions of the environment, while the studies on arousal-seeking tendencies have been concerned with a very specific personality dimension and its relationship to highly unusual situations. The studies on leisure have often mixed social and non-social situations, and have concentrated more on demographic variables than on individual differences (see p. 79f.).

This study was designed for three reasons: (*a*) to establish whether there is a coherent and meaningful pattern of differences in preference for a wide variety of social situations, across two commonly investigated personality variables, not exclusively related to arousal; (*b*) to determine whether those differences exist for situations which subjects had actually experienced as well as for hypothetical situations; (*c*) to determine whether those differences which occur are apparent using stimulus situations described at various levels of abstraction. A number of specific hypotheses were formulated after initial factor analysis of the various scales used. However, the general hypothesis to be examined is that there will be a number of meaningful and significant differences between the situations that different personality types, such as introverts and extroverts, neurotics and non-neurotics, either seek out or avoid.

Method

Subjects. In all there were 130 subjects drawn from three populations: ninety-one female second-year occupational therapy students (mean age 20.0 years, S.D. 3.2); thirty-five female second-year nursing students (mean age, 21.2 years, S.D. 0.8); and four female polytechnic students (mean age 21.0 years, S.D. 4.0). The mean age of the three populations together was 20.3 years, S.D. 2.8. All subjects were paid volunteers who were later debriefed as to the nature of the study.

The questionnaire. The questionnaire was divided into five sections.

(*a*) *The Eysenck Personality Questionnaire* (1975): a 90-item, yes/no questionnaire which provides four scores per subject – neuroticism, extroversion, psychotism and lie-scale. It was content-analysed to ensure that there was no item overlap with the other scales used. Only one item in the extroversion factor was similar to a Leisure Scale item, and was removed from the latter.

(*b*) *The Leisure Scale*: a 21-item scale derived from the Opinion Research Corporation study (1962) and Neulinger's (1978) review of the psychology of leisure, which requires subjects to report how much time they have spent in each leisure activity during the previous week.

(*c*) *The Free-Time Activity Scale*: a 9-item rank-order preference scale devised by Neulinger and Raps (1972), based on the work of Murray (1938) and his needs/press construct.

(*d*) *The Social Situation Scale*: a 30-item scale, piloted for this study, asking subjects to what extent they choose or avoid situation types. The situations are described primarily in terms of a single adjective and derived from dimensional labels used in other studies.

(*e*) *The Stressful Situation Scale*: a 15-item scale devised and used by Furnham and Argyle that asks subjects to indicate the extent to which they seek out or avoid stressful social situations.

Procedure. The questionnaire was administered to groups of fifteen to twenty people in the presence of an experimenter. The questionnaire was filled in anonymously and took approximately 1 hour to complete.

4.3. Personality and the choice of situations

Results

The results were analysed in three stages.

1. Subjects with a lie-scale score of 8 or above were discarded. The mean
and standard deviation for the extroversion score (mean = 13.98, S.D. 4.84)
and the neutroticism score were calculated (mean = 11.11, S.D. 4.91). It was
decided to use 0.5 of a standard deviation to establish groups. Subjects with
an extroversion score of 17 and above were allocated to the extrovert group,
and those with a score of 11 or below to the introvert group; similarly, those
with a neuroticism score of 14 and above were classed as neurotics and those
with a score of 8 or below as non-neurotics. Subjects were randomly
discarded from the larger groups until the numbers in all groups were equal
to that in the smallest of the four groups (introverted, non-neurotics), which
was fifteen. Thus, sixty subjects were retained for the remainder of the
analysis.

2. Secondly, because of the large number of items in the Leisure Scale,
the Social Situation Scale and the Stressful Situation Scale, these were
factor-analysed using a varimax rotation. Also factor scores were calculated
for each subject on the first three factors in each scale.

(a) *The Leisure Scale*. Table 4.5 shows the results of three factors from the
Leisure Scale factor analysis. These factors (with eigenvalues of above
1.50) accounted for approximately 45 per cent of the variance. It can
be seen that the first two factors involved social leisure activities though
the first factor contained more social and interactional activities than
the latter, which seems to involve more physical activity. Thus the first
factor was labelled 'social interaction' and the second 'physical pursuits'.
The third factor contained more passive activities with minimal interaction and this was called 'reading'. It was predicted that there would
be a significant difference on all three factors, extroverts participating in the
first two types of leisure activities more than introverts, the reverse being
true of the third factor. No predictions were made about the neuroticism
factor.

(b) *The Social Situation Scale*. Table 4.6 shows the results of the Two
factors from the Social Situation Scale factor analysis. These factors (with
eigenvalues of above 3.00) accounted for approximately 27 per cent of the
variance. Both appeared to be bipolar: the first factor was labelled 'stimu-
lating/unstimulating' because of the loading of active/passive and consistent/
inconsistent, and the second factor was labelled 'formal/informal'. Both of
these dimensions have arisen in previous studies. It was predicted that there
would be a significant difference on both personality traits in both situation
factors, introverts and neurotics preferring unstimulating and formal situations significantly more than extroverts, who would seek out stimulating
informal situations.

(c) *The Stressful Situation Scale*. Table 4.7 shows the results of the two factors

TABLE 4.5. *Factor analysis (varimax) results for the Leisure Scale*

Factor	Item	Loading[a]	Eigenvalue	Variance
Social interaction	2. Visiting friends and relatives	0.52		
	6. Listening to records	0.69		
	7. Going pleasure-driving	0.47		
	11. Going out to dinner	0.52	5.04	25.2
	14. Going to the cinema	0.68		
	15. Spending time in cafés, Wimpy bars	0.71		
	16. Going to discos, dances, parties	0.77		
Physical pursuits	2. Visiting friends and relatives	0.42		
	8. Going to club, group meetings	0.43		
	10. Active hobbies: crafts, mechanical work	0.66		
	11. Going out to dinner	0.46	2.27	11.4
	12. Playing cards, chequers, board games	0.68		
	17. Going to plays, operas, concerts	0.53		
	19. Going for walks or hikes	0.79		
Reading	4. Reading magazines	0.79		
	5. Reading books	0.63	1.70	8.5
	12. Playing cards, chequers, board games	0.68		

[a] Items with a loading of above +0.4 were retained.

from the Stressful Situation Scale factor analysis. These factors (with eigenvalues of above 1.50) accounted for approximately 32 per cent of the variance. The first seemed to involve two aspects, 'counselling' and 'entertaining', both of which are concerned with helping others. The second factor, which is bipolar, also has two factors, 'assertiveness' and 'intimacy', both involved with the expression of emotion towards others. It was predicted that extroverts and non-neurotics would seek out both these types of situation more than introverts and neurotics.

3. Thirdly, a two-way analysis of variance was calculated with the subjects' factor scores and with the press variables in the Free-Time Activity Scale.

TABLE 4.6. *Factor analysis (varimax) results for the Social Situation Scale*

Factor	Item	Loading[a]	Eigenvalue	Variance
Stimulating/ unstimulating	1. Active	−0.41		
	4. Inconsistent	−0.73		
	6. Open	−0.47		
	8. Organised	0.73	4.84	16.1
	10. Serious	0.43		
	12. Unusual	−0.45		
	14. Passive	0.47		
	21. Consistent	0.70		
Formal/ informal	3. Formal	−0.42		
	19. Informal	0.71		
	26. Simple	0.72	3.34	11.2
	29. Lighthearted	0.72		

[a] Items with a loading of above +0.4 were retained.

TABLE 4.7. *Factor analysis (varimax) results from the Stressful Situation Scale*

Factor	Item	Loading[a]	Eigenvalue	Variance
Counselling/ entertaining	5. Going to the funeral of a close relative, who you knew well	0.78		
	6. Going round to cheer up a depressed friend who asked you to call	0.66	3.08	20.6
	7. Being host or hostess at a fairly large party	0.60		
Assertiveness/ intimacy	2. Taking a person of the opposite sex out for the first time	−0.41		
	14. Attending a distant relation's wedding ceremony, where you know few people	0.82	1.71	11.5
	15. Apologising to a superior for forgetting an important errand	0.63		

[a] Items with a loading of above +0.4 were retained.

(a) The Leisure Scale. Table 4.8 shows the ANOVA results: on both of the first two factors there is a significant difference between introverts and extroverts, though there is no difference on neuroticism and no interaction between main factors. In both factors extroverts loaded positively on the factors and introverts negatively, indicating that extroverts take part significantly more than introverts in social and physical leisure activities. However, there was no introversion/extroversion difference on the third factor but a significant neuroticism and interaction effect. It seems that introverted neurotics prefer reading and competitive indoor games less than extroverted non-neurotics, whose need for stimulation may be higher.

TABLE 4.8. *Two-way analysis of variance on Leisure Scale factor scores*

Mean factor score			Source		F
Factor 1: Social interaction					
	High *N*	Low *N*	Extroversion	(A)	7.27***
Intro	−0.17	−0.95	Neuroticism	(B)	0.69
Extro	0.29	0.75	Interaction	(A × B)	0.13
Factor 2: Physical pursuits					
	High *N*	Low *N*	Extroversion	(A)	4.30**
Intro	−0.18	−0.30	Neuroticism	(B)	0.01
Extro	0.18	0.36	Interaction	(A × B)	0.33
Factor 3: Reading					
	High *N*	Low *N*	Extroversion	(A)	1.53
Intro	0.19	0.15	Neuroticism	(A)	3.57*
Extro	0.31	0.57	Interaction	(A × B)	3.19*

*** $P<0.01$; ** $P<0.05$; * $P<0.08$.

(b) The Free-Time Activity Scale: Table 4.9 gives the ANOVA results, which were calculated after it had been established that the assumptions for parametric analysis were met. Of the nine presses only two revealed significant differences on the introvert/extrovert scale. They were 'order', where introverts showed a significantly higher preference than extroverts, and 'affiliation', where the opposite occurred. Curiously, the activity press showed no significant difference. Although there was no significant difference in the rank-ordering between either of the two groups, the press activities which were seen as most desirable were those offering 'affiliation' and 'nurturance', and those that were least attractive those offering 'understanding' and 'order'. Presumably, both of these results reflect the needs of the general population from which they were drawn.

TABLE 4.9. *Two-way analysis of variance on the nine presses of the Free-Time Activity Scale*[a]

		Neuroticism		Source	F
		High N	Low N		
1. Order	Intro	5.93	5.86	Extroversion	8.29***
	Extro	7.53	7.53	Neuroticism	0.00
				Interaction	0.00
2. Autonomy	Intro	5.40	5.80	Extroversion	2.54
	Extro	4.80	4.26	Neuroticism	0.00
				Interaction	0.48
3. Sentience	Intro	4.60	4.06	Extroversion	0.36
	Extro	3.73	5.26	Neuroticism	1.32
				Interaction	1.11
4. Understanding	Intro	7.26	5.33	Extroversion	0.27
	Extro	6.73	6.53	Neuroticism	3.13**
				Interaction	1.87
5. Achievement	Intro	5.93	4.46	Extroversion	0.09
	Extro	5.53	5.20	Neuroticism	2.99**
				Interaction	1.14
6. Sex	Intro	4.06	5.66	Extroversion	0.08
	Extro	4.73	4.60	Neuroticism	1.16
				Interaction	1.63
7. Affiliation	Intro	3.86	4.00	Extroversion	5.20***
	Extro	3.00	2.53	Neuroticism	0.10
				Interaction	0.34
8. Nurturance	Intro	3.13	3.80	Extroversion	0.22
	Extro	3.83	3.53	Neuroticism	0.11
				Interaction	1.04
9. Activity	Intro	4.80	5.40	Extroversion	0.06
	Extro	5.00	5.53	Neuroticism	0.71
				Interaction	0.00

[a] Low score indicates high preference.
*** $P < 0.01$; ** $P < 0.09$.

(c) *The Social Situation Scale.* Table 4.10 gives the ANOVA results for the first factor. Both main effects were significant on this factor. Extroverts chose stimulating, active, unusual situations significantly more than introverts, while neurotics avoided these types of situations more than non-neurotics. Previous literature (Eysenck, 1975) would predict both of these results. However, there were no significant differences on the second factor, formal/informal situations.

(d) *Stressful Situation Scale.* Table 4.11 gives the ANOVA results for the first two factors. As predicted, on both factors extroverts avoid these situations significantly less than introverts, though there is surprisingly no

TABLE 4.10. *Two-way analysis of variance on Social Situation Scale factor score for stimulating/unstimulating situations*

	Mean factor score		Source	F
	High N	Low N	Extroversion (A)	7.62***
Intro	−0.63	−0.02	Neuroticism (B)	4.45**
Extro	0.13	0.52	Interaction (A × B)	0.21

*** $P<0.01$; ** $P<0.05$.

TABLE 4.11. *Two-way analysis of variance on Stressful Situations Scale factor scores*

Mean factor score			Source	F
Factor 1: Counselling/entertaining				
	High N	Low N	Extroversion (A)	6.65***
Intro	−0.18	−0.35	Neuroticism (B)	0.01
Extro	0.29	0.40	Interaction (A × B)	0.32
Factor 2: Assertiveness/intimacy				
	High N	Low N	Extroversion (A)	3.96**
Intro	−0.19	−0.29	Neuroticism (B)	0.04
Extro	0.18	0.32	Interaction (A × B)	0.21

*** $P<0.01$; ** $P<0.05$.

difference as a function of neuroticism. All these situations are avoided with the exception of situations 2 (taking out, or being taken out by, a person of the opposite sex) and 6 (going round to cheer up a depressed friend who asked you to call round for a chat).

Discussion

The main purpose of this study was to determine whether different personality types choose and avoid different social situations in which to participate. Despite the relatively weak criterion for the selection of the personality variables (0.5 of the S.D.), the introversion/extroversion factor consistently produced significant effects over past, actually experienced leisure situations, and hypothetical needs/press variables, social situations and difficult social situations. A number of significant differences also occurred along the neuroticism factor, as predicted by Eysenck and Zuckerman (1978), who found extroversion, though not neuroticism, to be a distinguishing factor on four measures of experience-seeking. Nearly all of the results are explicable in terms of Eysenck's personality theory.

Studies that attempt to resolve the trait–state or person–situation argument by apportioning variance to person, situation and interaction between them do not take sufficient cognizance of the person variable (Endler and Hunt, 1969). That is, the person variable operates twice – both before the situation, in that it partly determines whether a person will enter that situation, and during the situation, determining how he will behave.

The second implication of this study concerns assessment, of persons, situations and their interaction. From the results it can be seen that a person's life-style or interaction pattern reflects his personality. This may be very useful for the assessment of personality under certain circumstances, for example as an unobtrusive measure, as a technique to be used in psycho-historical studies of deceased people, or as a self-monitoring technique used in behaviour therapy. Thus, by a careful and sensitive assessment of the salient dimensions of both persons and situations we may be able to match them in work, social and leisure situations.

A third implication of the study concerns experimental work which randomly assigns people to laboratory situations. This misses the important factor of personality functioning, as well as placing subjects in unfamiliar settings. As a result, in certain social psychological, even cognitive experiments, artefacts may occur unless individual differences are considered. Indeed the very fact that people volunteer for psychological experiments may mean that they are a grossly biased sample. Zuckerman (1978) has shown that sensation-seekers are more likely to become subjects in a psychology experiment than are non-sensation-seekers.

Finally, one major reason why people might avoid certain situations is because they are socially phobic, or unable to 'read' or cope adequately with certain situations. This is not to say that all situations that people avoid are those they find difficult, but rather that for certain personalities (neurotics) their avoidance pattern reflects their inadequacy. This information may prove useful in assessing both the nature and extent of the person's problem and the success or failure of subsequent social-skills treatment.

4.4. The choice of situation and medium as a function of the message

A. FURNHAM

When people have specific messages, ideas or intentions to communicate to others, they choose to operate in situations that best help that communication. That is, a situation by virtue of its intimacy, spatial arrangement, social rules and conventions, opportunities for physical activity, etc., may help to control the interaction and hence the communication. Some messages of course may be context-free in the sense that they are of insufficient importance – so trivial, simple or everyday that they can be communicated in any situation. However, other messages that involve subtle, emotional, or unpleasant information may be greatly facilitated by their communication in certain situations rather than others. Many a messenger, in previous eras, paid dearly for delivering his message in inappropriate situations, that he could not select or control. Further, certain ritualised social situations exist for the exchanges of certain messages – presentation of credentials to an important figure, public political statements, confessionals, the business luncheon, etc.

Another important aspect in ensuring effective communication as well as controlling the situations in which it occurs is the medium in or through which communication takes place. Furnham, Trevethan and Gaskell (in press) have pointed out that people frequently communicate with each other through three media which provide a different number of types of cues: written media, e.g. letters, notes or telegrams (verbal cues only), the telephone (verbal and vocal cues) and radio (verbal and vocal cues). A judicious choice of medium may ensure, through a minimisation of interfering cues or emphasis on certain other cues (e.g. visual nonverbal), that a message is satisfactorily communicated. Short, Williams and Christie (1976) have reviewed a number of studies which demonstrated that the mechanics of interaction, and information transmission, are affected by the use of different media. They also showed that the decision of which communications medium is selected is dependent on such factors as the relationship between communicants, the importance of the meeting and the accessibility of the medium.

An experiment was designed to examine the thesis that people choose to communicate different messages in certain situations, and through certain media, in order to ensure the effectiveness of that communication. Four *a priori* categories of messages were examined and there were four examples in each category. These involved messages concerning the counselling of others, the disclosure of personal information, interpersonal assertiveness, and impression management/information exchange. The description of the situations varied according to three criteria: whether there were more than two people present; whether the people were engaged in some displacement activity other than talking, i.e. whether there was opportunity for bodily movement; and whether the situation was open or closed, i.e. whether it was public and observable or private and enclosed.

Three media were examined in the choice of communication medium: letter (verbal), telephone (adds auditory nonverbal) and face-to-face (adds visual nonverbal). A number of specific hypotheses were tested:

1. That all the messages are perceived as situationally specific with regard to appropriateness of delivery.
2. That the likelihood of delivering specific messages in specific situations is determined by the people present in the situation, the

presence or absence of some activity, the open or closed nature of the situation, and the particular type of message.

3. That in order to communicate messages associated with counselling, self-disclosure and assertiveness, subjects will select closed situations where they were alone with the other person and with no distracting activity.

4. That subjects will prefer to communicate all the messages by face-to-face interaction, rather than by telephone or letter.

Method

Subjects. Thirty-three subjects were used, twenty females and thirteen males. All subjects were adult and were drawn from the subject panel of the Psychology Department at the University of Oxford. All subjects were between forty-one and fifty years of age. They were paid volunteers, who were later debriefed about the nature of the study.

Materials. Each subject had a three-page questionnaire. The first page consisted of instructions. The second page consisted of a 16 × 16 grid with situations along the top and messages down the side, which the subject was required to fill in using a seven-point scale to indicate the likelihood of their giving each message in each situation (1, highly likely; 7, highly unlikely). The third page consisted of a grid where the subject was asked to indicate his or her preference between three media in communicating the sixteen messages, by rank-ordering the media.

Procedure. The questionnaire was administered by post to the subjects (who were used to this system). Pilot work and subject answers indicated that the questionnaire took approximately half an hour to complete.

Results

Four separate analyses were performed on the data:

Cluster analysis. The situations were clustered in terms of the likelihood scores on the messages, and vice versa. This produced two cluster analyses, one for situations and the other for messages. These provided a clear picture of how the subjects perceived the messages and situations, and allowed for a check of the *a priori* categorisation. The cluster analysis of the situations is shown in Fig. 4.5.

Five clusters emerged in the analysis of the social situations. Of the three closest clusters the largest one (items 10, 12, 15 and 16) involved predominantly 'closed' situations, with other people co-present. The

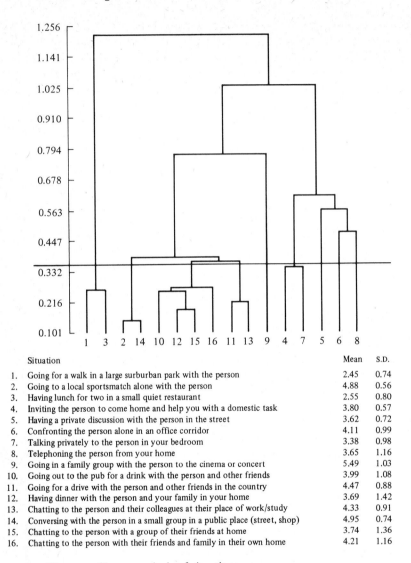

Fig. 4.5. Cluster analysis of situations.

	Situation	Mean	S.D.
1.	Going for a walk in a large surburban park with the person	2.45	0.74
2.	Going to a local sportsmatch alone with the person	4.88	0.56
3.	Having lunch for two in a small quiet restaurant	2.55	0.80
4.	Inviting the person to come home and help you with a domestic task	3.80	0.57
5.	Having a private discussion with the person in the street	3.62	0.72
6.	Confronting the person alone in an office corridor	4.11	0.99
7.	Talking privately to the person in your bedroom	3.38	0.98
8.	Telephoning the person from your home	3.65	1.16
9.	Going in a family group with the person to the cinema or concert	5.49	1.03
10.	Going out to the pub for a drink with the person and other friends	3.99	1.08
11.	Going for a drive with the person and other friends in the country	4.47	0.88
12.	Having dinner with the person and your family in your home	3.69	1.42
13.	Chatting to the person and their colleagues at their place of work/study	4.33	0.91
14.	Conversing with the person in a small group in a public place (street, shop)	4.95	0.74
15.	Chatting to the person with a group of their friends at home	3.74	1.36
16.	Chatting to the person with their friends and family in their own home	4.21	1.16

second (items 11 and 13) involved situations with others present, yet the situations in the third appeared to have little in common except that both were 'open'. All the situations in these clusters had high mean scores, indicating that they were perceived as not being specifically appropriate for the imparting of many messages. By contrast the two remaining clusters had lower mean scores indicating that they were perceived as being more appropriate for the delivery of the messages. One (items 1 and 3) involved situations where both communicants were alone and engaged in some activity and the other (items 4 and 7) involved closed situations where the communicants were alone. Thus although the situation clusters did not exactly confirm the *a priori* classification, a meaningful pattern emerged.

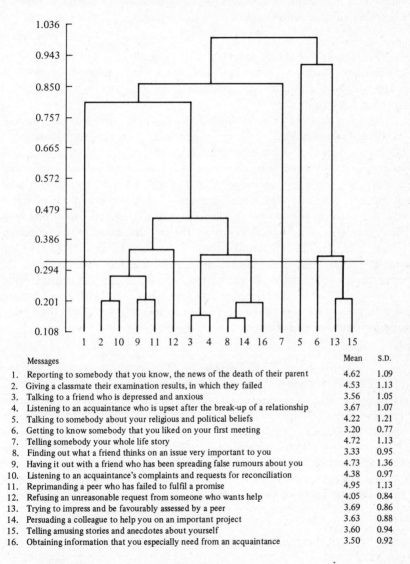

	Messages	Mean	S.D.
1.	Reporting to somebody that you know, the news of the death of their parent	4.62	1.09
2.	Giving a classmate their examination results, in which they failed	4.53	1.13
3.	Talking to a friend who is depressed and anxious	3.56	1.05
4.	Listening to an acquaintance who is upset after the break-up of a relationship	3.67	1.07
5.	Talking to somebody about your religious and political beliefs	4.22	1.21
6.	Getting to know somebody that you liked on your first meeting	3.20	0.77
7.	Telling somebody your whole life story	4.72	1.13
8.	Finding out what a friend thinks on an issue very important to you	3.33	0.95
9.	Having it out with a friend who has been spreading false rumours about you	4.73	1.36
10.	Listening to an acquaintance's complaints and requests for reconciliation	4.38	0.97
11.	Reprimanding a peer who has failed to fulfil a promise	4.95	1.13
12.	Refusing an unreasonable request from someone who wants help	4.05	0.84
13.	Trying to impress and be favourably assessed by a peer	3.69	0.86
14.	Persuading a colleague to help you on an important project	3.63	0.88
15.	Telling amusing stories and anecdotes about yourself	3.60	0.94
16.	Obtaining information that you especially need from an acquaintance	3.50	0.92

Fig. 4.6. Cluster analysis of messages.

Similarly a meaningful, but not perfect pattern emerged from the cluster analysis of messages. The largest cluster (items 2, 9, 10 and 11) contained one counselling and three assertiveness messages. Another (items 8, 14 and 16) included a self-disclosure and two impression management messages. Two others, which contained self-disclosure messages (items 3 and 4) and impression management messages (items 13 and 15), also emerged. Overall there was an interpretable clustering of messages.

Slater's PREFAN program. This program analyses grids in terms of elements (situations) only. It allowed for a dimensional, as opposed to a categorical, plotting of the situations (Fig. 4.7), through the use of a different algorithm.

This analysis reveals clearly, with a few minor exceptions, the grouping of the situations according to the three factors. Apart from situation 2 (Going to a local sportsmatch alone with the person) all the situations where the two people were alone are to be found in the two right-hand quandrants, while the situations involving others are in the two left-hand quadrants. Similarly the 'open' situations, with the exception of items 1 and 10, are in the top two quadrants, and the 'closed' situations with the exception of 4, 7 and 8 are in the bottom quadrants. Situations in which there is the opportunity for activity are predominantly in the top left-hand and bottom right-hand quadrants, whereas those without the opportunity for activity are in the top right-hand and bottom left-hand quadrants. Thus a dimensional analysis reveals a slightly different pattern of results from a categorical analysis, but supports more clearly the *a priori* categorisation of situations.

Slater's (1977) SERIES program. This performs one-way analysis of variance for each construct (message) across all the elements (situations). We are thus able to determine whether each message is seen to be significantly different in its appropriateness for being delivered in the sixteen specified situations (Table 4.12).

The messages that revealed the highest significant differences were those concerned with giving bad news (2), important self-disclosure (5) and confronting somebody with their previous behaviour (9). Other messages that involved very similar processes were also perceived as being

4.4. Situation and medium as a function of message

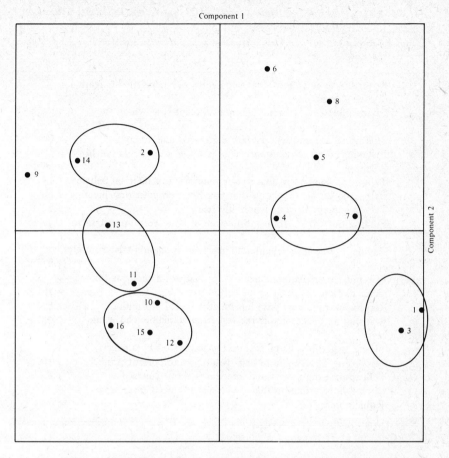

Fig. 4.7. Graphical representations of the situations from the **PREFAN** analysis in terms of the first two components, which accounted for 26.9 and 14.3 per cent of the variance respectively. Situations as in Fig. 4.5.

differently appropriate across widely different situations. Only five messages revealed no significant differences; three of these concerned impression management/information exchange, which partially confirms the first hypothesis.

TABLE 4.12. *Analysis of variance for each message across all sixteen situations using Slater's SERIES program*

	Message	F
1.	Reporting to somebody that you know, the news of the death of their parent	2.48**
2.	Giving a classmate their examination results, in which they failed	3.32***
3.	Talking to a friend who is very depressed and anxious	2.09*
4.	Listening to an acquaintance who is upset after a relationship breakup	2.46**
5.	Talking to somebody about your religious and political beliefs	3.44***
6.	Getting to know somebody that you liked on your first meeting	1.69
7.	Telling somebody your whole life story	2.29*
8.	Finding out what a friend thinks on an issue very important to you	2.37*
9.	Having it out with a friend who has been spreading false rumours about you	3.87***
10.	Listening to an acquaintance's complaints and requests for reconciliation	2.10*
11.	Reprimanding a peer who has failed to fulfil a promise	2.60**
12.	Refusing an unreasonable request from someone who wants help	0.94
13.	Trying to impress or be favourably impressed by a peer	1.37
14.	Persuading a colleague to help you on an important project	2.16*
15.	Telling amusing stories and anecdotes about yourself	1.84
16.	Obtaining information that you especially need from an acquaintance	1.50

*** $P<0.01$; ** $P<0.025$; * $P<0.05$.

Sign test. This was performed on the means of the rank-ordered media preferences for the communication of the separate messages.

It can be seen from Table 4.13 that most people prefer to communicate messages face-to-face, rather than by letter or phone. There is, however, one exception, and that is refusing an unreasonable request for help, where the letter seems to be the preferred medium. This is possible due to the opportunity to choose words more carefully, and to be excluded from the difficulty of coping with the other person's anger or embarrassment. It is also interesting to note that only 50 per cent of the letter versus phone differences are significant, whereas over 80 per cent of the face-to-face versus letter and face-to-face versus phone differences were highly significant. The difference between face-to-face interaction and communication by letter or telephone lies predominantly in the nonverbal cues, which are

TABLE 4.13. *The means and Z scores derived from the sign test, for the preferred choice of medium for each message*

	Mean[a]			Z score		
Message	Letter	Phone	Face-to-face	Letter versus phone	Letter versus face-to-face	Phone versus face-to-face
I	2.3	2.2	1.4	0.00	2.09*	2.43*
2	2.2	1.9	1.5	2.43*	2.43*	2.09*
3	2.3	2.2	1.3	1.74	2.09*	1.39
4	2.7	2.1	1.1	3.48***	5.22***	4.52***
5	2.1	2.6	1.2	1.74	3.48***	4.87***
6	2.5	2.1	1.3	2.43*	3.13**	3.13**
7	2.9	1.9	1.1	1.39	5.22***	4.87***
8	2.6	2.1	1.2	2.43*	4.52***	4.18***
9	2.5	1.9	1.2	2.43*	2.09*	3.48***
10	2.8	2.0	1.1	4.52***	4.87***	4.52***
11	2.6	2.0	1.3	3.13**	4.52***	3.13**
12	1.7	1.6	2.5	0.69	1.04	3.13**
13	2.3	2.3	1.3	0.00	2.78**	3.83***
14	2.2	2.0	1.7	0.69	1.74	1.04
15	2.4	2.3	1.1	0.69	4.52***	4.52***
16	2.6	1.8	1.4	3.48***	3.48***	2.09*

*** $P<0.001$; ** $P<0.01$; * $P<0.05$.
[a] Low score indicates high preference.

excluded in the letter and take only a vocal form on the telephone. It thus seems that vocal cues are not as important as the combination of other nonverbal cues in facilitating communication. Messages 3 and 14 are particularly interesting because of the large amount of individual difference and hence lack of significant differences between media. Although people seemed to prefer a face-to-face encounter to a letter for talking to a depressed, anxious friend there was no significant difference regarding letter versus phone or phone versus face-to-face communication, perhaps indicating the lack of confidence or skill on the part of some people in counselling a friend – especially in interpreting and responding to the other's nonverbal communication, etc. The only message for which no significant preference for any of the three media occurred was 14, persuading a colleague to help one, where wide individual differences occurred. It is possible that people had discovered that they were personally most assertive and influential in one medium rather than others and hence preferred it. Finally, the messages that distinguished most between the three media were 4 and 10, which both involve listening more than talking. It seems that the vocal and nonverbal cues afforded by the telephone and visual medium respectively are greatly appreciated by people seeking to understand another's emotions.

These results have demonstrated that people are likely to choose particular situations not only in terms of their personality and needs but also in order to achieve certain goals in the communication of certain messages. That is, people have a clear idea of the norms, constraints and advantages of some social situations over others for imparting or receiving information. This is not true of all messages however. It seems that where communication involves persuasion to do or to refrain from doing something, or involves a display of emotion or self-disclosure, the situation can help to control or encourage that message. This is also true of the medium of communication, where wide differences may occur in the preferences for different media, possibly as a function of social skill.

4.5. Choice of situation as a function of relationship with others

M. ARGYLE AND A. FURNHAM

This study was designed to test the general hypothesis that choice of situations is affected by the role relationship with those expected to be present. The range of relationships chosen included some from the three domains of family, friends and work. Within each domain, same and different status relationships were included. Within the work domain, liked and disliked colleagues were also used.

We had a number of hypotheses in mind about the functions of different relationships. Husband and wife, we expected, would be concerned with joint family tasks, and with mutual support and companionship. Friends would meet for leisure, and for eating and drinking. Colleagues would meet in work situations, and in such work social settings as morning coffee. Different status colleagues would meet at different sorts of work situation, and less at work social events. Disliked colleagues we expected to be avoided, met mainly in formal work situations, and rarely on work social occasions.

The procedure adopted was to ask subjects about the frequency with which they entered a wide range of situations in the company of specific others with whom they had different relationships.

Method

Subjects. There were forty-two subjects: twenty-four males and eighteen females. They ranged in age from their mid-twenties to over sixty, the majority being in their mid-thirties. The subjects were drawn from three populations: nurses and health administrators, housewives, and a number of different professionals (mainly engineers).

Materials. Each subject completed a two-part questionnaire. They were first required to specify seven people described in terms of whether they were work colleagues, family or friends, and in terms of age, sex, status and whether they were liked or disliked. They then stated how often they had met each person in twenty-six separate social situations over the previous month. Finally subjects were required to use seven rating scales about the nature of the typical situation in which they met each specified person (duration, whether food or drink was taken, numbers of people present, etc.).

Procedure. Approximately half the subjects were given the questionnaire in small groups, while half were sent the questionnaire by post. The questionnaire took about forty-five minutes to complete. Previous pilot work had established any ambiguities which were likely to occur, and these were removed.

Results

Do relationships affect choice of situation? A MANOVA was calculated for the twenty-six situations and seven role relationships: this was significant at $P < 0.025$. Separate one-way ANOVAS were then worked out for the twenty-six situations and the seven rating scales concerning the nature of the situations in which the seven people were seen; seventeen of the situations and all the rating scales were significantly affected by relationship at $P < 0.001$, and six more at $P < 0.01$ or $P < 0.05$. Examination of the means showed that two relationships had a particularly strong effect – spouse or equivalent and disliked colleague. The situations which were most affected by relationship were doing domestic jobs together, watching TV, helping and intimate conversation. The average range for these five situations was 3.48 on a five-point scale; without the spouse relationship the average fell to 2.10, and without disliked colleagues as well it fell to 1.53.

The detailed analysis of relationships in terms of situations chosen and avoided. Several different analyses were carried out.

1. The thirty-three one-way analyses of variance, where significant, were followed by a large number of Sheffé tests to find out which pairs of relationships differed significantly in choice of each situation.
2. In order to find out which situations were most characteristic of a relationship, ratios of frequency/average frequency for all seven

situations were worked out for each situation. In comparing pairs of relationships the ratios were examined as well as the Sheffé tests.

3. An INGRID principal-components analysis was computed for situations and relationships together after a SERIES analysis (Slater, 1977).

The situations with highest and lowest frequencies for four relationships are shown in Table 4.14, giving the ratios as described above, and the ratios for the ratings are given in Table 4.15.

(*a*) *The spouse relationship.* We asked about 'A family member of similar age to yourself (spouse, or nearest equivalent)'. This relationship had the most powerful effect on choice of situations, and produced the most frequent choice (twenty-two out of twenty-six). The INGRID also shows that this relationship is set apart from all the rest, particularly on the first component, which accounts for most of the variance. If we compare spouse with equal status colleague and similar-age friend, in terms of situations chosen, then for spouse the following situations are chosen more often at $P < 0.001$: intimate conversation, do domestic jobs together, informal meal together, one helps the other, watch TV, go shopping, go for a walk, play chess or other indoor game, have argument or disagreement. The situations which are chosen most often compared with all the others are shown in Table 4.14 (watch TV, do domestic jobs together, and so on).

The rating ratios, given in Table 4.15, show that spouse situations are much more frequent, and last longer, more is eaten and drunk, and they are less formal and task-oriented than for other relationships (most at $P < 0.001$, but all are significant at $P < 0.05$).

(*b*) *Friends* (and acquaintances of similar age). We can make a detailed comparison of friends with spouses and colleagues. Compared with spouses, friends are met much less frequently in general, and in nearly all situations. The biggest differences are for shopping (ratio $= 4.06$), domestic jobs (3.88), watching TV (3.53) and arguing (2.91), all at $P < 0.001$. Also, friends have lower scores on all the work-type situations. Compared to those with colleagues, friendship situations have a higher social/task rating (2.58, $P < 0.001$), more food is eaten, there are more visits to the pub, more informal meals and more intimate conversation.

Friends are intermediate between family and colleagues on most scales, and on the main dimension from the INGRID analysis defined by intimate and familial situations. However friends are different from *both* family and colleagues on many of the work scales, such as work together, morning coffee and negotiation. Friends do sometimes 'work' together, but in our sample they did not.

To summarise, friends meet much less often than spouses; when they do meet the situations are less domestic and less task-oriented, consisting mainly of eating, drinking, talking and playing games. Compared with

TABLE 4.14. *Relative frequencies of situations for four relationships*

Spouse
High (over 1.50)
   Watch TV: 3.35
   Do domestic jobs together: 3.14
   Going shopping: 2.81
   Go for a walk: 2.74
   Play chess, or other indoor
     game: 2.60
   Intimate conversation: 2.38
   Go to the pub: 2.28
   Informal meal together: 2.20
   Joint leisure, e.g. producing a
     play: 2.06
   Have argument, disagreement: 1.96
   Dancing: 1.85
   One helps the other: 1.83
   Work together on joint task: 1.76
   Negotiation, work out
     compromise: 1.61
   Morning coffee, tea: 1.51
   Casual chat, telling jokes: 1.50

Disliked colleague
High (over 1.00)
   Attend lecture, etc: 1.68
   Together in a committee: 1.00
Low (under 0.25)
   Dancing: 0
   Play chess, or other indoor
     game: 0
   Go shopping: 0
   Play tennis, squash, etc.: 0.07
   Watch TV: 0.09
   Informal meal together: 0.15
   Go to the pub: 0.16
   One helps the other: 0.22
   One teaches, instructs the
     other: 0.22

Friend
High (over 1.25)
   Dancing: 1.79
   Play tennis, squash, etc.: 1.45
   Attend lecture, or similar event
     together: 1.44
   Go for a walk: 1.39
   Go to the pub: 1.35
   Joint leisure, e.g. producing a play: 1.28

Colleague
High (over 1.25)
   Attend lecture, or similar event
     together: 2.61
   One interviews the other: 1.63
   Together in a committee: 1.54
   Work together on joint task: 1.42
   Morning coffee, tea: 1.41
   Negotiation, work out
     compromise: 1.38
   Meet at sherry party: 1.30
   Casual chat, telling jokes: 1.27
Low (under 0.50)
   Dancing: 0
   Watch TV: 0.09
   Do domestic jobs together: 0.20
   Go for a walk: 0.30
   Play chess, or other indoor
     game: 0.44
   Go to the pub: 0.48

colleagues also, there is less work and more eating, drinking and intimate conversation.

   Effects of like–dislike on situational choice. The workplace is one of the main domains in which it is necessary to deal with people who are disliked.

TABLE 4.15. *Ratios between ratings for each situation and averages for all situations*

	Spouse	Friend	Colleague	Disliked colleague
Frequency	1.72	0.76	0.89	0.75
Food eaten	1.34	1.14	0.81	0.69
Duration	1.25	1.18	0.98	0.71
Drink	1.18	1.13	0.98	0.69
Formal	0.85	0.89	1.02	1.43
Task	0.67	0.58	1.51	1.55

We compared situational choice for liked and disliked colleagues of the same status. Every situation was chosen less frequently for the disliked person. The highest *ratios* were for intimate conversation, playing tennis, etc., since these situations were almost never entered with a disliked person. The next highest ratios were found for helping the other (5.80, $P < 0.001$), teaches/instructs (4.65, $P < 0.001$) and the other work situations (in the range 5 : 1 to 2 : 1).

Which situations *are* chosen for a disliked colleague? Every situation was said to be chosen less often. Situations with the disliked colleagues were more formal (1.43, $P < 0.01$) and less was drunk (0.69, $P < 0.001$). The highest *absolute* frequencies were for morning coffee, casual chat and telling jokes, working together on a joint task, trying to persuade the other, together in a committee, and negotiation – though in all these cases the frequencies were much lower than for a liked colleague. The lowest ratios, i.e. where liking had least effect on situational choice, were for being together on a committee (1.54), and attending a lecture or similar event (1.55). To summarise, disliked colleagues are avoided, but if they must be encountered this occurs in short, infrequent and formal meetings, e.g. at morning coffee, committee meetings and lectures.

Effects of status differences. Within each of the three domains we included relationships of same and different status. The only common significant effect was of reduced frequency for different status. The greatest effects were in the family; however since this probably reflected spouse and child relationships, it is perhaps not right to interpret it simply in terms of status. Most of the other situations characteristic of spouse were much less frequent for a different status family relation. For friends, different status resulted in less intimate conversations, fewer informal meals and less food eaten. For colleagues, different status resulted in more direction by one, less working together and less morning coffee.

4.5. Situation as a function of relationship

Conclusions

Relationship with others has a strong effect on choice and avoidance of everyday social situations. The strongest effects are due to spouse and disliked colleague. There is a general dimension of intimacy, and family–friends–colleagues fall along it in this order, though friends are distinctive in the avoidance of work settings. It is therefore possible to define each relationship in terms of the characteristic situations in which people choose to interact with others: e.g. friends eat, drink, talk and engage in joint leisure activity. Liking results in more frequent interaction, especially more intimacy and helping. Status differences result in less frequent interaction, and choice of less-intimate situations.

5
Rules

Introduction

We propose to use the concept of rules as a central explanatory device in the analysis of situations. People come together in social situations so that certain goals can be attained; rules develop to coordinate the behaviour of interactors so that these goals can be met. But what exactly is meant by a 'rule'? By a rule we mean 'behaviour which members of a group believe should, or should not, or may be, performed in some situation, or range of situations'. This is based on the notion of appropriateness; when a person breaks a rule he has made a mistake (Winch, 1958).

Rules in this sense can be distinguished from 'norms', which are often used by social psychologists to refer to modal behaviour, i.e. what most people do; sometimes most people break the rules. Rules can also be distinguished from 'conventions', which refer to arbitrary customs such as fashion in clothes. It is a rule in cricket that the batsman should use a bat (rather than, say, a tennis racquet), but a convention that he shall wear white trousers. Conventions are elements of shared culture which can vary without affecting task performance or attainment of goals. This distinction is investigated empirically in experiment 5.2. Some rules emerge during the life of a particular group, such as a family or a research group. Some are imposed on members of a group from above, like the laws of the land or the regulations inside organisations.

Rules have been used in several different parts of the social sciences during recent years. (1) Wittgenstein (1953) argued that languages are rule-systems, like games, in which communication is made possible because the rules are shared. (2) Piaget (1932) showed how children come to treat the rules of games with increasing sophistication as they grow older. (3) Lévi-Strauss (1969) interpreted the elaborate kinship systems of primitive societies in terms of underlying rule-systems. (4) Chomsky (1957) showed how the structure of language could be interpreted in terms of the rules of a generative grammar. (5) Harré and Secord (1972) argued that most human social behaviour is rule-governed.

To speak of rules, in our sense, is to put forward a hypothesis. When we say that someone is following a rule we imply that he knows the rule (although there are different ways of knowing a rule), recognises that it applies in some situations, and that this has affected his behaviour. That is he is aware or conscious, in some way, of the rules – though there may be different reasons for his following the rules. We want, therefore, to contrast rule-following behaviour with behaviour which is the product of instinctive reaction, conditioning, reinforcement learning, or other processes which do not involve rules.

To speak of rules also implies a certain philosophical model of human behaviour. It implies, for the types of behaviour to which rules are said to apply, that people have a choice of different behaviours and that their decision is affected by their knowledge of the rules. However there are some rules that are learnt by children during socialisation, and become unthinking habits; perhaps children only realise there is a rule when someone breaks it. They may suffer from culture shock when they visit another country and find that some rules no longer apply. We want to extend the notion of rule to include this kind of rule-following.

Do animals follow rules? Reynolds (1976) compared the incest taboo in certain groups of primates with the marriage rules of very primitive human societies. He concluded that the main difference is that men can conceptualise, symbolise and use words for the social relations involved. It is possible that men use sanctions for rule-breaking where the non-human primates do not. Rules are not the same as empirical laws: rules are the practices of particular groups, they could be different and usually are so in different groups or situations, and they can be broken.

Can we speak of the personal rules of an individual? He may certainly follow a personal rule of life – it may be a rule of some group to which he once belonged – but we shall only consider it a rule if there is some consensus about it at the time of use. The point of a rule is that it coordinates behaviour or facilitates communication in a group.

The concept of rule opens the door to a whole range of empirical phenomena. In this chapter our main interest is in studying the differences between the rules in different situations. We shall also consider why particular rules develop in situations, what happens when rules are broken, and why people react differently to rule-breaking. There are other issues, such as how rules are learnt, how rules are created and changed, and so on, which we shall not deal with.

There are several different kinds of rule: some are prescriptive, others are proscriptive; some are categorical, others are guides to behaviour; there are laws, morals, etiquette and conventions; some rules are laid down by authority, others emerge from the group; some are stated in words, others have never been put into words (Twining and Miers, 1976).

We cannot rely simply on knowledge of the rules to predict people's behaviour. Were we to do so we would stand in danger of conjuring up a way of life

in which men tip their hats to ladies; youths defer to old people in public con-
veyances; unwed mothers are a rarity; citizens go to the aid of law enforcement
officers; chewing gum is never stuck under tables and never dropped on the
sidewalk; television repairmen fix television sets; children respect their aged
parents. (Harris, 1968, p. 590)

Such rules are obviously very 'weak'; though we should still regard them as
rules if people still believed that these things should or should not be done.
Jackson (1966) proposed that rules have two dimensions of strength: the
degree of consensus about them, and the strength of approval or disapproval resulting from their being kept or broken. However even when a
person does not keep a rule his behaviour may still be influenced by it, in
that he may feel guilty, or feel aware of having failed to behave properly.

Rules often sound restrictive – do this and don't do that. These restrictions often bring obvious benefits – for example, driving on a certain side of
the road, or not talking during concerts. But rules do far more than this –
they make whole realms of behaviour possible.

Using language, playing games, courting, getting married, reasoning in mathematics, making decisions in committees, buying and selling a house, passing sentences
on a person convicted of crime and even fighting a war are all to a large extent
rule-governed activities. (Twining and Miers, 1976, p. 57)

These are all examples of what Berger and Luckman (1966) described as
'the social construction of reality', in which rules play an important part.
It is the repertoire of behaviour, combined with the rules, that makes
each activity possible. In complex rule-systems, like the one that governs
cricket, the regulative rules are stated in terms of concepts such as 'declare',
'not out', etc., which themselves require definition. So there is a subsidiary
type of rule (constitutive rule) which defines the terms needed to apply
regulative rules; for example, rules are needed to define what counts as or
constitutes a 'try' in rugby football, as well as to regulate what happens
when one has been scored. As Collett (1977) concluded, 'while constitutive
rules do not regulate behaviour, nevertheless regulative rules do require the
assistance of constitutive rules' (p. 6).

Rules are related to each other. If one rule is changed in a game, other
rules may have to be changed too. For example, the rules of rugby football
were changed to reduce the extent to which games were won by penalty
kicks. The change was to give a free-kick (i.e. a drop-kick rather than a
place-kick) for certain minor infringements. This did not reduce the
number of points won from penalties, so the nature of a free-kick was
altered, so that the ball had to be played with the foot before being kicked at
goal. This in turn has led to the strategy of passing the ball to the best kicker
– but a third change of rule has not yet been made (Gordon Mangan,

personal communication). This is not a matter of logical implication, it is rather that in the context of the goals, elements, etc. of the game, one rule affects another.

What about 'informal situations', such as sitting around at home chatting, where rules are much less in evidence? Do they have rules too? Price and Bouffard (1974) found that situations could be ranked in terms of the number of things that could not be done in them. The least rule-bound situations in their study were: in own room, in a park, in the dormitory lounge. The most rule-bound were: in church, at a job interview and in the lift. In a very informal situation fewer things are prohibited, and probably fewer things are demanded; there is more freedom to do what you like, and probably weaker sanctions if the rules are broken. As we shall see in experiment 5.4, although informal situations have fewer rules than formal ones, they may still have special rules of their own, as well as the universal rules which apply to all situations. There is probably more latitude for variation in informal situations, for example in clothes and style of social behaviour.

Experiment 5.2 is concerned with the distinction between rules and conventions. It was found that breaking rules in a number of situations was judged as more disruptive, unacceptable, etc., than not abiding by conventions. Breaking universal rules which apply to all social situations was also very disruptive. However there was no sharp cut-off point, and some norms which had been classified as conventions were just as disruptive to break as some rules. There are some conventions, e.g. wearing clothes, which it is very disturbing to break, since breaking them brings about a change in the nature of the situation.

Is there a difference between 'generative' rules, like those of grammar, and rules that are more directly prescriptive or proscriptive? Rules of grammar are generative in the sense that they state how sentences are built up, in a hierarchical fashion, how negative and passive sentences are produced, how the same idea can be expressed in alternative ways. Examples are 'rewrite' rules of the form:

sentence → noun phrase + verb phrase

verb phrase → noun phrase + adjective

There are also transformational rules for generating negative and passive sentences (Lyons, 1969).

Such rules are discovered by special methods – postulating rule-systems, generating sentences from them, and making progressive corrections to the rules by seeing if they generate proper sentences and only proper sentences. This is like testing a highlevel scientific hypothesis: deductions from generative rules include more accessible 'surface' rules. We shall see that similar principles may govern sequences of social behaviour. For sentences and social behaviour we think that generative rules can usefully be regarded as rules in our sense.

As we have defined rules, members of a group must 'believe that x must be done', i.e. must in some sense be aware of the rule. But what is meant by 'knowing' a rule? The requirement that people shall be able to state the rule is perhaps to ask too much; in the case of grammar only students of linguistics can usually do this. A weaker criterion is that members of the group can recognise instances of rule-breaking – which most speakers of a language can do. The underlying rules of kinship structure may not be known even in this sense, in which case we should not call them rules at all.

Research methods for the study of rules

There are several ways of finding out whether rules are operating.

Observation of behaviour. Regularities in behaviour can easily be revealed by observation. But how can an observer decide whether the regularity is due to rules or to some other cause? Sometimes there is use of sanctions when people depart from the regular pattern – as at games of football or ice-hockey. This can happen in situations other than games, where verbal or nonverbal signs of disapproval can be seen; for example, Mann (1969) found some of the rules governing behaviour in Australian football queues by observing what happened if people tried to jump the queue etc. In polite social circles, however, it is common for no immediate sanctions to be used at all (see p. 139f.). Rule-breaking may lead to visible disruption of the flow of events, as it would if someone tried to argue during a sermon, or play a musical instrument during a lecture. Again, on some polite occasions there may be rapid restorative action, so that the rule-breaking is less evident. Rules can also be inferred if the behaviour which seems about to take place in fact does not. Fox (1977) observed that 'fights' on a certain Irish island almost never involved any actual blows, so he deduced that there were rules governing the conduct of these so-called fights. Marsh, *et al*. (1978) interpreted the very low level of actual violence at football matches in the same way.

Another kind of difficulty arises in the case of complex rule-systems, like those of cricket or of language. Cricket rules involve a number of concepts defined by constitutive rules; in the case of language the rules are of a complex generative type, so that inference of the rules is very difficult.

For several reasons, therefore, it looks as though the observational method of studying rules needs to be supplemented by other methods, to which we now turn.

The effects of deliberate rule-breaking. It is possible to verify the existence of a possible rule by finding out what happens when it is broken; the resulting sanctions can be observed or those present can be asked if they disapprove of what has happened. Garfinkel (1963) was the first to use this as a method of research; students behaved towards their parents as if they were lodgers, tried to buy books from other customers in a bookshop, and put their marks on the lines instead of in the boxes at noughts and crosses.

Experiment 5.3 was concerned with the rules governing interruption of speech, and used an experimentally controlled procedure. Two hypotheses were put forward, of which one was supported and the other not. It was found that interruption is allowed when a person reaches the end of a sentence, but not at grammatical breaks or within phrases. This study shows that it is possible to discover quite new information about rules by means of controlled experiments on rule-breaking.

Interview and questionnaire methods. It is possible to find out about rules by asking people how they would react to hypothetical instances of rule-breaking. In experiment 5.5, subjects were shown scenarios of a variety of situations in which rule-breaking occurred and asked to rate their reactions of disapproval, anger, and so on.

A more direct method is simply to ask people whether a certain rule applies. Price and Bouffard (1974) asked subjects to rate the appropriateness of fifteen forms of behaviour in fifteen situations. In experiment 5.4 we report an investigation of this kind: subjects were asked to rate on five-point scales the relevance of rules to different situations.

Another method is to interview members of a group about acceptable forms of behaviour. For example Marsh *et al.* (1978) interviewed football hooligans about how to 'put the boot in' and allied matters. In these interviews a number of rules were stated more or less directly by informants: e.g. it was not acceptable to injure members of the opposing gang though it was desirable to frighten them. Another study was concerned with the rules about fighting among schoolgirls, borstal girls and women in prison. Some of the results are shown in Table 5.1. It can be seen that there is a fairly high degree of agreement about some of these rules.

Study of the socially mobile. Garfinkel (1967) studied Agnes who was undergoing a sex change, and who thus became aware, to an unusual degree, of the different rules for males and females. This method could be used for less dramatic changes of status, such as upward or downward movement in the social scale, visiting other countries, and indeed joining any new group or organisation.

TABLE 5.1. *Rules for fighting among females*

1. Should not use a bottle to hit the other person
   schoolgirls 85% (borstal girls 58%)
2. Should not ask friends to call the police
   borstal girls 85%
3. Should not use a handbag to hit the other person
   69%
4. Should not use a knife on the other person
   schoolgirls 89% (borstal girls 52%)
5. Should not report it to the police later
   86%
6. Should not ask friends to join in
   81%
7. Should not tell the school later
   85%
8. It is OK to kick the other person
   borstal girls 78%
9. It is OK to slap the other person
   prison women 85%
10. It is OK to punch the other person
    borstal girls 90%

Survey of 251 schoolgirls, borstal girls and prison women, from Campbell (1980).

Study of rule-books. To discover the rules of a game the easiest way would be to look at the book of rules. Can the same method be used for non-game situations? Schools, colleges, clubs and other organisations often have printed lists of rules, though these would not be complete. For example, the very elaborate rules of London clubs do not mention the clothes that should be worn. Etiquette books which provide lists of rules were used by Goffman (1963) as a source of data. However these rules tend to describe the ideal behaviour of a certain social group, rather than the rules for which there is a real consensus.

Study of the development of a group. To discover how rules develop, change and are enforced one might study a small group over time. For various task-related or social reasons, rules emerge to control or restrict certain forms of social interaction. These rules are often situation-specific and relate only to a limited group of people. Homans (1951) reported a number of rules that developed among the fourteen workers in the Bank Wiring Room at the Hawthorne Plant, in the 1930s. The rules referred to production rates, interaction with the inspector, helping one another, and exchanging jobs.

Study of conformity and obedience. Experimental studies of conformity often reveal very dramatically the operation of various social rules. It is only when there is nonconformity that the rules become more explicit and apparent. These studies also reveal how far people will obey rules that have been imposed. Milgram (1974) demonstrated very forcefully the extent to which people will follow the orders of an experimenter.

A functional theory of rules

The theory we propose is simply this: rules are created and changed in order that situational goals can be attained. It is a familiar psychological principle that an individual person or animal will discover routes to desired goals, either by trial and error or by other forms of problem-solving. We are now proposing an extension to this principle: groups of people will find routes to their goals, and these routes will be collective solutions, including the necessary coordination of some behaviours and the exclusion of other behaviours by means of rules. Unless such coordination is achieved group goals will not be attained. For example in order to play a game of football, croquet, etc., it is necessary for a number of people to follow the same rules, otherwise no game is possible. Children's games provide a good example of creating rules as you go along – 'you're not allowed to hide in the next-door garden', etc.

Some functionalist writers have offered examples of the functional analysis of rules. For example Parsons (1951) suggested that the rules of etiquette surrounding professional people have the functions of structuring the relationship so that they can obtain intimate information without becoming too familiar or becoming too involved. Harris (1975) offered an explanation of the Indian rules protecting cows in terms of the value of cow-dung as fertiliser and fuel, of oxen for pulling farm implements, and so on.

Llewellyn (1962) has also proposed a functional theory of rules, in this case the rules of social groups. He suggested that the needs met by rules are the avoidance of conflicts within the group, the settling of disputes when they arise, the adjustment of the behaviour and expectations of members when the circumstances of the group change, and the regulation of decision-making. Twining and Miers (1976) add a number of further functions to this list, such as the need to educate in respect of values or standards (as in the case of school rules), to express disapproval at some forms of behaviour (as in the case of prohibition in the USA) and to manage social affairs.

What are the functions to be satisfied by rules in social situations? We shall postulate that there are three main kinds: (1) universal functions, which apply to all social situations; (2) universal features of verbal communication; (3) situation-specific rules, based on the goal structure of the situation. While some of these 'functional prerequisites' can be discovered from interviewing people, others cannot, and must be regarded as 'latent' functions (Merton, 1949).

It is sometimes possible to satisfy functions in more than one way, by more than one set of rules. For example, buying and selling can be done by (1) fixed-price sales, (2) bargaining, (3) auction sales and (4) barter. Why should one system develop rather than another? Perhaps because further goals are met, such as sustaining social relationships. The answer to these questions lies in historical factors – the use of money, the development of mass sales, and so on.

Rules which meet universal requirements of social situations

There are several requirements that apply to nearly all situations and lead to the formation of general rules.

Make communication possible. Social interaction is possible only if people can communicate with one another. So there is a rule that they must use or try to use a common language or signalling system. This was found empirically in experiment 5.2. Similarly there is a rule that interactors should adopt spatial positions from which they can communicate. If they are speaking to each other without optical or electronic assistance, this means that they must be within certain limits of distance and orientation, though these vary somewhat between cultures (Argyle, 1975).

Prevent withdrawal by other interactors. If interaction is insufficiently rewarding for an interactor he will withdraw and seek alternative ways of meeting his needs. Unless people are kept by force, like prisoners, soldiers, schoolchildren and mental hospital patients, there are rules about ensuring that they have adequate rewards. Thibaut and Faucheux (1965) found in a game-playing experiment that when players had unequal chances of winning, rules were created to guarantee some gains by the low-power players. In experiment 5.4 we found universal rules such as 'don't embarrass people' and 'don't make other people feel small' – all cases of avoiding negative consequences for others.

Prevent aggression. If interaction is to continue without a complete breakdown of communication, aggression must be avoided, even though there may be conflict of interests and mutual dislike. The rule 'be polite' has emerged as universal in our research (experiment 5.4). The main exception to this rule is that ritual aggression may be allowed, as in the case of opposing groups of football fans, who give an impressive display of aggressive attitudes and intentions but rarely, apparently, hurt anyone (Marsh *et al.*, 1978). Another exception is rule-governed aggression, as in, for example, boxing and wrestling, and up to a point in war.

Begin and end encounters. In order to start an encounter two or more people must signal their willingness to take part and must establish their relationships, in terms of intimacy, relative status and roles. Interactors must be changed to a state of readiness to interact. This 'ritual work' is performed by greetings rituals; when an encounter ends there are parting rituals (Goffman, 1971). Greetings and partings take somewhat different forms in different cultures, but there are some underlying similarities. For example the following nonverbal components are very commonly used in greetings:

> close proximity, direct orientation
> smiling
> mutual gaze
> bodily contact (with the exception of some non-contact cultures such as India and Japan)
> presenting palm of hand, either visibly or for shaking
> head-toss (or head-nod, bow)

Rules which meet universal requirements for verbal communication

A further set of rules are generated to meet the requirements of all situations in which there is verbal communication. This includes the first rule in the previous section, that interactors shall speak a common language.

Synchronisation of utterances. Verbal communication breaks down if everyone speaks at once, or if there are very long pauses between utterances. There is a rule that not more than one person should speak at a time. There is an exception to this rule: simultaneous speech is permitted if it is intended to supplement the other's speech. Ferguson (1977) found that many 'interruptions' were really cases of the listener helping the speaker to finish his sentences, or making comments like 'I see' which were not intended to stop the other's flow of speech. Research has shown how synchronising is achieved (e.g. Duncan and Fiske, 1977), but the important point is that it should take place.

Adjacency pairs. There are rules about how one utterance should follow another. As Grice (1975) said, 'Our talk exchanges do not consist of a succession of disconnected remarks and would not be rational if they did' (p. 45). He put forward the general cooperative principle: 'Make your conversational contribution such as is required, at the stage at which it occurs, by the accepted purpose or direction of the talk exchanges in which you are engaged' (p. 45). This is spelt out in a number of more detailed maxims (see below, p. 214).

There are also rules about how one class of utterance should lead to another, e.g. questions should lead to answers under certain conditions (p. 215f.).

Generating longer sequences of utterances. There are rules about the construction of sequences longer than two utterances, such as the episodic structure of situations, the four-step social-skill sequence and characteristic cycles found in some situations (p. 216f.)

Rules which meet the requirements of particular kinds of situation
So far we have considered rules that are universal to all or most situations in our culture. Now we turn to rules that are generated by the goal structure of particular situations.

Coordinate behaviour so that goals may be attained. An interactor who is pursuing a goal will make use of two-step sequences like question–answer. He will also use longer 'social-skill' sequences, in which he corrects his behaviour in response to feedback: e.g. asks a revised question in order to get a better answer (p. 217). He may also use planned sequences, where one of his moves is linked to the next, like:

Doctor : take your clothes off, please (D_1)
Patient : takes clothes off (P_1)
Doctor : examines patient (D_2)

The link between D_1 and D_2 is definitely rule-governed: it would be absurd if the doctor had lunch or wrote out a prescription at this point, because D_1–D_2 is part of the same social act, one move being necessary for the other. When a person is pursuing a goal there may be a number of steps which can logically come only in a certain order. A doctor must question or examine a patient before he can treat or prescribe; he could not reverse the order of events. Cooking a meal must come before eating it, and washing up after eating it. These are logical principles about the order of the main episodes – not exactly rules in our sense.

In cases where no participant is taking the whole initiative, the sequence of moves may have to follow a certain order in which two or more people must collaborate. In a sales situation, the salesperson (S) may ask the customer (C) what he wants, or C may ask S what he has; S may produce samples of goods, and C may ask questions about them, or ask to see others; if C decides to buy, S wraps the goods up, and C pays. The situation generates (*a*) the repertoire of elements, (*b*) adjacency pairs and (*c*) the order of the main episodes.

Some of the results of experiment 5.4 can be interpreted as rules linked to goals. In the classroom, at the doctor's and when making a complaint, there were rules about careful, formal, polite behaviour and avoiding gossip. For a hostess, someone on a first date or at a wedding, behaviour should be cheerful and show positive affect.

Guard against temptation. Many rules make possible the general pursuit of certain goals, but involve restrictions on the activities of individuals. For example a queue makes it possible for people to obtain tickets in a manner which is orderly and fair, but any one person could do better for himself by pushing to the front, asking friends at the front to buy him a ticket, or asking people to keep his place for long periods of time. Another example would be the rule of silence in a library that enables the goals of reading and studying to be pursued without disturbance. In Mann's (1969) study of queues for football matches in Australia, which last for twenty-four hours or more, he found that rules developed, and were enforced, to restrain such behaviour and make the queues tolerable, e.g. by allowing some time out. Indeed these were the main rules governing behaviour in the queues. He does not report that there were any rules about such things as not making a noise, making love or getting drunk (as there are in many other situations); these are not necessary since they would not interfere with the goals of queueing.

There could be an indefinite number of rules about what should not be done in a situation, but unless people are commonly tempted to do these things, and unless they would interfere with the goals, such rules are not necessary. There is no rule about letting off fireworks in chamber music concerts, about attending lectures on horseback, or wearing suits of armour at committee meetings.

One of the findings of experiment 5.4 provides an example of an anti-temptation rule among young female subjects: on a first date one should not touch the other.

Help with common difficulties. We earlier mentioned rules of the type 'don't embarrass people' that are a way of preventing withdrawal, and of the type 'be polite' that are a way of preventing aggression. Rules of etiquette appear to be designed to prevent such difficulties. For example, sending invitations not more than three weeks before the event makes it possible for the recipient to refuse, and coughing before entering rooms containing young couples is recommended (Goffman, 1963). In the 'Boston switch' the hostess speaks to the person on her right during the first course at dinner, and everyone else pairs off accordingly; during the second course she turns to the person on her left, and everyone switches (George Homans, personal communication). Rules of etiquette are sometimes used, however, to distinguish between those who know them and those who do not – which does *not* ease social difficulties though it does serve a different function.

It appears from the work on the perception of 'stressful' situations that people find situations difficult where the rules are complex or ambiguous (see Chapter 12).

There are some examples of this kind of rule from experiment 5.4. When making a complaint one should be especially polite (to avoid the danger of a row), and at an interview one should be cheerful (to avoid the anxiety perhaps).

Govern status differences. In many situations there are rules governing the behaviour expected by those of different status, and towards people of different status. Such rules are most important in formal and public situations, least important in informal and private situations. The use of title and last name in addressing others is most marked in formal work settings (p. 301), for example. Status or rank often requires conformity to certain styles of dress, and to certain forms of verbal and nonverbal behaviour. The behaviour expected of judges and bishops is different from that expected of prisoners in the dock and choirboys. There are proper ways of addressing superiors and subordinates, verbally and nonverbally; some degree of deference may be required.

The creative construction of complex rule-systems. The rules of football, for example, are very complex, and cannot be explained simply as functioning to help people get some exercise on Saturday afternoon. The game existed in many countries in the ancient world, and usually consisted of large mobs, often from different villages, kicking a ball about with virtually no rules, and often with great violence, so that the game was sometimes suppressed by law. Over a long period the different versions of the game developed, with gradual additions, changes and refinements to the rules, which in each form of the game have now developed into an elaborate system. The designers of board games such as Monopoly invent the whole set of rules at once, but these have to be tried out and modified so that they produce a satisfactory game. The rules of social situations other than games – e.g. seminars, dinner parties and committee meetings – are also modified in the course of history. Are there any completely new social situations, parallel to Monopoly and Scrabble? Psychologists have invented some new kinds of group activity, such as T-groups, encounter groups and 'brainstorming' (see p. 379). The counter-culture has produced some new situations with new sets of rules, such as the sit-in and squatting. The possibilities are endless, however, an awareness of how rules function could make possible the creation of a wide range of new situations.

5.1. The rule-breaking episode

M. ARGYLE AND G. P. GINSBURG

Rules cannot be fully described or understood unless we know the conditions and attendant consequences of their breakage. The consequences of breakage, especially the sanctions that are applied, often depend upon the reasons for the breakage as expressed by the rule-breakers or as attributed to them by observers. Therefore, we must consider the conditions under which people break rules, why they do so, and what happens when they do. Furthermore, it is important to recognise that an instance of rule-breaking (RB) occurs in a context of situated action; that is, RB necessarily occurs in some particular setting, is preceded by particular events and is followed by other events. Thus, an adequate description and understanding of rules requires an understanding of the rule-breaking episode (RBE) in which RB occurs and has consequences. We shall review here the nature of RBEs, starting with why people break rules and then considering what happens when they do so.

A common impression is that people break rules for selfish reasons, and that when they do so other people impose sanctions. If a football player is offside, the other team receives a free-kick; if a taxpayer does not report some of his income, he is given a heavy fine; if a gangster squeals to the police, he is put in a concrete overcoat. However, this impression notwithstanding, cheating to their own advantage is neither the only nor the most common reason for people breaking rules, and the breaking of a rule does not necessarily lead to the imposition of sanctions. Goffman (1971), for example, has provided an account of how RB may be followed by a 'remedial sequence' which restores normal social interaction without sanctions being applied (see p. 142f.)

Why do people break rules? We carried out a series of case studies, in which informants were asked to describe in some detail a RBE at which they had been present. These RBEs could be classified in terms of the different reasons for them, as follows:

1. Selfish, antisocial short-cut (e.g. a person who pushed his way into a queue).
2. Ignorance of the rule, or of the conditions for its application (e.g. a newcomer to an Oxford college who passed the port across the table; or the US President who called the West German Chancellor by his Christian name on their first meeting, in public).
3. Trying to be funny (e.g. a person who turned up at a committee meeting in fancy dress).
4. Serious attempt to improve procedures (e.g. picking up the ball in football, thus inventing rugby football).
5. Incompetence due to forgetfulness or oversight (e.g. a man who

met Princess Margaret at a party but forgot who she was: Man: 'The old firm still flourishes, eh?' Princess: 'You could say that.' Man: 'Your sister still well, I hope, still flourishing?' Princess: 'Still Queen.').

6. Incompetence due to physiological factors (e.g. drink or fatigue) or to irrational motivation (e.g. bizarre, insane behaviour).

7. Situational factors: ambiguity, overload or conflict of applicable rules (e.g. a person trying to take command of a carriage on the London underground in an overcrowding crisis).

In reviewing these seven categories of reasons, which are not meant to be exhaustive, it might be noted that the first six pertain to intentions and shortcomings of the rule-breaker, while the last refers to features of the situation. Furthermore, the intrapersonal reasons differ between the categories. Categories 1, 3 and 4 reflect deliberate RBs; 5 and 6 reflect inability on the part of the rule-breaker to recognise the applicability of the rule or to perform behaviours reflective of it; and 2 reflects ignorance of the rule or of the conditions for its application. These differences might be expected to be related to people's reactions to the RBE, and indeed they are.

As will be developed further in experiment 5.5, the RB may not be noticed; but if it is noticed, the immediate reactions to it are likely to be anger, embarrassment or laughter. According to our case studies, anger is most common as a reaction to category 1, the selfish short-cut; embarrassment to 5 and 6, the two types of incompetence; and laughter to 2 and 3, ignorance and deliberate attempts at comedy or humour, respectively. RB of type 4, an attempt to improve procedures, may well be received with approval if it is thought to be a good idea, but there is some question as to whether such approval reflects immediate reactions. Moreover, most RBs are unexpected and may be momentarily incomprehensible.

One class of RBs that has become known to social scientists but was not mentioned by our case study informants is deliberate 'Garfinkelling', in which background rules are broken in an apparently arbitrary manner for research purposes (Garfinkel, 1963). This kind of RB has a particularly pointless and incomprehensible character, whereas most RBs, as we know them, are for a good reason. Furthermore, it may be misleading as a method for studying RBs, since its usefulness seems limited to a demonstration of the existence of background rules. The technique does not seem dependable as an elicitor of *usual* reactions to RBs or of typical sanctions and corrective sequences to a more broadly defined RBE: 'experimenter-breaking-rule-for-no-apparent-reason-in-a-socially-routine-situation'. In any case, because Garfinkelling is uncommon in ordinary experience and was not mentioned by our informants, we shall not give it further attention.

The immediate reactions of observers to RBs may be concealed or displayed overtly, and even the overt displays may range from inadvertent nonverbal 'leakages' and autonomic reactions such as flushes, to fully developed verbal expressions. The voluntary and non-voluntary aspects of the immediate reactions, and the conditions which influence their temporal duration, have not yet been investigated, although experiment 5.5 provides some information regarding their intensity.

A RBE does not end with the immediate reactions of other people. The subsequent sequence of events is complex and can take several forms. Sanctions of various forms and contents may be applied, there may be a variety of verbal and nonverbal communications, order may be restored by various means and with a range of consequences, and the RBE may in fact continue well beyond the immediate situation.

Sanctions may be expressed verbally, by such nonverbal signals as a frown, or physically, as in a spanking. Nonverbal signals are probably the most common, but RBEs can occur in which no sanctions are applied. For example, a psychologist attended a British civil service committee meeting wearing a flowered shirt open to the navel, together with a large iron cross, and proceeded to eat chips from a dirty newspaper, explaining that it was his breakfast. The civil servants gave no hint of their reactions and applied no sanctions.

In addition to the form in which a sanction is expressed, attention must also be given to its contents and duration. The possible contents of sanctions include private and public criticism, retribution, restitution, and ejection from the group or society. A particularly powerful form of the last is 'shunning', as practised by such religious groups as the Amish in the United States; one may be 'sent to Coventry' by British workers; one may not be invited again. A member of the community who has transgressed seriously may be shunned by the whole community; although the transgressor continues to perform his responsibilities and to earn or receive physical sustenance, no-one converses with him or shares personal worlds with him.

RBs are often puzzling, at least briefly, and RBEs may entail communication among the people present to 'disambiguate' the occurrence and negotiate an agreed reaction to what has happened. Examples of such disambiguating communications include a brief mutual gaze with raised eyebrows, a patient smile which is visible to the others, and any of a number of expressions – surprise, puzzlement, disdain, annoyance or disapproval – which is held long enough to be noticeable as a signal rather than an unselfconscious affective reaction. These can be considered to be nonverbal solidarity processes in that they signal one's immediate reaction and negotiate a potential group solidarity regarding the RB and reactions to it. Some of the gestures used in southern Italy between second and third parties seem to function this way (Morris *et al.*, 1979). This process can be used by a majority to affirm the majority view of the world and to agree on an interpretation of the RB; or it can be used by a minority to sustain its deviant view (Moscovici, 1976). Even the rule-breaker can participate in this process, after the RB. For example, if he notices a brief eye contact and a disapproving expression exchanged by two group members immediately after his RB, that exchange could affect his subsequent actions. Or, if the rule-breaker finds himself in a briefly sustained mutual gaze with just one group member who shows a supportive expression, he may be less prone to display embarrassment or offer an apology for the RB. In any event, RBEs are likely to contain fairly complex communications which serve to establish the focal action as an RB and to affirm either a majority or minority value relevant to it.

RBs disturb the smooth flow of a situated act. The disturbances created by an RB, and the magnitude of reactions to it, appear to be greater (*a*) for rules than conventions, (*b*) for categorical rules, (*c*) in formal situations, and (*d*) when people of different status are present. However, reactions to RBs are themselves guided by rules. In groups of adolescents, for example, sanctions are often applied immediately, both verbally and nonverbally. Moreover, sanctions are more likely if the offender has not expressed his regrets or offered any explanation, and if the RB was of category 1, i.e. deliberate, antisocial and selfish. It is likely that the rules guiding reactions to RBs will include some that are very general and many that are specific to the culture, group and setting. At present, only the barest start has been made toward discovering such rules.

Given the fact that RBs disrupt the order of the situated activity, how is that order restored? Sometimes the situation simply cannot be restored, because the RB involved intrinsic rules which are essential to the successful accomplishment of the situated act. If a student sitting for an examination refuses to answer the questions presented to him and insists on posing and answering his own questions, the examination cannot be accomplished. More commonly, however, order can be restored. This is generally achieved through some sort of corrective sequence embedded in the larger act. For example, someone may make a socially skilled move which solves the problem presented by the RB. When a guest of King Edward VII drank the water in his finger bowl, the King did the same, and everyone else followed suit. Or a particular person of status in the situation may take charge and explain the rules or elicit an apology. Such a person might be the chairman of the committee, a senior member of the group or the hostess of the party, or it may be someone having special standing with the rule-breaker, such as a spouse.

An especially interesting form of embedded corrective interchange is the 'remedial sequence' described by Goffman (1971).

1. A commits error (e.g. steps on B's toe).
2. A apologizes, gives excuse or explanation ('I'm frightfully sorry, I didn't see your foot').

3. B accepts this ('It's OK, no damage done').
4. A thanks B ('It's very good of you to be so nice about it').
5. B minimises what A has done ('Think nothing of it').

Remedial sequences are important in RBEs, not only because they appear to be a common process by which order is re-established, as Goffman argues, but also because they are undertaken collaboratively by the perpetrator and the recipients of the RB. The collaborative restoration of order reaffirms the solidarity of the group and its continuing commitment to whatever activity had been disrupted by the RB. Goffman (1967), too, recognises the importance of joint participation in re-establishing smoothness and spontaneity of interaction.

The RBE does not end here. The episode may be discussed further, after the immediate situation has ended. The rule-breaker may receive instruction from a spouse or a senior member of the group. A British visitor to an American university, well known for his aggressive behaviour at seminars, was told, 'Ve Americans do not do eet like zat.' There may even be further negotiation as to whether a RBE actually had occurred, with the possibility of redefinition. Furthermore, the story of the RBE may be retold many times, until it becomes a kind of folk tale within the group. This can have the effect of continually reaffirming a value challenged by the RB or of denigrating a value implied by the RB, and it can extend the sanctions indefinitely by forming and maintaining particular attitudes and feelings toward the rule-breaker.

5.2. Rules versus conventions in everyday situations
M. ARGYLE

The distinction between rules and conventions was discussed above. The present experiment was designed to find out whether people could distinguish between them in relation to a number of everyday situations. The method used was to ask subjects to describe their reactions to the breaking of various rules or conventions in several common situations. The instances included some conceived by us as 'deviation from conventions', some conceived as 'rule-breaking', and a third category of breaking of universal rules, basic to all social situations.

Hypothesis. Deviation from conventions will be rated as the least disturbing, difficult to deal with, etc., followed by rule-breaking, followed by breaking universal rules.

Method

Subjects were asked to rate a number of episodes in different situations along five rating scales. The situations and the episodes were as shown in Table 5.2.

Two sets of subjects were used. The main study used thirty-four boys and forty-six girls, from two grammar schools, of average age seventeen.

TABLE 5.2. *Rule-breaking episodes*

Interview

You are interviewing someone for a job, and he behaves in one of the following ways:

1. He puts his feet on the desk.
2. He asks you questions all the time, but doesn't want to answer your questions.
3. He repeatedly speaks while you are speaking.
4. He wears clothes that are too dirty and informal for the occasion.
5. He smokes uninvited.
6. He tells what are obviously lies or gross exaggerations.
7. He treats the interview as a friendly chat, and does not give serious replies to questions.
8. He wants to discuss his sexual or other personal problems.
9. He is clearly not at all interested in the job.

Conversation

You are having a conversation with someone to whom you have been introduced, whom you would like to get to know, and where it is difficult to leave; he acts in one of the following ways:

1. He speaks in an unknown language.
2. He lies on the floor.
3. He faces in the opposite direction.
4. He replies to what you say by speaking on a totally different topic.
5. He suddenly shakes hands in the middle of the encounter.
6. He makes meaningless hand signals or gives bizarre facial expressions.
7. He is aggressive, and not at all friendly or interested in you.
8. He keeps touching you.
9. He sits much too close or much too far away.

Guest at a meal

You are the host at a meal and a guest acts in one of the following ways:

1. He eats with the wrong implements.
2. He wears a hat.
3. He gets very drunk.
4. He helps himself to much more than his share of the food.
5. He is unpleasant to the other guests.
6. He tells highly unsuitable stories.
7. He belches loudly, without apology.
8. He eats in a disgusting way.
9. He refuses to eat anything.

5.2. Rules versus conventions

At a party

You are at a party, and someone else behaves in one of the following ways:

1. He pretends to ask for help or advice but ridicules every suggestion you make.
2. He wears a ridiculous and obvious wig.
3. He appears to invite some sexual advances, but reacts with anger and contempt if one is made ('Rapo').
4. He is extremely hostile.
5. He makes comments on your personal appearance.
6. He makes no attempt to reciprocate the interest you have shown in him.
7. He insists on talking about boring and detailed matters connected with his work.
8. He asks you very personal questions, e.g. about your sex life or financial position.
9. He refuses to talk.

Playing a game

You are playing some games, and the other person acts in one of the following ways:

1. He moves your piece, instead of his own.
2. He is extremely slow, or very quick, to move.
3. He shouts or laughs all the time.
4. He makes no attempt to win.
5. He goes all out to win, at all costs, and plays very aggressively.
6. He follows some curious conventions about style of play.
7. He cheats, e.g. 'castles' when in check at chess.
8. He makes two moves instead of one.
9. He wears very odd and unsuitable clothes, or uses odd equipment

The rating scales were as follows:

Does not disrupt the situation	— — — — — — — — —	Totally disrupts the situation
Easy to deal with	— — — — — — — — —	Very difficult to deal with
Can be left or dealt with later	— — — — — — — — —	Needs to be dealt with first
Not annoying	— — — — — — — — —	Extremely annoying
Acceptable under some conditions	— — — — — — — — —	Never acceptable

A second study used seven faculty members from an Oxford college; a larger number declined to participate.

Results

From inspection of the results it was clear that there was a very high correlation between the five scales, though there were differences in means, the last scale for example producing more ratings at the 'acceptable' end of the scale. A principal-components analysis of these scales showed that disruptiveness was a major dimension of rule-breaking.

The disruptiveness scores (i.e. on the first scale) for the three *a priori* categories of episodes were compared. The investigator divided them into instances of breaking universal rules, situational rules and conventions. There was some support for the hypothesis that rule-breaking is found more disruptive than deviation from conventions, but not for the hypothesis that breaking postulated universal rules is even more disruptive. Furthermore there was less difference between deviation and rule-breaking and more overlap than was expected. A post-hoc classification was therefore made of the most and least disruptive episodes. This is shown in Table 5.3.

TABLE 5.3. *Post-hoc classification into rules and conventions*

Least disruptive (conventions)	Most disruptive (rules)
Interview	
Dirty clothes (1.8)	Asks questions (4.9)
Smokes uninvited (1.8)	Speaks while you are speaking (4.9)
	Tells lies (4.2)
Conversation	
Lies on floor (2.7)	Very aggressive (5.7)
Shakes hands (2.7)	Uses unknown language (4.6)
Guest at meal	
Wrong implements (1.8)	Gets drunk (5.5)
Wears hat (2.1)	Unsuitable stories (5.2)
	Unpleasant to guests (6.1)
Party	
Wears wig (1.9)	Hostile (5.9)
	Refuses to talk (5.8)
Game	
Too fast or slow (2.8)	Cheats (6.1)
Odd clothes etc. (2.5)	Makes two moves (5.6)
	No attempt to win (4.8)
	'Rapo' (5.1)

The less disruptive episodes are clearly cases of breaking arbitrary conventions, e.g. about clothes. The more disruptive episodes involve either (*a*) breakdown of communication, e.g. telling lies, speaking at the wrong point in time, etc., (*b*) aggressiveness, or (*c*) literally breaking the rules of games.

There are a number of other episodes which do not fall clearly at either end of the scale, so perhaps if there is a true distinction between rules and conventions it is a matter of degree. Or there may be conventions which it is very disturbing to break (e.g. belching at a meal, wearing *very* unsuitable clothes).

There were a number of quite interesting differences between the schoolchildren and the faculty members, which can be explained fairly easily on grounds of different experience. For example the faculty members were more tolerant of belching, disgusting table manners and the speaking of unknown languages, probably as a result of extensive experience of students from many parts of the world. On the other hand the faculty members were more disturbed by cheating etc. at games, perhaps because they come from a generation which took games more seriously. There were also a number of sex differences: the girls were more disturbed than the boys by aggressive behaviour, and by being touched.

5.3. The rules about interrupting

M. ARGYLE AND M. McCALLIN

The purpose of this study was to find out whether there are rules governing interruption, and if so what these rules are. Two possible rules were explored: (1) interruptions should not occur until another person has been speaking for a certain period of time, and (2) interruptions should take place only at certain grammatical points.

Method

Twelve short conversations were tape-recorded, in which one speaker clearly interrupted another, his interruption forming the final utterance.

Manipulation of independent variables. (a) Length of interrupted utterance. The lengths of utterance before the interruption took place were 2, 5, 10 or 30 seconds.

(b) Point in the sentence. This was either (1) at the end of a complete sentence, (2) at a pause and grammatical break where there was clearly more to come, or (3) in the middle of a clause.

The twelve conversations were presented in random order. Six subjects were used, all students, though not of psychology.

Subjects were asked to rate the behaviour of the interruptor along a scale of appropriate–inappropriate.

Results

The average ratings for appropriateness of the twelve interruptions are given in Table 5.4.

TABLE 5.4. *Ratings of appropriateness of interruptions*

Time of interruption	Length of utterance interrupted (seconds)			
	2	5	10	30
End of sentence	12.45	13.33	14.03	12.70
End of clause	11.72	7.53	7.72	6.05
Middle of clause	4.35	5.87	3.45	4.18

$N = 6$. The greater the value, the more appropriate the interruption.

An analysis of variance showed that 'point in the sentence' was the only significant source of variance ($P < 0.01$). The only result out of line is that for an interruption after 2 seconds at the end of a clause, which was rated as more appropriate than other interruptions at ends of clauses. On replaying the tape we realised that the phrase which was interrupted was in fact not very different from the phrase intended as a completed sentence in one of the other 2-second conditions.

Discussion

This experiment shows that the rule about interruptions used by our judges was that interruptions should occur only at the end of a complete sentence; it made no difference how long the other person had been speaking. It is possible that the length of speaking might be relevant after rather longer speeches.

This experiment is interesting since it shows that this method of experimentation – graduated rule-breaking – can be used to discover rules which are being used; the investigators were not able to state beforehand which of the two possible factors was more important. This method may be open to the criticism that the kind of rule-breaking looked at here is not generated by any of the usual causes – antisocial short-cut, ignorance of the rule, etc. – and that this might lead to epiphenomenal results.

5.4. The rules of different situations

M. ARGYLE, J. A. GRAHAM, A. CAMPBELL AND P. WHITE

[We are indebted to David Clarke, Gregory Young and Peter Hancock for help with the statistical treatment of the data. A fuller version of this paper was published as Argyle *et al.* (1979).]

It has been suggested that rules are one of the important features of situations. It ought to be possible to find the rules for different situations by asking people what should and should not be done in them. In this exploratory study it was intended to investigate several aspects of rules in relation to situations. (1) Do members of a subculture agree on the rules for common situations? (2) Are there some general or universal rules? (3) Are there also some very specific rules, only applying to one situation? (4) Can rules be grouped in terms of the situations to which they apply? (5) Can situations be classified and understood by the rules which apply to them? (6) Do situations vary in the number of rules which apply to them? (7) Do the rules help us to understand situations? Do they fulfil functions in these situations?

Method

A pilot study was carried out, using the twenty-five situations found by Forgas (1976) to be the most common ones for Oxford psychology students. Ten subjects were shown pairs of situations and asked to differentiate between them on the basis of proscriptive and prescriptive rules, by stating rules which applied to one and not to the other. This was repeated with pairs of situation clusters, using each level of clustering of situations found by Forgas. The list of rules obtained was reduced by the avoidance of duplication and the elimination of rules that referred to attitudes rather than to actual behaviour. This left 124 rules.

In experiment 5.4A subjects were presented with the grid of 124 rules by twenty-five situations and asked to tick each case in which they thought a rule applied. The subjects were fifteen Oxford psychology students. This method was not wholly satisfactory, since some rules could only apply to certain situations (e.g. 'should offer to carry heavy bags', 'should not step on people on way to seat'). Also, it looked as though subjects were using different criteria for deciding whether or not a rule applied.

In experiment 5.4B, the rules were reduced to twenty and the situations to eight, so that each rule could apply to any situation. And a five-point scale was used of 'How important do you think it is to keep to various rules in each situation?', in order that a better statistical measure of concordance could be obtained. The subjects were fifty female students of occupational therapy.

Results

Subjects had no difficulty in reporting rules in any of the three procedures used to elicit them. The nature of the rules so obtained does give a certain face validity to the methods used.

Agreement between subjects. In experiment 5.4A the 124 × 25 ratings were reshuffled by computer in a random matrix, against which the real ratings were compared. The numbers of cells with different levels of agreement were as shown in Table 5.5. It can be seen that there is far more agreement than would be expected by chance. A level of agreement of eleven or more subjects was chosen for use in later analyses.

TABLE 5.5. *Numbers of actual and random subjects reporting rules in different situations*

Number of subjects reporting rule[a]	Actual number of rule–situation cells	Number of rule–situation cell in random matrix
15	15	0
14	40	0
13	55	5
12	84	5
11	103	32
10	144	46
9	169	113
8	188	174

[a] Out of a total of fifteen.

In experiment 5.4B a similar random matrix was constructed, but this time standard deviations were also computed for each rule–situation cell. The lowest 5 per cent of the 160 standard deviations (the number of cells in the 8 × 20 matrix) was taken for comparison: thirty-one of the actual standard deviations were below this level, compared with eight for the random matrix, again showing the above-chance degree of concordance.

General rules. Experiment 5.4A produced a number of rules of high generality. These are shown in Table 5.6. Column A shows the number of situations, out of twenty-five, to which eleven or more subjects out of fifteen thought a rule applied. Column B shows the average number of agreements for all twenty-five situations.

For experiment 5.4B we show in column C the number of situations out of eight which had an average rating of 4 or above on the five-point scale, and in column D the average score across all eight situations.

TABLE 5.6. *The most general rules*

	Experiment 5.4A		Experiment 5.4B	
	A No. of situations[a]	B Average no. agreements	C No. of situations[b]	D Average no. agreements
Should be friendly	16	11.4	6	4.1
Should not try to make other feel small	12	10.0	6	4.2
Should be polite	12	10.7	6	4.1
Should try and make it a pleasant encounter	10	10.9	5	4.1
Should not embarrass others	9	9.6	5	3.9

[a] Number of situations (out of twenty-five) checked by eleven or more subjects.
[b] Number of situations (out of eight) checked at scale point 4 or above.

It can be seen that there is good agreement between 5.4A and 5.4B. What were the situations to which these general rules did *not* apply so strongly? In 5.4A there was only one situation to which these rules were not thought to apply – JCR meetings. In 5.4B there was also only one situation – visiting the doctor.

Specific rules. Having looked at the most general rules, we turn now to the most specific ones. Rules of all degrees of generality were found. In 5.4A a lot of rules applied to only one situation (at eleven out of fifteen subjects agreeing). Of these we looked at those which also had very low levels of applicability to the remaining twenty-four situations. Most of these could only have applied to one situation: e.g. 'should offer to carry heavy bags' (when shopping with a friend), and 'should visit when he is unlikely to be working' (visiting a friend in a college room). Others could have applied more widely but did not do so.

Listed below are some of the rules which applied to one situation, had a low average score for all other situations, and were not uniquely determined by the nature of the situation, as in the example just given:

74: Should dress smartly (at a wedding): number of ratings was 13; average number of ratings for other situations 0.88

89: Should address other by second name (doctor): 11 versus 1.44

121: Should be quiet (at a play): 18 versus 2.76

There were also some specific rules in 5.4B. The best examples were:

6: Should do whatever the other person says (doctor): mean rating on the five-point scale was 3.9, mean rating for other situations was 1.81

7: Should keep to cheerful topics of conversation (at a wedding): 3.8 versus 2.31

4: Should not comment on the other's behaviour or appearance (at an interview): 4.1 versus 2.99

Only one specific rule item from 5.4A was used in 5.4B, and this was 'should dress smartly'; this applied now to the hostess and interview situations as well as to the wedding.

Grouping rules by situations. For both investigations hierarchical cluster analyses were carried out on the rules. These were based on the degree of similarity of ratings for the rules when applied to different situations. Experiment 5.4A produced very large clusters, one of which consisted of the very general rules and one of the very specific ones. Experiment 5.4B did not suffer from this artefactual result, perhaps because the rules did not vary so widely in generality or because of the use of a five-point rating scale.

The clusters of rules in 5.4B were as follows:

A. 'Should be friendly', 'should be polite', etc. (the five most general rules: 1, 5, 8, 11, 20).

B. 'Should not make long speeches', 'should avoid personal chat or gossip', etc. (2, 4, 9, 17, 19).

C. 'If the other asks a question it should be answered', 'only one person should speak at a time', etc. (3, 10, 15).

D. 'Should do what the other person says', 'speak only when spoken to' (6, 12).

E. 'Should keep to cheerful topics', 'should dress smartly', etc. (7, 13, 14).

F. 'Should display positive affection' (18).

Grouping situations by rules. For both experiments hierarchical cluster analyses were carried out for the situations, based on degree of similarity of ratings of the applicability of different rules to situations. The results from 5.4A are shown in Fig. 5.1.

The results for 5.4B were similar. In both cluster analyses the main division of situations was into work and social. Social divided into formal versus intimate and casual; work divided up differently in the two studies, but with an intimate group (e.g. seeing doctor) and a less personal group (e.g. going to the bank) in each. It is interesting, however, that the twenty-five situations of 5.4A produced a quite different structure from the Forgas study, in which they were rated along other dimensions of situations.

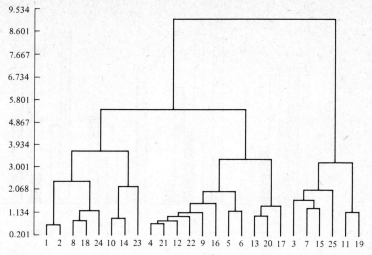

1. Morning coffee	14. Meeting new people at a sherry party
2. Drink in pub	15. Visiting your doctor
3. Discussing an essay in a tutorial	16. Chatting with acquaintance who gives you a lift
4. Meeting acquaintance while checking mail	17. Visiting a friend in a college room
5. Walk with a friend	18. Going to see a play
6. Shopping with a friend	19. Going to the bank
7. Acting as a subject in a psychology experiment	20. Having an intimate conversation with boy/girlfriend
8. Going to the pictures	21. Chat with acquaintance on street
9. Having a short chat with shop-assistant	22. Chatting at launderette
10. Dinner in Hall	23. Attending a wedding
11. Going to JCR meeting	24. Watching TV with friends
12. Chatting before lecture	25. Playing chess
13. Discussing work topics with friends	

Fig. 5.1. Clusters of situations in experiment 5.4A.

We can understand these groups of situations by examining the rules which apply to them. This can be done by studying which rule clusters apply to which clusters of situations. The procedure is more satisfactory for 5.4B and for 5.4A, since the rule clusters here were clearer. This interaction between clusters of rules and clusters of situations is shown in Fig. 5.2.

Complaint, class, doctor. High (over 3.5) on general rules (A) ('be polite', etc.) and on conduct-of-conversation rules (C), low (under 1.5) on expression of positive affect (F).

Interview. Very high (4.4) on general rules (A), and on conduct-of-conversation rules (C), low on expression of positive affect (F).

Friendly chat. High on general rules (A), fairly high on positive affect (F), low on formal speech rules (C), low on obedience rules (D).

Hostess, wedding, date. Very high on general rules (A), high on cheerfulness rules (E), low on obedience (D).

153

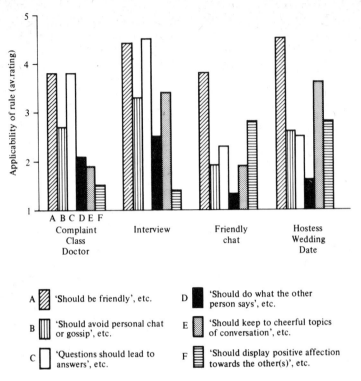

Fig. 5.2. Clusters of rules in relation to clusters of situations.

Situations with different numbers of rules. It is of interest to compare the situations with many rules, which can be regarded as 'formal', and those with fewer rules. The situations in experiment 5.4A which had the largest and smallest numbers of rules are shown in Table 5.7. The situations with the most rules are work situations and formal social situations. Morning coffee is an apparent exception; however coffee in the Psychology Department is closely connected with work, and people of different status frequently meet here. The situations with few rules are conversations with friends and acquaintances; these situations are social and informal.

Is there more variation between situations in this respect than would occur by chance? The numbers of rules rated 4 or more for each situation were compared for the real and shuffled data in experiment 5.4B.

Real data   10, 6, 6, 5, 5, 4, 3, 1

Shuffled data   4, 3, 3, 1, 1, 0, 0, 0

Clearly the variation actually found between situations was much greater than that expected by chance.

TABLE 5.7. *The situations with most and least rules*

Most rules		Least rules	
Situation	Number of rules[a]	Situation	Number of rules[a]
Tutorial	27	Walk with friend	0
Doctor	23	Chat before lecture	4
Sherry party	18	Meet acquaintance while checking mail	6
Play	18	Shopping with friend	7
Dinner in Hall	17	Chatting at launderette	7
Morning coffee	17	Chat with shop assistant	7
		Intimate conversation with boy/girlfriend	7

[a] Eleven or more subjects agreed.

Do the rules perform the function of helping interactors to realise situational goals? A classification of goals was presented above (p. 134f.). Is it supported by the set of rules which we have found?

(i) Rules which meet universal requirements of social situations. 'Make communication possible' is not represented by any rules, perhaps because the method of eliciting them prevented any completely universal rules from appearing. Our cluster of universal rules clearly fits the categories 'Prevent withdrawal by other interactors' and 'Prevent aggression' ('should be friendly', etc.), though they could also be looked at in terms of exchange theory – providing a sufficiently high level of rewards. Two rules of the kind 'Begin and end encounters' appeared – 'knock before entering' and 'should not leave without saying goodbye and thanks' – but there was no mention of greeting, again perhaps because of its complete universality.

(ii) Rules which meet universal requirements for verbal communication. In both studies a cluster of common rules of this type appeared ('don't interrupt', 'questions should lead to answers', etc.), and these applied to formal verbal encounters like interviews and classes. However they did not apply so clearly to friendly chats, dates, and other primarily social events. No rules appeared for the construction of longer sequences of interaction, perhaps because our original informants did not think of them.

(iii) Rules which meet the requirements of particular kinds of situation. There are certain examples of the kinds of rules that were expected; on the other hand this is simply a case of post-hoc classification, not of prediction proper. We should expect the clearest examples of 'Coordinate behaviour so that goals may be attained' to occur when there is a definite task. In the

tutorial there are a number of such rules, e.g. 'don't pretend to understand when you don't' and 'should say what problems you are having'. At the doctor's there are 'make sure your body is clean' and 'answer truthfully'. Some of the rules just mentioned could also be classified as 'Guard against temptation'. Others of this type are 'don't touch', on a first date, and 'don't leave others to pay', at the pub. At an earlier period of history rules of etiquette were of the 'Help with common difficulties' type. Possible examples from the present study are 'introduce yourself', at a sherry party, 'don't treat it as a social visit', at the bank, and 'don't outstay your welcome', when visiting a friend in a college room.

5.5. Reactions to rule-breaking

G. P. GINSBURG, M. ARGYLE, J. P. FORGAS AND T. HOLTGRAVES

The understanding of rules, and often their identification, is frequently based on studying reactions to rule-breaking (RB). In fact, the only evidence of RB may be reactions of others which imply its occurrence. From this perspective, we undertook an exploratory study of reactions to RBs, in which selected features of the RB and setting were systematically varied.

Method

A written scenario format was used, in which four features of the RBs were varied and the effects assessed on seventeen scales. A factorial 2^4 multivariate analysis of variance (MANOVA) with seventeen dependent variables constituted the major analysis framework, and factor analyses and a path analysis were used to assess the relationships between the dependent variables.

Independent variables. The four features of rule-breaking episodes selected for the test were gender of actor, reason for rule-breaking (deliberate or accidental), instrumental effect (whether or not there was interference with completion of ongoing activity or episode) and specific RB (to assess the impact of the preceding three factors relative to two instances). Since these features were selected from a list of thirty-two likely to be important for the understanding of rules and RBs, the amount of variance for which they account will necessarily be moderate – but they can be assessed for the dependability of their impact.

The factors were incorporated into the following paraphrased scenarios, each of which appeared in two gender-forms:

1. P deliberately (or by accident) coughs a mouthful of potatoes back onto his own plate, or into the serving dish.

2. P wittingly decided to shop (or unwittingly lost track of the time) and was late for the theatre where friends were waiting. P was so late that they almost missed the start of the play.

Dependent variables. The dependent variables can be summarised as dealing with (1) labelling the RB, (2) estimating the reactions of others, (3) estimating one's own reactions and (4) judging the comprehensibility (not the likelihood) of each of four possible extended consequences. The latter include two remedial sequences (discuss and continue; discuss and move on).

The seventeen dependent variables contained four subsets, all of which used four-point rating scales. The first subset asked whether the RB was odd, rude, funny, irritating, understandable, insulting and embarrassing, each being rated as 'not at all', 'fairly', 'quite' or 'extremely'. The second and third subsets asked whether 'most of the other people' or 'you', respectively, would laugh, be angry or be embarrassed, using the same scales as in the first subset.

The fourth subset explored more extended consequences of the RB and asked whether it would be understandable if the other people present (*a*) simply continued as planned, (*b*) discussed the incident and then continued as planned, (*c*) discussed the incident and then went on together to do something else or (*d*) discussed the incident and then broke up and went home. The detailed phrasings were made appropriate for the particular incident.

Subjects. All subjects were drawn from the Introductory Psychology Subject Pool, University of Nevada, Reno; $N = 128$.

Results

The seventeen dependent variables constitute a set of judgements about plausible immediate and delayed reactions, and can therefore be examined as a set. The use of the MANOVA instead of a univariate ANOVA on each dependent variable is supported by tests of the overall pattern of results. Specifically, the determinant of the variance/covariance matrix approximated 0 (0.087) and the Bartlett test of sphericity was very highly significant (257.74, d.f. = 136, $P < 0.00001$), jointly indicating the existence of common themes among the dependent variables. Therefore, only those factorial effects that were significant in the MANOVA will be discussed, along with univariate effects within those MANOVA effects.

MANOVA results. Four effects displayed reliable influence by the independent variables in the MANOVA. These four were specific RB, reason, specific RB × reason interaction and gender × specific RB interaction. The relevant statistics for these effects are shown in Table 5.8. Each effect will be considered in turn.

The main effect of *specific RB* shows that lateness at the theatre is more irritating and more likely to make people angry than the dinner incident. The dependent variables which correlated $\geqslant 0.40$ with their canonical variate are 'irritating' (0.462), 'others angry' (0.437), and 'you angry' (0.454).

According to the main effect of *reason* (accidental versus deliberate), incidents that are due to deliberate actions by the perpetrator are ruder and more difficult to comprehend than those that occur involuntarily or by accident. Interpretation of this effect must be qualified by the two interactions discussed below.

TABLE 5.8. *Multivariate statistics of significant MANOVA effects*

Effect	Statistic[a]		
	P	r_c	B_c
Specific RB	<0.001	0.895	−1.875
Reason	<0.001	0.676	0.857
Specific RB × reason	<0.001	0.574	−0.655
Gender × specific RB	0.054	0.482	−0.515

[a] r_c, canonical correlation for the effect; B_c, regression coefficient of the canonical variate, as a dependent variable, on the factorial effect as an independent variable.

The *specific RB* × *reason* interaction indicates that the understandability of the dinner incident is especially sensitive to the reason for its occurrence. The reason also influences the comprehensibility of one of the extended consequences. If the incident were accidental, then leaving the table for another room would not be understandable, but leaving the theatre for another theatre would be highly so.

The interaction *gender* × *specific RB* suggests that people are more likely to laugh and to be embarrassed at the dinner incident than at the theatre incident, especially when the dinner incident is enacted by a woman. This interaction is the only line of the MANOVA containing a significant gender effect and, as can be seen in Table 5.8, it is the weakest of the four significant MANOVA effects.

In summary, then, the MANOVA effects suggest that incidents that are perpetrated deliberately are seen as rude and insulting and are likely to anger people. Moreover, a fairly ordinary event such as lateness for the theatre is more likely to be seen as irritating and to anger people than is the unusual act of spitting out a mouthful of potatoes at a dinner party. The unusual nature of the dinner incident is reflected in its nearly total lack of understandability if done deliberately, and ready understandability if an accident. Furthermore, if the dinner incident is perpetrated by a woman, it is especially likely to lead to embarrassed laughter.

Given the limited number of incidents studied, and the somewhat arbitrary nature of the independent variables, these results are illustrative rather than definitive. However the findings clearly show that reactions to rule-breaking can be studied empirically and result in meaningful and interpretable data. Further statistical analyses confirmed this impression.

ANOVA results. The significant univariate effects were consistent with those MANOVA effects discussed above. In addition, the ANOVAs show that a discussion of the RB incident, followed by a simple continuation of the original activity (the dinner, or attending the intended play), is more understandable for the theatre than for the dinner incident. Discussing the incident and then moving to another setting (another room for coffee, or another play at a different theatre) also is more understandable for the theatre incident, but especially and most clearly if the incident is accidental. In the accidental case, it is hardly understandable to move to another room for coffee but quite understandable to move to another theatre.

A priori predictions. The analysis of rule-breaking episodes (RBEs) presented in experiment 5.1 suggests certain predictions, some of which can be assessed against the results of this RB study. First, since angry reactions should be the most likely reactions to selfish short-cuts, we should find anger, but not embarrassment or laughter, to be greater in the face of deliberate RBs. The present data clearly and strongly support this prediction. Moreover, we would also predict more anger in response to deliberate theatre lateness than to the deliberate dinner incident, since the former more clearly than the latter conveys the idea of a selfish short-cut. This prediction is supported by examination of the pertinent means for 'others angry' and 'you angry'. In both cases, the deliberate theatre means exceed the deliberate dinner means (3.12 versus 2.16 and 3.13 versus 1.75, $P <$ 0.10 and $P < 0.05$, respectively).

The discussion of RBEs also leads to the prediction that embarrassment is a likely reaction to RBs that are based on oversight or physiological events. Accidental RBs at both the theatre and dinner represent these sorts of incompetencies, but there is no difference in any of the embarrassment variables as a function of 'reason' (deliberate versus accidental). Therefore, under the conditions of this study, the hypothesis concerning embarrassment is not supported.

The third affective reaction discussed in experiment 5.1, laughter, was specified as a function of RBs which were due to ignorance or were attempts to be funny. Unfortunately, the design of the present study does not allow a test of that hypothesis.

Analysis of dependent variables. We examined the relationships between the seventeen dependent variables (DVs) factor-analytically and through path analysis. As noted earlier, the seventeen DVs were comprised of four subsets: (1) labelling the RB, (2) estimating the reactions of others, (3) estimating one's own reactions and (4) judging the comprehensibility of each of four possible extended consequences. A separate principal-components analysis was conducted on each of the subsets, and two factors were extracted in each analysis and rotated to a varimax criterion. The rotated factor matrices for the four subsets of DVs are shown in Table 5.9.

The two factors extracted from the labelling subset are roughly equally important, and together explain about 45 per cent of the total variance. The first dimension is bipolar and very clearly differentiates funny from irritating RBs. The second factor differentiates odd from understandable RBs. Rude and insulting RBs load jointly on the two dimensions, containing roughly equal contributions of oddness and irritatingness. Embarrassing RBs, meanwhile, have no clear meaning in the extracted factor space, perhaps through lack of clarity as to who was embarrassed.

The factor matrices of the 'reactions of others' and 'one's own reactions' subsets are quite similar. They each explain a little over 40 per cent of the total variance, and the first factor in each is much more important than the second. The first factor is bipolar and clearly differentiates reactions of laughter from reactions of anger. The second factor somewhat less clearly differentiates anger from embarrassment.

The fourth subset pertains to the comprehensibility of various extended consequences of the RB. The matrix explains about 35 per cent of the total variance, with one dimension capturing the two remedial sequences (discuss the RB, then continue as planned; discuss the RB, then shift jointly to another setting).

Thus, the factor analyses of DVs suggest that RBs can be differentiated

TABLE 5.9. *Factor matrices (varimax rotation)*

Subset	Variables	Factor loadings		Per cent variance per factor		
		I	II		I	II
Labelling the RB	Odd	−0.09	0.73	Common	53.5	46.5
	Rude	0.41	0.59	total	24.0	20.8
	Funny	−0.57	−0.13			
	Irritating	0.88	0.09			
	Understandable	−0.24	−0.54			
	Insulting	0.59	0.49			
	Embarrassing	0.05	0.08			
Reactions of others	Others laugh	0.73	−0.01	Common	84.0	16.0
	Others angry	−0.70	−0.29	total	32.3	6.6
	Others embarrassed	0.04	0.34			
One's own reactions	You laugh	0.74	0.21	Common	79.1	20.9
	You angry	−0.70	−0.38	total	34.9	9.2
	You embarrassed	0.10	0.29			
Comprehensibility of extended consequences	Continue as planned	0.01	−0.29	Common	58.2	41.8
	Discuss, continue	0.65	−0.19	total	20.2	14.5
	Discuss, shift setting	0.62	0.39			
	Discuss, go home	0.02	0.55			

reasonably well on the basis of two dimensions – oddness, and whether they are funny or irritating. Affective reactions to RBs lie primarily along one dimension – laughter versus anger – which matches the second labelling dimension. Naturally, the validity of these two dimensions needs to be confirmed by further research. We feel that there is a considerable need for studies constructing descriptive taxonomies of rule-breaking episodes, and reactions to them.

It is reasonable to expect that the nature of an RB will influence the reactions of the people caught up in it, and that one's own reactions in turn will be affected by the reactions of the others. Moreover, the comprehensibility of various extended consequences should be influenced by all of those factors. These expectations were assessed in a path analysis, the results of which are shown in fig. 5.3. It should be noted that the path analysis is based largely on factor scores (see Table 5.9) rather than on original variable scores.

The humorous versus irritating nature of the RB incident has a moderate influence on one's own affective reaction. The more influential impact of the RB on one's own affective reaction is a mediated one, as reflected by the

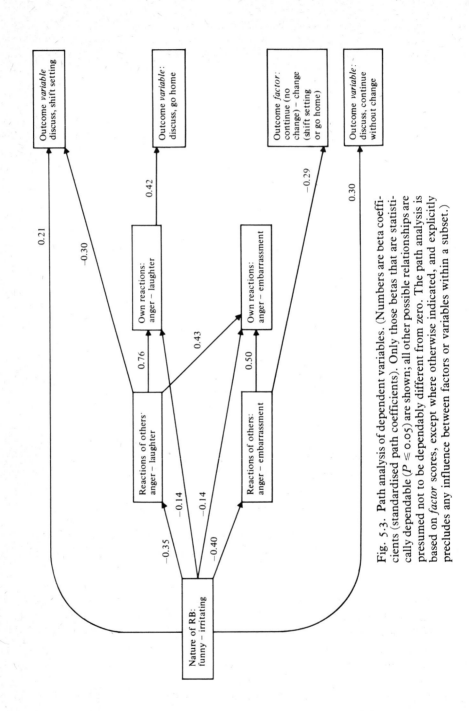

Fig. 5.3. Path analysis of dependent variables. (Numbers are beta coefficients (standardised path coefficients). Only those betas that are statistically dependable ($P \leqslant 0.05$) are shown; all other possible relationships are presumed not to be dependably different from zero. The path analysis is based on *factor* scores, except where otherwise indicated, and explicitly precludes any influence between factors or variables within a subset.)

moderate to high influences of others' reactions upon one's own. Funny RBs lead people to laugh and to be embarrassed, while irritating RBs elicit anger; and one's own reactions are directly influenced by the comparable reactions of others, and only indirectly by the nature of the RB itself, at least in the context of the particular RBs of this study. Clearly a broader range of RBEs needs to be looked at to resolve this issue.

One finding is somewhat anomalous: disbanding and going home is more comprehensible when one laughs at the RB than when one is angry. Quite possibly, the RB incidents were not of sufficient magnitude to make an angry disruption of the occasion comprehensible, but this interpretation is speculative.

Summary

We have explored the applicability of a scenario methodology to gain knowledge about the impact of gender, intention, instrumental interference and specific identity of two quite different RBs upon the labels assigned to the RBs, the affective reactions to them and the extended social consequences. We found that RBs can be differentiated on a dimension ranging from humorous to irritating and also on a dimension of oddness. The affective reactions of people to the RBs can be captured adequately by a single dimension of laughter versus anger, complementing the humour/irritation dimension noted above. One's own affective reactions are largely a function of the reactions of others, and only slightly due to the humorous or irritating nature of the RB itself.

The characteristics of the RB, and to a limited extent of the rule-breaker, clearly influence the reactions of involved observers. People are angered by deliberate RBs and see them as rude and insulting. This is especially true for an ordinary RB, and less so for an unusual, relatively incomprehensible one. In fact, if the unusual RB is done deliberately it becomes very difficult to understand; but if it is an accident it is readily understandable. Very little in the way of gender effect was demonstrated, the only reliable effect being that embarrassment was most likely under the combination of the dinner incident being perpetrated by a woman. Finally, the finding that anger, but not laughter or embarrassment, is augmented by the deliberateness of an RB supports our analysis of RBEs, discussed earlier in experiment 5.1. However, accidental RBs do not generate greater embarrassment than deliberate RBs, which also had been suggested by our RBE analysis. These tentative findings suggest that empirical methods and statistical analysis can be readily applied to the study of such complex events as RBEs. However, further work is clearly needed to substantiate the external validity and scope of our results in other kinds of RBEs.

6

Role-systems

Introduction

The system of roles is an important feature of most situations. Examples are salesman–customer, teacher–pupil and chairman–committee member. By a role is meant the pattern of behaviour associated with, or expected of, the occupants of a position. If we define roles in terms of expectations, a role is defined by the rules that apply to an occupant of a position. Positions include age, sex, class, and job or rank in organisations (e.g. doctor, nurse, patient). There is a problem in that there may be disagreement between the occupant and others, or between different groups of others, over how the occupant should behave; this creates role-conflict.

Some situations have very clear role-systems, for example court-rooms, churches and hospital wards. But we want to extend the concept of role to include informal roles in small groups, where there are no pre-existing patterns. Examples are task leader, socio-emotional leader and leader of the opposition. These roles are the distinctive patterns of behaviour which commonly occur in certain kinds of group or situation. In the case of formal roles, occupation of a position exposes the occupant to pressures to adopt the role; in the case of informal roles, adopting the role behaviour (e.g. engaging in a great deal of task activity) makes him the occupant of a kind of informal position. It is useful to combine these two sorts of role, since there is continuity between formal and informal situations; there can be a gradual growth of formality, as roles become more established and rules fixed.

Roles are interlocked with other features of situations that have been discussed in previous chapters. The occupant of a particular role has *goals* (e.g. customer versus shopkeeper), can use only part of the *repertoire* (e.g. umpire versus bowler), is constrained by certain *rules* which may define the role, occupies a special part of the *physical environment* (e.g. prisoner versus judge), and is faced by special *difficulties* and requires special *skills* (e.g. performer versus audience). To use a previous analogy: at cricket each player occupies several distinctive roles, e.g. third batsman, bowler, point. We shall see that in order to cope with common situations such as going to a restaurant it is necessary to understand the roles involved.

Roles fit together to form role-systems; they are often complementary. It is impossible to play the role of teacher unless others are prepared to play the role of pupil; doctors need patients, and leaders need followers. In sociology the system of interlocking roles is seen as an enduring social structure. We propose to adopt the same analysis for situational roles.

There are several dimensions of roles; Wish, Deutsch and Kaplan (1976) made an interesting attempt to classify a wide range of role relationships using multidimensional scaling. The dimensions they found were (1) cooperative and friendly versus competitive and hostile, (2) equal (power) versus unequal, (3) intense versus superficial, and (4) socio–emotional and informal versus task-oriented and formal. In a later study, Wish and Kaplan (1977) included different situations as well as different role relations; the last factor from the earlier study now divided into (1) socio–emotional versus task, and (2) formal versus informal.

Occupancy of different roles is one of the main determinants of the relationship between two people. Their relationship may vary along the above dimensions. There are further complexities of relationships based on the personalities of the two people, and the history of their past interactions.

In our analysis below we shall start with power and status roles (equal versus unequal) and go on to sociometric roles (friendly versus hostile), division of labour (in task situations), informal roles (mainly in socio-emotional settings), and the selection of formal roles (in formal situations).

Roles may be assessed in a number of ways.

Study of expectations and rules. For formal situations, such as games and committees, the rules also describe the roles. In formal organisations, where there are positions, it is possible to carry out surveys of role-holders and others to discover their beliefs about what behaviour is correct in different situations for the occupants of each position. It may be useful to interview the socially mobile, who have experienced other situations or subcultures, since they will be sensitised to less obvious aspects of roles, e.g. those for males and females (Garfinkel, 1967).

Study of behaviour. For both formal and informal roles it is possible to observe, categorise and compare the behaviour of different role-holders. Hitherto the study of roles has been mainly concerned with describing the behaviour associated with different roles (Biddle and Thomas, 1966). It has sometimes been objected that 'role theory isn't a theory', and we are inclined to agree. However if it could be shown how role-systems are generated from other variables it could be a theory. We shall explore the influence of situations upon roles.

Roles are a product of situations in different ways. (1) Constantly recurring situations generate repertoires of elements and rules, as we have seen. They also generate role-systems. Committee meetings require a chairman and a secretary, games need two sides and a referee, juries need a foreman but also generate an (informal) leader of the opposition. These situational roles may be formal or informal. (2) Everyone occupies a number of different formal roles – age, sex, class, family relationships, work relationships, positions in religious, political and voluntary organisations, and so on. The same two people might be able to relate to each other as, say, doctor–patient, pupil–teacher (e.g. of pharmacology), rival squash players, or just friends. A particular situation will result in certain role relationships becoming salient. We shall investigate in this chapter how far these different role-systems are functional in relation to situational goals.

One general function of role-systems may be to provide a clear guide to behaviour for everyone; in an informal group it takes time to work out what each person will do, whereas in a formal role-system it is clear from the beginning (Kelvin, 1969). Role-systems are functional in a number of more specific ways as well (cf. Parsons *et al.*, 1953). When two or more people enter a situation with different goals, they often adopt different roles, as in the case of salesman and customer, doctor and patient. These roles are usually complementary. Differences of power and status emerge, when the group task requires it. There are sociometric roles, such as the formation of cooperative subgroups and coalitions. When there is a cooperative task there is division of labour, and different kinds of communicative structure appear, depending on that task. Various informal roles appear to satisfy various individual needs, and to create feelings of distinctness.

Some individuals evidently have a 'need for structure' (Cohen, Stotland and Wolfe, 1955); unstructured situations are found to be uncomfortable and are ineffective if a task is to be performed. Initially unstructured groups rapidly develop a structure: the hierarchy is the first aspect to be established, followed by friendship choices and division of labour. T-groups and encounter groups often make the members very uncomfortable at first, because there appear to be no rules and the person in charge does not play the usual role of leader (Bennis and Shepard, 1956; Tuckman, 1965).

So far we have discussed roles as generated by goals. However, roles may be generated by other features of situations, such as the environmental setting. For example, the relationship of judge, defendant, jury, etc., in a court-room is probably affected by the physical layout; but this environmental design is itself constructed to fulfil the aims of that situation.

Power and status roles

One of the main ways in which roles may be distinguished is in terms of power and status. (There are other role-systems that have no clear differences of this kind, e.g. boyfriend–girlfriend, customer–shopkeeper.) By power is meant an individual's ability to influence other people, that is, to make them do things they would not otherwise have done (Kelvin, 1969). By status is meant the extent to which an individual or position is valued, admired and approved of by others in the group or community.

What functions, if any, are served by hierarchical role-systems? In a dyad, if an agreement can be reached about power relations, then conflict within the dyad is reduced. In a group of three or more, if there is a leader then he can coordinate the activities of the others. We shall describe below how a leadership structure emerged in groups which could communicate only by messages, even when the communication system had no central position, as in the 'circle' pattern (p. 173). In any group, if the people who are most skilled and knowledgeable about the group's task are allowed to take charge, the group would be expected to be more effective. It can be predicted, from these considerations, that hierarchical roles would develop under certain conditions.

(a) *In a larger group*. It is found that there is a more definite hierarchy in larger informal groups, as shown by the amount of inequality in frequency of speaking (Bales *et al.*, 1951). Hemphill (1950) found that directions from leaders are more acceptable in larger groups.

(b) *When a group is concerned with task as opposed to primarily social activities*. Fisek and Ofshe (1970) found that in task groups there was rapid formation of a status hierarchy, often during the first minute of interaction. There is evidence that triads of females do not form a hierarchy while triads of males do (Robson, 1967); this supports the idea that women are more concerned with social relationships, men with tasks.

(c) *When decisions must be made quickly*. Hamblin (1958) found that under these conditions an ineffective leader was rapidly replaced, and leaders were allowed to be more influential.

This gives a certain amount of support to a functional explanation for hierarchical roles. Bales (1950) put forward a more general theory of the emergence of roles in groups. He suggested that a number of roles appear in groups in order for the group to deal with its tasks. Some of these roles carry more authority than others. However, this disturbs the cohesion of the group, which starts to disintegrate, so that forces for integration are created and there is a state of equilibrium between those forces producing hierarchy and those producing integration.

Hierarchies form in groups of animals and children. Animals form pecking orders, as do children in nursery schools. Groups of adolescents form very definite hierarchies of informal leadership and influence. However there is more than one hierarchy, and each situation produces one set of leaders rather than another; groups of delinquents have different leaders for crime and football (Whyte, 1943). Similarly in families there are often different domains: for situations like cooking and infant care the mother is usually the leader; for gardening, family finances and looking after the car, father is usually in charge (Herbst, 1952).

Informal hierarchies also depend on the characteristics of the individuals concerned. When two people meet, the person who is older, male, or of higher social class is likely to dominate (Breer, 1960). The effects of personality variables are relatively small, though the person who has the highest IQ and who is more extroverted and better adjusted tends to dominate (Mann, 1959). In a task situation the relative skills of the two people at the task or activity in hand are particularly important. A number of studies have shown that leadership rotates when the task facing the group changes (Carter and Nixon, 1949). These personal factors interact with the 'domain' factors mentioned above; Blood and Wolfe (1960) confirmed Herbst's findings about the domains of husbands and wives, but found that husband dominance was greater when he was successful and had a high income, when the wife was not employed, when she was older than him, and when she had a strong need for love and affection. These findings can be explained in terms of exchange theory: the partner who contributes more has more power over the other (Chadwick-Jones, 1976).

We turn now to formal hierarchies. Studies of the growth of industries and other large groups show that at a certain stage the informal leadership hierarchy becomes formalised into a series of ranks and other positions, with their associated roles. This is partly a function of sheer size: it is difficult for one man to supervise more than about fifteen others efficiently, so if there are many more than this number there are a series of first-line leaders, and eventually two levels of leadership. The size of the span of control varies with the technology of the task. At a simple level of technological development, as in craft work, working groups are small and cohesive, but there is little supervision and as many as twenty-five to thirty workers per supervisor or manager. In assembly-line and machine-tending technologies there is a more hierarchical structure, more use of incentives and machine pacing, and fourteen to eighteen workers per supervisor. Under automation there are about eight workers per manager; the numbers involved are less and relations are better (Blauner, 1964; Woodward, 1965). The extent of hierarchical development depends also on the culture; for example in Japanese industry there is a very hierarchical structure, with a small span of control, many levels in the hierarchy, and great differences of status between levels. It also depends on the development of ideas about organisations; there has been a great deal of criticism of bureaucratic hierarchies, since they produce communication problems and poor morale in the lower ranks, and more recent thinking has led to flatter hierarchies and smaller industrial firms (Argyle, 1972).

There are several kinds of power, each of which varies between situations. Expert power is effective mainly in the area of expertise, though there is a tendency for power to generalise to related areas (Allen and Crutchfield, 1963). When power is based on rewards or punishments (coercive power) it is more effective in situations where there is surveillance; while there is much less influence on private than on public behaviour, there is some influence due to other kinds of power (Deutsch and Gerard, 1955). Referent power is based on the desire to identify with the influencing source; this is greater when the source is similar in age, sex, attitudes, or group membership (Collins and Raven, 1969).

Sociometric roles

The second main dimension of roles is cooperation versus competition, and the correlated dimension of friendly versus hostile (Wish *et al.*, 1976). We shall consider cooperative roles first. It would be expected that in certain situations it is functional for pairs of people, or members of a larger group, to cooperate and help each other. This should happen if individuals depend on a group effort to realise their own goals. Cooperative reward conditions have been set up in experiments and in group incentive schemes; they exist naturally in families, groups in primitive societies, and in numerous other group situations – some research groups, committees and military groups, for example. Joint reward conditions have been found to produce cooperative roles – more friendly and helpful behaviour, more agreement, better communication, smoother social interaction and more division of labour (e.g. Deutsch, 1949).

It would be expected that situational conditions which make cooperation instrumental to common goals, lead to greater cooperation. There is more cooperation when a division of labour is created so that group members play complementary roles (Thomas, 1957), when the work-flow system brings people together in a rewarding way, and when the group members like one another (Argyle, 1972).

Similar considerations apply to the appearance of coalitions within larger groups. This happens when two or more people realise it is to their advantage to pool their resources and divide the rewards. For example if two members of an experimental triad are given less power or a smaller individual stake in scarce resources than the other, they will form a coalition against the third member (Collins and Raven, 1969). An example of real-life coalitions was found by Burns (1955) in a factory. There were 'cliques' consisting of older men with no hope of promotion; these provided social support and formed a kind of alternative organisation. There were also 'cabals' consisting of ambitious younger men; these helped them in their careers by providing information not otherwise available and useful social contacts. Cabals are similar to experimentally created coalitions, while cliques are more like sociometric groups (discussed below).

Competitive roles have been created experimentally by the setting up of situations in which only one person can win and the others must lose. This state of affairs exists in many real-life situations, such as competition for mates or food, selling goods, winning prizes or making scientific discoveries.

Friendly role relationships have been extensively studied by sociometric methods, in which members of a group are asked to nominate their preferred companion for some activity. Somewhat different choices are made for leisure and task activities (Tagiuri, 1958). Furthermore it is clear from a number of studies that people prefer others who are of about the same standing as themselves in ability, attractiveness, etc.; the salient dimension for such evaluative purposes varies with the situation. Similarly people reject those who deviate from group norms; again the norms that are salient vary between situations. Thus inside the hospital a doctor will prefer the company of doctors rather than of patients or ambulancemen; in the squash club he will prefer the company of those at a similar point in the squash ladder.

The famous detailed study of the Bank Wiring Room (Homans, 1951) revealed how the job role and the room layout led to such developments as friendship and clique formation. Homans distinguished between the external system – that established and conditioned by the environment – and the internal system – a set of dynamic relationships and roles that develops within the external system. The Bank Wiring Room had three official job roles: two inspectors, nine welders and three soldermen. Fig. 6.1 illustrates how friendships formed.

What is the basis for friendly roles? These have a functional basis in that friendly roles produce cooperation, but affiliative motivation has developed as an additional source of friendly behaviour, and appears to be aroused by rather different situational conditions. Certain situations are created and

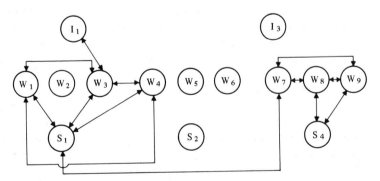

Fig. 6.1. Friendships in the Bank Wiring Room. I, inspector; S, solderman; W, welder. (After Homans, 1951.)

defined as 'social': the cues include the presence of food and drink, together with appropriate furniture, decoration, lighting, and perhaps music, for relaxed social encounters, though the precise social signals vary between cultures.

Hostile role relationships can be studied in the same way as positive ones. They are brought about in various ways but particularly by one person or group frustrating another person or group. Sherif and Sherif (1953) created conflicts between groups of boys at a camp by arranging things so that, for example, one group ate more than its share of the food. Hostile role relations could be functional to an individual or group that is led to pursue its own goals to the point of victory. Parsons (1942) suggested that the tradition in the USA of adolescent rebellion against parents serves the function of securing independence from parents. It is of course more debatable whether conflict is functional for the whole group involved.

There are a number of possible individual roles within a sociometric structure, which are partly due to situational factors. The popular person, or 'star', may be popular because of his social skills and rewardingness, because his job gives him the power to reward others, or because his position in the environment produces a high level of interaction with everyone else; for example, students in rooms at the bottom of staircases were found to be more popular than those at the top (Festinger *et al.*, 1950). Similarly a person may be unpopular because he is difficult and unreward-ing, or because his job is unrewarding to others, or keeps him from interacting with others. Another sociometric role is that of belonging to each of two groups, which may place the occupant in a 'marginal man' position, under different pressures from each side, or may make him a valued mediator between the groups.

Division of labour

This is one of the main sources of roles in groups that have a task to perform. Parsons *et al.* (1953) argued that groups divide up the jobs in order to perform tasks better. This is certainly supported from the study of problem-solving groups. If problems are divided up, each part can be tackled by the member best able to do it; members often have different and complementary skills or knowledge. This is the main reason for the superiority of groups over individuals at such tasks (Kelley and Thibaut, 1969).

If we are considering problem-solving groups, or any other task groups, the amount of division of labour that takes place depends on the complexity of the task and the extent to which it can be divided up. We should expect more division of labour in larger groups because of the greater variety of skills and knowledge present, and this is indeed found (Thomas and Fink, 1963).

Industrial groups usually have a high degree of division of labour, with various complementary relationships between the roles. The different jobs in a large restaurant provide an example (Fig. 6.2) There are perhaps eleven role relationships here:

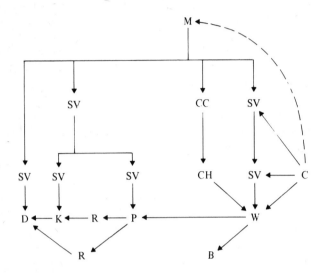

Fig. 6.2. The social system of a restaurant. B, bartender; C, customer; CC, cost-control supervisor; CH, checker; D, dishwasher; K, kitchen worker; M, manager; P, pantry worker; R, runner; SV, supervisor; W, waitress. (After Whyte, 1948.)

1. parallel behaviour: waitresses
2. cooperative performance: cooks
3. cooperative and complementary performance: waitresses and barmen
4. sequential performances: cooks and dishwashers
5. supervision: at several points
6. inspection: e.g. checkers and waitresses
7. assistance: probably in kitchen, but not shown
8. conveying objects and information: e.g. runners take food from kitchen to pantry, and orders from pantry to kitchen
9. discussion: between supervisors
10. negotiation: between waitresses and customer
11. providing expert advice: no example here

We shall see later that the 'scripts' for performance as a customer require information about some of these roles and the proper sequences of interaction between them (p. 222).

In the most primitive communities there is division of labour between men and women. Women look after the children, do the cooking, carry water, grow crops and make clothes. Men do the hunting, fighting and herding, clear land, and build houses and boats (D'Andrade, 1967). Division of labour at work has increased with the complexity of industrial processes, and was enshrined as one of the central principles of classical management theory: the work should be divided up so that no-one has duties that are too varied and unrelated. However the division of work into very simple, often repeated jobs proved to be dysfunctional, and there has been a move towards creating larger and more meaningful tasks by various kinds of job enlargement. But there is still a very high division of labour in modern industry (Argyle, 1972).

Communication networks

In most situations there are certain 'channels' of communication. In a restaurant customers can speak to waitresses but not to the cook, in a hospital to the nurses but not always to the doctor, and so on. Experiments in this area have been concerned mainly with the performance of groups that have different imposed communication channels, such as the wheel or circle:

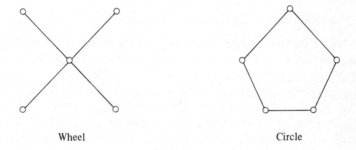

Wheel   Circle

It is found that, for simple tasks, centralised structures like the wheel are superior in that they need less time or fewer messages (Collins and Raven, 1969). However for more complex problems the decentralised patterns do better (Shaw, 1964).

Our main concern here is to establish the conditions under which different communication networks are established, i.e. to consider networks as dependent rather than independent variables. Shaw and Gilchrist (1956) used a situation in which members of groups of five had to communicate by writing. Every group decided quite early that they needed a leader or coordinator; in effect they all adopted the wheel pattern. Shure *et al*. (1962), found that when a two-minute planning period was introduced, groups were faster at subsequent task performance.

Mulder (1960) measured achieved centrality by comparing the number of solutions to set problems that were sent from each position. He found that this correlated with performance better than did imposed centrality; efficiency depended on how rapidly a centralised structure was established. Faucheux and Moscovici (1960) found that groups of four tended to develop a centralised structure for deductive problems and a decentralised structure for inferential ones. Guetzkow and Simon (1955) argued that the effect of imposed structures was only indirect, in that it handicapped certain groups in achieving the best structure; if groups can attain a satisfactory organisation there will be no differences in efficiency. They found little difference in efficiency between different group structures by trial 20, though the circle groups had still not fully organised themselves. Burgess (1968) found no difference in problem-solving efficiency between wheel and circle groups after 500 trials.

In centralised structures the person in the middle nearly always becomes the leader. Mohanna and Argyle (1960) compared groups that had popular and unpopular central members. It was found that after a few trials the wheel-pattern groups with unpopular central members had overcome their initial organisational problem, had overtaken the circle groups, and nearly caught up with the wheel groups that had popular central members.

Other informal roles in small groups

Our basic hypothesis is that groups will develop the roles they need in order that individuals can achieve their goals. Informal roles are functional in a different way. Different people have different personalities and needs; these may be satisfied by formal roles but they can also be catered for by the taking up of one of a number of possible informal roles. This has the additional function of creating a feeling of distinctness and reducing feelings of de-individuation. Examples are the roles found in large families and other settings, which will be described below.

Discussion groups. Bales and Slater (1955) found evidence for the appearance of two different leaders in five-man discussion groups – a task leader and a socio-emotional leader. The member who was most liked was often not the person who was rated highest on 'guidance' and 'best ideas', and the task leader was sometimes the most disliked member of the group. But the groups varied in this respect, and in some cases the same person was rated highest in both areas. The separation of affective and leadership ratings has been found in a number of other studies. However it is not clear that these ratings describe *roles*; Bonacich and Lewis (1973) found that those who were rated as task leaders did not always have a high rate of interaction in the task area. Burke (1967) found that the separation of task and socio-emotional ratings occurred only if group members did not accept the legitimacy of the task. Talland (1957) found that the two sets of ratings coincided in therapy groups – where the task is virtually a socio-emotional one. Where there is an appointed leader he is often able to fulfil both functions: the most effective leaders are found to be rated high both on 'initiating structure' and on 'consideration' (Fleishman and Harris, 1962).

There is a certain amount of evidence, then, that there are two separate functions for leaders to perform, which under some conditions produce two separate leaders. This may be because the two jobs are rather difficult to combine; if a leader gives too many orders he will be liked less, if he is too popular and becomes 'one of the boys' he loses his authority. The solution to this problem may lie in the use of democratic-persuasive leadership skills (Argyle, 1972). Another possible basis for the two leadership roles is the behaviour of parents; fathers usually act more like task leaders while mothers are primarily socio-emotional leaders, and these two roles are learnt by children (Parsons *et al.*, 1953).

T-groups. Mann, Gibbard and Hartman (1967) reported the informal roles often found in the T-groups run by Bales at Harvard, typically with twenty to thirty students as members. There roles were: (1) *hero*, a male informal leader who tries to take over from the trainer; (2) *moralistic resister*, a male who rejects the trainer's plans and acts as spokesman for more 'balanced, sane discussion'; (3) *paranoid resister*, a more rebellious and hostile version of the last, acting as main leader of the opposition; (4) *distressed female*, passive and dependent on the leader, but who does not get on with the job; (5) *sexual scapegoat*, an inconspicuous male who is uncertain of his masculinity and asks the group to study him (he may become the spokesman for the distressed females); (6) *male enactor*, who accepts the leader and the task; (7) *female enactor* who is similar to the male enactor but more dependent on the leader.

Family roles. As well as the roles of father and mother, there are those of older and younger son and daughter. In families with six or more children Bossard and Boll (1956) reported that further roles develop. These are: (1) *responsible*, looks after others (often oldest daughter); (2) *most popular* (often second-born); (3) *socially ambitious*, social butterfly (usually later-born daughter); (4) *studious*; (5) *self-centred isolate* (often the only one of a sex); (6) *irresponsible*; (7) *not well*; (8) *spoiled* (often the last-born). The first two correspond to task and socio-emotional leaders, though of course the father and mother are the main performers of these roles.

Prison. Mitchell (1957) reported the following roles among the inmates of American prisons. (1) *Big shots*, of which there are three subdivisions: politicians, who have the highest prestige and do various assistant administrative jobs; strategists, who have certain work skills which make them useful and enable them to gain certain advantages, such as better accommodation; and hoodlums, who are a small, close-knit, anti-authority group and consider themselves the true bearers of prison tradition. (2) *Con-wise* is the second rank, and consists of professional criminals or old lags, who know the ropes and keep away from both the authorities and the prisoner leaders. (3) *Hoosiers* form the lowest rank, consisting mainly of younger offenders; they are exploited and not treated as equals.

Football fans. Marsh *et al.* (1978) reported on the roles they found among football fans at British football grounds. These are: (1) *rowdies*, aged twelve to seventeen, who make the most noise, produce the most violent displays of aggression and wear the most spectacular costumes; (2) *town boys*, aged seventeen to twenty-five, who have graduated from being rowdies, are quieter, dressed in a normal way and are deferred to by boys in the other roles; (3) *novices*, younger than the rowdies, set apart from them and keen to join them; (4) *part-time supporters*, a varied group not so fully involved in aggressive displays and despised by the others; and (5) *nutters*, extremely aggressive boys who often behave in a crazy way and break the rules accepted by the majority of fans.

How can these systems of informal roles be interpreted? Groups have needs, for example for task leaders and assistant task leaders; they also require socio-emotional leaders to hold the group together. Different group members have different needs; in prison some want to get in with the authorities and make themselves more comfortable, while others want to be left alone and not be involved. Group members may have different ideas, and hence there are often people in opposition to the leadership, and a spokesman for the opposition. It is not known how far these roles represent group tasks, or how far they represent the main preferences by different personalities. The two leader roles are probably roles that have to be done by someone, but the same may not be true of the other roles.

A third possible source of role differentiation is the desire of members to present themselves as unique individuals. It is found that there is greater specialisation in different aspects of the group task in larger groups (Thomas and Fink, 1963), though this could be explained by division of labour. On the individuation hypothesis, if a number of very similar personalities are put together in a group then there should be divergence of behaviour.

Social performance in a role-system

Selection of a role

Since everyone has learnt and is capable of performing a variety of different roles, we must explain how roles are selected in different situations. Even one role, like 'father' or 'professor', produces a great variety of behaviours in different settings (Kelvin, 1969).

Situations, with their basic goals, and tasks, activate relevant roles. The first thing a participant in a situation needs to decide is which is the main role-system operating – e.g. is it football or crime? This can be inferred from the nature of an invitation, the environmental setting, or simply by observation of the action (Sarbin and Allen, 1968).

He then decides which role to play himself. He may have a regular position in the football team, hospital or other role-system. He may be able to infer the roles of the others from their uniforms or spatial positions – hospital patients sit in bed wearing pyjamas, while doctors stride about in white coats. If another person adopts a particular role, the participant may be forced to adopt the complementary one. If the other plays doctor he may have to adopt the patient role. If the other plays the pupil role, he may have to be a teacher. This has been described as 'altercasting', and is a very powerful form of social influence. It can be resisted by the 'put-on', in which the proffered role is rejected by the use of absurd reactions (Brackman, 1967).

The role-demands of situations are pervasive and subtle, and are an important source of error in psychological experiments (Orne, 1962). For example when Officers' Training Corps students were given a vocational guidance inventory in a room decorated with art posters they gave different replies from those tested in more military surroundings (Kroger, 1967). The institutional setting is another factor: within a hospital the roles that count are medical ones; within university buildings, or at the football ground, other roles are more important. Roles can be made salient by the combination of people present. If there are large differences of age or social class, if half are black, or speak with a strong Welsh accent, then these roles will become salient.

Training of social behaviour in role-systems can be carried out by role-playing, in which trainees experience specimens of the role they are to play. Role-reversal enables them to experience roles other than those they would normally have, which can give them insight into the problems of the people who do have those roles. Customers might understand shopkeepers better, for example, if they could experience their role.

Dealing with role-conflict

The occupant of a position may be exposed to conflicting pressures from other people, to play different roles. A doctor may find that his patients and his research colleagues have different expectations of him; a husband may find that his wife and his work-mates make conflicting demands on his time; an adolescent usually finds that parents and friends make different demands; a salesman may recognise the different demands of his customers and his colleagues. Role-conflict is extremely common in organisations; Kahn *et al.* (1964) found that 45 per cent of a sample of American industrial employees experienced definite role-conflict, and that 35 per cent were disturbed by lack of clarity about the scope and responsibilities of their jobs ('role-ambiguity'). Role-conflict and role-ambiguity make people tense and unhappy, and ineffective in their jobs.

Individuals may decide how to deal with these conflicting pressures by going along with what seem the most legitimate demands, or with the person who can cause most trouble for them (Gross, Mason and Mc-Eachern, 1958), or they may go through a process of 'role-bargaining' in which they try out various compromise solutions to see how far these are acceptable to those in interlocking roles. It is also possible to alter the role-system as a whole in such a way as to reduce role-conflict. Diplomats are under extreme role-conflict – from officials in their home country and from those in the country in which they are living. This is minimised by the system of diplomatic immunity, whereby they cannot be prosecuted for breaking the local laws. If a member of an organisation can be directed by two or more superiors, conflict may easily arise; this can be avoided by redesigning the supervisory hierarchy.

Altering role-systems

There is constant change of roles and role-systems in organisations. As organisations grow, there are more levels in the hierarchy and more division of labour. Technological change has led to new organisations and roles, connected, for example, with TV, computers and aeroplanes. New ideas produce changes in roles, for example by creating new kinds of group (T-groups, etc.) or organisational structures with roles such as worker-directors or sports animateurs. In many cases new or greatly modified situations are involved, as in the situations created by TV, with their roles of 'anchor-man', political interviewer, and performer in panel games.

In Chapter 13 we shall give some examples of the deliberate reconstruction of role-systems that has been done by industrial consultants in order to improve the functioning of industrial organisation (see p. 380).

Conclusions

Situations, like groups and organisations, develop role-systems. This is partly because people have different and complementary needs (e.g.

doctor–patient). It is also partly because situational tasks require some division of labour, or special communication systems. Leardership roles appear under certain conditions – e.g. in a large group and when there is a definite task – and can be regarded as functional. There are sociometric roles, such as coalitions, which produce cooperation and increase the power of those involved. Informal roles develop in addition, in order to cater for the different needs of individuals and to reduce feelings of de-individuation.

7

Repertoire of elements

Introduction

Early devisers of category schemes (e.g. Bales, 1950) hoped that their schemes would be equally applicable to all social situations. Bales' scheme has indeed been used to analyse group discussion, classrooms, management–union negotiation, psychotherapy, doctor–patient encounters and family life. The hypothesis that the repertoire of social behaviour is universal to all situations is attractive; it would reflect the constant structure of the nervous system, and enable us to look for universal principles of social behaviour. Beneath the differences between tennis, table tennis and squash, for example, are basically equivalent moves, and the same may be true of social behaviour. We shall examine the alternative hypothesis that the repertoire of social acts is different in different situations; connected with this is the functional hypothesis that these repertoires are related to the goals being sought, for example by forming the steps that bring about those goals, and by providing the distinctions that need to be made between otherwise similar acts in particular situations.

We shall study several different kinds of elements: verbal categories, verbal contents, nonverbal communication and bodily actions. And we shall discuss the question of the size of units of social behaviour. Duncan contrasted the structural approach and the external variable approach to the study of nonverbal communication. By the structural approach he meant 'studies which have sought to identify fundamental elements (or units) of nonverbal behaviours, and to explore the systematic relationships among these units' (1969, p. 121), as have been carried out by Birdwhistell, Scheflen, Kendon and others. This approach has often been criticised as being inadequate in research methodology, but we shall attempt to look at some of its concerns. One hypothesis is that the elements in different situations will be structured differently in ways that can be predicted.

The structuralist approach to nonverbal communication is derived from structuralism in linguistics, and initially from Saussure (1916). The meaning of a word is partly derived from the other words with which it is contrasted; for example, the meaning of a colour word depends on the other colour words used in a language. We shall refer to the way in which elements are grouped and contrasted as their 'semiotic structure'.

In this chapter we shall be concerned with the structure of the main kinds of speech acts and other social actions, i.e. behaviour which produces social consequences (Austin, 1962). If a functional approach is taken to situations, then the elements of a situation can be understood in terms of how they enable the goals of that situation to be attained; this has been done for rules and role-systems. The elements can be seen as the steps used to attain the goals; presumably elements will be grouped together if they lead to the same goal, and contrasted if they lead to different goals.

How can the repertoire of elements for a situation be decided upon? There may be no one agreed set of categories; for social behaviour in the classroom over a hundred schemes are in use, reflecting different points of view, and many of them are in use for training teachers (Simon and Boyer, 1974). The same is true, on a smaller scale, of other situations such as committees and psychotherapy. However a number of systematic methods have been used for defining category sets, and the following principles may be suggested:

1. Is an element actually used in this situation? For example, committee members do not usually kiss each other or throw tennis balls about – if they did we should probably want to redefine the situation. Some common category of behaviour might simply not be used in a situation, so that the category set could be retained though one of the categories is empty. On the other hand extra categories may be needed, as is found to be the case in the doctor–patient situation (see p. 188f.). Sometimes elements are mentioned in the rules, e.g. of games or of committees; when the rules of less formal situations are found they often refer to elements of behaviour that should be performed, or that participants are tempted to do. In experiment 7.1 we used the criterion of agreement between judges to decide whether an element normally occurred in a situation. We questioned a sample of subjects from a subculture about a long list of possible elements and took 40 per cent agreement between judges as the cut-off point as to whether an element normally occurred in a situation. This led to lists of between sixty-five and ninety-one categories for different situations.

2. The method described above results in rather large category sets. Some of these categories may be equivalent in one sense or another, and could with advantage be grouped together, e.g. 'drinks tea', 'drinks coffee'. On the other hand, rather broad categories like 'asks question' may need to be subdivided for various purposes. One way of deciding on the grouping of elements is to ask judges to rate elements on a number of scales, and to use similarity statistics such as hierarchical cluster analysis to find the main divisions between elements. An example of the use of this method is given in experiment 7.2. In this study it was found that work and social situations had rather different similarity structures.

3. Another way of deciding on the similarity of elements is to study their

interchangeability in the sequence of events, i.e. the extent to which they have similar antecedents and consequences. Van Hooff (1973) found the transition probabilities between fifty-three elements of chimpanzee behaviour. The lists of transition probabilities for each pair of elements were then correlated; the correlations led to a cluster analysis, showing the main groupings of chimpanzee behaviour. This method was used in experiment 7.2, in which subjects were asked to judge the extent to which one element could plausibly be substituted for another in the stream of social behaviour.

4. In several of the fields we have examined, investigators wanted to find categories of behaviour that would make a difference in the attainment of situational goals. Research workers wanted to discover the most effective forms of behaviour, and trainers wanted to teach these to young teachers, doctors, etc. Naive practitioners might not be aware of the importance of certain kinds of behaviour, so methods 1 and 2 would fail to produce these categories. From this point of view elements which have similar consequences may as well be combined into a single category. Furthermore it is usually necessary to have different categories for, for example, teachers and pupils, or doctors and patients. The categories of behaviour which make a difference range from broad, global styles of behaviour, like 'warm' and 'enthusiastic' (ratings for a specified time period), to small nonverbal elements like gaze shifts and head-nods. Observer reliability is higher for these smaller units. Most interaction recording schemes are at an intermediate or 'speech act' level, with elements such as 'asks question', 'agrees', etc. One source of variability between repertoires is the theoretical outlook of the investigator. However we are primarily concerned with the repertoires that have been found useful in different situations. We assume that they reflect the repertoires actually used by people in these settings.

When a category system is used to record social behaviour, it is necessary to decide on the units to be coded. For verbal behaviour the complete utterance may be used. However a long utterance may contain several different kinds of message, and it is usual to divide utterances up, either into different speech act types, e.g. information followed by a question, or into units of definite duration, e.g. 3 seconds. Another sub-utterance unit is the 'phonemic' clause – chunks of seven or eight syllables with pauses before and after, with distinctive pitch patterns, and change in rhythm and loudness between clauses (Boomer, 1978). Nonverbal communication is more difficult to divide into units; facial expressions or interpersonal distance may change quite slowly. They can be rated within time intervals, e.g. every minute. Or the behaviour stream can be 'parsed' by observers, who indicate where they think the main points of change are (e.g. Newtson, Engquist and Bois, 1977). Larger units of social behaviour can be found by sequence analysis methods, revealing repeated cycles for example. Or they can be found by parsing, showing the main episodes.

If factor analysis is carried out on perception of the elements of social behaviour, two main dimensions are usually found: friendly–hostile and dominant–submissive (Foa, 1961). Bales (1950) also supposed that one of the main distinctions between elements is between positive and negative. The main factor in the semantic differential is between high and low evaluation (Osgood, Suci and Tannenbaum, 1957); dimensional analysis of facial expressions produces a pleasant–unpleasant factor (Ekman, Friesen and Ellsworth, 1972). It looks as if in the interpersonal sphere, for primarily social activities, positive versus negative, or friendly–hostile, will be an important distinction. In functional terms this can be understood if it is assumed that one of the main goals in such social situations is to elicit positive responses from others.

The second main dimension is dominant–submissive; this is related to the activity and potency dimensions of the semantic differential. It is probably important in those situations in which orders are given and received, where there are differences of power and status between people.

Bales distinguished between task and socio-emotional behaviour (Fig. 7.1). It is common to distinguish between task and social *situations*; in task situations both kinds of behaviour should be found, whereas social situations contain little task behaviour, and task versus social should not be an important distinction. Where there is a definite task this will probably affect the groupings of social acts. Acts that take those present nearer to the goal will be contrasted with those that interfere. The meaning of acts may be changed by the nature of the task. If a man touches a woman, this act will be grouped differently if it is in a doctor's surgery rather than in her flat.

When people are playing a game, or are in some formal situation with rules, the rules will affect the grouping and contrasting of elements. If they are playing rugby football it makes a difference whether the ball is thrown forward or back; if they are playing association football it makes a difference whether they use hands or feet. At a committee meeting there is a difference between a vote and a 'straw' vote.

Our plan in this chapter is to examine closely the hypothesis of a universal repertoire, and also the hypothesis that repertoire varies with situations. This will be done for several different kinds of elements. If we find any evidence of situational variability we shall then ask whether this can be given a functional explanation in terms of situational goals. Since no previous studies have compared repertoires in different situations, we shall look first at a number of situations for which repertoires have been obtained – the behaviour of young children, socialisation and family interaction, committees and negotiation, doctor–patient communication, behaviour in the school classroom and psychotherapy interviews.

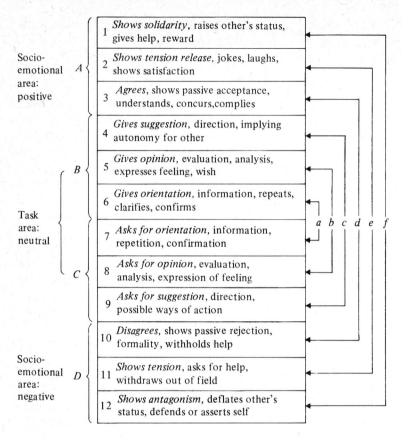

Fig. 7.1. The Bales (1950) categories. *a*, problems of communication; *b*, problems of evaluation; *c*, problems of control; *d*, problems of decision; *e*, problems of tension reduction; *f*, problems of reintegration; *A*, positive reactions; *B*, attempted answers; *C*, questions; *D*, negative reactions.

Categories in six situations

(1) *The social behaviour of young children*

Verbal categories. Research on children in the ethological tradition sometimes uses only one category of verbal behaviour, 'verbalise' (McGrew, 1972). In fact children aged two to five talk a good deal, increasingly with age. The earliest uses of speech are (1) egocentric monologues, accompanying action, (2) questions, sometimes to keep the other's attention, to sustain the relationship, (3) to influence behaviour of others, e.g. asking for things, (4) to convey information, e.g. in answer to questions, (5) as part of games and routines, like pat-a-cake.

Verbal contents. No category schemes have been developed for contents, but it is known that children ask questions about the causes of events, names and classification, and about social relations (Thompson, 1962).

Nonverbal behaviour and bodily actions. A number of ethologists have produced category schemes for the behaviour of nursery-school children. McGrew (1972) has forty-five categories and Blurton-Jones (1972) has thirty-one. Part of McGrew's set of categories is shown in Table 7.1. Brannigan and Humphries (1972) made finer distinctions and listed 136 categories.

(2) *Socialisation and family interaction*

Verbal categories. The Bales scheme has been used here, but reliable coding has been found difficult and it fails to distinguish between families producing very different kinds of deviance in the children (Winter and Ferreira, 1967). The most important variables in socialisation are combinations of verbal and nonverbal, such as warm–cold, strict–permissive, or direct–indirect forms of influence (Sears, Maccoby and Levin, 1957). Adolescents do better under 'democratic' styles of parental supervision (Elder, 1962). So distinctions need to be made between different degrees and forms of direction.

Verbal contents. The contents of parental exhortations, instructions and disciplinary comments are most important. Moral exhortation and punishment have little effect unless reasons are given. Achievement motivation requires the setting of standards, as well as help and encouragement with actual tasks. There are class differences in the production of long-term goals, and indeed in bringing about the verbal control of behaviour (Klein, 1965). The motivation to work may be based on the internalisation of the Protestant Ethic; other long-term values depend on the communication of cognitive contents. Parents communicate the importance of goals and the means to attain them.

Nonverbal communication. Studies of the socialisation of infants are entirely concerned with nonverbal communication. This includes the usual range, but the most important categories are looking, smiling, laughing and crying by the infant, and looking, holding, feeding and rocking by the mother (Ainsworth, Bell and Stayton, 1974). Psychoanalytically inspired research on growing children has focused on feeding methods and toilet training. The delivery of rewards and punishments, which are primarily nonverbal, is of great importance in socialisation, as is the form of punishment (physical, psychological, deprivation, isolation, etc.). Up to adoles-

TABLE 7.1. *Elements of behaviour for nursery-school children*

1. *Back:* walk backwards
2. *Back step:* one unit of *back*
3. *Beat:* overarm blow with lightly clenched fist
4. *Bite:* hold object forcefully between teeth
5. *Chew lips:* press teeth against lips
6. *Chin in:* face forward and down, chin pressed to neck
7. *Flee:* run with arms flailing, frequent veering and direction changing, quick glances over shoulder
8. *Flinch:* shoulders flexed, face down and to side, arms flexed to shoulders
9. *Forearm raise:* forearm raised to horizontal position in front of head
10. *Gaze fixate:* eyes oriented to another's eyes, usually prolonged
11. *Hand on back:* palm placed on another's back
12. *Head nod:* head moved forward and down, then back and up
13. *Head shake:* head moved from side to side
14. *Head tilt:* head leaned sideways to diagonal position
15. *Hold hands:* grasp another's hand, palm-to-palm
16. *Hug:* arms flexed horizontally and toward trunk, encircling an object
17. *Jump:* extension of legs launches body into air, landing on flexed legs, two feet
18. *Kick:* leg rapidly extended toe-first
19. *Kiss:* protruded lips contact another
20. *Laugh:* series of short, rapid, open-mouthed vocalisations
21. *Lean away:* trunk extended at hips
22. *Low frown:* brows lowered and brought together
23. *Pat:* palm repeatedly touched to object
24. *Pinch:* thumb and forefinger pressed together
25. *Play crouch:* arms and legs partially flexed, feet wide apart, shoulders slightly hunched
26. *Play face:* mouth opened wide with corners up, teeth only partially visible
27. *Pucker face:* forehead and nose wrinkled, brows together with inner ends up, eyes screwed up
28. *Pull:* arms flexed to body, hands hold object
29. *Push:* arms extended from body, palms pressed to object
30. *Red face:* facial skin flushed
31. *Rock:* trunk moved back and forth or sideways, rhythmically repeated
32. *Shoulder hug:* arm is flexed around and on another's shoulders
33. *Shrug:* shoulders flexed and extended in rapid succession
34. *Shuffle:* feet moved repetitively while standing
35. *Sidle:* walk sideways
36. *Slap:* palm-first, sidearm blow with hand open
37. *Slope:* shoulders hunched, chin in, hands clasped together at waist
38. *Smile:* mouth partially open and corners up, eyes partially closed, teeth partially visible
39. *Stamp:* sole of foot moved forcefully down onto object
40. *Suck:* lips closed around object inserted into mouth
41. *Turn:* trunk rotated
42. *Vocalise:* laryngeal sound production

From McGrew (1972, p. 154).

cence, family life with children has a wider range of nonverbal expression than have other social situations; there is more violent emotional expression, greater intimacy and aggression, more bodily contact, less restrained proper behaviour than elsewhere.

Bodily actions. As in children's play, there is no clear distinction between actions and nonverbal communication here. Any actions of parents may become the object of imitation by children; any actions of children may be the object of approval or disciplinary action by parents. Life in the home consists of a characteristic range of actions concerned with eating and sleeping, housework, gardening, homework, TV and other leisure activities, and control of these is divided between the parents (p. 168). The extent to which parents play with children, and the extent of joint family activities, are important in socialisation.

(3) *Committees and negotiation*

Verbal categories. The best-known set of categories is the Bales list of twelve categories, divided into task and socio-emotional, and into positive and negative. The main criticism that has been made of this is that some of the categories are too broad, and Borgatta (1962) brought out a revised eighteen-category version. Morley and Stephenson (1977) point out that the scheme does not distinguish between different kinds of content, e.g. of information accepted (category 3 'agrees') or rejected (category 10). Their Conference Process Analysis scheme is summarised in Table 7.2. Every utterance is classified in three ways. There are four *modes* – offer, accept, reject and seek – in the Bales tradition of a problem-solving sequence. There are nine *resources*, indicating the function of the information exchanged. And there are seven *referents*, indicating who is being talked about. So '£2 a week should boost the morale of the workers considerably' is coded as 1/4/5 (1 = offer, 4 = positive consequences of proposed outcomes, 5 = opponent referred to).

Rackham, Honey and Colbert (1971) devised another scheme for recording group discussions, and training in committee skills. Their categories focus on the interpersonal aspects of utterances – supporting, disagreeing, building, criticising, bringing in, shutting out, innovating, solidifying, admitting difficulty, defending or attacking, giving information, seeking information.

Verbal contents. Several schemes code the contents of negotiation. Morley and Stephenson's Conference Process Analysis has the nine resources and seven referents listed in Table 7.2.

Research on the skills of committee chairmanship show that a number of verbal contents categories are important here too. A chairman should make

TABLE 7.2. *Conference Process Analysis scheme*

Mode	Resource	Referent
1 Offer	*Structuring activity*	0 No referent
2 Accept	1 Procedure	1 Self
3 Reject	*Outcome activity*	2 Person
4 Seek	2 Settlement point (*a*) initial (*b*) new	3 Other
	3 Limits	4 Party
	4 Positive consequences	5 Opponent
	of proposed outcomes	6 Both persons
	5 Negative consequences	7 Both parties
	of proposed outcomes	
	6 Other statements	
	about outcomes	
	Acknowledgement	
	7 Acknowledgement + (*a*) own and	
	both sides, (*b*) other side	
	8 Acknowledgement − (*a*) own and	
	both sides, (*b*) other side	
	Other information	
	9 Information	

From Morley and Stephenson (1977).

sure that minority views are expressed, focus on points of disagreement, try to arrive at a creative solution, evaluate a solution in relation to agreed criteria, secure group support for each solution and beware of risky solutions being accepted (Hoffman, 1965).

The rules of committee procedure introduce a number of divisions within categories, for example between proposals and amendments, votes and 'straw' votes, unanimity and *nem. con.*

Nonverbal communication is the same as elsewhere.

(4) *Doctor–patient communication*

Verbal categories. A number of investigators have used the Bales categories (e.g. Korsch and Nygrete, 1972). Byrne and Long (1976) produced a set of fifty-five categories of doctors' behaviour (they did not categorise patient behaviour). Many of these categories are subdivisions of broader categories of the kind found in the Bales scheme. For example there are several different kinds of question. Other categories use interpersonal speech acts, e.g. encouraging, doubting, chastising. Some reflect strategies of interaction, such as refusing the patient's ideas, challenging, evading the patient's questions. Several other schemes combined verbal categories, verbal contents and actions; these will be discussed below.

Verbal contents. Freemon *et al.* (1971) carried out a Bales analysis and a content analysis of consultations, and related the contents to some of the goals of the encounter (e.g. patient satisfaction and compliance with instructions). The results of this and several similar studies suggest the following set of guidelines for doctors (Ley, 1977, p. 19):

1. Find out what the patient's worries are. Do not confine yourself merely to gathering objective medical information.
2. Find out what the patient's expectations are. If they cannot be met, explain why.
3. Provide information about the diagnosis and cause of the illness.
4. Adopt a friendly rather than a businesslike attitude.
5. Avoid medical jargon.
6. Spend some time in conversation about non-medical topics.

Non-verbal communication. Several schemes for recording non-verbal communication in doctor–patient interviews have been used, but they are identical with those used in other kinds of encounter.

Bodily actions. Doctors do other things besides talk. In experiment 7.1 we found that activity items comprised 55 per cent of doctor–patient interaction, which was higher than for the other situations studied. Some of these activities, such as various forms of examination and treatment, are unique to this situation.

(5) *Behaviour in the school classroom*

More category schemes have been devised for this situation than for all others put together; Simon and Boyer (1974) present ninety-nine of them.

Verbal categories. The most extensively used scheme is that of Flanders (1970), and many of the others are derived from it (see p. 190). There are seven categories for teacher behaviour and two for pupils. This system has been criticised by Dunkin and Biddle (1974) on the grounds that most of the individual categories and contents derived from them (e.g. 'indirection') are not consistently related to the attainment of situational goals, i.e. successful teaching. The only exception is 'criticising', which is negatively related. This may be because the categories are too broad (e.g. 'asks questions'), or because no account is taken of the contents, or because it is important *when*, for example, praise is given.

If this criterion of relation to goal attainment is adopted, we can look for categories of teacher behaviour which have been found to be consistently

TABLE 7.3. *The Flanders categories for teacher and pupil behaviour*

Teacher talk

Response
1. *Accepts feeling.* Accepts and clarifies an attitude or the feeling tone of a pupil in a non-threatening manner. Feelings may be positive or negative. Predicting and recalling feelings are included.
2. *Praises or encourages.* Praises or encourages pupil action or behaviour. Jokes that release tension, but not at the expense of another individual; nodding head, or saying 'um hm?' or 'go on' are included.
3. *Accepts or uses ideas of pupils.* Clarifying, building or developing ideas suggested by a pupil. Teacher extensions of pupil ideas are included but as the teacher brings more of his own ideas into play, shift to category 5.

4. *Asks questions.* Asking a question about content or procedure, based on teacher ideas, with the intent that a pupil will answer.

Initiation
5. *Lecturing.* Giving facts or opinions about content or procedures; expressing *his own* ideas, giving *his own* explanation, or citing an authority other than a pupil.
6. *Giving directions.* Directions, commands or orders with which a pupil is expected to comply.
7. *Criticising or justifying authority.* Statements intended to change pupil behaviour from non-acceptable to acceptable pattern; bawling someone out; stating why the teacher is doing what he is doing; extreme self-reference.

Pupil talk

Response
8. *Pupil-talk: response.* Talk by pupils in response to teacher. Teacher initiates the contact or solicits pupil statement or structures the situation. Freedom to express own ideas is limited.

Initiation
9. *Pupil-talk: initiation.* Talk by pupils which they initiate. Expressing own ideas; initiating a new topic; freedom to develop opinions and a line of thought, like asking thoughtful questions; going beyond the existing structure.

Silence

10. *Silence or confusion.* Pauses, short periods of silence and periods of confusion in which communication cannot be understood by the observer.

From Flanders (1970).

related to higher rates of learning or academic achievement. Rosenshine (1971) reviewed a large number of studies in this area, and the following categories emerged as most important:

praises, rewards
explains with examples
asks higher-order questions
encourages pupil participation, uses pupils' ideas
structures

Verbal contents. A number of researchers have recognised that it is misleading to code all 'questions' in a lesson as identical, when there is in fact a planned build-up of complexity and sophistication in the questions being asked. Several schemes, such as that of Smith *et al.* (1967), distinguish between the elements of behaviour at different points of a longer strategy; these will be discussed below.

Nonverbal communication. Many schemes have included nonverbal categories. The main point of interest is that several nonverbal variables in teacher behaviour have been found to be related to successful teaching. The most important are warmth and enthusiasm.

Bodily actions. Many schemes have contained different kinds of classroom activity, by individuals and groups, with various kinds of materials. They include different physical arrangements of pupils, at desks or tables, and the use of various kinds of teaching equipment. Categories are needed for reading, looking at films, doing laboratory experiments, and so on.

(6) *Psychotherapy interviews*

A great deal of research has been carried out in this field, and a number of category schemes have been used (Marsden, 1971). These schemes reflect an interest in comparing the styles of therapists from different schools of thought and also of discovering which kinds of therapist behaviour are most effective.

Verbal categories. The Bales scheme has been used in this setting, though the majority of research workers have preferred to use other sets of categories which differentiate more clearly between different kinds of therapists. The difference between psychoanalysts and non-directive therapists, for example, requires categories such as:
depth of interpretation (degrees of inference)
directiveness
use of clarification
specificity (i.e. limiting patient's reply)
For example, Strupp and Wallach (1965) used six categories for therapist behaviour: facilitating communication, exploratory operations, clarification, interpretative operations (three degrees of intensity), direct guidance

and activity not relevant to therapy. Mintz, Luborsky and Auerbach (1971) factor-analysed measures of behaviour in psychotherapy sessions, and found the following factors:

      warmth, spontaneity, relaxed manner

      directiveness

      depth of interpretation

Rogers and his followers have been concerned with three particular dimensions of therapist behaviour, and Truax and Mitchell (1971) found that successful therapists scored high on genuineness, warmth and empathy, these qualities being rated from segments of tape-recordings. However these dimensions are not easily translated into categories of interaction.

Verbal contents. A number of category schemes have been constructed for contents. Dollard and Auld (1959) devised a set of seventy-eight patient categories and six therapist categories; these consist, following Murray's earlier work, of interpretation of the motive involved, including unconscious motivation. Holzman and Forman (1966) developed a scheme which included twelve objects of concern, five types of difficulty and three degrees of approval/disapproval. Mann *et al.* (1967) used twenty categories for therapy groups, including four for symbolic feelings towards the leader, and other categories for affection, hostility and other authority feelings. Another approach is direct analysis of verbal contents; the most sophisticated version is the General Inquirer program, as used by Psathas and Arp (1966), which carries out a computer analysis of words spoken.

Nonverbal communication. Psychotherapy interviews have been the source of much of the research on nonverbal communication. Many of the categories used have been found to be applicable in other situations, but there are some kinds of nonverbal communication which may be more or less unique to psychotherapy. Mahl (1968) and others have described the symbolic behaviour of patients: postural changes indicating commitment to the therapeutic couch, removal of wedding ring, protective clutching of the body, etc. Scheflen and Scheflen (1972) described sequences of behaviour which they interpreted as flirtation with the therapist. A number of phenomena occur in therapy groups which are not commonly observed elsewhere, such as the 'condenser phenomenon', in which shared emotions, normally repressed, are suddenly released.

Four kinds of categories

Verbal categories

Most category schemes have focused on utterances as the basis for categories. The Bales scheme is like this, though nonverbal aspects of utterances are taken into account. The categories fall into two groups: those concerned with the task (i.e. verbal problem-solving) and those concerned with social relationships. It is clear that any set of verbal categories will need to cover these two areas. In experiment 7.2 we found that subjects recognise task versus social as one of the main divisions between elements of behaviour. The Bales system also distinguishes between positive and negative; in experiment 7.2 it was an important division for social elements, but not so clearly for task elements.

Bales hoped that his scheme would be applicable to any social situation. It has in fact been used by researchers in a variety of settings, but has generally been abandoned in favour of other category sets which are tailor-made for particular situations and usually involve finer subdivisions of certain categories. It might be expected that these would be most needed for task categories. For psychotherapy interviews the Bales scheme fails to differentiate between different kinds of therapist; 'makes suggestion' can be subdivided into different degrees of interpretation and directiveness, and the use of clarification, on the part of the therapist.

A further problem with this kind of scheme is that the contents of communication are not recorded. For the analysis of negotiation this is found to be important: one category set distinguishes stating settlement point, stating limits, describing positive consequences for various people, and so on. In the same way, categories of teacher behaviour, like that of Flanders, have been found to be unsatisfactory since all questions are coded as identical, whereas in the course of a lesson there is a systematic shift in the complexity of what is discussed, and one question builds on another. We shall discuss verbal contents below.

Some formal situations have special moves, which may be mentioned in the rules. At committee meetings it is necessary to distinguish between proposing motions and proposing amendments, and between taking true votes and 'straw' votes. In less formal situations traditions may come to define certain classes of acts, e.g. 'interpretation' and 'reflection' in psychotherapy.

It would be expected that the interpersonal categories of verbal behaviour would be less variable between situations. This may well be so, but there is no one category set that has been used successfully in a variety of settings. The Rackham scheme for committees could be widely used, with its categories of supporting, disagreeing, building, criticising, etc. Any scheme should include, either directly or by inference from other measures, the main dimensions of relationships: friendly–hostile (rewardingness), and dominant (directive)–submissive.

Austin (1962), Searle (1969) and others have compiled categories of speech acts, i.e. utterances that act as signals and influence other people. Below is a list of forty-three speech acts devised by Clarke (in press), intended to apply to all situations:

accept	comply	permit
accuse	confess	praise
advise	continue	prohibit
agree	defer	promise
answer	deny	question
apologise	fulfil	refuse
assert	greet	reject
attend	joke	request
bid farewell	justify	sympathise
blame	laugh	terminate
boast	minimise	thank
challenge	offend	threaten
cheer	offer	warn
command	pacify	
complain	pardon	

Verbal contents

We have just said that the omission of verbal contents is a weakness of verbal category schemes. Obviously the contents of conversation are going to vary between situations, and no set of categories has been thought of which could apply to different kinds of situation. There is, however, a universal procedure for analysing verbal contents – the General Inquirer program – which has been used for psychotherapy interviews, but so far not for the other five situations (Stone *et al.*, 1966). The contents of negotiations are about the size and nature of offers, statement of limits, etc.; the contents of psychotherapy are about the patient's symptoms and worries, and the reasons for them. The sequence of events in each case consists of discussion of these contents, but in one case it is a matter of bargaining, in the other of cooperative exploration.

Nonverbal communication

Since nonverbal communication is mainly used in establishing and maintaining social relationships (Argyle, 1975), it would be expected that the same categories would be used in all situations. This is generally found to be so, and very similar sets of categories have been used in all the situations that we have examined. However the full range of nonverbal communication is not used in all settings. There is not much bodily contact at committee meetings for example. In the analysis of children's social behaviour it is not very useful to distinguish between nonverbal communication and actions; during play there is a lot of gross bodily movement, like climbing and running, which is directed simultaneously towards the play materials and other children. Research on nonverbal communication in psychotherapy has emphasised features which have not been noted in other contexts. This is nonverbal communication of a symbolic kind, e.g. removal of wedding ring. The scientific status of these interpretations is rather weak as yet, but assuming that they are broadly correct it seems likely that similar kinds of nonverbal communication occur in other settings. Finally there is one aspect of nonverbal communication which is situation-specific: the use of conventional gesture languages by, for example, tick-tack men, broadcasters and under-water swimmers.

Bodily actions

These are bodily movements that are part of the performance of a task; some of these tasks are interpersonal, as when a doctor takes a patient's temperature. At first sight it looks as if actions are highly situation-specific – there is little in common between the actions of doctors and teachers. However there are only a limited number of possible bodily movements, and it might be possible to devise a universal set of categories. The analogy of ball games may be illuminating. All ball games involve four basic moves – throwing, kicking, catching, or hitting balls with a foot, hand, bat or racquet – though these take different specialised forms. The repertoire used in ergonomics for the movements of industrial workers could be the basis of actions in social situations. These include elements such as:

search	position
select	inspect
group	assemble (Barnes, 1958)

However we should have to add actions specific to situations. Teaching might include:

write on blackboard	show slides
give out books	move chairs
operate tape-recorder	set up scientific equipment, etc.

Eating a meal would involve quite different actions, and cooking a meal a further set.

Another approach to actions is in terms of the skills used, which can include social skills. Saskatchewan Newstart (1972) helped people to find jobs by listing the job skills they had used in past jobs; an example is given in Table 7.4.

To summarise so far: some areas of categories are universal, especially those dealing with interpersonal relations; other aspects are not, especially

TABLE 7.4. *Categories of job skills*

Surveying marketable skills
On this sheet list the jobs you have done in the first column, the job skills which you have performed well in the second column, and any 'hidden skills' you feel relevant to the job in the third column.

Jobs I have had	Job skills I performed well	Hidden skills I performed well
Example: Barman	1. Pouring drinks correctly 2. Cellar work 3. Mixing drinks 4. Charging correct amount 5. Working the till 6. Giving efficient service 7. Keeping bar stocked up	1. Sociable 2. Good memory (stock layout, prices, etc.) 3. Good at mental arithmetic 4. Good timekeeper 5. Got on with workmates

From Saskatchewan Newstart (1972).

those concerned with tasks. Some of the differences can be interpreted in terms of the varied use made of particular categories; some can be interpreted as the need for finer subdivisions of certain categories in different situations.

Can these similarities and differences be given a functional interpretation? Clearly they can, but partly because the constructors of category sets have wanted to find categories of behaviour that would be related to goals. Would the functional hypothesis be supported if we examined the natural categories used by naive interactors?

In experiment 7.1 we found that repertoires as used by members of the public did vary between situations, particularly the bodily activity elements. For example those used at the doctor's are quite distinctive. The elements also varied in type, the visit to the doctor having the largest proportion of activity elements and the smallest proportion of feeling and conversation elements (compared with the evening at home, etc.). The 'date' was found to be highest on feeling elements and lowest on activity elements. This pattern of findings is compatible with what we know about the goals of these situations in that it suggests that, for example, a visit to the doctor is mainly concerned with the activities of the task (dealing with the patient's illness) and a date is mostly social-emotional in nature, with a large proportion of feeling elements.

If we look at the goals or basic characteristics of situations in terms of whether a situation is predominantly task-oriented or socio-emotional in nature, in the situation 'evening at home with husband', which is both social in nature and involves some tasks, the elements in the repertoire are mostly socio-emotional, with a few task-oriented elements such as 'attend to domestic chores' and 'prepare meal'. The situation 'visit to the doctor' consists mostly of items concerned with dealing with the patient's possible illness, which is the basic task-oriented goal of this situation.

In experiment 7.2 we were able to test the semiotic hypothesis about the grouping and contrasting of repertoire elements in different situations. In the work situation, where there is a definite work task, there is a much clearer division of work-related and personal/socially-related elements than there is in the dating situation. The findings from this study also suggested that (for males taking the role of boss rating the behaviour of a secretary in the office) both negative and social elements interfere in different ways with the main goals of the situation, since a large 'negative' cluster of elements was linked with a 'social' cluster to form a large 'social and negative' cluster separate from the cluster of work-related elements.

Conclusions

Categories of verbal behaviour of the Bales type can be applied to all situations, though they are not always very useful. Verbal categories for interpersonal behaviour can be applied fairly generally, though there are probably better category sets for this purpose than Bales'. The task categories are more variable, mainly because more subdivisions are needed in some situations; for example in families different degrees of direction are important, in teaching different kinds of questions, and in psychotherapy different degrees of interpretation; in committees various subdivisions are created by the rules. In all situations it is important to record the contents of speech in addition to broad categories of speech acts. Verbal contents vary greatly between situations, and it seems unlikely that any general set of categories could be found.

Nonverbal communication takes similar forms in all situations, though different ranges of it are used, for example in the family and in committee meetings. For children's play and family life there is no clear distinction between nonverbal communication and bodily actions.

Actions vary a great deal between situations, but it seems possible that a set of general categories could be found into which they all fall, as is the case for ball games.

7.1. The repertoires of behavioural elements in four social situations

J. A. GRAHAM, M. ARGYLE, D. CLARKE AND G. MAXWELL

[A fuller version of this study is given in part of Graham *et al.* (in press).]

Preliminary studies

To begin with we wanted to select a number of common but quite different situations to look at, so we asked some male and female social psychologists in the Oxford research group to list commonly occurring social situations. From these lists four situations which had been experienced by most of the subjects were chosen.

The four situations were:

A. An evening at home with your husband – just the two of you (when children are not present).

B. Visiting a doctor with whom you are familiar (i.e. your regular doctor).

C. A sporting activity with a friend of the same sex.

D. A first date with a member of the opposite sex whom you find, or found, attractive.

We then wanted to find out from what segments of behaviour these situations are made up. Using several groups of subjects (research workers, housewives and ourselves) we collected together a list which would cover as wide a range as possible of behavioural elements which could occur in these situations.

Some subjects were asked simply to describe particular situations in more detail, others were asked to write prose accounts of the typical course of events in each of the four situations. Most subjects described behavioural elements which included not only the main activities but also types of conversation and feelings relevant to the situation. (This was later explicitly requested.)

A list was then drawn up of the behavioural elements that had been elicited for each situation. We did this by taking the simplest form of the elements and rephrasing them in a standardised, unambiguous way and sometimes describing the element in a more general form (e.g. 'have a sherry' became 'have an alcoholic drink'). Furthermore, which person(s) in the situation the behaviours referred to was not specified; e.g. 'is encouraging', 'have tea' may refer to the subject himself, the other person, or both. We combined the four individual lists of elements in a randomised order to produce a collective elements list consisting of 194 elements (elements which had been elicited in more than one situation, e.g. 'feel relaxed', were represented once only in the collective list).

Main experiment

The aim of the main experiment was to find out which elements were thought to be important in all of the situations and which were important in particular situations.

Method

Subjects. Subjects were a group of ten housewives who were all less than thirty-five years of age and who had some experience of each of the four situations.

Procedure. Each subject was given a copy of the collective elements list. They were told that we were interested in what they saw as normally happening, or the typical course of events, in each of four situations – including alternatives, i.e. the fact that sometimes one thing happens and sometimes another. Subjects were asked to consider each situation in turn and decide for each element whether they thought it was of some importance or commonly occurred in that situation. After all of the subjects had finished the task and checked their responses they were asked to think of any behavioural elements that they thought were important or commonly occurred which were not present on the list. These elements were added to the original list and were then treated by the subjects in the same way as the original elements.

Results

Frequency counts (out of ten) of 'yes' responses were obtained for each element within each of the three behavioural classes (activity, conversation and feeling) in each situation. These were drawn up as twelve frequency distributions by rank-ordering the elements according to number of 'yes's' they obtained. These twelve distributions were all rather similar; one of these (the frequency distribution for choices of activity elements in situation B) is shown in Fig. 7.2.

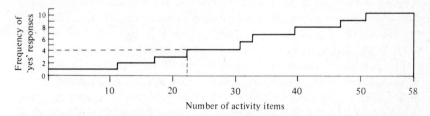

Fig. 7.2. Frequency distribution for choices of activity elements in situation B, a visit to the doctor. The dashed line shows the 40 per cent cut-off point.

From inspection of the distributions it was clear that there was no obvious point at which there was substantial agreement. A fairly low, conservative cut-off point of 40 per cent of the subject sample (equivalent to about 40 per cent of the original set of elements) was chosen to safeguard against dropping any elements which might be crucial. The total number of elements of each class thus agreed to be important in each situation are shown in Table 7.5.

TABLE 7.5. *The important elements of each class occurring in each situation*

Situation	Activity	Conversation	Feeling	Total items considered salient per situation
A	40.6%	38.5%	20.9%	91
	37	35	19	
B	55.4%	29.2%	15.4%	65
	36	19	10	
C	34.2%	46.1%	19.7%	76
	26	35	15	
D	34.1%	40.6%	25.3%	91
	31	37	23	

Percentage values represent number of items of each class, expressed as a proportion of total number of items, considered salient in a situation.
Numerical values represent number of items of each class considered salient in a situation.

These elements were listed within their behavioural classes and their situations. Within the lists, items occurring in all four situations, in different subgroupings of two and three situations, and only in a particular situation, were grouped. Inspection of these lists revealed that large proportions of the activity elements were specific to particular situations only; few were common to more than one situation – e.g. 'prescribe medicine' was specific to the visit to the doctor. Only three activity items (e.g. 'sit and watch other people') were common to all situations.

The pattern for conversation elements and feeling elements was somewhat different. A fairly substantial proportion of these elements was common to three of the situations (A, C and D): e.g. 'discuss interests' and 'feel relaxed'. The proportion of conversation elements specific to individual situations was relatively small for these three situations; indeed, for the date situation there were none. Those elements that were specific to the visit to the doctor tended to contain reference to particular aspects of this situation, such as 'explain how treatment works'. The proportion of feeling elements which were situation-specific was relatively small for all situations (e.g. 'worry' was peculiar to the doctor–patient situation).

Discussion

In this experiment the repertoire of behavioural elements making up four different situations has been discovered by the use of the 'emic' approach, i.e. from the viewpoint of the participants. As we have seen, some elements are specific to one situation only and others apply to some or all of the situations. The elements specific to one of the situations and not to others tend to be activity items – that is, rather different activities distinguish the different situation. The elements thought to be important in all of the situations tend to be conversation and feeling elements.

For situation B, the visit to the doctor, it seems that the actual consultation part of this situation is seen rather more simply from the patient's viewpoint than the detailed behavioural repertoire reported by Byrne and Long (1976). However, it is quite likely that further 'emic' research on this situation would extend the list of elements as seen from the patient's viewpoint. It seems that Bales' (1950) behavioural categories of task and socio-emotional behaviour, and their subcategories, are not really appropriate to the much wider range of behavioural elements elicited here using the emic approach. The elements used in this experiment were fairly specific in so far as they were derived directly from detailed descriptions of each situation.

The goals and basic characteristics of each situation are reflected to some extent in the relative proportions of the elements of each type and also in the elements which were situation-specific (these were mostly activities). For example, the visit to the doctor had the largest proportion of activity elements and the smallest proportion of feeling and conversation elements. This situation consisted mostly of elements concerned with dealing with a patient's possible illness, which is the basic goal of this predominantly task-oriented situation. The situation highest on feeling elements was the date, which was also lowest on activity elements, reflecting the basic person-oriented goals of developing intimacy and liking for the other, and getting to know and understand the other person better.

7.2. The structure of behavioural elements in social and work situations

M. ARGYLE, J. A. GRAHAM AND M. KRECKEL

The central hypothesis of this study was that the verbal and nonverbal elements in different conditions (situations and sex roles) would be structured differently in ways that could be predicted, i.e. that the ways in which acts are grouped and contrasted would vary in the different conditions. In the investigation reported here we used two situations: a boss–secretary encounter in an office, and a 'date'. In each situation there were two roles: male and female.

There are several ways in which the structure of elements might be expected to vary between conditions. It could vary in terms of the distinctions of Bales' (1950) positive–negative and task–socio-emotional dimensions or Foa's (1961) friendly–hostile and dominant–submissive dimensions.

Both these distinctions are likely to be more salient in the more social situation (the date). In functional terms this can be understood if we assume that one of the main goals of such social situations is to elicit positive responses from others.

The task-oriented/socio-emotional distinction would be likely to be more important in the work situation, where both types of behaviour would be found but would be seen as quite separate compared with the social situation. The date should contain little task behaviour and it would be much less important to separate the two types of behaviour here.

Also, where there is a definite task in a situation (as in the office) behavioural acts that take the participants nearer to the goal are likely to be contrasted with those that interfere. In general, the meaning of a particular act may be changed by the nature of the situation.

The following expectations developed, based on a common-sense analysis of the goals and nature of the two situations:

1. That the general structure of clusters would differ in the different conditions. In particular it was expected that the positive–negative distinction would appear in all conditions but more clearly in the date, and that the task versus social distinction would be clearer in the work situation.

2. That the similar clusters of elements which appear in different conditions would be likely to have different profiles.

3. That specific pairs of elements would be seen as similar in one situation but not in another:
   (i)   Asking about work and private life (element 1 versus element 6) would be seen as similar on a date but different at work.
   (ii) Invitations to home and pub (9 versus 18) would be seen as similar on a date but different at work.
   (iii) Giving information about work and private life (20 versus 13) would be seen as similar on a date but different at work.
   (iv) Teasing and making favourable comment about appearance (7 versus 3) would be seen as similar on a date but different at work.

7.2. Elements in social and work situation

Method

Subjects. Ten males and ten females all aged about twenty-five years were the volunteer subjects. Subjects of each sex were run in separate groups.

Procedure. We chose twenty-six elements of behaviour which we thought covered much of the repertoire of both situations and which could occur equally well in either. And we used ten different seven-point rating scales which we hoped would cover the main forms of reaction to these elements. The elements and dimensions were derived partly from our previous studies.

The subjects were asked to imagine typical examples of the two situations: a date (between a young man and young woman) and a boss–secretary encounter in the office. The subjects were required to take the viewpoint or role in each situation that corresponded to their own sex and to rate how they would react to each of the twenty-six elements of behaviour if it were emitted by the *other* person in the situation; for example, a male subject would be required to rate how desirable it would be for a female secretary to 'ask about work' in the work situation. The set of twenty-six behavioural elements can be seen in Fig. 7.3. The ten seven-point scales (the ends of which were labelled with polar opposites (e.g. frequent–infrequent) were: frequent, desirable, socially skilled, relevant, emotionally arousing, friendly, dominant, easy to deal with, pleasant and predictable.

The order of presentation of situations was reversed for half of the subjects, and within each of these groups of subjects the order of presentation of the rating scales was reversed for half of the subjects.

Results

Several methods may be used to find out how elements are related in the minds of raters, by grouping together elements perceived as similar or as invoking similar reactions. Ward's technique for hierarchical cluster analysis (Wishart program) was used since it shows groupings and contrasts of elements most clearly. Four such analyses (one for each condition) were carried out on the rating scale scores and the results were presented in the form of a dendrogram for each condition.

General structure of clusters. An example of one of the four dendrograms, for males' ratings of the secretary in the work situation, is shown in Fig. 7.3. The items which join at the top part of the dendrogram are dissimilar and those which join at the bottom part are similar. A similarity coefficient of 2.3 was used as the cut-off point below which adjoining elements were treated as subclusters of highly similar elements. The

203

combinations of subclusters joining above the cut-off point were regarded as clusters (these were larger/of a higher order).

For males' ratings of secretary at work there was a large 'positive' cluster made up of 'work' and ('positive') 'nonverbal' subclusters. Subclusters of 'invitations' and 'intimacy' formed the 'social' branch of a larger 'social and negative' cluster; 'withdrawal' and 'conflict' made up the 'negative' part of it (see Fig. 7.3).

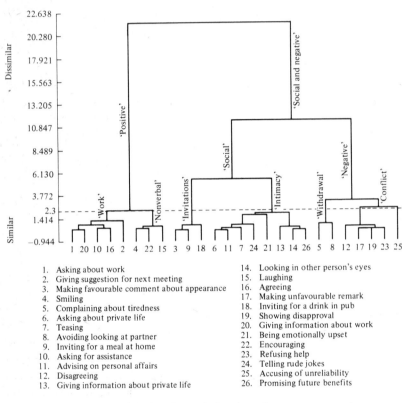

1. Asking about work	14. Looking in other person's eyes
2. Giving suggestion for next meeting	15. Laughing
3. Making favourable comment about appearance	16. Agreeing
4. Smiling	17. Making unfavourable remark
5. Complaining about tiredness	18. Inviting for a drink in pub
6. Asking about private life	19. Showing disapproval
7. Teasing	20. Giving information about work
8. Avoiding looking at partner	21. Being emotionally upset
9. Inviting for a meal at home	22. Encouraging
10. Asking for assistance	23. Refusing help
11. Advising on personal affairs	24. Telling rude jokes
12. Disagreeing	25. Accusing of unreliability
13. Giving information about private life	26. Promising future benefits

Fig. 7.3. Dendrogram for males' rating of secretary at work.

For females' ratings of boss at work there were two clear-cut higher-order clusters – 'positive' and 'negative'. Subclusters of 'work' and 'intimacy' made up the 'positive' cluster and subclusters of 'intimacy' and 'conflict' made up the 'negative' cluster.

For males' ratings of girlfriend on date there were two large clusters – 'positive' and 'negative'. The 'positive' cluster was made up of 'support' and 'approach' and the 'negative' cluster of 'conflict' and 'avoidance'.

For females' ratings of boyfriend on date there was a 'positive' cluster made up of 'work', 'intimacy' and 'approach' subclusters, and a 'negative' cluster made up of 'withdrawal', 'conflict' and 'avoidance'.

There was more differentiation for males' perceptions of females in the work situation than vice versa (six versus four subclusters). For the date, the outcome was reversed; there was more differentiation for females' ratings of males than vice versa.

Do similar clusters of elements which appear in different conditions have different profiles? The profiles of the scale ratings for clusters which occurred in more than one condition were plotted. As most of the clusters given the same label were not identical in terms of their component elements, only those elements which were common to more than one condition were used in plotting the mean rating. For example, the 'negative' cluster had a slightly different composition in each condition but it always contained the elements 12, 17, 19, 13 and 25 (disagreeing, making unfavourable remark, showing disapproval, refusing help, accusing of unreliability). The profiles for these elements (of the 'negative' cluster) were found to be fairly similar in each of the four conditions. The main divergence was on the scale 'difficult to deal with'; males rated females as more difficult to deal with than females rated males, in both situations.

The profiles for the common elements which occurred in the 'intimacy' cluster for ratings of males and females in the work situation were also plotted; these profiles were again found to be very similar to each other. None of the differences appeared to be as great as those for the 'negative' cluster. Similar findings occurred for the 'approach' clusters.

Are specific pairs of elements seen as similar in one situation but not in another? The approximate similarity scores (read off directly from the dendrograms) for the elements relevant to the expectations about the perceived similarity of specific pairs of scales in each condition, are shown in Table 7.6. These values are the points along the similarity scale at which the clusters, containing each of the two behavioural elements being compared, join. The higher the score, the more different are the two behaviours thought to be, in that condition. The criterion for whether two elements were similar was that they should appear in the same cluster.

From the table it can be seen that there appears to be some support for the expectations:

(i)   Asking about work and private life (1 versus 6) would be seen as similar on a date but different at work. This was confirmed.

(ii) Invitations to home and pub (9 versus 18) would be seen as similar on a date but different at work. This was confirmed for females rating males. (For males rating females they were seen as similar in both work and the date.)

TABLE 7.6. *Approximate similarity scores for ratings of certain pairs of elements between four conditions*

	Date		Work	
	Males rating girlfriend	Females rating boyfriend	Males rating secretary	Females rating boss
Elements				
1 and 6 (asking about work versus asking about private life)	5.3	5.3	21.0	28.0
9 and 18 (inviting for a meal at home versus inviting for a drink in pub)	1.8	5.2	1.0	28.0
20 and 13 (giving information about work versus giving information about private life)	5.3	5.2	21.0	28.0
7 and 3 (teasing versus making favourable comment on appearance)	5.3	5.2	5.0	28.0

Scores shown are approximately similarity scores. Low score means the two elements are very similar (form part of the same cluster).

(iii) Giving information about work and private life (20 versus 13) would be seen as similar on a date but different at work. This was confirmed.

(iv) Teasing and making favourable comment about appearance (7 versus 3) would be seen as similar on date but different at work. This was confirmed for females rating males. (For males rating females they were seen as similar in both work and the date.)

Discussion

The first expectation was that the general structure of clusters would differ in the different conditions, in particular that the positive–negative division would be found in all four conditions but more clearly in the more social situation (the date). There was indeed a positive–negative division for all four conditions but more clearly in the date condition: the separation of the divisions within the 'positive' and 'negative' clusters occurred at a lower point on the scale in the date than for work, so the positive and negative aspects were more tightly clustered within each division for the date.

Furthermore, the 'negative' branch (in males' ratings of secretary at work) was not separate in itself but was linked with a 'social' branch to form a large 'social and negative' cluster. The explanation in this condition may be that both negative and obviously social elements interfere in different ways with the main goals of the situation. This is seen more clearly by the boss (evaluating the secretary's behaviour) than vice versa.

It was also expected that the work versus social distinction would be clearer in the work situation. In fact there were no clear 'work' clusters for the date situation. In the office situation the next division of clusters after 'positive' and 'negative' was into 'work' and 'social'. In the date, males saw work-related elements of behaviour from their girlfriend not as separate but as forming part of a 'support' subcluster which linked with an 'approach' subcluster to form an overall 'positive' group of behaviours. In females' ratings of the boyfriends' behaviour on a date, the work-related items were grouped with 'inviting for drink' and 'agreeing' in the 'work' subcluster. In addition, this cluster was strongly similar to the 'intimacy' subcluster (these two joining to form a branch of the 'positive' cluster).

One of the unexpected findings was the overall pattern of the work and date situation as perceived by males and females. Males saw the work situation in a more differentiated way than did females (six versus four clusters), whereas females made finer distinctions within the date situation than males (six versus four clusters). One is almost tempted to say that both males and females perceive their 'culturally allocated domain' in a more differentiated way.

Surprisingly, perhaps, it was found that the profiles (of mean scores on each of the ten rating scales) for the 'negative', 'intimacy' and 'approach' clusters were all rather similar in the different conditions; the main exception was that males found 'negative' behaviour in females difficult to deal with.

Of particular interest in the comparisons of the approximate similarity scores for some of the pairs of elements is that the distinction between work and social behaviours appears to be more salient in the work situation than in social situation. For example, asking about working and asking about private life were seen as very similar on a date but totally different when at work.

8

Sequences of interaction

Introduction

Social psychologists have long been trying to understand the principles underlying sequences of interaction. It has often been assumed that there will be some universal principles, or 'grammar', common to all situations, although very little progress has been made so far in finding them. It is fairly obvious that interaction sequences take different forms in different situations, and this is what we shall explore in this chapter. But are they fundamentally different, or are there universal principles underlying these different kinds of sequence, in the way that the same grammar underlies different kinds of conversation? We saw in the last chapter that the repertoire of social acts varies with the situation, and that the repertoire for a situation is functional – it consists of the steps needed to attain the situational goals. A related hypothesis is that the repertoire elements, the steps to the goals, must be used in a special order. It is fairly obvious that the moves made by *one* person to perform a task must often be in a certain order, though this is not always so: it is true for climbing mountains, or building a house, less true for getting dressed or cooking a meal. What we are saying is that the alternating sequence of moves made by two or more people is similarly ordered.

The most widely used method of studying behaviour sequences is the analysis of transitional probabilities, as developed in ethology. This leads to empirical generalisations, from which later behaviour in a sequence can be predicted. We shall see that this method has rather limited application to human interaction sequences, since it cannot deal with long or complex sequences. The methods of linguistics have been tried – looking for rules of combination and sequence of behaviour elements, on the analogy of the rules of grammar in relation to the order of words in sentences. This has led to the development of a number of new research techniques and some interesting findings, but has not produced a grammar of social behaviour. Another approach is that of the ethnomethodologists, who have the more limited 'hermeneutic' goal of interpreting particular conversations, and cataloguing different ways of ending them, of speakers correcting themselves, and so on. This is an area in which social psychologists are not agreed about the appropriate methodology; previous methods have failed to produce results, and new ones seem scientifically inadequate.

The approach we have been following makes use of ethological methods; it also uses ideas from linguistics in looking for more complex structures; it looks for rules rather than for predictive generalisations; it uses rigorous empirical methods, while accepting a greater variety of empirical procedures than have formerly been used; and it tries to explain sequences of behaviour in terms of the other properties of situations. This approach has already proved successful in one way: the findings have been used to train people in social skills. Indeed the analysis of common forms of failure in social performance is a useful method for studying sequences of behaviour.

Ethological methods

Ethologists have often used Markovian methods; Markov chains can account for many sequences of animal behaviour (Slater, 1973). Most forms of sequence analysis of human social behaviour consist of finding the main categories of behaviour used in a situation, and producing a Markov chain of the transition probabilities of a particular behavioural act by one person leading to certain other acts by himself or another person. In the example of a behaviour matrix shown below it can be seen that behaviour A would have a high probability of leading to behaviour B, and B would have a high probability of leading to behaviour C.

	A	B	C
A	5	90	5
B	10	10	80
C	35	35	30

This method leads most directly to the study of two-step links, 'adjacency pairs', such as question–answer. Longer sequences can be constructed out of two-step units, but there is plenty of evidence for embedding (see p. 215f.) and phrase structure, for utterances as well as words. Clarke (in press) asked subjects to contribute to artificial dialogues, in a method similar to that for the statistical approximation to sentences, where one, two, three, etc., previous utterances were supplied. The rated realism of these dialogues increased up to the fourth order, i.e. where three previous utterances were provided, and these were judged as slightly more realistic than real dialogue. There are ways of dealing with sequences longer than two within the Markovian approach. One method is 'chain analysis' (Dawkins, 1976). If two elements, A and B, repeatedly occur in sequence, A and B can be regarded as a new, higher-order, unit AB, and the analysis can be repeated including AB as an element. If this principle is repeated many times, larger and larger units and more elaborate hierarchical structures of behaviour can be revealed. Chain analysis had not been applied to human behaviour in social situations before our use of it in experiment 8.1. In this experiment we asked people to provide typical orderings of the elements for each of four situations. These orders were the basis for a transitional probability matrix which was then treated by chain analysis. The 'visit to the doctor' situation yielded the most higher-order units, and these were longer than for other situations. The structures obtained were quite different for each situation.

Animal studies have shown that the pattern of transition probabilities may shift as the action enters a new phase and a repeated cycle of behaviour gives way to a different one. These large units, in turn, have their own transitional probabilities. Dawkins (1976) describes this as a hierarchy of decisions – first to enter a particular phase and then to select a move. The high transition probabilities occur within the larger phases and so there is greatest uncertainty at the beginning of a phase. This is non-Markovian because there is a series of decisions and an earlier decision affects a larger chunk of following moves. Newtson and Engquist (1976) found that break-points provide more information than points within units (or chunks). In the study of nonverbal behaviour in humans it has been found that there is often increased gaze and mutual gaze at transition points in social encounters, e.g. at greetings, farewells and at the ends of utterances (Steer, 1972). Argyle and Cook (1976) suggested that this may be because of the greater amount of information available at these points.

A number of studies of human nonverbal behaviour have used Markovian methods. Kendon (1976) found that for a couple kissing on a park bench the girl had two main kinds of smile in terms of its consequences: one led to her being kissed, the other led to her withdrawal. The two kinds of smile would therefore not be grouped as equivalent. Collett and Marsh (1974) studied the bodily movements of people on a London pedestrian crossing, to find out how they managed to avoid colliding. It was found that most people crossed giving their left shoulder; if they were going to give their right shoulder they gave a visible lurch to the left to signal this. Men offered the front of their body, women the back.

It must be admitted that ethological methods have not been very successful in the analysis of sequences of human social behaviour, though they have had some success for animals, children, and human nonverbal behaviour. The main difficulty is that human sequences are too long and complex; an earlier move can affect another move much later in the sequence. Sequences depend on the plans and ideas of participants and the rules and other features of the situation. And, as we have seen, the elements vary from situation to situation. Consider people playing cricket or any other complex game; it is not possible to predict from the previous act, or twenty previous acts, when one team will 'declare'.

Linguistic methods

We turn now to the linguistic approach to behaviour sequences. Birdwhistell (1970) in the field of nonverbal behaviour, and Goffman (1971) in the field of conversation, observed the success of linguists such as Chomsky in formulating an adequate set of the generative rules for ordering words in sentences, and hoped to do likewise for other units of social behaviour. The linguistic model has suggested several lines of research into sequences.

Categories of elements which can be substituted. The ethological approach can lead to the discovery of items with similar antecedents and consequents, which can therefore be regarded as equivalent (p. 181f.). The linguistic approach uses groups of elements which could be substituted at a particular point in the sequence without breaking the rules and producing a meaningless sequence. Ratings of equivalence of elements by subjects can be obtained in two quite distinct ways. One procedure used in the past to construct category sets is for subjects to rate the perceived similarity of, or difficulty of discriminating between, different elements of behaviour; this can be done either by interactors or by observers. Alternatively a procedure used in linguistics is for judgements to be made about which elements could substitute for one another in a sequence. For example, in the sentence 'The boy ate a bun', 'boy' could be replaced by 'girl', 'dog', etc., but not by 'ate', 'slowly' or 'blue'. Fries (1952) describes this procedure under the name of test-frame analysis for the identification of word types in sentences. Mendeleev (1879) used this kind of procedure in substituting chemical elements in crystal lattices to discover the main groups of elements. The same principle was used in experiment 8.1.

The logic behind this procedure is that if sequences have a structure, then some combinations of elements will form or not, according to the relevant properties of the elements that affect how they combine with each other. In trying to discover what these relevant properties are it can be argued that any two elements that are interchangeable in a structure must be identical in these relevant properties and distinct only in properties that are unaffected by the principles of combination. Similarly, elements that are not interchangeable must differ in terms of the properties that are relevant to combination.

We used substitution methods in experiment 8.1. Subjects rated the substitutability of items in each of four social situations. Cluster analyses were carried out, and inspection of the dendrograms (showing the percentage of subjects who rated different elements as equivalent) revealed that the pattern of clustering of equivalent or substitutable elements was rather similar for three of the situations. Clusters were few and large and there was a high degree of agreement about them. In the 'visit to the doctor' clusters were small, more numerous and weaker in terms of agreement.

One of the questions of interest in the equivalence experiment was whether or not this procedure would generate something like parts of speech and semantic categories for each situation, and this is indeed the pattern for three of the situations. However, we do not find a small number of large categories, as there are for parts of speech, though there could still be a grammar with a larger number of categories. Perhaps the 'visit to the doctor' is different because it is a specialised task-oriented situation which employs peculiar constructions. It produced the clearest clusters of elements. The equivalence experiment also showed that elements that formed clusters (above a cut-off point of 65 per cent subject agreement) belonged to the same behavioural class – activity, conversation or feeling – but we did not obtain a few simple types like the parts of speech in verbal grammar.

Rules of composition. Clarke (1975) recorded a number of informal conversations, transcribed them, and placed utterances on cards which were then shuffled into random order. A second group of subjects was asked to put the utterances back in the right order, and they were able to do so with far above chance accuracy. This shows that people have a good intuitive idea of the way conversations are ordered. It is obvious, for example, how the following conversation should be rearranged:

1. Oh, nothing much.
2. Did you have a good day at the office, dear?
3. What's been happening at home then?
4. No, bloody awful.

Parsing and episode structure. It has been found by Newtson (1973) and Dickman (1963) that judges agree fairly well about the main divisions or breakpoints in verbal and nonverbal behaviour. The main disagreement is over the size of the units to employ. In one of our experiments we found the main episodes and sub-episodes for some common kinds of encounter (p. 221).

The linguistic approach to social behaviour sequences has so far been only moderately successful. We have not found any equivalent of parts of speech, or of grammar. If there are any universal principles they seem to be too abstract to be helpful, like the principle that people take turns in conversations. On the other hand this model has led to the opening up of a variety of new research methods, such as constructing artificial dialogues and asking subjects to rate their acceptability. The studies we shall discuss in this chapter fall within an extension of the linguistic model, taking account of the rules, goals and other features of situations. And it should be said that the linguistic model has been used to try to understand far more complex sequences than those to which Markovian analysis has been applied.

Effect of different repertoires on sequence

If the elements are different, the sequence is usually different. The order of moves in knitting is different from the order of moves in cooking a meal or mowing the lawn, except perhaps in the very abstract sense of: make plan, assemble materials, do job, check, clear up (or something of the kind). On the other hand if the elements belong to the same abstract type, the order may be the same – like the order of moves at tennis and squash, and the order of events in four-step social-skill sequences (p. 216f.).

Just as situations have characteristic repertoires of elements, so also do they have characteristic sequences of these elements. The sequence of acts forms the route to the goals of the interactors. In the case of games the sequence usually takes the form of alternative moves, each responsive to the last, which attempt to defeat the other player. An auction sale has a similar structure of alternating, competitive moves. So do sessions of boasting, or story-telling. Most social situations, however, are more cooperative and less competitive. In selling, for example, there are such cooperative sequences, between customer C. and salesperson S, as:

(1) C: asks to see goods
    S: produces, demonstrates goods
(2) C: asks for price, or other information
    S: gives information
(3) C: asks to buy, pays
    S: wraps up and hands over goods

Consider a more complex kind of negotiation: management–union bargaining. Morley and Stephenson's scheme (p. 188) has nine main categories – procedure, settlement point, limits, positive consequences of proposed outcomes, negative consequences, other statements about outcomes, acknowledgement (praise, etc.), acknowledgement (blame, etc.) and information (other statements of fact or opinion). This repertoire makes for a much more intricate sequence than in the auction sale, where only one move is possible.

Two-step sequences

We saw that ethological methods of sequence analysis lead most readily to the discovery of two-step linkages, in which move A often leads to move B, either by the other person ('reactive') or by the same person ('proactive'). Ethnomethodologists have attached importance to 'adjacency pairs', where there is a rule that move A should lead to move B (Schegloff and Sacks, 1973).

Clarke (in press) asked people to construct artificial dialogues consisting of strings of speech acts labelled as 'question', 'threat', etc. He found a number of common two-step sequences, where the first very often led to the second:

question–answer	complain–sympathise
joke–laugh	greet–greet
accuse–deny	apologise–pardon
praise–minimise	offer–accept or reject
request–comply or refuse	

However there are other ways in which acceptable conversation can be constructed. Questions may lead to questions (e.g. about the meaning of the first question); questions may lead to irrelevant impassioned outbursts (in psychotherapy), etc.

When a social psychologist looks at these pairs, it is evident that several different principles are involved. (1) The speech act types are related in terms of rules of discourse, whereby a question more often leads to an answer rather than to a question, and a joke leads to a laugh rather than to an apology – though a very bad joke could perhaps lead to a farewell or to sympathy. (2) The meanings of successive utterances are linked, as described by Grice's (1975) maxim of relevance. (3) Some two-step links are based on principles of social behaviour, such as reinforcement, response-matching or equilibrium maintenance; these are not rules, but are more like empirical generalisations or laws. (4) Some two-step links are based on the rules of particular situations such as auction sales, card games or committee meetings.

We can specify in more detail the rules about how one utterance should follow from another. Grice (1975) put forward four maxims (i.e. rules):

1. *Maxim of quantity.* Make your contribution as informative as is required, but give no more information than is required.
2. *Maxim of quality.* Try to make your contribution one that is true. That is, do not say anything you believe to be false or lack adequate evidence for.
3. *Maxim of relevance.* Make your contribution relevant to the aims of the ongoing conversation.
4. *Maxim of manner.* Be clear. Try to avoid obscurity, ambiguity, wordiness, and disorderliness in your use of language.

Rommetveit (1974) suggested that there is a rule that a speaker should take for granted, i.e. not repeat, knowledge that is shared by him and the listener, and should add something new to it: 'the new is nested in the old'.

214

Of all two-step sequences the question–answer link is the most important. Kent, Davis and Shapiro (1978) carried out an experiment based on Clarke (1975) in which subjects were asked to re-order scrambled dialogues. They found that if the original conversationalists were not allowed to ask any questions it was impossible for judges to discover the original order. On the other hand if we use finer divisions of social acts, these simple sequences become more complicated. Thus rhetorical questions, rude questions or impossible questions (e.g. 'Have you stopped beating your wife?'), will produce anger, silence or further questions, which are not usefully classified as 'answers'. Perhaps it is only genuine enquiries that produce answers.

However the question–answer sequence does not always work. In the Gonja, and elsewhere, people do not ask questions unless they have the power to extract an answer (Goody, 1978); there, schoolchildren do not ask questions in class. Information is regarded as a form of property in some cultures, not to be given away for the asking. In Japan, questions are not asked when the answer might be 'no', since the person answering would lose face. Similarly in our own culture people will not give answers to personal, intimate questions unless the person asking them is in a relationship which entitles him to ask such questions. There are some questions that may be asked by doctors, parents, bank managers or interviewers, and some that may not. The answering of questions may be upset by considerations of politeness. To disagree may be to insult the other person. To give him information that he does not like is avoided, and inaccurate information given instead. In South American countries subordinates in business organisations do not speak their minds when more senior officials are present, so less use is made of group meetings.

Other sequences may change as a result of situational factors. Patterson *et al.* (1967) found that interaction sequences that commonly led to aggression or other undesirable behaviour by children did not do so if parents established regular sanctions for these forms of behaviour. The pay-offs for various kinds of behaviour may change for a number of reasons. Huesmann and Levinger (1976) showed how such pay-offs change as the relationship between two people develops, so that, for example, a reward for one is partly shared by the giver of the reward.

Two-step sequences can act as the building blocks for longer sequences. It is legitimate to insert subordinate clauses in sentences, bracketed by commas. Embedding is also allowed in conversation. For example:

A_1 What'll you have?
B_2 Ya got those almond things?
A_2 Not to-day honey.
B_1 Black coffee and a toasted muffin.

(Goffman, 1971, p. 146)

215

Clarke (in press) presented instances of embedding to judges and found that they were nearly as acceptable as question–answer, question–answer sequences. However cross-over sequences ($Q_1 - Q_2 - A_1 - A_2$) were not acceptable at all. It is not known how acceptable double or treble embedding would be.

Longer strings can be put together by combining adjacency pairs; however, principles of 'phrase structure' operate, whereby account has to be taken of the situation, its goals and longer sequences of conversation in order to decide what utterances would be appropriate at a particular point.

Goals and feedback

The order of moves by an interactor depends on the goals which he is trying to attain. If one move does not provide quite the right result, feedback leads to corrective action. This is the essence of the motor-skill model of social behaviour (Fig. 8.1). The model fits best situations such as interviewing

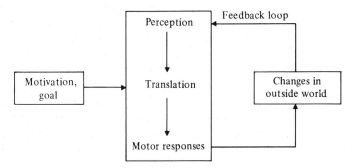

Fig. 8.1. The motor-skill model of social performance. (After Argyle and Kendon, 1967.)

and teaching, where one person is in charge. The social-skill model generates a characteristic kind of four-step sequence, though further pairs of feedback moves followed by corrective action can follow indefinitely.

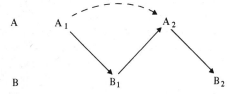

The diagram above shows a case of asymmetrical contingency, with A in charge. A's first move, A_1, produces an unsatisfactory result, B_1, so A modifies his behaviour to A_2, which produces the desired B_2. Note the link

216

$A_1 - A_2$, representing the persistence of A's goal-directed behaviour. This can be seen in the social survey interview (Brenner, 1980):

I_1: asks question
R_1: gives inadequate answer, or does not
understand question
I_2: clarifies and repeats question
R_2: gives adequate answer
or
I_1: asks question
R_1: refuses to answer
I_2: explains purpose and importance of survey;
repeats question
R_2: gives adequate answer

The model can be extended to cases where both interactors are pursuing goals simultaneously, as in the following example, from a selection interview:

I_1: How well did you do at physics at school?
R_1: Not very well, I was better at chemistry.
I_2: What were your A-level results?
R_2: I got a C in physics, but an A in chemistry.
I_3: That's very good.

There are two four-step sequences here: $I_1 R_1 I_2 R_2$ and $R_1 I_2 R_2 I_3$. There is persistence and continuity between R_1 and R_2, as well as between I_1 and I_2. Although I has the initiative, R can also pursue his goals.

The destructive social techniques which Berne (1966) called 'games' are instances of social-skill strategies used by one person to another's disadvantage. For example in 'Rapo' a woman signals that she is available and a man pursues her: as soon as he has committed himself she rejects him. The woman enjoys both the pursuit and the pleasure of rejecting her pursuer.

It has long been recognised that in the performance of motor skills there is a hierarchy of plans and goals, and this was embodied in the Miller, Galanter and Pribram (1960) account of behaviour. A motorist has the main goal of driving to some destination; subgoals are the points in between; these in turn have several levels of subordinate goals before the level of the actual manipulation of the car's controls is reached. At the higher levels there are consciously chosen plans; at the lower levels automatic sequences of behaviour are run off.

The selection interview referred to above has four main episodes, as shown in Fig. 8.2: (1) greeting, informal chat; (2) interviewer asks questions; (3) candidate asks questions; (4) ending. Each of these episodes has subgoals, each of which may in turn have further subgoals. Some of these units of the interview consist of repeated cycles, as will be shown below.

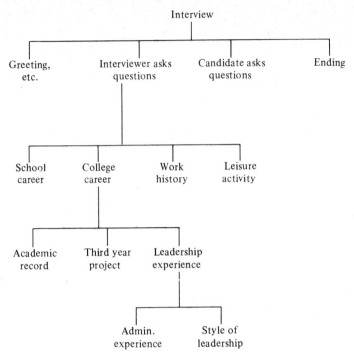

Fig. 8.2. Episodes of a selection interview.

Cycles and episodes

Ethological research into sequences has often located repeated cycles of behaviour, for example in individual grooming and in pairs of courting birds. Repeated cycles are also found in human social behaviour, and they vary with the situation. We have already seen a typical interview cycle: question–inadequate answer–revised question–better answer. Bellack *et al.* (1966) found that the commonest cycle in teaching was solicit–respond–react. Flanders (1970) found a variety of teaching cycles, as shown in Fig. 8.3, and maintained that the skill of teaching consisted in part in the ability to shift from cycle to cycle.

The earliest social behaviour of infants shows the repetition of complete cycles, such as peek-a-boo, and other mother–infant games such as the mother labelling objects for the child (Ninio and Bruner, 1978). An episode may be defined as a segment of a social encounter which is characterised by some internal homogeneity, such as the pursuit of a particular goal, a particular activity, topic of conversation or mood, a particular spatial location, or individuals taking particular roles. Episodes may be identified by the investigator, or a sample of judges may be used to determine the

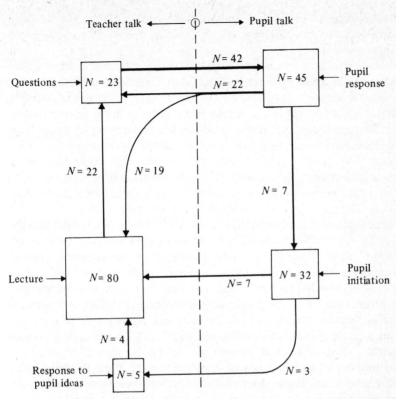

Fig. 8.3. Flanders' (1970) cycles of interaction in the classroom. Numbers inside boxes, and the sizes of the boxes, show how often a 3-second unit of e.g. lecture is followed by a second unit of the same kind. (© 1970 Addison–Wesley Publishing Co. Reprinted with permission.)

episode boundaries. Judges observe the action, or a video-tape of it, and mark the main breakpoints. As we said above, there is a high level of agreement between judges over where these breakpoints are. Episodes are like miniature situations in that they have a beginning and an end, and have to be signalled and often negotiated. An interviewer might indicate that the serious part of the interview has started by a change of expression and the picking up of some relevant papers; a hostess might announce the end of dinner by rising from the table. An episode is a larger unit of behaviour than a cycle, and may consist of repeated cycles.

Some social episodes e.g. greetings, farewells and Goffman's (1971) remedial sequence, do not involve repeated cycles but a once-through series. These are non-Markovian. Kendon and Ferber (1973) described greetings as a sequence of four main moves: mutual gaze–wave–smile–voc- alisation/physical approach–aversion of face–grooming/mutual gaze–bodily contact–smile–vocalisation/orientation shift–conversation. Gazing and smiling occur at two different points in the sequence as parts of more complex social acts.

Episode structure is found in the play of young children. In her study of fantasy play in three- to five-year-olds, Garvey (1977) found that this took the form of complete episodes, e.g. of shopping or going to the doctor's; each participant would take a special role and speak in the proper tone of voice. Blurton-Jones (1972) factor-analysed his elements of play on the basis of the frequency with which they occurred during five-minute observation periods. The factors therefore represent elements that occur together in time. There were three factors: (i) rough-and-tumble play (laugh, run, wrestle, etc.) versus work (i.e. painting, etc.); (ii) aggression (frown, hit, push, etc.); and (iii) social (point, give, receive, talk, smile).

In the study of behaviour in the classroom it has been pointed out that the cycles are not really repeated, since different questions and answers are involved. Taba (1966) introduced the concept of the 'complex chain of reasoning', referring to sequences of classroom interaction that lead to higher levels of pupil thought. Teachers could be trained to generate such sequences. Smith *et al.* (1967) identified the 'venture', which is 'a segment of discourse consisting of a set of utterances dealing with a single topic and having a single overarching content objective' (p. 6). Eight different kinds of venture are distinguished – reason, evaluation, interpretation, etc. Each has a number of special kinds of moves within it. Nuthall (1968) had a similar scheme and found that certain kinds of venture were more successful than others. For concept learning, greater success was obtained with a combination of descriptive and instantial moves.

It has often been suggested that doctor–patient interviews fall into a series of fairly distinct phases or episodes. Byrne and Long (1976) reported the following phases:

1. relating to the patient
2. discussing the reason for the patient's attendance
3. conducting a verbal or physical examination or both
4. consideration of patient's condition
5. detailing treatment or further investigation
6. terminating

They found that all six phases occurred in only 63 per cent of interviews, and that sometimes part of the sequence was repeated.

Bales (1950) thought that there were three phases to group meetings, which came in a certain order (orientation, evaluation and control), though the Bales and Strodtbeck (1951) study showed that these are not clearly separate phases. Something like these phases can be found whenever there is problem-solving and decision-taking, as in committee work and negotiation. The doctor–patient episodes can be seen as finer divisions of the Bales phases: evaluation divides into (*a*) discovering the reason for the patient's attendance and (*b*) conducting a verbal or physical examination. These episodes have to come in the order they do – it would be impossible to give the diagnosis before the examination. In teaching, on the other hand, there may be a number of fairly independent episodes, and the order may be unimportant. We suggest that social encounters usually have a five-episode structure:

1. greeting
2. establishing the relationship, clarifying roles
3. the task
4. re-establishing the relationship
5. parting

The task, episode 3, in turn often has several episodes, which may come in a fixed order, depending on the task. And each of these in turn has repeated cycles built out of two-step adjacency pairs and four-step social-skill sequences.

Social encounters start with a greeting episode and end with a parting episode. Kendon and Ferber (1973) showed how greetings consist of three main parts: the distant salutation, the approach phase and the close phase. Collet (1980) has found that partings in Anglo-American society have three similar phases, in reverse order; in an African tribe, the Mossi, he found a similar symmetry in their very different forms of greeting and parting. Schegloff and Sacks (1973) have described the ways in which people start the endings of a conversation with, for example, 'OK', 'We-ell' or 'So-oo', making arrangements for the next meeting, or suggesting something the other person should do at this point.

We have conducted a study of episode structure. The beginnings of a number of situations were briefly introduced, and subjects asked to write a sketch of how the situation might develop. They were then asked to parse their scripts into the main episodes, and to parse the episodes into sub-episodes. There was considerable agreement on the main episodes; these were described in fewer words than the sub-episodes, and the episodes fitted the schema above. In the case of purely social encounters it is not clear whether the task is omitted, or whether the 'task' consists of eating and drinking, or of information exchange. There was considerable agreement on the phase sequence for each situation. For example when a wife calls on a new neighbour, it was agreed that the following episodes would occur: (1) greeting, (2) wife admires house, (3) neighbour provides coffee etc., (4) exchange of information about jobs, husbands, interests, etc., (5) arrange to meet again, introduce husbands, (6) parting. In our scheme the 'work' can be identified as episode 4, information exchange, though it could be argued that hospitality (episode 3), the provision of food and drink, is the equivalent of work here.

Rules and roles

The rules of a situation influence the sequence of events. We discussed the sequence in an auction sale earlier. This is most obviously true of games, and a not very helpful example from some of the rules of cricket is given below:

CRICKET

(as explained to a foreign visitor)

You have two sides, one out in the field and one in.
Each man that's in the side that's in goes out and when he's out he comes in and the next man goes in until he's out.
When they are all out the side that's out comes in and the side that's been in goes out and tries to get those coming in out.
Sometimes you get men still in and not out.
When both sides have been in and out including the not outs
THAT'S THE END OF THE GAME
HOWZAT!

(from an anonymous tea-towel)

The sequence of events in formal situations is also greatly affected by the rules, but this is true in addition of less formal situations. Schank and Abelson (1977) have given an account of this in terms of the knowledge a person would need to have, or how a computer would need to be programmed, to cope with common social situations, like going to a restaurant. It needs a certain body of knowledge to understand stories like the following:

'John went to a restaurant. He ordered a hamburger. It was cold when the waitress brought it. He left her a very small tip.'

'Willa was hungry. She took out the Michelin guide.'

Schank and Abelson say that we know the 'scripts' for these situations, i.e. have organised knowledge about them.

The script is their central concept: the restaurant script, for example, describes the sequence of events at a restaurant for the four main episodes – enter, order, eat and exit. Scripts incorporate the kind of features we have been considering: *goals*, and the relations between them; *plans*, knowledge of the sequence of elements which will realise the goals; *elements* of behaviour, e.g. order, eat, pay, leave, tip; *roles*, e.g. of waiter and diner; and *physical equipment*, such as menu, food. The *rules* are implicit in the scripts, especially role scripts. And there are 'interpersonal themes', which are scripts for love, father–son interaction, etc. This scheme does not include the skills or difficulties of situations, but it does formalise much of the conceptual knowledge needed in a situation.

The way in which one utterance or other element would follow another depends on the properties of the situation. Thus the significance of 'Can I pay the bill?' would be quite different and lead to different answers if addressed to (*a*) a waiter, (*b*) another diner, (*c*) a bank manager. The same applies to the sequence of events in a game of cricket; it is necessary to understand the game to know what will happen next after (*a*) six balls have been bowled, (*b*) ten men are out, (*c*) the ball reaches the boundary, etc.

Sequences also depend on the role relations between people, as the example of paying the bill showed. Victorian parents liked their children to be 'seen and not heard', which is one kind of discourse (Fishman, 1972). Wittgenstein (1953) thought that the conversation between a builder and his assistant would consist solely of directions from the builder. With more enlightened skills of supervision, the builder would ask the assistant for his suggestions, listen to his ideas, and ask him how he was getting on. The motives of the builder here are more complex: he wants to tell the assistant what to do, but he also wants to motivate him, make use of his skills and knowledge, and keep him happy (Argyle, 1972).

Jones and Gerard (1967) suggested that there are four different kinds of dyadic encounter, in terms of who is reacting to whom. Their scheme is shown in Fig. 8.4.

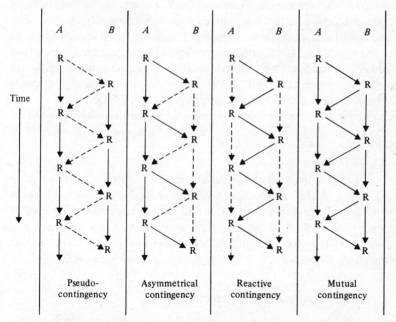

Fig. 8.4. Classes of social interaction in terms of contingency. (After Jones and Gerard, 1967.)

Pseudo-contingency. Here neither interactor is reacting to the other, except as regards timing. Examples are people acting in a play, or enacting a ritual, such as greeting or saying farewell. Greetings and farewells are a little different, in that there is some variation and interaction. Such formal sequences are taken by Harré and Secord (1972) and Goffman (1971) as a model for other situations; our view is that they lack some of the key properties of other kinds of sequence. In pseudo-contingencies the sequence is totally predictable from the rules; there is no variation within the rules, except in style.

Official ceremonies have a complete plan of the interaction from the outset. It requires more skill to design such ceremonies than to take part in them. The same is true to some extent of such formal occasions as birthday parties, retirement presentations, dances and conferences.

Asymmetrical contingency. Here only one person has a plan, while the others are mainly reacting to what he does. Examples are teaching and interviewing. However the person being interviewed does have some initiative; he gives longer or shorter replies, he may pursue his own plan, e.g. to impress the interviewer (see p. 217), and he may ask questions.

Reactive contingency. Here each person reacts to the last move by the other. Examples are rambling conversations. The sequence is limited by the universal rules of all social behaviour, and the particular rules of the situation, which will allow only certain kinds of utterances, for example, and certain sequences. Thus a conversation in a pub is somewhat different from a conversation at a polite dinner party. In either case the sequence could be described, and to a limited extent predicted, by the rules governing which sequences are allowable as sensible sequences of social behaviour, and the probabilities (in each situation) that the allowable moves will be made.

Mutual contingency. Here each interactor is pursuing his own goals and is reacting to the moves made by the other, and neither is in charge of the situation. Examples are negotiation and serious discussion. There are no sharp dividing lines between this kind of encounter and asymmetrical contingency (where the subordinate person has *some* initiative) or reactive contingency (where neither person is pursuing a particular goal).

Skilled sequences of interaction

There is considerable skill in the construction of single utterances. Bates (1976) found that Italian children aged two would say the equivalent of 'I want a sweet', but by six, could say 'please', rephrase it as a request, with question intonation, as a conditional ('I would like'), and use formal pronouns in addressing the other. Adult polite speech goes a long way beyond this, as in 'If you're passing the letter box, could you post this letter for me?', for which it might be hard to provide grammatical rules. Being polite cannot be reduced entirely to grammar however; how polite is 'Please could you tell me why you gave use such a terrible lecture this evening?'? Giving orders or instructions needs skill: 'do X' does not get things done, in most settings, even when the speaker has the power to command. Orders are usually disguised as suggestions, or even questions.

What is usually regarded as 'tact' requires more social skill. Tact could be defined as the production of socially effective utterances in difficult situations; these are usually utterances that influence others in a desired way, without upsetting them or others present. How do you congratulate the winner without upsetting the loser? What do you say to a child who has just been expelled from school? This is clearly an area of social skills, where the skill consists in finding the right verbal message; again it seems to have little to do with grammar. McPhail (1967) presented teenagers with written descriptions of a variety of difficult social situations and asked them what they would say. The younger ones opted for boldly direct, often aggressive ('experimental') utterances, but the older ones preferred more skilled, indeed 'tactful' remarks (Fig. 8.5).

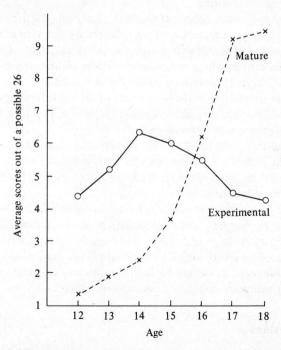

Fig. 8.5. Experimental and mature solutions to social problems. (After McPhail, 1967.)

In our work with socially unskilled neurotic patients, we often found them unable to sustain a simple conversation (Trower, Bryant and Argyle, 1978). Here are some common types of failure:

1. Failure to make nonverbal responses and give feedback (head-nods, smiles, uh-huh noises) as a listener.
2. Failure to pursue any persistent plans, producing only passive responses.
3. Attempts to make conversation by producing unwanted information ('I went to Weston-super-Mare last year').
4. Failure to make proactive move after replying to a question ('Where do you come from?' 'Swansea . . .': end of conversation).

In order to identify these forms of failure it is necessary to understand the structure of normal conversation. It is then possible to train people in how to do it. The general procedure is instruction and demonstration followed by role-playing and play-back of tape- or videotape-recordings. Sometimes special exercises are used. For example, lack of persistent planning can be tackled by practice at a simple skill, such as interviewing, where the performer is in charge. He is asked to make notes beforehand, and plan the whole session. Failure to make nonverbal responses can be dealt with by playing back a video-recording (Trower *et al.*, 1978).

In the WAIS, and some other intelligence tests, one of the subtests consists of several series of pictures, which subjects are asked to put in the right order to make a story (Psychological Corporation, 1957). Complex professional skills require the construction of quite elaborate sequences. Here are some of the points we have made about teaching:

1. A teacher should follow the statement of a principle by an example.
2. He should be able to establish certain cycles of interaction, such as lecture–question–answer–comment.
3. He should use a series of cycles to build up educational episodes, intended to teach a certain body of knowledge.
4. He should be responsive to feedback, and modify his style of behaviour when necessary.

In some professional skills the episodes have to come in a certain order, as in doctor–patient encounters, and in negotiation. In some cases the time scale extends beyond a single encounter, as in psychotherapy sessions. In making friends there is a very long time scale: there is a gradual increase in self-disclosure and trust, discovery of shared views and interests, and the establishment of mutually rewarding patterns of interaction.

Conclusions

We have not succeeded in uncovering the principles of sequence construction to the point where we could predict how a sequence would develop, or to the point where we could write the rules of composition. On the other hand we have identified some of the main structures out of which interaction sequences are composed, and these have been found to be useful in training those who find social behaviour difficult. These structures include the sequence of episodes, putting the episodes of task performance in the right order, the different contingencies, repeated cycles, four-step sequences directed towards goals, the rule-system of the situation and two-step linkages. Some situations, such as going to the doctor, are more highly structured and predictable than more informal situations such as a casual chat. Sometimes there are alternative routes to the same goals.

Several of these principles indicate that sequences vary between situations. Are there any universal principles? Some two-step links are very common, though not universal, like question–answer, request–comply or refuse, joke–laugh, etc. The four-step goal-directed sequence is probably universal, though the actual goals and sequences vary. Similarly the details of repeated cycles vary between situations. We suggested earlier that encounters have a basic five-episode structure, though episode 3, the task, divides up into a series of sub-episodes specific to each task.

Can the situational variations between sequences be given a functional explanation? In our study of doctor–patient interaction we found that one of the main goals of patients is 'seek help, advice, reassurance', and that a common two-step sequence is 'ask if disease is serious–reassure that illness/disease is not serious'. Four-step goal-directed sequences are clearly functional. Cycles of the type 'lecture–question–answer–comment' (in the classroom) are processes of social interaction which have been found to be successful, in this case in attaining the goal of teaching. Rules governing the order of events have presumably emerged, like other rules, because they help in goal attainment. Episodes are often ordered – e.g. the six doctor–patient episodes – because tasks have to be done in a particular order.

8.1. A study of sequential structure using chain analysis

J. A. GRAHAM, M. ARGYLE, D. CLARKE AND G. MAXWELL

[A fuller version of this study is given in part of Graham *et al.* (in press).]

The stimulus material used in this experiment was derived from experiment 7.1. In this study the number of elements considered important, in each of four situations, was reduced by collapsing into categories the elements thought to be equivalent by 65 per cent of more of the subject sample. Equivalence was based on the substitutability of a set of elements (not equivalence of meaning). The criterion for substitutability of elements was that they could always sensibly and acceptably replace one another at any point in time in the typical order of events in a particular situation. For example, the elements 'drink tea' and 'drink coffee' could be thought to be substitutable for each other, but not for 'drink alcohol', if every time it was appropriate to drink tea it was also appropriate to drink coffee without changing the nature of a typical 'evening at home' and if drinking alcohol would not be usual but would make it a special and different situation.

Aim

The aim of this experiment was to discover the sequential structure of elements (some of which were single elements and some of which were categories of equivalent elements) for four situations by asking subjects what they saw as the typical sequence or order of events occurring for most people in each situation (i.e. to capture the shared idea of what happens).

Method

A group of housewives who had some experience of the four situations was tested individually. The elements were each typed on a separate card, except that where the element formed part of a group of equivalent items several of the most general items were shown on the card as examples. Subjects were told that we were interested in finding out the typical sequence of events in each situation for people in general. They were told to consider each situation in turn, and arrange the cards in a row in the order in which the events usually occur in the situation (like a time-table of events). They were also given blank cards to duplicate any elements they thought should occur more than once in the sequence.

Results

Transitional probability matrices. The sequential order of events given for each subject was transferred to an $N \times N$ matrix for each situation (where N is the total number of elements or categories arrived at from the equivalence stage). The matrix recorded the frequencies with which each element was followed by each element. The matrix was then treated by chain analysis to find the larger units, i.e. strings of two, three, four, etc., elements. This is done by finding the highest cell frequency (e.g. nine of the ten subjects) with which one element is followed by another, and renaming this pair of elements with a letter, e.g. A, as a new two-item unit. The data are then rescanned and every occurrence of the pair of elements making up this new unit is deleted and replaced by the letter A. The matrix is then extended to incorporate the new unit by deleting the old frequency for one element following another, and recording the frequencies with which the two-item unit precedes and is followed by other elements or units.

Larger units (of three, four, five items) are dealt with in a similar way. For example, if the next highest cell frequency in the matrix is eight and this is recorded for the new two-item unit A followed by element number 13, then (A–13) would become a new three-item unit, renamed B in the original data. The matrix is extended to incorporate the new unit B by deleting the old frequency of eight for (A–13) and recording the frequencies of B preceding and following other items.

The sequential structure. The highest frequencies were recorded for the visit to the doctor situation and the lowest for the evening at home. The highest-order units (five-item units) were also obtained for the visit to the doctor; four-item units were obtained in the sport and date situations, and the smallest units (two items) for the evening at home. The number of sequential units (irrespective of size) was highest for the visit to the doctor situation, for which twelve units were obtained, and lowest for the evening at home, where only four units were obtained. In all situations except the evening at home certain elements tended to appear early or late in the sequence, but these were mainly concerned with arrival and departure.

The sequential structure of the elements making up the visit to the doctor situation is shown in Fig. 8.6. This shows how elements and categories of equivalent elements are joined sequentially in time to form higher-order units of behaviour. The key shows details of the elements and the relationships between them.

The elements which make up the higher-order units in the later part of the situation are listed below in order:

n: i–17 (three-item unit)		take off clothes → examination of patient → put clothes on again
j: 48–49 (two-item unit)		ask if illness/disease is serious → reassure that illness/disease is not serious
x: 1–h (four-item unit)	(two-item unit)	suggest treatment → explain how treatment works → prescribe medicine → explain how to take medicine/tablets
v: 46–47 (two-item unit)		discuss domestic problems → discuss personal needs
s: 12–k (three-item unit)	(two-item unit)	give cue to departure → thank → leave doctor's surgery
t: 23–25 (two-item unit)		make further appointment if necessary → check out with receptionist

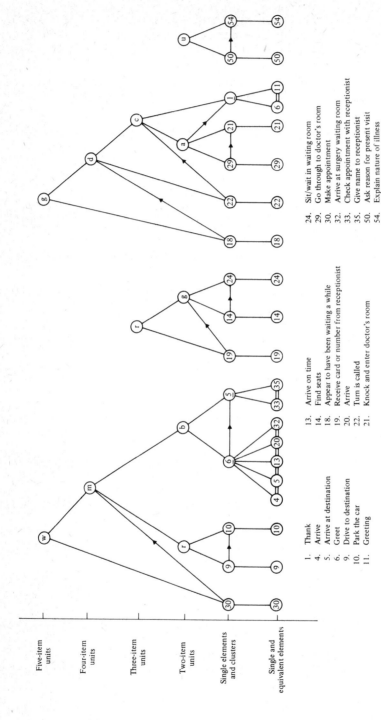

Fig. 8.6. Sequential structure of part of the visit to the doctor situation. The early part of the situation only is represented. Numbers represent single elements; these do not have other elements equivalent to them. Underlined numbers represent clusters; these consist of elements that are equivalent/substitutable at the same point in the sequence. Letters represent two-, three-, four- or five-item units; these consist of single elements that are linked sequentially in time to form higher-order units. Arrows

1. Thank
4. Arrive
5. Arrive at destination
6. Greet
9. Drive to destination
10. Park the car
11. Greeting

13. Arrive on time
14. Find seats
18. Appear to have been waiting a while
19. Receive card or number from receptionist
20. Arrive
22. Turn is called
21. Knock and enter doctor's room

24. Sit/wait in waiting room
29. Go through to doctor's room
30. Make appointment
32. Arrive at surgery waiting room
33. Check appointment with receptionist
35. Give name to receptionist
50. Ask reason for present visit
54. Explain nature of illness

o: 16–27	depart →	
(two-item	go to dispensary to collect prescription	
unit)		

e: 7–8	drive home →	
(two-item	arrive home	
unit)		

Discussion

We have shown that use of a hierarchical classification scheme can yield larger units of behaviour made up of lower-order units. However, the chains are not very long and are in some cases rather obvious. The findings suggest that there is more agreement about some situations than others. The finding that the visit to the doctor was the most structured situation in all respects and provided the least room for variation is not surprising because in this primarily task-oriented situation (dealing with the patient's illness) some elements *must* logically follow others, e.g. the medicine should be prescribed after the patient has been examined, not before. For the evening at home it appears that a lot of variation in the order of events is possible without disruption of the situation.

9

Concepts and cognitive structures

Introduction

In order to behave effectively in any situation people need to possess appropriate concepts. It would not be possible to play cricket without knowing the meaning of 'out', 'over', etc., or to play chess without knowing what a queen is, and what 'check' means.

We can see how concepts are related to the goals of behaviour, in terms of the motor-skills model of social behaviour (Argyle and Kendon, 1967), as shown in Fig. 8.1. In the first place an interactor needs to perceive and interpret the behaviour of others, in a relevant way. A motorist needs to perceive the traffic signals and signposts rather than the contents of shops, and to watch the speedometer reading rather than the state of the car's carpet. And he needs to know what the traffic signals and the speedometer reading mean. In a social situation an interactor needs categories in order to classify:

1. *Persons*: e.g. a teacher needs to distinguish between pupils of different intelligence and motivation, since they would need to be handled differently.
2. *Social structure*, i.e. the relations between those present, in terms of status, role, friendship, etc.
3. *Elements of interaction*: e.g. between friendly and hostile, and further categories in particular situations (discussed in Chapter 7).
4. *Relevant objects* of attention: e.g. parts of the physical environment and task-related objects, such as the pieces at chess.

In addition, people need sufficient cognitive equipment to understand what is happening, and to decide how to deal with the situation. A motorist needs to understand something about the workings of cars, and something about local geography. When, for example, he sees a signpost he can then understand where he is, and what direction he should take to reach his goal. In social situations an interactor needs a similar kind of understanding.

Interpreting another's behaviour. He needs to understand why another person is, for example, aggressive, depressed or uncooperative.

Planning his own behaviour. When he has correctly perceived and interpreted another's behaviour, he has to decide how best to

232

proceed. This can be seen in terms of expectancies – he has to know which behaviour will probably have the desired consequences. It also involves understanding, just as a motorist needs to understand engines and maps.

It is unfortunate, from our point of view, that most research in the field of cognitive structures has concentrated on individual differences. However it has also been found that when people have similar constructs they can communicate better. Runkel (1956) devised a measure of the similarity of cognitive dimensions between two people, and found that the greater the similarity the more effective the communication was. For example, students with similar dimensions to their instructors obtained better grades. It was not necessary for two people to have the same opinions, i.e. to place objects at the same points on dimensions, provided they used the same dimensions. Triandis (1960) found that people in laboratory situations and in industry could communicate better if they had similar personal constructs; Landfield and Nawas (1964) found that there was greater improvement in psychotherapy when patients and therapists shared more personal constructs, though again it was not necessary for them to agree in their evaluation of objects. These studies show, therefore, that shared constructs in situations are desirable; we shall show later that situations produce characteristic sets of constructs which are related to the goals of situations, and we shall also show that situations defined by the same term are not always similarly perceived (experiment 9.3).

One of the most important approaches to the analysis of constructs is the repertory grid method of Kelly (1955). Here an individual's 'own constructs' are elicited by the triad method and a grid of constructs and objects is completed, followed by factor analysis to reveal the main factors; a measure of complexity can be obtained from this. It is possible to extract a 'consensus grid' of the constructs shared by most group members. It is clearly recognised that constructs have a limited 'range of convenience', i.e. that they only apply to a limited range of objects. It does not make sense to ask people to rate false teeth as 'religious' or 'atheist', for example (Bannister and Mair, 1968). Applying this to situations we can see that the concepts needed to distinguish between cricket bowlers may not apply so readily to politicians, and that the conceptual schemes for understanding committee meetings may not be of much help in restaurants. Further the way people construe others is partly dependent on the situation in which they are perceived (experiment 9.3).

In the semantic differential (Osgood *et al.*, 1957) subjects are asked to make ratings on scales provided by the investigators, and the same scales are used for all objects to be rated. Jaspars (1966) found that normals were more able than neurotics to express themselves in terms of such provided constructs; Harvey, Hunt and Schroder (1961) distinguished between persons with 'concrete' cognitive structures, who had more difficulty in extending the range of constructs, and 'abstract' people. However Osgood *et al.* recognised that there is 'scale–concept interaction', i.e. that certain scales may load on the evaluative dimension for one object but not another, so that a separate set of scales may have to be devised for each object or range of objects.

There are several aspects of cognitive structure which we should consider.

(*a*) *Dimensions or constructs.* These can be established by repertory grid techniques followed by factor analysis, by semantic differential and factor analysis, and by multidimensional scaling of ratings, or simply by asking people to rate dimensions for relevance.

(*b*) *Relations between constructs.* Two constructs may be related in several ways. They may be correlated with one another – perhaps forming part of a larger factor. There may be asymmetrical relations, as when one construct is subordinate to a broader one, in a hierarchical cluster. One construct may imply another logically, through empirical causation, or emotional association.

(*c*) *Division of dimensions into categories.* The same dimension may be divided into large or small categories, and in different ways. Hovland and Sherif (1952) found that people with extreme judgements rejected a larger number of scale items, the rejected ones being regarded as equivalent.

(*d*) *Explanatory concepts.* There are many possible explanatory systems, including the whole of psychology, not to mention astrology, phrenology and black magic. There is no one way of discovering these, though depth interviews have been used most often (e.g. Smith, Bruner and White, 1956).

As Tajfel (1978) and others have shown, cognitive constructs are functional in relation to action. Individuals categorise objects as equivalent if they are going to be treated similarly, and distinguish them if they are going to be treated differently. Categorisation simplifies, in order to act as a guide for action. Gardeners need to be able to distinguish 'weeds' from other plants. Cliff and Young (1968) did a multidimensional scaling classification of judgements of simulated air-raids by US naval officers; the raids were clustered in three groups, each corresponding to a definite course of action. An important principle in selecting constructs is social consensus – every culture and subgroup selects different categories, related to the life and needs of that society.

Constructs for persons

The traditional method of discovering the dimensions which people use to conceptualise and discriminate between each other is factor analysis. Subjects are asked to rate a number of target persons on a series of seven-point scales, and these ratings are factor-analysed. If the repertory grid method is used, then instead of the investigator imposing his constructs, the subjects' own constructs are elicited, and ratings on them are factor-analysed. Another method is multidimensional scaling: similarity judgements, or ratings on scales, are analysed to reveal the underlying dimensional structure.

The functional hypothesis here is that other people will be categorised in ways that are relevant to the purpose of the encounter, the goals of the situation. For example, if the situation is primarily a social occasion it would be expected that evaluation would be important; in a task situation ability at the task would be expected to be important.

In the majority of studies subjects have been asked for ratings of other people without the situation being specified, so presumably the raters would average across a range of situations. If members of groups are asked to rate each other, they use dimensions such as:

1. leadership, influence, initiative
2. evaluation, liking
3. task competence (Tagiuri, 1958)

Recent studies using multidimensional scaling have produced other dimensions. Davison and Jones (1976) studied ratings of Officers' Training Corps members by other members and students, and found these dimensions:

1. status
2. professional orientation, group membership
3. political affiliation

Members of groups assess each other in terms of status, liking, etc. They also perceive the structure of the group, in terms of perceived choice and rejection, dyads and cliques, and status differences. Tagiuri (1958) found that (1) group members think there is more reciprocation of positive and negative choices than there actually is, (2) if they choose someone they think he is more popular than he actually is – because they think that the people whom they like choose each other, (3) if they reject someone they think he is more unpopular than he actually is.

How far are these dimensions universal, and how far do they vary between situations? Forgas, Argyle and Ginsburg (1979), as reported in experiment 9.1, used multidimensional scaling for ratings of behaviour in four situations. In two of the situations (pub and morning coffee), 'evaluation' was found to be the first dimension, followed by 'extroversion' and 'self-confidence'; in the third situation (a party at the boss's house) the dimensions were 'self-confidence', 'warmth' and 'ingratiation'. In the work situation (a seminar), the dimensions were 'dominance', 'creativity' and 'supportiveness'. This study clearly confirms the hypothesis, though the

235

party involved the unanticipated dimension of self-confidence. In this experiment it was also found that the perceived structure of the group varied with the situation. For example status was important mainly in the seminar situation; here the senior academics were clearly above the graduate students. At the party there were no dominance differences apart from the position of the host.

In a second study, by Argyle, Ginsburg, Forgas and Campbell, reported as experiment 9.2, subjects were asked to rate the relevance of constructs to situations. A 'friendly–extroversion', or evaluation factor was important in all four situations; however work-related scales were judged to be much more relevant to the work situations compared with the social situations. This study suggests that the evaluative dimension is used in all situations; the previous study found this factor in three situations, but not in the seminar.

When people are engaged on specific tasks, do they use constructs for persons that are directly related to those tasks? We have already had one example of this: the dimensions of dominance, creativity and supportiveness at a seminar. Cohen (1961), following the Zajonc theory of cognitive tuning, found that when subjects thought they would have to transmit their impressions of someone to a third person, they overlooked contradictory components, and formed a simple, homogeneous impression. Woodward (1960), in an interview study of shop-assistants, found that they developed categories of difficult customer – 'elderly frustrated spinsters', 'peppery colonels', etc. Another source of evidence in this area is research on leadership in informal groups; it has been widely found that such leadership has little relation to personality traits, but depends mainly on ability at the group task (Argyle, 1969). It follows that group members can distinguish between one another on the basis of possession of these situation-relevant abilities.

People in a number of professions have to learn to categorise others in specialised ways. Policemen are trained to distinguish those who are engaged in illegal behaviour from others (Sacks, 1972); selection interviewers are trained to look for evidence of properties such as stability, achievement motivation, creativity, etc. (Argyle, 1978b); doctors, dentists, psychiatrists, all have their category systems for classifying their clients.

Another situational source of constructs for others is the nature of the relationship with them, which may reflect different patterns of motivation toward them. Argyle *et al.* (experiment 9.2) found that 'friendly–extroversion' was judged to be relevant for all nine target groups used. The other constructs varied greatly between target groups, and seemed to reflect the relationship with them. For children, for example, 'well-behaved' and 'noisy' were used (but not 'radical–conservative', etc.); for professional people 'competent' and 'intelligent', and for opposite-sex friends 'attractive', 'considerate' and 'well-behaved', were relevant constructs.

A further feature of the situation which affects the use of constructs is the presence or absence of norms for various kinds of behaviour. If a person behaves in an unusual, or rule-breaking way, then his behaviour is attributed to him rather than to the situation. Sometimes he will be categorised as a deviate of one kind or another. Calhoun, Selby and Wroten (1977) found that a young woman seen as crying and mumbling in a job interview was thought to be more psychologically disturbed than when the same behaviour took place in her own room.

When different social groups come into contact, or expect to do so, the salience of constructs is affected. Tajfel (1970) proposed the following theory: members of groups attempt to attain and preserve a positive social identity; this is done by a favourable evaluation of properties possessed by the group which distinguish it from other groups; comparisons between the group and other groups are focused on these value-laden dimensions. Doise (1979) showed how this is partly a matter of (*a*) selection of relevant negative attributes, (*b*) justification of own behaviour, and (*c*) anticipatory representation. In each case group goals lead to certain cognitive representations of the two groups, which in turn direct or justify behaviour.

(*a*) *Selection.* Avigdor (1953) arranged different relationships between youth clubs rehearsing for a theatrical performance. Where there was unfavourable interaction, e.g. having to rehearse at the same time on the same stage, each group rated the other as cheating, selfish, etc., but not as slovenly or depressed, i.e. they selected features which might reasonably induce hostile behaviour. Wilson, Chun and Kayatani (1965) used an experimental game with two pairs of subjects; after interaction the opposing pair were seen as more competitive and hostile, ratings of partner moved in the opposite direction, and ratings on other scales were unaffected.

(*b*) *Justification.* Racial stereotypes can often be interpreted as justifying hostile behaviour. Groups will try to find negative constructs for other groups, and favourable concepts for their own group. Mann (1963) found that South African Hindus accept their inferiority in economic and scientific fields, but believe that they are superior in spiritual, social and practical fields. Lemaine (1966) created competitions between groups of children at a holiday camp in such a way that one group was always at a disadvantage through having fewer resources. The disadvantaged groups managed to discover dimensions of success such that they could claim to have done better than the other group, e.g. by having made nicer surrounds when building a hut.

(*c*) *Anticipation.* Doise (1969) found that subjects who knew that they were shortly going to play a competitive game devalued the opposite side, by rating them as low in cooperative motives, before the game started.

237

Doise and Weinberger (1972–3) found that when pairs of boys were about to enter a competitive situation with pairs of girls they formed a more negative and more feminine image of the girls than when boys and girls were going to act together.

Tajfel (1957) also argued that the effect of categorisation is to exaggerate differences between the groups thus contrasted. Tajfel and Wilkes (1963) found that if the four largest of eight lines were labelled A, and the four shortest B, subjects underestimated the differences within each group and exaggerated the difference between the groups. Secord, Bevan and Katz (1956) found that prejudiced American subjects exaggerated the blackness of blacks – magnifying the true black–white difference. Leach (1966) observed that often there *are* intermediate cases, for example between categories of animals (pets, vermin, farm animals, etc.), but that in these cases the animal in question becomes taboo because no-one knows how to react to them.

Other experiments by Tajfel and colleagues have shown how minimal labelling of random groups by the experimenter can create preferential behaviour towards members of the in-group (e.g. Tajfel, 1970). Turner (1973) found that subjects gave preferential rewards to themselves: as if 'I–other' was the main categorisation. At a second stage in-group favouritism was evoked: now 'in-group versus out-group' was the main categorisation. After this had occurred subjects were willing to award money against their own interest to a member of the in-group.

Many studies have supported the theory that there are pressures for individuals to achieve a state of balance, or congruity, between their attitudes towards different objects. Incongruity or imbalance would occur if person A liked B but did not like something B had done, or if A liked B but B had an attitude towards X that differed from A's attitude. Jaspars (1966) pointed out that these ideas of balance hold only if a single attitudinal dimension is used, e.g. if A uses the same dimensions to evaluate B and B's behaviour. Cognitive conflicts can be resolved by the use of new dimensions. Cohen (1971) found that if, for example, a judge is asked to assess the intelligence of a student who does well in written examinations but badly in orals he will make use of new concepts such as 'difficulties of verbal expression' or 'examination anxiety' to resolve the imbalance. Different dimensions are used to conceptualise people in different spheres of behaviour. Stroebe *et al.* (1970) found that when subjects were asked to rate 'Dr M. as a scientist' and 'Dr M. as a person' (in relation to his wife) they used quite different attributes.

Dimensions for classifying others are organised into more complex structures. The perceived correlations between traits are known as 'implicit personality theories'. Most studies show that there is a strong evaluative factor, i.e. traits are correlated if they have similar evaluation implications.

Peabody (1967) showed that descriptive similarity is also important. The upshot appears to be that both descriptive *and* evaluative consistency are important (Eiser and Stroebe, 1972). Implicit personality theories are found to vary with situation, or at any rate with role: Warr and Knapper (1968) found that bank managers assumed that people who were impulsive were also careless, but students did not think this.

Attribution and explanation

Sometimes it is not sufficient just to perceive what has happened; it is necessary to know why it has happened. Unless events are explained and understood, it is impossible to deal with them effectively. What are the occasions on which such explanations are required? There are several different, though related, conditions.

(*a*) Another person's behaviour may be difficult to deal with: for example he may be aggressive or uncooperative. Unless the reasons for his behaviour can be found it is hard to know how to deal with him.

(*b*) It may be necessary to apportion responsibility or blame; this makes it necessary to decide whether one person or another was responsible, or whether events were due to chance or to environmental pressure.

(*c*) There may be conflicting cues: for example a person might behave in one way in one situation and in a quite different way in a second situation. This makes person perception difficult, and requires some explanation.

(*d*) A person may feel the need to defend his own behaviour; this happens particularly in cases of conflict of interest or where there is a danger that others will evaluate his behaviour negatively. The actor believes that the account he gives justifies his behaviour (Orvis, Kelley and Butler, 1976).

What kinds of explanation do people give? Attribution theory research has found that people offer explanations which vary in three ways. (1) Internal versus external: internal factors are within the person, especially his abilities and efforts; external factors are outside the person, such as the difficulty of the task and chance variations in the situation. (2) Stable versus unstable: ability and difficulty are stable, effort and luck are unstable. (3) Intentional versus unintentional: this cuts across the other classes of explanation, for example internal, unstable and unintentional would include variations due to mood and fatigue (Ickes and Kidd, 1976).

Behaviour may be attributed primarily to the person or to the situation. Jones and Nisbett (1972) found that observers attribute responsibility primarily to situational factors. The currently accepted explanation for this is that observers have a different perspective from actors: observers see actors from outside, see them as fixed and static, and assume that they will behave in a similar way in future situations; actors on the other hand direct their attention to the situation and think that their own future behaviour will depend on the situation. Storms (1973) found that these attributions could be reversed if observers saw video-tapes taken from the actor's point of view, and vice versa. Duval and Wicklund (1972) similarly found that people attribute behaviour to themselves when in a state of 'objective self-awareness', i.e. when in front of mirrors or TV cameras. These differences in attribution have been explained in terms of focus of attention. They could also be interpreted in a functional way: there is no point in attributing one's own behaviour to properties of the self as these are very hard to change, whereas it is useful to be able to seek or to avoid certain situational influences. When other people are observed to behave in different ways, it is easy to focus on individual difference variables; it is necessary to treat them differently, i.e. to suppose that their behaviour is due to dispositional properties.

Individuals often provide attributions of their own behaviour or experiences, either for themselves or for others. The experiments by Schachter and Singer (1962) showed that people decide what emotion they are experiencing partly on the basis of contextual cues. Studies by Storms and Nisbett (1970) and others showed that subjects can be induced to reattribute experiences of unpleasant emotional arousal to external stimuli (e.g. a placebo pill) rather than to internal stimuli. In later experiments it was found that subjects who had been aroused in dissonance experiments sought alternative ways of explaining their arousal, e.g. chose to wait in a room with 'new fluorescent lighting' which made people 'feel very tense or uncomfortable' (Zanna and Cooper, 1976). There are individual differences in the extent to which people feel that they are in control of events, rather than that events are being controlled by other people or by chance (internal versus external controllers). This also depends on the situation. Wortman (1975) found that subjects felt more in control when they had in fact controlled the outcomes, and knew beforehand what outcome they were aiming for. Langer (1975) found that people had a greater feeling of control over a lottery when they could choose a ticket, had become involved with the situation, and were familiar with it. This manipulation is produced by telling subjects that outcomes at a laboratory task are due to skill or chance; alternatively they may find this out in the course of an experiment (Phares, 1976).

Individuals may use what correspond to psychological theories to explain behaviour, particularly if they are psychologists. Bierhof and Bierhof-Alferman (1976) asked German teachers to judge different kinds of explanation for the behaviour of stimulus persons, for which written descriptions were provided. The most widely accepted explanation was in terms of roles, followed by reinforcement and modelling, effects of external conditions, and lastly unconscious motivation. External conditions were chosen more for the stimulus person who made an overall good impression than for a negative stimulus person. Lockhart, Abrahams and Oskerson (1977) found that older children could distinguish between conventions and physical laws better than younger children. Older children realise that conventions can be changed.

What happens if it is impossible to explain another person's behaviour? We have seen that observers make strenuous efforts to do so, for example by inventing extra dimensions. If this fails they may decide that the other person is mad. Scheff (1966) proposed the theory of 'residual rule-breaking': forms of deviance which fall outside familiar categories (delinquency, drink, drugs, etc.) are categorised as 'insanity'.

People may also provide accounts of behaviour that are primarily intended for others. Lyman and Scott (1970) suggested that actors provide such accounts to explain behaviour that might otherwise be misunderstood or disapproved of, and that they have to be of a kind that is acceptable to the audience in question. Sykes and Matza (1957) list the kinds of account given by deviates and delinquents. These consisted of (1) denial of responsibility ('I didn't mean it', 'It was an accident'), (2) denial of injury ('I didn't really hurt him', 'I was only borrowing it'), (3) denial of the victim ('He deserved it'), (4) attacking the accuser ('The police are corrupt and stupid'), (5) appealing to higher loyalties ('It wasn't for me, it was for the gang').

There is a certain amount of evidence that the accounts people give of their own behaviour are different for different recipients. It seems likely that the delinquents studied by Sykes and Matza would have given rather different accounts of their deviant acts to one another, for example. There are perhaps two principles here. (*a*) Accounts are adjusted to the intellectual capacity of receivers; garage mechanics, for example, give a rather simplified version of the mechanical problems of cars to customers compared to those given to other mechanics (Moscovici, 1967). (*b*) Accounts are usually presented that will be evaluated favourably by the hearer. This may involve selecting, out of the many actual causes of behaviour, the one that will appeal most to the listener. Thus lateness might be excused, when one is talking to the boss, by tiredness due to overwork, or failure of public transport, rather than by reference to late-night drinking or too much sex. Accounts can be made acceptable by being cast into the conceptual schemes of the hearer, whether psychiatric, medical, astrological, etc. Accounts would be phrased in terms of concepts in normal use in the group, and for the situation in question.

Understanding situations

What cognitive structures do people need to have in order to behave appropriately and competently in a situation? Do they need to have a full understanding of the goals, the repertoire of elements, the roles, rules, physical setting, behaviour sequences and skills? They probably do need to have some conceptual representation of all these features, and without it they are likely to be socially ineffective.

Let us start with cricket. Clearly a person would not be able to play this game merely by putting on some white trousers and wandering onto the pitch; he would need to have mastered the main features of the game. He would need to know the *goals* of the game (to make more runs than the other side), the main *elements* used (batting and bowling), the *rules* (e.g. how to get people out), the *roles* (wicket-keeper, slips, etc.), the *physical equipment* (bat, ball, crease-lines, etc.). He would need to be able to categorise balls bowled (as leg-breaks, etc.), the bowlers and batsmen, and the condition of the pitch. There are also concepts for various states of the game, or of the players – 'out', 'not out', 'l.b.w.', 'no-ball', 'century', etc. He would need to understand the principles that govern 'declaring' – taking the risk of losing in order to have a chance of winning. He would need to understand something of the strategic interplay between batsmen and bowlers, and much more beside. An experienced and competent player would have very complex conceptual structures. In the case of games it seems that unless a person possesses certain constructs he will not be a very competent performer. Do similar considerations apply to situations other than games? Schank and Abelson (1977) tried to formalise the conceptual information a person would need to have in order to go and eat a meal at a restaurant, how he would need to understand such things as 'menu', 'tip', 'waiter', 'bar', 'dessert' and so on (see p. 222).

The knowledge that interactors have in a situation may vary with their role. Goffman (1956) showed how in many situations in professional life the client is kept in some degree of ignorance of what is going on, and indeed does not understand how the professional performance is managed. This is particularly true of encounters with undertakers, doctors, waiters, and others. Glaser and Strauss (1967) describe the different degrees of awareness on the part of hospital staff and dying patients and their relatives. The staff use a number of techniques to prevent these patients from understanding the true situation. The conceptual schemes used vary in other ways with role. Sewell (1971) compared the perceptions of the environment of engineers and public health officials. The ways in which they thought about problems such as water pollution were quite different, as were the solutions they considered. Sewell and Little (1973) found that environmental activists produced a greater number of repertory grid dimesnions in areas such as pollution and environmental degradation.

The social construction of reality

We have argued so far that constructs are partly a product of situations, and are devised to enable participants to attain situational goals. However there is often more than one set of constructs which will make this possible, as can be seen from the diverse sets of ideas to be found in different cultures and subcultures. Berger and Luckman (1966) have spoken of this process as 'the social construction of reality', and their point of view has been widely adopted. The meaning of events and objects, indeed of every aspect of life, is partly provided by shared social constructions; they tell us the significance of, and how to use, altar and incense, tennis racquets and balls, vintage wine and cars, red flags and hammers and sickles, and so on. The social construction of reality often includes sets of concepts, sometimes very elaborate ones. The point of interest here is that these concepts and constructions are partly arbitrary; they are indeed constrained by situational goals, but a variety of alternative cognitive structures will do the job.

Let us take a number of situations where there are alternative sets of concepts.

1. *Manufacture of e.g. clothes.* This can be done in a great variety of ways, corresponding to different stages of technology; compare an automated factory making artificial fabrics with primitive methods of spinning and weaving. There would probably be some shared concepts, to do with thread thickness and quality, and the design of clothes; otherwise the differences are immense.

2. *Healing.* There are a variety of methods that have been used to heal – magical methods, modern medicine, psychoanalysis, faith healing and acupuncture, for example. Psychoanalysis and their patients use concepts such as projection, transference, denial, sexual symbolism, father figure, etc., as part of their normal vocabulary, to interpret the patient's behaviour and what is happening in the therapeutic session. Psychoanalysts interpret a variety of physical illnesses in terms of unconscious motivation and symbolism. The same illnesses are likely to be interpreted very differently by members of certain religious sects (in terms of devils or punishment), by orthodox doctors (in terms of germs, glands, the contents of the blood) and by eastern doctors who use acupuncture. This example fits our functional model rather well: in each case there is a clear goal – to heal the patient – but the means used are very different and the concepts used are directly related to the proposed means. If the intended method is acupuncture, then the concepts needed are quite different from those where the intended method is injections and surgery.

3. *Games.* Let us suppose that the main purposes of games are taking exercise, stimulating cooperation within a group, competing with other individuals or groups, achieving fame for exceptional skill, and so on. These

purposes can be attained by a great variety of games. In order to play these games, the relevant concepts must be understood and used. We discussed the concepts for cricket above; those for the different kinds of football or hockey are quite different, though there are some similar concepts for each – 'side', 'score', 'referee' or 'umpire', and 'foul' or its equivalent, for example.

We can also see from the games example how competence in a situation depends on mastering the concepts. The novice at chess learns the 'fork' move, whereby he can attack two pieces simultaneously, and likewise the move 'check by discovery'. Until he has understood these ideas he will not be able to make the moves. Concepts may help in the mastery of larger sequences of behaviour; in Scottish country dancing the novice must learn the concepts of 'reel of three', 'poussette', 'allemande', etc. Concepts may enable the performer to make finer distinctions, e.g. between 'leg-break', 'yorker' and other balls bowled at cricket. Finally concepts enable the player to grasp the state of the game.

Formal situations, such as the examples of games above, can be taken as models for less formal social situations. Symbolic interactionists have emphasised the dependence of behaviour on the 'definition of the situation', that is to say, the way the situation is perceived and interpreted, including the conceptual schemes involved. They also maintain that the rules and other aspects of a situation have to be negotiated, and interactors cooperate to achieve a shared set of meanings and concepts (Stone and Farberman, 1970). However these shared meanings may become more or less institutionalised and taught to newcomers to the situation; for example, an abortion clinic was found to be ostentatiously equipped with the symbols of medicine, to create the desired perception on the part of clients and to legitimise the enterprise (Ball, 1970*b*).

Different subcultural groups attach different meanings to events and use different concepts. The members of deviate groups are of interest from this point of view. These include groups of delinquents, drug-takers, homosexuals, religious sects and football fans. New members are taught how to behave, how to perceive and interpret events – e.g. how to get 'high' on 'pot'. They come to live in a new cognitive world, very different from that of those outside. Marsh *et al.* (1978) investigated the conceptual worlds of football fans and disruptive schoolchildren. Some schoolchildren have 'rules' for teachers, e.g. teachers should be fair, not have favourites, not demand too much work; if teachers break these rules they must be 'punished'. This is very different from the teachers' view of the class-room. Football fans spend several hours on Saturday afternoons engaged mainly in aggressive displays against groups of rival fans. We discussed the rules in Chapter 5 (p. 130f.); they depend on the possession of relevant concepts – the hierarchical ranks in the football fan group, ideas of what is desired (humiliation and ridicule of rivals), and what is not generally acceptable (physical harm to rivals), of 'tough' and feeble behaviour, and so on.

In addition to subcultural variations in concepts, there are rather greater differences between cultures. In Japan there are elaborate rules about gift-giving, and to understand these it is necessary to use three concepts. (1) *On* applies in a hierarchical relation, as in parent–child: the debt must be returned, but is never completely repaid. (2) *Giri* obtains between friends and neighbours: there are rules of etiquette about the giving and reciprocation of gifts. (3) *Ninjo* governs gifts based on natural feelings and inclination (Morsbach, 1977).

In our culture we disapprove of what we call 'bribery', i.e. giving presents to businessmen or officials. In many other cultures this is thought of in quite different terms – as the normal and legitimate exchange of gifts. When car accidents happen in West Africa they are explained in terms of magical spells operating at a distance, whereas we should explain them in terms of mechanical failure or inattention. In some Mediterranean countries people believe in the Evil Eye, and think that whenever old ladies with squints look at people they are placing a curse on them. The Australian aboriginals have many ideas that are strange to us. Some groups believe that a fire in the home is of spiritual importance, even when the smoke is making people ill; they think it is wrong to cross another person's territory uninvited, for example crossing his front garden to knock at the door (O'Brien and Plooij, 1980).

Conclusions

We have found a certain amount of evidence that concepts and cognitive structures vary between situations, and are developed to enable performers to attain situational goals. The constructs used for persons include an almost-universal evaluative dimension, but abilities and other task-related constructs vary with the task.

The relations between groups affect the constructs used, in order to maintain self-esteem or justify hostile behaviour. Attribution and explanation vary between actor and observer roles, with the implicit personality theories shared in a group, and with the intended recipients of accounts. Different situations require sets of concepts, such as those needed to play cricket or visit restaurants. Competence in a situation requires the mastery of these concepts. The goals of a situation may be pursued by different methods, aided by different sets of concepts, as in alternative methods of healing.

9.1. Person perception and the interaction episode
J. P. FORGAS, M. ARGYLE, AND G. P. GINSBURG

[A fuller version of this study is given in Forgas *et al.* (1979).]

The aim of the present study was to demonstrate that person perception is situation-specific, and that judgements of people depend not only on the relatively invariant characteristics of the persons to be judged but also on the more volatile attributes of the episode context. It was hypothesised that in the academic group studied here, the complexity of the social structure (the number of dimensions necessary to represent the group) and the nature of the underlying attribute dimensions would both vary with the episode specified. Further, it was expected that the group structure in the different episodes would differentially reflect formal, *a priori* status differences between faculty, staff and students. Finally, it was hypothesised that group members would be differentially sensitive to these cross-situational differences: for example, faculty, research students and staff would have systematically different ways of reacting to the episode contexts.

Method

Subjects. Members of a subsection of a large psychology department at a British university ($N = 16$) were both the subjects and the objects of this study. The group included males and females, and consisted of five faculty members, three first-year research students, six advanced research students and two other staff. This group was a cohesive and well-established social unit, with its members in regular contact with each other inside and outside the department for at least six months before the study.

Procedure. The selection of the social episodes (in effect, the independent variables) to be studied was crucial: ideally, they should be both representative of the normal social interaction patterns of the group and maximally different in their characteristics and requirements. In making this decision, data obtained from a previous study by Forgas (1978) were used as empirical guidelines. In this study, multidimensional scaling procedures were used to represent group members' perceptions of a representative sample of their commonly occurring social episodes. From this empirically derived 'episode space', four episodes were selected such that they (*a*) were maximally different from each other, and (*b*) included both work and non-work, superficial and more involved situations. The four episodes selected were the following:

1. Having a drink together in the pub on a Friday night, after the regular weekly seminars ('pub').
2. Having morning coffee with other group members in the department ('morning coffee').

246

3. Being a guest at a faculty member's house for drinks ('party').
4. Participating in one of the research seminars, with only group members being present ('seminar').
   (NB: These episode labels have been altered slightly in order to eliminate personal references to individuals.)

A questionnaire was constructed, containing all instructions in a written form, that asked subjects to rate every member of the group, including themselves, on ten scales in each of the four selected situations (Table 9.1). (These scales were constructed on the basis of open-ended judgements in a pilot study.) The complete anonymity of respondents was emphasised throughout, and returned questionnaires were processed and coded by a specially hired outside research assistant, who removed names and all other identification from the completed questionnaires. Only the status category of the respondent was preserved and coded (faculty member, first-year research student, advanced research student or other staff).

Results and discussion

Ratings were analysed by multidimensional scaling, using the INDSCAL programme (Carroll and Chang, 1970). In the first instance, four separate INDSCAL analyses, each representing the group as seen by its members in one episode, were carried out.

Two dimensions were necessary to represent the group in episodes 1 and 2 (pub and morning coffee), while a more complex, three-dimensional representation was necessary to represent the group in situations 3 and 4 (party and seminar). The structure and complexity of intragroup perception was thus found to be episode-specific: situations 1 and 2 appeared to call for less complex representations than situations 3 and 4.

The first two episodes, going to the pub after a seminar and having morning coffee in the department, are obviously fairly regular, easygoing and simple episodes, mostly socio-emotional rather than task-oriented in character; two dimensions in each case were sufficient to represent most of the perceived differences between group members in these situations. Being invited to a faculty member's house for drinks or participating in a seminar were clearly seen as more complex and involved activities calling for a more complex and multifaceted representation of the relevant characteristics of group members.

The interpretation of the four group spaces showed that not only the complexity but also the quality of the perceived relationships between group members varied with the episode. In the two 'simple' episodes, the pub and coffee time, the major dimension differentiating group members was evaluation. Even within this category, however, the pub situation seemed to call for evaluation in terms of interpersonal qualities (being interesting, humorous and friendly), while the morning coffee situation

TABLE 9.1 *Multidimensional scaling of personal constructs in four situations*

Scale	Dimension 1	Dimension 2	Dimension 3	R^a
Situation 1: Pub				
	Evaluation	*Extroversion*		
Self-confident/shy	0.682	0.390		0.921
Talkative/silent	0.665	0.395		0.908
Interesting/boring	0.731[b]	0.318		0.915
Tense/relaxed	0.425	0.511		0.794
Humorous/humourless	0.868[b]	0.107		0.919
Warm/cold	0.667	0.204		0.803
Friendly/unfriendly	0.771[b]	0.005		0.773
Generous/stingy	0.671	0.211		0.786
Reserved/disclosing	0.242	0.764[b]		0.838
Drinks a lot/drinks little	0.037	0.709[b]		0.814
Situation 2: Morning coffee				
	Evaluation	*Self-confidence*		
Self-confident/shy	−0.089	0.756[b]		0.717
Talkative/silent	0.827[b]	0.176		0.926
Interesting/boring	0.834[b]	0.155		0.919
Tense/relaxed	0.182	0.761[b]		0.865
Humorous/humourless	0.538	0.548		0.937
Warm/cold	0.009	0.763[b]		0.768
Introverted/extroverted	0.563	0.506		0.923
Annoying/pleasant	0.869[b]	0.186		0.974
Slow/quick	0.868[b]	0.155		0.954
Intelligent/dull	0.557	0.395		0.826

Situation 3: Party

	Self-confidence	Warmth	Ingratiation	R[a]
Self-confident/shy	0.796[b]	0.174	0.167	0.973
Talkative/silent	0.729[b]	0.196	0.184	0.962
Interesting/boring	0.373	0.549	0.191	0.927
Tense/relaxed	0.312	0.507	0.201	0.844
Humorous/humourless	0.619	0.425	0.096	0.977
Warm/cold	0.004	0.791	0.238	0.917
Reserved/disclosing	0.204	0.447	0.272	0.756
Poised/awkward	0.334	0.195	0.519	0.867
Articulate/inarticulate	0.774[b]	-0.023	0.295	0.948
Ingratiating/not ingratiating	-0.046	-0.140	0.759[b]	0.694

Situation 4: Seminar

	Dominance	Creativity	Supportiveness	R[a]
Self-confident/shy	0.718[b]	0.336	0.011	0.955
Talkative/silent	0.713[b]	0.289	0.169	0.945
Interesting/boring	0.434	0.532	0.025	0.363
Annoying/pleasant	0.035	0.073	0.743[b]	0.758
Intelligent/dull	0.629	0.376	0.013	0.902
Articulate/inarticulate	0.522	0.499	-0.028	0.906
Critical/supportive	-0.017	0.055	0.835[b]	0.899
Creative/uncreative	0.254	0.754[b]	-0.004	0.924
Dominant/submissive	0.771[b]	0.300	0.108	0.925
Patient/impatient	0.325	0.129	0.719[b]	0.841

[a] R = Multiple correlation coefficient.
[b] Dimension weights >0.7, used in labelling INDSCAL dimensions.

called for evaluation more in terms of intellectual as well as personal qualities (being talkative, interesting, pleasant and quick) (Table 9.1). The second dimension in the pub was a fairly straightforward extroversion dimension, while in the more demanding morning coffee situation self-confidence, tenseness and warmth were seen as important. In the two more complex episodes, the differentiating dimensions appeared to be more idiosyncratic and situation-specific. At a party at a faculty member's house, self-confidence, warmth and ingratiation were seen as the three most salient personal characteristics. The last dimension, surprisingly, was most salient to faculty members, indicating that they evaluated this episode in terms of how others behave in it. In the research seminar situation, which was seen by many group members as a highly competitive and demanding episode involving a fair amount of exposure to criticism, dominance, creativity, and supportiveness were seen as relevant.

It was also expected that perceived differences between status groups such as faculty, students and staff might be more relevant in some situations than in others. Superficially, status in an academic setting could be expected to be a most pertinent dimension differentiating individuals (Jones and Young, 1973). According to the present findings, however, this is only true for some episodes. In a research seminar status differences were strongly reflected in the perceived group structure, indicating that in academic life status was primarily supposed to reflect intellectual capability, most relevant to behaviour in a task-oriented, work episode. Status was also seen as relatively important in a purely interactive episode, such as a party, if the senior position of the host was specified. Presumably, status differences became relevant in a setting in which the status of the host was high, and interaction with him was fairly clearly regulated along status lines; similar purely interactive situations in other settings, without a specified 'host', did not bring forth status differences. This is reflected in perceptions of the group in the pub and the morning coffee situation, where *a priori* status differences were of no significance.

The differences between faculty, staff and students as judges were also evaluated (Fig. 9.1). There were no significant differences in judgements of the group in the pub episode. At a seminar, however, students, most likely to be exposed to criticism, judged a critical as against a supportive attitude as of high salience, while faculty and staff perceived self-confidence and dominance as more important. These results tend to support some previous findings by Forgas (1976, 1978) indicating that the subjective meaning of a particular social episode depends not only on the subcultural background of the subjects but also on the particular position of the individual within his reference group. Students and faculty differed in their judgements of the group in the morning coffee situation; here evaluation was the more salient dimension for faculty members and self-confidence a more important

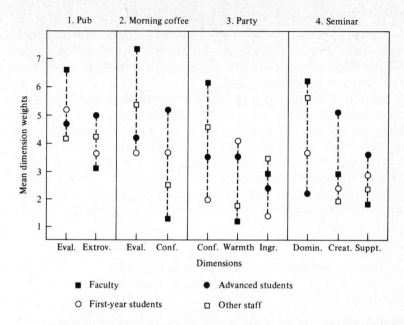

Fig. 9.1. Differences between formal status subgroups (faculty, students, staff) in their perception of the group in each of four social episodes. Eval., evaluation; Extrov., extroversion; Conf., self-confidence; Ingr., ingratiation; Domin., dominance; Creat., creativity; Suppt., supportiveness.

dimension for students. Also, in the party situation, self-confidence and ingratiation were seen as more relevant dimensions by faculty than by students, while warmth was relatively more salient for students in their judgements of the group. In short, although ingratiation may be a relevant *behaviour* to low-status individuals, it is more likely to be of interest to high-status people in their judgements of the group.

The various dimensions found here, derived in the context of specified episodes, may be compared with dimensions constructed without the specification of the situation. Jones and Young (1973) found that political persuasion, research interests and status were the three dimensions best describing the academic group they studied. Further, these dimensions were found to be rather stable over time, and not affected by minor changes in group membership. All three dimensions reported by these authors refer to rather abstract, enduring, permanent characteristics of the members. They do not describe personal characteristics directly relevant to everyday functioning and behaviour within the group. The same point can be made about Davison and Jones' (1976) comparable study. It appears that interpersonal judgements made in a contextual vacuum may be qualitatively different from judgements based on experience in a specified episode. If these differences could be reliably replicated in a wider population, it would strongly suggest that the lack of predictive validity of much research in social perception may be at least partly due to the investigators' failure to specify the relevant episode context.

In summary, the results indicated that (*a*) the traits used were different in the four episodes, (*b*) the number of dimensions used varied with the episode, (*c*) the status of group members was differentially relevant in different episodes, and (*d*) status groups differed in their perceptions of the group structure in each of the four episodes. This shows that interpersonal perception is strongly influenced by the episode context. These findings contradict the tacit assumption of cross-situational invariance and individual consistency employed in most studies in social perception.

9.2. Personality constructs in relation to situations
M. ARGYLE., G. P. GINSBURG, J. P. FORGAS AND A. CAMPBELL

Does the situation influence the set of constructs relevant to making discriminations between people? We expected that it would, and we also expected that the relevance of descriptors would vary as a function of who was doing the discriminating and who was being described. We designed a study to test the hypothesis that the relevance of personality constructs would vary as a function of judge, target and interactional context in which the target is located.

Method
The subjects were asked to rate thirty-six seven-point personality construct scales for their relevance in four situations and for seven target groups. The four situations were:
1.   Chatting casually on the street (casual, social)
2.   Having an intimate conversation at home or at a party (involved, social)
3.   Discussing some minor work problems (casual, task-oriented)
4.   Working closely together on a project or activity (involved task-oriented)

These represent the two dimensions task–social and casual–involved.
   The seven target groups were:

Students	*Housewives*
1. Members of your family and close relatives	Same

Students	Housewives
2. Your immediate circle of friends	Same
3. Your friends of the opposite sex	Same
4. Children of your acquaintance who are less than thirteen years of age	Same
5. Casual acquaintances (people whom you do not know well)	Same
6. Students in your college	Neighbours
7. University dons and other senior academics you know	Professional people (e.g.) doctors, lawyers

For each target category, subjects listed five people actually known to them. The subjects' task was to rate the *relevance* of each descriptor scale to the behaviour of the five people they had listed in each of the twenty-eight episode × target category combinations. We used two groups of participants: fifteen housewives from the paid Subject Panel of the Department of Experimental Psychology at the University of Oxford, and fifteen Oxford students – very different groups. The overall design thus generated relevance ratings for thirty-six dependent variables (the construct scales), based on three classes of independent variables (four situations, seven target categories and two groups of participants).

Results

We analysed the data first by a 36 × 4 × 7 × 2 MANOVA, and subsequently by selective ANOVAs and factor analyses. In the MANOVA, all main and interaction effects were significant, as expected. That is, relevance ratings of the descriptors varied as a function of situations, target categories and participants. The subsequent factor analyses revealed several bases for the MANOVA results.

Factor analyses were worked out for all situations together, and for each separately. Each had a similar factor structure, but there were interesting differences. The overall factor analysis produced three factors: friendly–extroversion (or social evaluation), status–appearance and competence–dependability. The casual chat situation produced a large friendly–extroversion factor, in which 'good-natured', 'talkative' and 'self-confident' had the highest loadings. In the minor work problem, on the other hand, instead of a social evaluative factor there was a first factor which combined work and status scales with some evaluative ones. For the situation of working closely together the evaluative factor was combined with

253

'dependable' and 'consistent'. It looks as if the evaluative scale combines with whatever is most important in each situation.

Situation affected construct relevance at $P < 0.001$ in the MANOVA. The friendly–extroversion factor was judged highly relevant in all situations, except the minor work problem (Fig. 9.2). In the involved work situation the 'competence–dependability and 'social evaluative' factors were most important. We also looked at the relevance of selected scales in each situation. 'Intelligent' was rated quite relevant in all situations, especially the intense ones; 'neurotic' was also most relevant in intense situations, 'extroverted' in social situations (see Table 9.2).

TABLE 9.2 *Means for the three factors, and for certain scales, for the four situations*

	Episodes				
Factors and selected scales	Social casual	Social intimate	Work minor prob.	Working closely	Overall mean
I. Friendly–extroversion	4.43	4.52	3.71	4.46	4.28
II. Status–appearance	2.63	2.89	3.57	2.65	2.94
III. Competence–dependability	3.34	3.67	3.47	4.74	3.81
Extroverted	3.70	4.01	3.30	3.57	3.65
Neurotic	3.26	3.94	3.70	4.05	3.74
Intelligent	4.11	4.60	4.10	4.88	4.42

Different target groups required different constructs ($P < 0.001$), and thirty-four of the thirty-six scales varied in relevance between groups at this level of significance. The friendly–extroversion factor was again relevant for most groups, dons being lowest. Status–appearance was much less relevant, but was highest for housewives assessing professional people. 'Competence–dependability' was most relevant for professional people, least relevant for children and students (see Table 9.3).

The pattern of relevance scores reflects closely the nature of the interaction with target groups. Here are some examples of this for children: *Above-average:* 'well-behaved' ($+1.00$), 'noisy' ($+0.74$). *Below-average:* 'competence–dependability' (-0.40), 'competent' (-1.01), 'radical' (-0.98), 'considerate' (-0.73), 'awkward' (-0.71). (These are differences from the means for all target groups.)

We think that the best explanation of the variation of constructs with target groups is that the nature of the social interaction with each group makes different traits relevant. This theory can provide a post-hoc explanation for many of the findings. It explains why professional people are thought of in terms of 'competence', children as 'well-behaved' and 'noisy', and friends of the opposite sex in terms of 'attractive', 'well-behaved' and 'considerate'. It could also explain the situational differences in a similar way.

The MANOVA showed a significant interaction between situation and target group ($P < 0.001$), i.e. certain constructs are relevant for certain target groups in particular situations. To explore this interaction we factor-analysed the twenty-eight situation–target group interactions, for housewives and students separately. We present here the results for the students only. There were four main factors:

I.   Involved task episodes
II. Episodes with children
III. Casual social episodes with family or friends
IV. Casual episodes with acquaintances

When the construct factors were plotted against these situation–target group types, for students (Fig. 9.2) the friendly–extroversion factor did not vary much. The 'dependable' factor was high for involved task episodes, low for episodes with acquaintances and children. The 'intelligent' factor was highest in casual social encounters with family and friends, lowest for children.

Finally, as predicted, housewives and students regarded different constructs as relevant. The housewives rated 'status', 'well-behaved' and 'warm' as more relevant than did students. The two groups of subjects produced similar factor structures of constructs.

Summary

Fifteen housewives and fifteen students rated the relevance of thirty-six personality constructs in four situations for seven target groups. (1) There was a similar factor structure in all situations, with the factors friendly–extroversion, status–appearance and competence–dependability. However the factors varied between situation, and evaluative scales combined with whatever was important in each situation. (2) Situation affected the relevance of constructs: a friendly–extroversion factor was universally relevant, the 'competence' factor was more relevant in the involved work situation, 'extroversion' in social situations, 'intelligent' and 'neurotic' in intense situations. (3) Target group also affected relevance of constructs. Friendly–extroversion was relevant for most groups; 'competence' was relevant for professional people, not for children. The pattern of relevant constructs could be explained in terms of the pattern of interaction with each group. (4) Construct relevance was affected by situation–target group interaction; students had four factors of episodes each of which had its

255

TABLE 9.3. *Mean relevance ratings for the three components and for certain scales fo*

| | Target groups and means | | | | |
Factors and selected scales	1 Family	2 Friends	3 Opp. sex	4 Children	5 Acquai
I. Friendly–extroversion	4.51	4.67	4.61	4.39	4.26
II. Status–appearance	2.91	2.73	3.09	2.50	2.67
III. Competence–dependability	4.17	4.25	4.11	3.55	3.71
Extroverted	3.61	3.92	3.98	4.08	3.64
Neurotic	4.33	4.10	4.04	3.40	3.56
Intelligent	4.13	4.61	4.59	3.98	4.16

Column 6 contains means for all target groups. Column 9 contains means for students o
[a] Rated by students. [b] Rated by housewives.

group of relevant constructs. (5) Housewives and students differed in their ratings of some constructs, but produced similar factor structures.

9.3. Construing social situations

A. FURNHAM

Most of the studies that have been published on the perception of social situations have required subjects to rate brief descriptions of social situations on various dimensions. The obvious inadequacy of this approach is that, firstly, subjects may have little or no experience of the situations they are asked to judge. Secondly, they may interpret short ambiguous descriptions radically differently or in terms of abstract stereotyped dimensions. Thirdly, the rating scales provided by the experimenter may not be relevant to the situation or to the cognitive constructs or systems of the subjects. The results may therefore be invalid, artefactual or unrepresentative.

In order to investigate the social psychology of social situations and perhaps build a taxonomy it seems important that subjects provide and describe actual social situations in their current lives, and also judge and compare situations in terms of their own cognitive constructs. This implies the use of a more clinical idiographic approach. It is possible that certain situations have similar subjective meanings and elicit certain behaviour patterns across different subject groups, but one must make sure not to impose loose subcultural definitions on what are specific, complex, subtle, dynamic episodes by too short, inadequate or unspecific a description. The extensive, though somewhat inconclusive, sociological literature on the

256

e target groups

an	7 Students[a]	8 Dons[a]	9 Mean[a]	10 Neigh.[b]	11 Professionals[b]	12 Mean[b]
	3.87	3.66	4.05	4.19	4.36	4.58
	1.94	2.21	2.16	2.70	3.63	3.33
	3.42	3.69	3.62	4.06	4.60	4.27
	3.60	3.17	3.66	2.68	3.20	3.65
	3.38	3.08	3.55	3.23	3.85	3.95
	4.25	4.90	4.32	4.42	5.48	4.52

umn 12 contains means for housewives only.

definition of the situation points to the subtleties involved in situational perception and definition.

The technique that seems most applicable here is the *repertory grid*, which can be administered individually or in larger groups and analysed in various ways. The repertory grid has been suggested as the most useful technique by De Waele and Harré (1976) and Kelly (1955) for showing the structure and process of situation perception.

The advantage of the repertory grid method is that it allows each subject to rate situations in his own way, while the experimenter's hypotheses and constructs are considerably removed, unlike other methods where situations and rating scales are provided by the experimenter.

Two experiments were carried out using the repertory grid, to investigate two aspects of the concepts people have of certain social situations. Each addressed itself to a different question.

1. Are situations that are labelled similarly perceived more similarly than situations that are labelled differently? Can we talk of situation types being homogeneously defined in a subculture by a shorthand term (dinner party, wedding), or are they quite unique and dependent on a number of other circumstances and variables? All situations have a number of different elements and their individual weights and arrangement might radically affect one's perception of them, although they are defined by the same term.

2. How is the perception of a person influenced by the situation in which he or she is perceived? Is there more similarity in the perception of the same person known to the subject across different situations in which the subject has observed this person, or of different people in the same type of social situation? Person perception experiments and the repertory grid have

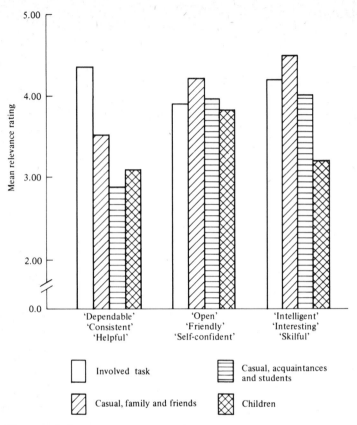

Fig. 9.2. Relevance ratings by students for clusters of scales in clusters of situations.

usually ignored the immediate situation in which the person is 'perceived', which might well bias their perception.

Part I

This study was designed to find out whether situations or episodes which are defined by the same term are actually seen as more similar than those that are defined by different terms. Is it the case that weddings by virtue of their sharing of a common label are seen as more similar than any particular wedding is to any particular dinner party? We know what is required of us at a dinner party and roughly what the rules, roles and sequences are, but dinner parties differ widely in terms of formality, length, number of guests, etc. Social occasions of one category, e.g. 'dinner parties', may in fact differ so widely that some are more like situations from other categories, e.g.

'wedding receptions' or even 'job interviews'. Thus when judging or clustering situations we must be sure how representative these are of a general group or type if one exists. That is to say, if we are asked to describe our perception of a dinner party we must know considerably more about it (people involved, setting, reason for celebration, etc.) before we can meaningfully describe or compare it with other situations described. A dinner party to a middle-aged executive may involve quite different rituals, behaviour and constraints from those in the mind of an undergraduate.

The hypothesis here is that situations of one type – that is, defined subculturally in terms of the aim/purpose of the interactions – will be perceived as more similar to each other than to situations of another type.

Method

Subjects. Twenty subjects completed the task; ten were undergraduates in their late teens and early twenties and ten were adults in their late twenties and early thirties, from the department Subject Panel.

Materials. Subjects were asked to complete a repertory grid which had twelve invitations to social functions provided as elements. The invitations were to three different types of function: four were to a dinner party, four to a wedding and reception, and four to a job interview. They were all typed on foolscap sheets, each being about ten to fifteen lines long and based on genuine invitations received by the experimenter. Invitations were used as stimuli for two reasons: firstly they gave a much lengthier and more detailed description of the anticipated episode (when, where, with whom) than had been used in previous studies, and secondly they were fairly realistic and conformed to Kelly's idea of man as a scientist anticipating future events (i.e. all the subjects had no experience of a particular episode, but the same amount of information on it). Invitations 1 and 2 are given as examples.

1.
Mr and Mrs Ken Smythe
hope that you can come
to the Wedding of their daughter
Susan
to
James Spring
at St Mary's Church, Watford
on Saturday, 15th April at 3.00

The reception afterwards will be at
the Royal Hotel, Church Street.

RSVP

2. Jenny and Brian invite you to either
or both of the following: their
marriage (at long last!) at the
High Street Magistrates' Court
(next to Woolies) at 5.00 p.m. on
Saturday 16th and/or the party in
the Skittles room at the King's Arms
from 7 p.m. till late. See you there.

The invitations were presented in fifteen triads, and fifteen constructs were elicited from each person. Each grid took about one hour to complete.

Results

(*a*) The grids were analysed individually and as a group using Slater's (1977) INGRID and PREFAN programs' designed to analyse group grids aligned by element and not construct. Also a cluster analysis was performed on the elements (situations). Two further aspects of the grids were considered – the *content* (the number and meaning of the constructs) and the *structure* (loadings in grid space). The group results of the PREFAN program are plotted in Fig. 9.3.

The first eight components were all significant, indicating the complexity of these perceptions of the situations. However the results of the Scree test, which extracts the predominant factors that account for most of the variance, reduced the results to two components which accounted for over 56 per cent of the variance (35 per cent and 21 per cent respectively).

The hypothesis of this study was that the three situation types would group together across all the components, while the alternative hypothesis was that the situations would not all group in the above pattern but in different ways in terms of other similarities. It is apparent that the alternative hypothesis is confirmed. Three clusters emerged:

1. Elements 1, 4, 7, 8 were two weddings (1, 4) and two dinner parties (7, 8); a post-hoc review of the invitations revealed that the common feature in these four situations was that they were large formal public episodes.
2. Elements 2, 3 and 6 were two weddings (2, 3) and one dinner party (6); these seemed to be fairly small intimate informal episodes.
3. Elements 5, 9 and 10 were a wedding and two job interviews.
4. Element 12, a two-day-long job interview, and element 11, a job interview which was a mere formality between colleagues rather than a structured formalised affair, were both uniquely perceived in construct space.

(*b*) The cluster analysis (Fig. 9.4) revealed very similar results, the only major difference being in the job interview cluster. Items 5, 9, 10 are

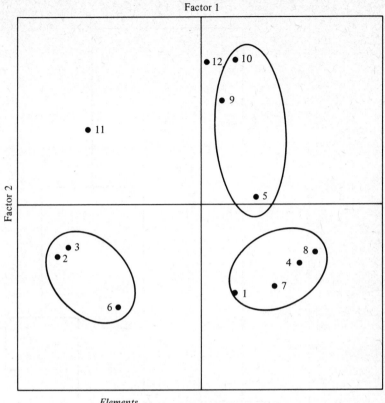

Fig. 9.3. PREFAN group graph.

clustered together (a wedding and two job interviews) whereas 11 and 12 are also perceived as fairly similar. It is apparent from the dendrogram that the four clusters are composed of situations with different labels.

(*c*) A content analysis of the constructs revealed that over fifty different constructs were used. Synonymous and similar constructs were grouped with four groups emerging: activity, potency, evaluation and invitation-specific. The most commonly occurring constructs were formal/informal (37), friendly/unfriendly (27), personal/impersonal (18), family/non-family (15).

Clearly we cannot rely on simple phrases like 'going to a wedding' in episode or situation perception, as weddings differ very widely between one another and people from different socio-economic and subcultural groups

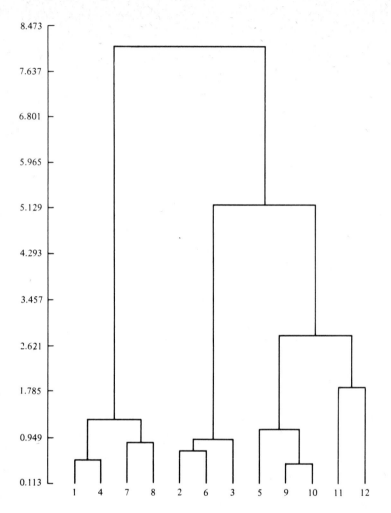

Fig. 9.4. Cluster analysis of situations. For a description of the situations see Fig. 9.3.

have very different expectations of them. The results indicate that some weddings are seen as being more like dinner parties than other weddings and that there is great heterogeneity in situation types labelled by the same term, some being a considerable distance away from others. This implies that the situation type labels should be revised. If we are to be able to compare and contrast situations we must be more specific about the nature, definition and description of the stimulus situations under review.

Part 2

This study was concerned with how much the perception of people known to the subject was influenced by the social definition of the episode in which they were described. Is there more consistency in the perception of the same person irrespective of the situation he is in (hypothesis), or are perceptions more similar as a function of the social episode that a person is perceived in (alternative hypothesis)?

Method

Subjects. Twenty subjects completed the task. Ten were male psychology undergraduates at the University of Oxford who were in their late teens and early twenties, and ten were female second-year occupational therapy students in the same age group.

Materials. All subjects were given a grid. The elements were divided into six groups of three – six role constructs (self, mother, father, same-sex friend, opposite-sex friend, sibling) in each of three situation types (group discussion with peers, a party with and for peers, and an argument with a stranger). The provided elements were thus 'yourself in an argument with a stranger', 'mother in a group discussion with peers', etc. Subjects were provided with twenty-four triads and twenty-four constructs were elicited. The grid took about one and a half hours to complete.

Results

(a) The grids were analysed individually and as a group, using Slater's INGRID and PREFAN (1977) programs, and both the content and the structure of the grids were analysed. The null hypothesis of the study was that the same people perceived in different situations cluster together in element space (1, 2, 3: self in group discussion, self at party, self in argument; 4, 5, 6: mother in group discussion, mother at party, mother in argument). The alternative hypothesis is that the situation will determine the grouping of stimulus people to the extent that elements will cluster mainly in terms of the social situation in which people find themselves.

Eleven components were found to be significant using the Barlett test; however the Scree test results provided justification for looking at the first two factors, which together accounted for 58 per cent of the variance (34 per cent and 24 per cent respectively). It is apparent from Fig. 9.5 that the alternative hypothesis is confirmed. Three distinct clusters emerged:

1. Elements 1, 4, 7, 10, 13, 16: all linked in terms of the same situation, a group discussion with peers.
2. Elements 2, 5, 8, 11, 14, 17: all linked in terms of the same situation, a party with peers.

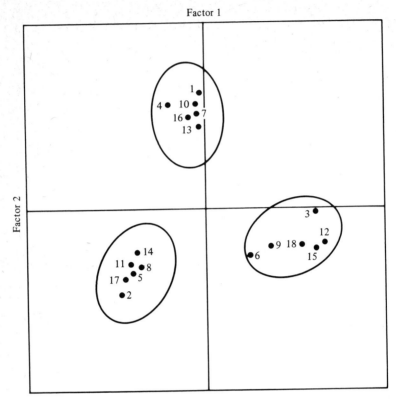

Fig. 9.5. PREFAN group graph.

Elements

	Group discussion with peers	Party with peers	Arguing with stranger
Self	1	2	3
Mother	4	5	6
Father	7	8	9
Opposite-sex friend	10	11	12
Same-sex friend	13	14	15
Sibling	16	17	18

3. Elements 3, 6, 9, 12, 15, 18: all linked in terms of the same situation, arguing with a stranger.

These results strongly support the alternative hypothesis, namely that the perception of people in specific situations is more strongly determined by the social context of that situation than by the personality of those people. However, it must be stressed that this result may be true for these situations only. As Argyle (1976) has argued before, if we generalise across people and situations when apportioning variance we must sample both persons and situations equally widely.

(*b*) The results of the cluster analysis (Fig. 9.6) exactly parallel the PREFAN results. It is interesting to note that group discussions with peers are perceived as more similar to arguments with a stranger than to a party for peers.

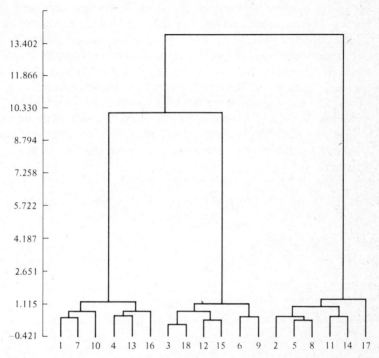

Fig. 9.6. Cluster analysis of situations. For description of situations see Fig. 9.5.

(*c*) The content analysis revealed that by far the largest category of constructs was evaluative. Over sixty constructs were used more than once, the most common being interesting/boring (28), restrained/unrestrained (25), relaxed/not relaxed (24), active/passive (20), quiet/noisy (20). Many constructs were common to the previous study though the stimulus situations were quite different.

There are two important implications of these results, one for person perception and one for repertory grid analysis. Firstly, it has been shown that the social situation (task–social, friendly–unfriendly) alters the way in which people are seen, and in fact leads to more uniformity of perception.

That is to say the process of person perception rarely occurs in a vacuum, and our ideas and perceptions are strongly influenced by background and contextual factors. Secondly, the repertory grid has traditionally required subjects to rate and compare role titles *in vacuo* (e.g. mother, liked person, sibling). It has been argued that we all carry about in our heads pictures of these people as sets of traits, abstracts of our observation of these people in a number of situations, but these are of necessity highly abstract, and so do not reflect how we see these people in particular situations and circumstances. This concept could well be purely artefactual because we ask of our subject only trait-like questions in our experiments, and these people may carry round memories of specific happenings or outstanding situations. If we asked subjects to rate the role titles in social contexts with which they are familiar, the picture of the results might be quite different from the one in which they rate unfamiliar or different contexts, but it might be equally revealing. Constructs of specific people in specific situations are likely to be more specific and less abstract, and in this way we are able to compare a subject's perception of consistency of behaviour across persons and situations.

10

Environmental setting

Introduction

The feature of situations that has been most thoroughly investigated is the physical environment. We suggest that the physical features of situations can be looked at in terms of four concepts.

1. Boundaries (the physical enclosures within which behaviour takes place).
2. Props (the furnishings, decorations and objects contained in that boundary).
3. Modifiers (the quality and quantity of conditioners in the boundary).
4. Spaces (the use and meaning attached to spaces between people and objects within the boundary).

The scientific analysis of the structure and function of the physical environment is a comparatively recent development for psychology. In 1966 Craik defined environmental psychology as 'the psychological study of behaviour as it relates to the everyday physical environment', and which addresses itself to three related questions:

1. What does the everyday physical environment do to people?
2. How do people comprehend their physical environment?
3. What do people do to the everyday physical environment?

The relationship between social and environmental psychology is close theoretically and methodologically, as social psychology's traditional focus on perception and behaviour has been broadened to include contextual orientation in which the transaction between people and their socio-physical settings is emphasised. Altman (1976) has suggested that both the two subdisciplines might benefit from looking at people × place units, as the new social unit of enquiry. He maintains that this approach will have three advantages: it would encourage the study of interrelationship of various modes of behaviour; it calls for the analysis of patterns of simultaneously occurring behaviours; and it would underline the dynamic nature of behaviour which changes over time and circumstances.

The obvious relevance of the P×S debate and research into various psychological aspects of social situations has not escaped environmental psychologists, a number of whom have considered the interrelationship

267

between environmental assessment and situational analysis. Craik (1979) has stated that increasing knowledge of situational perception can form the basis for developing techniques permitting the observational assessment of situations. 'Among the components of situations, the actors, the physical environment and the social environment can be conceptualized as relatively enduring entities, while the acts and the situation-as-an-episodic-configuration are ephemeral events' (p. 19). Craik also notes that situations can and do act as both dependent and independent variables simultaneously, a point much neglected in the literature.

Stokols (1979) proposed a study of group × place transactions which highlights the active role taken by individuals and groups in creating and modifying their environments. He maintains that a defining characteristic of a setting is the interdependence of its physical, social and personal elements, and he proposed to investigate settings by looking at the degree of interdependence between groups – shared socio-cultural images which are conveyed by physical environments. Thus environments or situations are to be studied in terms of their social imageability – their capacity to evoke vivid and widely shared social meanings among members of a setting. Stokols maintains that the perceived social field of a setting should be defined as the totality of *functional* (goal-specific activities, norms, roles), *motivational* (collective goals and purposes, weighted by their relative importance to members of the setting) and *evaluative* (occupants, physical features, social functions) meanings conveyed by the physical environment to members of the setting. Finally Stokols suggests a number of strategies for measuring the perceived field of a setting: the content, clarity, complexity, heterogeneity, and contradiction between actual and preferred social meaning of a setting.

We suggest that some of the concepts and methodological techniques developed in environmental psychology are particularly useful in the analysis of social situations. We differ from environmental psychologists, however, in our emphasis on the relationship between social and physical features, on the types and levels of social behaviour in which we are interested and in our concern with motivational and normative features in situations. To a large extent behaviours associated with, or considered appropriate to, certain places govern or direct behaviour in those places. Further the layout and ambiance of a setting substantially contribute to the way people perceive and act in these situations. To this extent people actively create and modify social situations to fulfil their own goals.

Bennett and Bennett (1970) described how environmental features in a room have behavioural consequences. They described situations which were identical only in terms of enclosure, number of objects and number of people, yet because of certain conventions and conditioners evoked predictable responses from specific population groups. The situations described below are settings for the following interactions: an interrogation, a social conversation and an interview.

Situation One: The walls, floors, and ceiling of the room are concrete and plaster, unpainted and bare of decoration. There is a single naked, bright electric bulb suspended above the table as the only source of light. The table and chairs are wood, bare, hard, and smooth. The temperature is relatively low (say 60 degrees Fahrenheit), and the relative humidity is high making the room chilly and damp. There is a slight odour of mildew. The predominant colours are grey and white.
Situation Two: Now the walls are hung with dark red curtains. The floor is thickly carpeted, and the ceiling painted a soft off-white. The light source is a light cove around the ceiling which gives off a soft, diffuse, dim light. The table is covered with a white cloth and the chairs are upholstered with a nappy material. The temperature and humidity are a little above the American Standard Engineering 'Comfort Range' (68° Fahrenheit and 45% relative humidity), making the room feel a little warm and humid. There is a slightly 'stuffy' odour in the room. The predominant colours are dark red, off-white, and a muted gold.
Situation Three: The ceiling is a luminous fluorescent ceiling such as may be found in many contemporary office buildings. Three of the walls are smooth white plaster; the fourth, a chromatic blue. The floor is covered with a dark grey carpet. The table is very low, its top no more than sixteen inches above the floor. Its base is polished steel, its top is glass. The chairs are polished steel frames fitted with black leather cushions. The room is cool and dry and, for all intents and purposes, 'odourless'. (pp. 192–3)

The authors point out that these situations are of a generalised type and that each can accommodate a number – but a very finite number – of different interactions in the context of our culture.

In addition to the work on environmental psychology, we suggest that in the analysis of social situations we may also profitably integrate material from three distinct areas that are concerned with the relationship between people and their environment, each with its own theoretical and methodological tradition. These are:

1. Ecological psychology, with its emphasis on behaviour, and using the Gestalt approach.
2. Experimental psychology, with its interest in specific physical variables (heat, light, sound) and their effect on behavioural processes.
3. Phenomenological psychology, with its interest in symbolism and meaning in the physical environment.

The results of the Hawthorne experiment, which demonstrated that the social milieu of work was considerably more significant than the physical milieu, was an important reason for psychologists dropping interest in the psychological effects of the physical environment. However the Hawthorne experiment did result in the development of interest in groups and the establishment of roles, norms and rules, all of which are relevant in the analysis of social situations.

The work of Barker and Wright (1949, 1951, 1955) preceded the work of most environmental psychologists and in fact grew out of the same early literature as the P×S debate. More recently environmental psychologists (Canter, 1977) have amalgamated constructs to produce a cognitive role-oriented approach to situations and settings. Canter has argued that a person's environmental role is the most appropriate construct for linking people to places, and that these roles lead to differences in conceptual systems and hence behaviour. He maintained that the concept of place might act as a bridge between various fields of enquiry such as geography, planning, psychology and architecture. However many different episodes might occur in the same place – such as a living room or an office – and we prefer to emphasise the social situation rather than concepts associated with place alone.

A functional model for behaviour and environments

In a famous remark in 1943, Churchill proclaimed: 'We shape our buildings and afterwards our buildings shape us'. As Canter *et al.* (1975) have pointed out, Churchill went on to demonstrate that the inefficiencies of the bombed House of Commons should be maintained as integral to Parliamentary government. They wrote: 'the rebuilding was not seen as brought about by simple functional necessity but as the need to maintain a form which complemented the social and psychological process of an institution' (p. 4). However what is particularly interesting and largely overlooked in Churchill's remark is the bidirectional implications of the statement, and its applicability to social situations as well as to buildings, rooms, etc. Environmental psychologists have for the most part regarded the physical environment as the *independent* variable and the related behaviour as the *dependent* variable, but it seems equally useful to use the variables in the opposite way: that is, to see how we use or shape our physical environments and attach certain meanings to them in order to facilitate or inhibit particular types of social behaviour. We have proposed a functional model of situations: situations are created and exist to fulfil certain goals. The physical component of situations may also be seen to fulfil goals.

Indeed it appears that one of the main reasons why certain buildings fail to meet their aims is that there is a very clear discrepancy between the ideas and aims of the people involved in building them and the way of life of the residents (e.g. high-rise buildings in the 1960s). Architects are often motivated by aesthetic, creative and innovative needs with certain practical constraints; city councils are motivated primarily by financial and political considerations; and the people who work or live in the buildings are motivated by a host of complex, even mutually exclusive, psychological needs (Canter *et al.* and Edwards, in Canter and Lee, 1974).

We have argued that one way to approach an analysis of social situations is to investigate their goal structure – the way that they are constructed to fulfil various needs or to achieve certain goals. When the goal of the designer (architect, planner) is in conflict with, or unrelated to, the goals of the users (clients, etc.), the latter might attempt to change or redefine the physical environment to make it more in line with their goals and needs. As we showed in Chapter 4, goal conflict often leads to difficulty and disrupted communication.

We suggest that it is possible to look at the way people change, create and react to their physical environment in terms of the goal structures of the social situations that occur in those environments. When people move into a house, a bedroom or an office that is in some sense theirs, they are often able to furnish and decorate it in a personal way according to their own tastes, values and self-presentation, and to achieve various goals. Some people are more conscious of their environment than others are, and consider their environment very important to the way they interact within it. People often arrange or rearrange a room to achieve various different ends: to encourage maximum communication at a cocktail party, to impress a superior coming to dinner, to prevent or discourage people from going into various spaces, to produce heightened levels of arousal. Thus within the physical environment people are able to select, arrange and manipulate various props – chairs, tables, books, paintings, ventilation, lights, spaces – for specific ends. Ruesch and Kees (1956) pointed out how social control can be attained through material objects. The placement of objects in strategic locations may be substituted for explanations or instructions.

Chairs faced obliquely attenuate direct confrontation. A table between two chairs sets up a sort of barrier. This obstacle, however, may reassure the participants that excessive closeness will not be forced upon them, and with this reassurance they may achieve more intimate communication than would otherwise be possible. Shape and arrangement of furniture provides clues about how easily and conveniently the furniture may be approached and what degrees of comfort may be anticipated. (p. 128)

The organisation of the material environment can be seen as a conscious expression of taste, value, personality, and as an unconscious revelation of orderliness, social skill, etc. Many personal idiosyncrasies occur, such as contact with the surface of objects, vertical versus horizontal orientation of objects and the way in which objects are stored (piling, shelving, spreading, dumping, aligning).

Goffman (1959) discussed the use of furnishings and environmental layout in terms of impression management. His well-known distinction between back and front stage has in fact been empirically verified by Canter (1977), who found that the main distinction between different regions of private homes was perceived to be between public and private rooms. There are also cultural variables – Canter and Lee (1974) showed how differently

Japanese people arranged their personal furniture compared with Western traditions.

In our society we have developed numerous physical signs of power, wealth, authority and status, which in social situations are extremely important. One of these is *height* – more important people are elevated physically as well as socially. Consider the Pope or bishop on his throne, the judge on his bench, the Master of college at high table, the priest at the altar. The increased height of authority figures gives them a better chance for others around to see them, and for them to see the less powerful. Hence there is a related variable of *visibility*. However, although the visibility of the authority figure or speaker may be encouraged, seating arrangements may be organised so as to prevent much external visibility and encourage interaction and concentration. Oxford college dining rooms, it seems, were deliberately designed to have as few windows as possible so as to encourage students to interact. This is quite contradictory to the concept behind revolving restaurants on towers, which seem to have been designed to maximise outside viewing.

Yet another physical variable related to importance is *light*. Often artificial or spot lighting is used to highlight an important person. The difference in colour of clothing between an authority figure (white) and those around him (black) might help visibility. Hence *size* and *colour* may be important ways in which people manipulate their environment for specific effects. Often the larger the size of a room or piece of furniture – desk, chair, painting – the higher the status of the owner or user. Size, however, is very much a relative variable; among great uniformity a difference in either direction (larger or smaller) stands out and can signal a variety of messages. The same is true of colour, in uniforms, furnishings or architecture. Furthermore certain colours such as gold, purple and white have symbolic significance in our culture. Canter (1977) has provided a good review of this material. He notes how certain objects, symbols or layouts symbolise a place or situation and considers the processes which make that representation possible.

The orientation and symmetry of the physical components of social situations also have implications for role, status and authority. Lower-status members/followers are usually arrayed one behind the other facing the powerful figure, who if most powerful (monarch, judge) faces the followers, and if not the most powerful, places his back to the audience interceding for, or leading the others (priest at the altar, officer at the flag). The symmetry of furnishings also has implications for interaction. Consider debating chambers like the British House of Commons, or the Cambridge Union, a law court, or some nineteenth-century non-Conformist churches which had two pulpits, actually separating two people or groups of people who were expected to be in some form of conflict or disagreement. If there is a platform or enclosure between two spaces, the occupant is the referee, or judge – a person said to be impartial and not aligned, but often the final authority.

Consider the following three examples that illustrate the functional model suggested: an Anglican church, a court-room and a restaurant. Each typical setting has considerable variety within it, but we shall consider traditional examples of each.

An Anglican church uses a great number of the variables we have mentioned to highlight or symbolise certain acts and relationships. The church is traditionally divided into two sections, the nave and the sanctuary. The nave is public and secular, the sanctuary private, though visible, and sacred. Only the preachers, celebrants and assistants are allowed into the sanctuary, which is usually higher than the nave, more elaborately decorated and with different light. There are two focal points, the altar and the pulpit; these are the two highest points in the church and are used for different functions. The font, used for baptism, is usually near the main door, symbolising acceptance into the church. Occasionally a family, usually of wealthy landowners, may own a pew over which they have control and exclusive use; such pews are near the front of the nave to symbolise the family's importance. The direction in which furniture faces clearly indicates its symbolic function. The use of such props as candles, bells and a myriad of vestments (mitre, stole, cassock) constantly help to symbolise and reinforce sacred and secular distinctions. Joiner (1970) has noted how the interiors of small Danish churches reflect not only the formality of the set liturgy but also the social status differences between the villagers who use the building.

Court-rooms also provide a good example of the functional model of social situations. The most prominent position in any court-room is the high bench used by the most important and powerful figure in the room, the judge, who is uniquely dressed in symbols of power and status. Opposite one another and below the judge are usually to be found the representatives of the opposing parties, who argue points with one another. Three other important zones are clearly signalled by their height, visibility and the direction in which they face. They are the dock, the walled, enclosed box for the person or persons accused; the stand in which the witnesses are questioned; and the seats in which the jury sits. Certain members of the court are restricted in their movement much more than others who are allowed to pace up and down. There are separate entrances to the court, usually leading to different levels of outside room which also symbolise status and position. Even an empty court-room signals a great deal of information about the structure, proceedings and values of the law. Similarly Joiner (1970) found that in government and commercial organisations occupants of single-person rooms arranged their rooms so that furniture served as cues for interaction – territoriality, zones, distance and personal orientation – as well as social status.

Goffman (1971) made a number of important distinctions about rituals, using restaurants as examples. The most commonly quoted is about back and front stage areas. Restaurants have public open areas decorated specifically for effect with appropriate colours, odours, ventilation, music, etc. They also have working areas in which the food is produced. The lighting, decoration, etc., are quite different in the back stage and front stage areas and hence so is the interaction of the people who are able to pass from one area to another (waiters, managers) with those who remain either back stage or front stage. The size and number of tables and chairs and the type of decoration used clearly indicate who the clientele usually are, the sort of food that is served and the types of interaction likely to occur (business lunches, family celebrations, romantic dinners). The use of other rooms for leaving coats, having pre-meal drinks, etc., gives a clue to the nature of the social interaction likely to take place in the restaurant. Finally, the different dress of restaurant personnel – the dress suit for the manager, special insignia for the head or wine waiter – also helps to show up numerous important distinctions.

The effect of the environment on interaction

From a very early age we are socialised into behaving appropriately in different physical settings, which often have strong symbolic meaning. We have a set of expectations about how to behave, cultural and group norms for verbal and nonverbal behaviours, and a number of concepts for interpreting and understanding the behaviour of others. We have a concept of place.

Ittelson *et al*. (1974) maintained that there are at least two possible ways of looking at how the environment shapes social interaction and vice versa. Firstly one can look at the idea of *place*, and at certain physical place types like the home, the office, the pavement, the restaurant, the hospital ward and so on. One might observe how the arrangement of different props leads to interaction patterns, and how different values or needs of certain groups had led them to structure a particular place in a unique way. For Canter (1977) a place is the result of relationships between actions, conceptions and physical attributes and an important unit for the study of environmental interaction. Secondly one could begin with the idea of *space*, and look at how we act or react to various situations as a function of certain spaces within them – distance, orientation, posture, height. Depending on other aspects of the situation, distances between people might signal threat, intimacy, affection, etc. Spatial differences maintained by people from different groups (classes, cultures, age groups, mental health categories) reveal that behaviour is normative to various groups and that it serves both functional and symbolic purposes. However, as Liebman (1970) pointed out, there are at least four factors influencing personal space norms and behaviour: the physical environment, the personality of the individual, situational tasks or relations, and the personality of other individuals. Yet another factor is cultural differences. Rapaport (1969) showed how the focal point and the spaces of seating in living rooms differed between cultures as a function of the position and necessity of the hearth.

Environmental psychologists, drawing on the work of social psychologists, anthropologists and sociologists as well as from their own observations, have come up with a number of interesting concepts regarding social behaviour and the psychophysical environment. These concepts may be very useful in the analysis of specific social situations, though it must be added that there is no clear consensus about the definition or necessity of all of these concepts within psychology or interested disciplines (architecture, planning).

Territoriality. This involves the ways in which individuals make temporary or permanent claims on various aspects of their environment – temporal and behavioural – and the way they control who may or may not enter a particular physical domain. There are at least two types of territory: personal territory, which might include permanent areas such as house, garden, car and office, and temporary areas such as hotel rooms, library tables, cinema seats; and 'home' territories, which are usually public places such as a particular street corner or pub bench normally used by members of a particular group. There are many reasons why people might lay claim to certain spaces – to reduce the possibilities of interaction, to establish status or role rights, protect possessions, maintain or preserve their sense of personal identity. Territoriality is most obviously manifest in living quarters such as homes, barracks, schools, etc., where numerous factors such as the size of the house and the number, age, status, personality, culture and habits of the people lead to the occupation and possession of space. Sommer and Becker (1969) demonstrated how people could claim public space by leaving certain markers. Territoriality is also a group phenomenon: for instance adolescent or ethnic groups mark certain territories by their presence. Altman (1975) has shown that territories can be classified by their association with primary, secondary and reference group functions. More recently, design principles have been derived from theories of territoriality. Clearly social situations that occur in marked private territory such as a bedroom will affect the social behaviour of the owner and invader of that territory.

Crowding. A great deal of research into crowding had recently taken place, and there are a number of models and theories to explain it, though a number of authors regard it as an ambiguous concept as it is context-specific (Canter, 1977). Crowding may be defined as a psychological state of stress that *sometimes* accompanies high population density (Stokols, 1972). The three most commonly quoted models of crowding are the following:

1. The overload model assumes that it is the excessive input of social and physical stimuli (too many interaction partners, prolonged interactions, heat, noise, personal-space invasions) that leads to the subjective experience of crowding.

2. The behaviour-constraint model assumes that in conditions of high density people's goals are blocked and their behavioural freedom curtailed and hence they show signs of frustration and reaction commonly associated with crowding.

3. The ecological model assumes that where settings are overpopulated, that is where there are more people than necessary to perform the requisite activities, subjective feelings of crowding arise.

Crowding does not refer exclusively to close physical contact and density, but is a psychological subjectively experienced phenomenon. The experience of crowding is determined by how space is organised and for what purposes; what are the nature of the activities, personalities and learning experience of the people involved? The most salient factor in crowding appears to be the frustration a person suffers in having his goals blocked by high density of people, together with a sense of depersonalisation. Crowding is, however, not always perceived negatively. In some activities, and with certain cultural groups, crowding may be experienced as exhilarating or as a sign of solidarity.

Crowded situations may lead to a number of possible psychological effects, depending on the intensity, duration and individual needs of the participants. These effects may include: heightened arousal, aggression, frustration, reduced task performance, embarrassment, laughter, etc. Stokols (1978) has suggested that crowding experiences will be most intense and difficult to resolve in psychologically important, rather than secondary, environments and in the context of perceived threat. The literature on the effects of crowding is often ambiguous: some studies using children have shown that normal children reduced their social encounters under crowded conditions, while brain-damaged children became more aggressive, and autistic children spent more time at the boundaries of the room (Hutt and Vaizey, 1966). McGrew (1970) showed that increased social density (group size increases, area size remains constant) rather than spatial density (area size decreases, group size remains constant) had a greater disruptive effect on free play in nurseries. Thus social situations which are socially and spatially crowded, such as shops, lifts and certain sporting functions, could have important consequences on the social behaviour of the participants.

Cohen, Sladen and Bennett (1975) demonstrated that students tolerated higher densities with acquaintances than with strangers and that they preferred high densities in recreational and cooperative activities than at work or independent activities.

      Privacy. Privacy includes all processes by which people control the flow of information and interaction; it is defined by Kelvin (1973) as the perceived limitation of the other's power over oneself. Privacy is the ability to choose freely what a person will communicate, and to whom, in certain situations, and is clearly related to motivational aspects of communication. Privacy is not necessarily the same as physical isolation, which might produce a contrasting feeling from that induced by privacy. Westin (1967) has isolated four states of privacy and related functions: *solitude*, where a person is free from the observation of others; *intimacy*, where a person needs privacy from surveillance and other sensory distraction; *anonymity*, where a person seeks freedom from identification; and *reserve*, where a person has the opportunity for minimal self-disclosure. According to Westin, privacy fulfils four distinct functions: personal autonomy (control over one's life and environment), emotional release (tension release for emotional unwinding), self-evaluation (integration and assimilation of information about oneself), and the limiting and protection of communication. Work in mental hospitals, schools and military establishments has very clearly pointed to the need for privacy and norms in certain situations. Altman (1975) has spelt out the way people employ behavioural strategies to maintain desired levels of privacy. Privacy, however, may be temporal in nature, people having very different privacy needs during the cycle of one day.

      Personal space. This refers to how people perceive and structure the space around them. There are various consequences when a person's body space is invaded, usually shown in measures of emotional arousal. Certain groups require more personal space or body-buffer zones than others. Horowitz, Duff and Stratton (1969) showed that male and female schizophrenics had a greater need for personal space than matched non-schizophrenics, while Kinzel (1970) found that violent prisoners had body-buffer zones almost three times as large as non-violent prisoners. Watson and Graves (1966) showed that when Arabs talked to one another they stood closer together and faced each other more directly than pairs of Americans. Watson (1972) also showed that Latin Americans, Asians and Indians were intermediate between Arabs and Americans in preferred personal space.

    Other important variables related to space are interpersonal distance, orientation, height and movement. Hall (1966) postulated the existence of four spatial zones that are used differentially as a function of setting and social relationship, though this has not been empirically tested. They were 'intimate' (o – 18 inches), 'personal' (18 inches to 4 feet), 'social consultative' (9 feet to 12 feet) and 'public social occasions' (12 feet and above). More recently empirical work and observation have been done on zones of co-presence. Ciolek (1979) in an observational study suggested that the field of co-presence is clearly limited and consists of five concentrically nested spaces that correspond to man's senses: vision, hearing, smell, touch mediated by tools, direct contact. The radii of these zones were found to be 100, 33, 10, 3 and 1 yard respectively.

Other aspects of the environment, more associated with objects than with spaces, have important effects on social interaction. These include barriers, furniture arrangement and the aesthetic appeal of rooms.

Barriers. The placing of barriers within and between buildings can influence many aspects of interaction. Festinger *et al.* (1950) demonstrated that the positioning of stairways in buildings can have clear effects on friendship formation. They found friendship formation to be a function of distance from and position on staircases. Gullahorn (1952) found that where filing cabinets acted as barriers in a large office people spent more time talking to fewer individuals than where there were no barriers. Some barriers such as screens or windows are designed to prevent communication of some, but not all, information (sight versus sound).

Furniture. Sommer and Ross (1958) demonstrated in a study in a geriatric ward that furniture arrangement can dramatically affect interaction – when the chairs were placed around small tables this facilitated interaction, but when they were placed side-by-side along the wall it was discouraged. Chair orientation has also been shown to affect various forms of affiliative behaviour. The more directly chairs faced the more affiliative people were (Mehrabian and Diamond, 1971). Steinzor (1950) showed that when sitting at a round table discussants addressed more remarks to people sitting opposite them than to those in any other, less accessible, position. Gullahorn (1952) observed twelve filing clerks in an office who sat in three rows. He found that the clerks tended to interact with members of the same row more than members of another row indicating that distance and orientation is a primary factor in interaction in offices. It was also found that people in closed, rather than open, offices tended to interact more with one another. Thus, as Wells (1965) has pointed out, organisations can encourage group communication within large departments by appropriately altering seating arrangements. Brookes and Kaplan (1972) noted that open-planned offices which kept small working groups together in the same space divided off by low movable barriers increased sociability but led to other distractions. Smith (1974), in a study of the relationship between space, play and equipment in nursery schools, found that behaviour was affected by the amount of spatial confinement of the nursery. The quantity of play equipment had a marked influence on social behaviour in that where there were fewer toys the size of the play group increased and more sharing occurred, though there was also more aggression. Later work revealed that the actual nature of the play equipment induced different amounts of cooperation behaviour: larger and more symbolic toys led to more activity and cooperation.

Aesthetic room appeal. In an early experiment Maslow and Mintz (1956) demonstrated that the aesthetic nature of a room can affect various interpersonal processes. Subjects judged photographs of others and of themselves less favourably while in an ugly room than when in a beautiful room. Mintz (1956) demonstrated that interviews did not last as long in an ugly room as in a beautiful one. Canter and Wools (1970) showed that furniture type was the most important factor in the perception of the friendliness of rooms.

Environmental stressors and behaviour

For some time environmental and social psychologists, human experimentalists and ergonomicists have been studying environmental modifiers that tax or exceed a person's adaptive resources and affect the emotional tone of behaviour being enacted within them. These environmental modifiers are also called stressors, and several studies have reported the direct effect of such stressors as temperature, light, noise, air pollution, colour, odour, humidity and exposure to novel stimuli, which at certain levels of intensity can have dramatic effects on behaviour. Modifiers seem to be particularly important elements in a situation when they are at extremes, though these extremes are determined by the situation itself (extremes of noise in a library are different from those in a playground, as are those of heat in a sauna and in an office). We have expectations about the levels of modifiers in a situation, and when these are infringed our behaviour is affected. To some extent these elements can take on a symbolic significance (light in a church or bedroom, odour in a restaurant) and become particularly noticeable by their absence or presence. Some modifiers, such as music ('muzak') or colour, may act subliminally or unconsciously.

Modifiers. A number of experiments have investigated the effects of modifiers upon certain aspects of behaviour:

1. *Heat*. A link has been found between heat and aggression. Goranson and King (1970) found that outbreaks of riots in the United States in 1967

occurred at the same time as rises in temperature, though the exact nature of the link is uncertain. Baron and Bell (1977) found that as the temperature rose, students were more likely to act aggressively toward an accomplice, but that beyond a certain temperature level (85°F) there was a decline in open aggressive responding. This was confirmed by Baron and Ransberger (1978), who in an archive study of the period 1967–71 found that the number of riots increased as the temperature rose to the mid-eighties Fahrenheit, but that further increments beyond this point were associated with a decrease in the number of civil disturbances. High levels of temperature have also been shown to affect interpersonal attraction. Griffitt (1970) demonstrated that at three levels of attitude similarity, subjects were more attracted to a stranger when the temperature was normal than when it was hot. The temperature, airflow and humidity of classrooms not only affect comfort but also learning. Higher temperatures have been shown to make children more easily distracted and less effective at arithmetic and learning tasks. Using teachers' judgements of their pupils' behaviour, Humphreys (1974) found that cool days were associated with high industriousness and moderate energy, hot days with low energy and low industriousness, and windy days with high energy and low industriousness.

2. *Light*. Many early industrial studies investigating the effects of light upon productivity revealed that the two were related, though it was demonstrated that in many studies the famous Hawthorne effect accounted for the relationship. Numerous psychological processes can be affected by various forms of light – the stroboscopes at discos, or the special lighting in supermarkets which makes food look more highly coloured. Champness (1979) noted that a subject's perception of the attractiveness of strangers was affected by the type of neon light under which they worked. Boyce (in Canter *et al.*, 1975) has reviewed many studies which have revealed direct and indirect effects of lighting on task performance and preferences for certain types of light.

3. *Noise*. There is a vast literature on the effect of noise upon behaviour (Glass and Singer, 1972). Uncontrollable noise has been shown to produce greater aggression (Donnerstein and Wilson, 1976), less altruistic behaviour (Sherrod and Downs, 1974), and a low tolerance for frustration (Sherrod *et al.*, 1977). Many studies have demonstrated the adverse effects of noise upon performance (Hamilton and Copeman, 1970). Smith and Curnow (1966) found that people spent less time in supermarkets in which there was loud, as opposed to soft, music in the background, though it did not affect the amount of purchasing. Wohlwill and Heft (1978) found that children from noisy homes performed less well on selective attention tasks and were less sensitive to auditory distraction than children from quiet homes. Lack of sound, however, can also be a stressor, as sensory deprivation experiments have demonstrated. It seems that certain types and levels

of noise may affect behaviour, the effect depending on the controllability, duration and predictability of the noise and the situation in which it occurs.

4. *Odour.* With the rise of urban industrialisation, applied psychologists have been concerned with the effects of pollution upon behaviour. Lewis *et al.* (1970) demonstrated that subjects who breathed clean air were more efficient on information processing tasks than matched subjects who breathed air heavily polluted by motor traffic. Rotton *et al.* (1976) demonstrated that college students who lived in offensive-smelling rooms expressed more negative attitudes about themselves, their peers and their environment than students in rooms with a normal odour. Clearly the appropriateness of odour to certain situations is important – the smell of food and cooking is considered inappropriate in a living room or bedroom, while the disinfectant smell considered satisfactory in a bathroom or lavatory is highly undesirable in a dining room.

5. *Others.* A number of other variables – colour, humidity, etc. – are also important. In an early review article Norman and Scott (1952) pointed to the effect of colour on emotion in specific situations. Wright and Rainwater (1962) found that the emotional responses to colours are determined almost entirely by the combination of hue, saturation and lightness. Thus happiness may be signalled by a combination of blueness, saturation and lightness, and warmth by redness, saturation and darkness. The controllability of and length of exposure to the stressor appear to be the most important factors in predicting how stressful the environmental conditions will be. However as Stokols (1978) has pointed out, the persistence and generalisability of stress responses across situations have not been adequately examined.

Overloading. Certain environments overstimulate sensory capacity so that people within them do not have the capacity to scan or process incoming information. Excessive stimulus information for extended periods might lead to a person becoming increasingly passive and withdrawn, and his behaviour routinised, simplified and unproductive.

Most writers on the subject have looked at behaviour in larger environments, such as living in crowded cosmopolitan cities, working in large organisations, or living in large institutions, but there are other situations that cause overloading, e.g. discos, industrial workshops, even supermarkets. Meier (1962) has argued that the variety and complexity of communication techniques and media in modern social institutions causes overload. As a continuous stream of information reaches people, backlogs accrue, more work is automated and less face-to-face interaction takes place. As more time is spent on coding and recoding information than on its simple transmission, overload occurs.

Milgram (1970) considered the effects and coping strategies that result from overloaded environments. He maintains that the concept of overloading helps to explain at least four major contrasts between urban and rural behaviour: role enactment, urban norms, cognitive processes and competition for facilities. Milgram identified five coping strategies: less time is given to each input; low-priority inputs are disregarded; the burden of social responsibility is moved on to others; social screening devices are interposed between the individual and the environment; and specialised institutions are created to absorb inputs. One of the most important consequences of overloading is the lack of bystanders' intervention in crises (Latané and Darley, 1970) and the unwillingness to trust or assist strangers.

However, it must be borne in mind that there are personality differences and demographic differences regarding coping with and avoiding sensory overload. Indeed some people actively seek out arousing environments (Mehrabian, 1978; Zuckerman, 1978). This was demonstrated in experiment 4.3, where the relationship between extroversion and neuroticism and the choice and avoidance of social situations was demonstrated. It is also wrong to assume that overloading always has a deleterious effect on social behaviour. In some situations heightened arousal may greatly benefit the behaviour of the participants.

The built environment. A number of writers have considered the nature of the built environment and the city as an unnatural habitat (Ittelson *et al.*, 1974). Ittelson *et al.* maintained that pleasant living in the built environment of a city or town is dependent on six basic requirements:

1. Reduction of stress from noise pollution, poor and inadequate housing, crowding and sensory overload.
2. Opportunity for community and sociability, in that the physical environment facilitates certain social and civic interaction.
3. Ease of movement between important places of work, recreation and habitation. Also the ability of the inmates to form an accurate and useful image of the city.
4. Environmental enrichment which provides vitality, novelty and movement and an assortment of sounds, smells and colours often with symbolic meaning.
5. Cultural and recreational activities that allow for a variety of interests – theatres, museums, sports facilities, etc.
6. An ability to take part in the decision process and have some control or say in the way their environment is changed.

A built environment provides a unique opportunity for certain types of interaction and social situations to occur. Neighbourhoods in big cities are very heterogeneous, allowing for the opportunity of mixing. The transience of settlement in built environments also has important implications for the way in which people interact. The need for open recreational areas and for less congestion in cities has been shown by the flight to the suburbs in many Western cities.

One very interesting research tradition that has grown out of an analysis of the built environment is the interest in mental maps (Lynch, 1960; Gould and White, 1974). The images people have of certain places can give us a very good indication of their perception of, and interaction in, those environments. Further, it can reveal patterns of ignorance, information and learning. Pearce (1977) showed that one could obtain information about a tourist's movements in a city by getting him to draw a mental map of the city.

Institutional living. The requirements of housing and caring for people in a variety of institutions – mental hospitals, military barracks, old people's homes, student dormitories, boarding schools, etc. – have a number of behavioural consequences. Most people work, play and live in different settings that have different inhabitants and authority structures, yet in institutions this is not so: living, working and sleeping all take place in the same setting, with the same group. Further, in order to coordinate activities a fairly rigid timetable has to be followed, usually to fulfil set goals of the institution.

Sommer and Osmond (1961) have isolated a number of institutional experiences in a mental hospital, such as disculturation and de-individuation, impairment and physical damage based on hospital experiences, estrangement from the civilian world, isolation from friends and family and stimulus deprivation. Goffman (1961b) has distinguished between two types of institutions: total and partial. The former may vary considerably: they may protect or care for people unable to look after themselves, detain those who threaten the community, provide facilities for those working in some group, form or provide a safe setting where people can remove themselves from the world. Goffman (1961b) paid particular attention to mental hospitals, which have been a recent focus of popular interest in drama ('One flew over the cuckoo's nest') and politics (Russian mental hospitals). Goffman maintained that behaviour in total institutions is affected in two respects: disculturation and a process of regression whereby the person becomes less and less able to control his own affairs both within and outside the institution; self-respect, autonomy and self-determination are all undermined. Zimbardo (1973) showed the dramatic effects of role pressure in prisons, which are usually total institutions. However the effects of partial institutions such as day care centres and schools are far less startling.

In most institutions there is a clear relationship between the physical form of the institution and its goals. The philosophy of the institution is often apparent in the combination of open spaces, opportunities for privacy, and barriers between staff and inmates. Prisons are often very similar to one another, as are mental hospitals, monasteries and private hospitals. A number of studies (Kennedy and Highlands, 1964; Sivadon, 1970) have shown that rate of recovery after illness is related to the physical environment. Canter and Canter (1979) have devised a set of seven questions which policy-makers and administrators should ask themselves: e.g. 'Can therapeutic processes be set in motion by changes in the physical surroundings?', 'Does the provision of the facility in this location tend to make it part of a larger setting or does it help to establish it as a smaller unit?'. Holahan and Saegert (1973) showed how adaptive behaviour could be encouraged in a psychiatric hospital simply by changes in the physical layout. Much the same is true of prisons. Gilbert (1972) showed that degree of confinement was a critical factor in prisoner satisfaction and good behaviour. In both prisons and hospitals, however, size was an important factor – the larger the institution, the more unsuccessful the attainment of goals.

Moos (1973*a*) has devised a number of rating scales for social institutions, as also has Stern (1969). Moos found three dimensions which best discriminate between different environmental institutions: relationships (involvement, support, expressiveness), personal development (autonomy, self-sufficiency, practical and problem-solving orientation) and system maintenance and change (order, clarity and control). Various scales have been devised for the assessment of specific environments: the Living Room Check List (Laumann and House, 1970), the Activity Pattern List (Craik, 1970), the Environmental Descriptor Scale (Kasmar, 1970), the Ward Atmosphere Scale (Moos, 1974), the Classroom Environment Scale (Moos, 1974), the Military Company Environment Scale (Moos, 1973*b*), etc. Price and Blashfield (1975) factor analysed 455 settings in a small mid-western town and found twelve distinct types of behaviour setting. Moos (1976) has suggested that these types of settings may provide insights concerning the socialisation, economic, political and behavioural control functions of social settings in the context of an entire community. He thus reclassified the findings of Price and Blashfield into four groups: those concerned with economic production, those oriented toward political goals, those concerned primarily with social integration and those concerned with behavioural pattern maintenance.

Environmental assessment and evaluation

The aim of environmental assessment is to develop techniques and tools that systematically and validly describe and evaluate the physical and social environment. Two approaches are traditionally used to assess the environment – the so-called 'subjective' approach based on impressions and observations by different groups of people, and the 'objective' approach based on a number of standard technical measures. The former includes ratings on prepared or generated scales of pictures, diagrams and models, free descriptions of environments, reports after tours, interviews with 'users' of various environments, etc. The latter includes the use of diverse and complicated instruments from light meters to colour charts. Environmental assessment and evaluation also has a temporal factor: environments may be assessed before they are constructed or changed, immediately after they have been created and also over long periods of time (Altman, 1975).

There are a great number of techniques available for use in the assessment and evaluation of social environments. Many of these are standard social psychological or clinical psychological in origin, while others have been specifically developed for and by environmental psychologists. They include the following:

Structured questionnaires and rating tasks. These can take many forms, ranging from a piloted set of rating scales for judging specific stimuli (the environment itself, photographs, drawings or models of the environment) to numerous rating tasks (sorting stimuli in groups, rating similarity, psychophysical scaling, etc.). To some extent the statistical technique that is to be employed dictates the type of task that is to be done. Questionnaires and rating task data can be used either to reveal dimensions in the perception of social situations or to compare differences in perception of the same environments between two groups. Recently a number of inventories have been psychometrically validated for use in certain institutional settings (Moos, 1979).

Interviews. These may be in-depth interviews with many open-ended questions, or market-research-type interviews concerned with specific reactions to the environment. Interviews with different groups of people who use an environment may provide a very useful starting point for further research into disparate perceptions and needs of users.

'Cognitive tests'. Two widely used tests for the assessment of social and physical environments are linked to clinical psychology and geography respectively. The repertory grid has been widely used to reveal the range and complexity of a person's constructs about the environment (Stringer, 1974). Although time-consuming, this test often provides very useful detailed information about how a person or group of persons perceives their environment, and may be useful for the development of rating scales. More recently, getting subjects to draw maps of their environment has been found to be an extremely useful technique for investigating people's experience and perception of various environments such as schools, neighbourhood, town or shopping centre (Lynch, 1960).

Diaries. By getting people to keep diaries of their free-time activities and movements one can form a good idea of how much people use certain environments, how regularly people interact in them, for how long, and with whom. Diaries may be prepared such that people record specific happenings in certain time periods. For example they may be required to state every two hours what they had been doing, where, with whom, what their feelings were, etc.

Observation. This may take many forms, such as detailed unstructured written or spoken observation of activities in certain environments, checking specific activities from a structured report sheet, participant observation with written reports afterwards, photographs, tape-recordings, video-tapes, etc. Usually the more rich the data in terms of the stimuli preserved (words, action, sounds) and the more accurate the data in terms of the original activity, the 'better' the observation, although this sort of coding and analysis is extremely time-consuming. In most instances observers need to be carefully trained in order to make useful observations of environments (Barker, 1968).

Unobtrusive measurements. Many unobtrusive measurements, from the amount and type of litter or of graffiti on buildings to the wear and tear on certain furnishings, enable psychologists to gain some idea of people's attitudes to, and experience of, certain environments. These techniques are particularly useful because they reduce or eliminate the amount of psychological reactance on the part of subjects, and provide reliable, accurate data on certain behaviours in the environments (Webb *et al.*, 1966).

Technical measurements. These include any of a great number of scales and devices that accurately measure one aspect of the physical environment – heat, light, damp, colour, etc. Though these instruments are widely used in building design and evaluation, they are not always particularly useful for environmental psychologists' assessment of people's subjective responses to the environment.

Canter *et al.* (1975) have summarised the major dimensions that arise out of environmental evaluation (Table 10.1). The first three are similar to those arising out of dimensional studies on the perception of social situations. Canter also noted that the medium of presentation of stimuli for evaluation – the simulations of the real environment – does not have a very noticeable affect on the evaluations themselves as long as the environment is simulated as adequately as possible.

Planning the environment

Environmental planners can plan environments so that to some extent they

TABLE 10.1. *Descriptors arising from work on environmental evaluation*

Building aspect title	Vielhauer Kasmar (1970)	Canter (1968a)	Craik (1968)	Hershberger (1972)	Collins (1969)
Aesthetic		Impressive Unique Interesting	Dynamic Different Interesting	Exciting Unique Interesting	Expressive Unique Interesting
Friendliness	Beautiful Attractive Appealing	Soft Friendly Welcoming	Civilised Cheerful Joyful	Soft Friendly Comfortable	Fun Happy Joyful
Organised	Organised Efficient Orderly	Tidy Coherent Clear		Ordered Controlled Clear	Equipped Coordinated Complete
Potency		Rough Coarse Dark		Rugged Massive Permanent	
Space	Roomy Large Wide	Spacious Changeable Flexible		Spacious Large Loose	Liveable Lived in Curtained
Ornate	Bright Colourful Gay		Conservative Colourful Bizarre	Generous Rich Lavish	Textured Bright colour Flashy
Neat	Clean Tidy Neat		Dirty Empty Broad		Cluttered Confined Roomy
Size	Large Huge		Big Huge Broad	Large Formal Proud	Big Large Roomy

From Canter *et al.* (1975, p. 194).

regulate, encourage or discourage social interaction. They could also plan for a maximisation of choice or flexibility. For instance it has been established that propinquity is an important factor in determining friendship formation and neighbour relations predominantly where the population is very homogeneous. Gans (1961) pointed out that if residents are homogeneous, the planner must decide whether to advocate homogeneous residential areas which will encourage friendship among neighbours, or heterogeneous areas which will encourage mixing of social classes and ages. Other important factors that can be planned for are uniformity, to discourage symbols of rank or status, or variety, to encourage interest.

We shall consider three of the many important aspects of planning: control of spaces, that is the amount of public and private space individuals have in their environments; under- and overmanning, that is the size of the population in any environment; and the use of symbolic signs and props.

Control of spaces. We have seen how central the concept of space is in the physical environment. The concepts of territoriality, crowding, privacy, personal space, overloading are all derived from the concept of space. Three problems might confront the planner in the design of space. Firstly, the costs of planning environments for optimal spaces that lead to the satisfaction of the inhabitants may be astronomical or plainly impossible. Secondly there may be curious contradictions in the ideas about space of both the planners and the inhabitants. Architects and councillors may have ideas about what is practical and necessary that are quite different from administrators and workers. People who live in environments may also have different needs for privacy and social stimulation, private territories and group areas. Thirdly needs may change over time as people change, get used to new conditions, or adapt to other changes.

Work in applied settings has shown the importance of spatial layout in social behaviour. Trites *et al.* (1970) compared three floor plans in general hospitals: the single corridor with a nursing station at the centre; the double corridor with nursing stations on either side; and the radial ward which has a nursing station at the centre with rooms encircling it. They found that staff on a radial ward spent less time moving about and more time with their patients, though they were more often working on 'non-productive' activities in the working station. Further there was a lower incidence of absenteeism and accidents in the radial ward.

Richardson (1967) pointed out that a teacher can arrange desks in a classroom in a number of ways for quite specific purposes:

1. Rows of desks, for exams or teacher-centred sessions with minimal discussion.
2. Groups of four desks facing each other, or a library table, for reading quietly by oneself.
3. A stage arrangement, with desks in a semi-circle around the teacher's desk which has a few rows of desks behind it for play reading.
4. A hollow square, for committee work or discussions.
5. Rows of desks facing on two sides of the room, with the teacher in the middle for a language lesson etc.
6. A semi-circle of desks for discussion.

Nevertheless planning spaces can be very important, as the dramatic reactions of people who are dissatisfied with their spatial arrangements have shown (Sommer and Peterson, 1967). Various populations have special

288

spatial needs and it is extremely important that planners should be aware of them. Planners may engineer various effects by the control of spaces. It does not require much imagination to construct situations that are a direct function of spatial arrangements, leading to group forming, to interpersonal attraction, to intergroup hostility, to the emergence of leaders, etc. Careful and judicial planning may lead to goals being achieved whereas the opposite can contribute directly to a serious breakdown in various forms of behaviour.

In a later section we discuss the ways in which large blocks of flats have been redesigned to deal with vandalism and other forms of crime which have been widespread in such buildings (p. 359f.)

Under- and overmanning. The number of people in any situation is clearly going to affect the quality and quantity of the interaction in that situation. This is particularly true of work situations, where inappropriate manning levels can cause industrial and political disputes over manning and job specification in certain job situations. In ecological psychology the concept and theory of overmanning was proposed by Barker (1968) and developed by Wicker (Wicker *et al.*, 1972; Wicker, 1973) who stressed the importance of the subjective experience of users of settings.

Barker (1960) proposed that occupants in undermanned settings:
1. Work harder and longer to support the setting and its function.
2. Get involved in more difficult and important tasks.
3. Participate in a greater diversity of tasks and roles.
4. Become less sensitive to differences between people.
5. Have a lower level of maximal or best performance.
6. Have a greater functional importance of individuals within the setting.
7. Become more responsible in the sense that the setting and what others gain from it depend on the individual occupant.
8. View themselves and others more in terms of task-related than social-emotional characteristics.
9. Set lower standards and fewer tests for admission into a setting.
10. Have greater insecurity about the eventual maintenance of the setting.
11. Have more frequent occurrences of success and failure, depending upon the outcome of the setting's functions.

A great many studies comparing small (usually undermanned) and large (usually overmanned) organisations have confirmed many of Barker's ideas – primarily that undermanning generates stronger forces towards participation in essential tasks or functions than optimal manning or overmanning does. Most of the earlier work was carried out in schools and churches. Wicker (1969) found that members of small churches contributed more money, attended Sunday worship more frequently, spent more time in church settings and were more approving of high levels of support for church activities than members of a large church.

Later work made a number of important distinctions in this area. Wicker *et al.* (1972) criticised the traditional index of degree of manning of an organisation and suggested that it should be replaced by a more precise measure which takes account of the capacity, the number of applications for positions and the minimum number of persons required in organisational settings. Secondly, they suggested a more complete specification of the degrees of manning: in terms of two mutually exclusive sets of setting occupants (performers and non-performers) and the minimum/maximum capacity for maintenance of a setting (Wicker, 1973). The maintenance minimum for performers is the smallest number of functions required to make a setting continue, with performers carrying out the necessary tasks in the proper sequence. Maintenance minimum for non-performers is the smallest number of people who must be present as consumers in the setting for it to continue. The capacity for performers could be constrained by either physical (space, seating) or social factors (roles available). Applicants for the performer role are people eligible to participate and who wish to do so while applicants for the non-performer role need only meet the requirements for those wishing to enter the seating. Hence undermanning occurs when applicants barely exceed the maintenance minimum. Such factors as the task structure and the authority setting need to be carefully matched.

In that manning is clearly related to goals, rules and roles, it is an important mediating situational variable. The more undermanned a social or work situation is, the more roles and goals there are for each person, and the higher the motivation they have for playing these roles. The important and large literature on organisational size (Warr, 1971) which elaborates on ecological studies, draws similar conclusions.

Symbolic signs and props. It is only when we visit a cultural group different from our own that we notice the constant use of symbolic signs and props in social interaction. Many are universal, others quite culturally specific. Some situations – such as formal ritualised events like religious and military ceremonies and royal occasions – are very rich in symbols and props, while others are relatively free from them.

People within the same group are usually able to read the language of signs or props, which often undergo changes in fashion. The ostentatiously placed car in the front drive, the name plaque on the house, the personalised number plate, the famous painting, the size of the desk and the number and style of telephones all carry a message to those who are perceptive (Harré, 1976). Some props have no practical or even aesthetic advantage except that they occasion admiration and carry status. Positively evaluated signs or props are usually different from others in their size, height, colour, ornateness, cost and abundance. Negatively evaluated signs are the opposite, and not as common. Props and possessions can also communicate other messages besides status – e.g. religious beliefs, orderliness, political beliefs, past history. Indeed any messages about one's self-image can be portrayed by possessions.

Providing for the use of props in the environment may be the job of the planner. He may thus provide in his planning the structure for various status relationships by the making available of various props. On the other hand he may try to abolish these distinctions by giving everybody the same facilities.

A number of researchers have mentioned the importance of symbolism in social situations. Richardson (1967) reported on the use of furniture as symbols in the classroom. Mead (1934) mentioned the importance of use of symbols in children's games and play.

Conclusions

For the most part environmental psychologists have considered spatial aspects of social and physical environments. However, as we have pointed out in Chapter 1, spatial arrangements between people or between people and objects are only one aspect of situations. All environments or situations have social rules, social goals or accepted repertoires of social acts, etc., which also affect social behaviour. In fact the relationship between space and social behaviour is mediated by other elements in the situation. That is, the role relationships and situational rules often determine the perception of and reaction to spatial arrangements between people, which in turn affects the social behaviour.

There are, therefore, not only differences in the subjective experience and objective measurement of certain spatial features (e.g. crowding) in an environment, but also situational differences which are often subculturally shared and understood. Hence the experience of overload or personal space invasion is different between different situations such as a lift, an office, a dormitory and a library. We have expectations of physical aspects of certain situations and when these are unfulfilled or broken various results may occur.

We have seen that a number of physical aspects in the situation adversely affect certain forms of behaviour that the environment was designed to facilitate – offices are too noisy for work, classrooms are arranged so as to prevent communication between pupil and teacher, etc. But we have also seen that these situations are relatively easy to change – the simple rearrangement of furniture or the addition of sound-proofing, for instance, may adequately change the nature of irritants or stressors in a social situation, allowing people to define it quite differently. Situations may be changed or redefined in other ways such as changing the rules, altering the role relationships or redefining the goals. However, it is often much slower and more difficult to change social attitudes and cognitions, and hence social behaviour, than it is to make changes in the physical environment. These must be accompanied by changes in the social relationships if the two are in contradiction. It is doubtful, for instance, whether Sommer could have encouraged interaction between the inhabitants of an old people's home so dramatically by any other method than the simple rearrangement of the furniture.

Finally, we have extended our functional model of social situations to include the relationship between behaviour and environment. The physical aspects of environment (space, conditions, colour) are designed to fulfil a number of specific social and other goals. These physical components may be changed by various people who live and work in the environment to fulfil other secondary goals or goals contrary to those envisaged by the original designer. To some extent the goals of the participants in any physical setting can be ascertained by an evaluation of the furniture arrangements and the decoration in specific social environments.

11
Language and speech

Introduction

Linguists since Saussure (1916) have distinguished between *language* (*langue*), the underlying system of shared grammatical and other rules, and *speech* (*parole*), which is the way people actually talk. While grammarians take as their data idealised utterances which are generally regarded as acceptable, sociolinguists have studied the actual speech systems used by different social groups, in different situations.

It is obvious that language is used in a variety of ways in different situations. The same individuals will talk quite differently when discussing a technical problem at work, playing a game, or drinking beer. In some cultures they use different languages for different situations; in most cultures there are 'high' and 'low' speech styles for formal and informal situations. The form of language used varies with the role relations of those speaking (e.g. parent–child, husband–wife), as well as with the physical channel used (e.g. the telephone). We have pursued a functional explanation of rules and repertoire, and we shall now explore a functional model of language in relation to the goals of situations.

Sociolinguists have collected samples of speech in different settings. For example, Labov (1972b) used the methods of informal interviews, group discussion between friends, unsystematic observation and asking people to read passages and word lists. He describes an 'observer's paradox', the difficulty of finding out how people talk when they are not being observed, which can only be overcome by systematic observation. The formal–informal, or personal–transactional dimension of speech has attracted most attention from research workers, but there are probably a number of other important aspects. If speech fulfils functions in social situations, we should expect it to vary with the goals of situations.

Speech is very complex, and varies in a number of different ways. We shall see that different features of speech reflect different aspects of situations. The speech variables we shall discuss are:
1. bilingualism (and multilingualism)
2. high and low forms of language (diglossia)
3. elaborated and restricted codes
4. vocabulary (lexicon)

5. grammar and sentence construction
6. accent, speed and volume
7. meaning (semantics)
8. sequences of utterances (discourse) (see Chapter 8)

A number of linguists have embraced the idea that, in one way or another, language is 'situated'. Writers on sociolinguistics all accept this point. Firth (1957) stressed the differences between language use in different situations. Pike (1967) observed that many utterances are meaningless if removed from their contexts. Hymes (1972) suggested a list of situational determinants. Halliday, McIntosh and Strevens (1964) suggested that situations differ in the 'register' or styles of speech that are used in them. The majority of linguists, however, have ignored the importance of the situation in speech, and have written as if utterances could stand by themselves; this is particularly true of those concerned with generative or other formal grammars. It is equally true to say that most social psychologists have failed to take account of the complexities of language. Most social behaviour includes verbal components, and it is quite inadequate simply to count the lengths or number of utterances, without asking what is said or how.

In previous chapters we explored the hypothesis that the rules, elements, etc., of situations are functional in relation to the goals of those situations. We shall now explore the hypothesis that speech is functional in the same way. This hypothesis has two parts to it: (1) individual speech acts are functional in relation to the immediate goals of the speaker, (2) the whole *speech system* used in a situation is functional in relation to the main, shared goals of that situation. This hypothesis is not tautological, since we have described in Chapter 4 how the goals of situations can be found. And it is possible, by varying the situation, to test hypotheses about the emergence of different forms of language.

Robinson (1972) produced a classification of fourteen different functions of language (e.g. expressing affect, giving instructions), each of which is more likely to be satisfied in certain situations than others. We can divide these fourteen functions into two main classes of (a) dealing with a task, and (b) dealing with interpersonal relationships – a familiar division of goals in social psychology, found in studies of leadership and elsewhere. As we have found, this second set of functions is performed more by nonverbal than by verbal forms of communications (Argyle, 1975).

Verbal utterances can be classified into different kinds of *speech act*; many linguists now believe that all speech acts have an illocutionary force, that is, they have an effect on others (Austin, 1962; Searle, 1969). Originally it was thought that this applied only to certain 'performative utterances' such as naming ships, voting, promising, etc., but it has been argued that all utterances are based on underlying performatives, such as declaring or ordering (Ross, 1970; Leech, 1974).

294

When two or more people are conversing, each tends to move towards a common code if they want to be accepted by the other, but a person will diverge from that code if he wants to emphasise his difference from others present (Giles and Powesland, 1975). It was found, for example, by Moscovici (1967), that a person talking about his car to a friend used a smaller vocabulary than when talking about it to a specialist. Adults talking to children, especially younger children, use a smaller vocabulary than when talking to adults (Granownsky and Krossner, 1970). Giles, Taylor and Bourhis (1973) found such accommodation when English-speaking and French-speaking Canadians in Quebec met. However, the extent of accommodation is limited by the linguistic repertoires of the speakers; in addition there may be norms about appropriate speech styles for different roles, such as male and female, old and young.

Speech is affected by many aspects of situations. There is not yet an agreed set of categories or dimensions from this point of view, but the following are generally accepted (Hymes, 1972; Coulthard, 1977):

1. setting and scene, e.g. church, pub
2. participants, and their role relationships
3. goals
4. key, e.g. serious, light-hearted
5. channel, e.g. telephone, TV with studio audience
6. rules, e.g. governing proper behaviour at committees

This list has considerable overlap with the set of features of situations that we have adopted as chapter headings in this book. However there is one feature of situations that has been found to have a great impact on speech – the degree of formality versus informality – which could come under several of the headings set out above.

Bilingualism (and multilingualism)

Bilingualism is the term given to the situation where two languages (rather than dialects) are used in one society, and where some people are able to use both of them. Examples are French and English in Quebec, Welsh and English in Wales, and the speech of migrant workers and immigrants such as Pakistanis in Britain or Turks in Germany. In each case first the language is learnt from the parents, while the second language is learnt at school or as a result of emigration. In fact few people have equally effective control over more than one language, but many people will switch from one language to another between different situations. Fishman and Greenfield (1970) found that Puerto Ricans in New York use English in education and at work, but use Spanish in the home and with friends. In the USA many languages are used by immigrant groups, but they have to use American-English in schools, at work and in offices. The situation for an Asian immigrant to Britain is shown in Table 11.1

TABLE 11.1. *Languages used by an Asian immigrant to Britain*

Domain	Language		
Family			P
Friendship			P
Religion	A		P
Shopping		E	P
Work		E	P
Government agencies		E	

From Bell (1976, p. 131).
A, Arabic; E, English; P, Punjabi.

Where there is a choice, the language used depends on further factors, such as the native language of shopkeepers and co-workers.

There are two main reasons for the variation of language with situation. Where there are a number of different languages in use, it is necessary to have a *lingua franca* for official purposes, and for different groups to communicate with one another. In addition, a language may be imposed for political purposes, to enhance feelings of national identity, or to perpetuate a particular subculture. Examples of this are French in Quebec and Welsh in Wales.

The main situational function we have seen so far in these language shifts is that of facilitating communication between speakers of different tongues. In addition, divergence has the function of emphasising the difference between groups and hence increasing feelings of group identity. Languages have certain images, which affect their use. In Paraguay, the local language is used for intimate conversation, while English is regarded as the 'voice of intellect'. Here mixed-sex couples speak English because there is restraint on the expression of sexual involvement in public (Rubin, 1962). One language may be regarded as the 'in-group' code, and is used in the family and between friends. Use of this language is associated with friendly, informal contexts. In South India there is a choice of high and low Tamil, and English. These codes are used in situations of different formality, and so can be used to signal the way a situation is perceived. While formality of setting is the main cause of code-switching, different dialects may be used for festive occasions, fighting, or other special settings (Giles and Powesland, 1975).

High and low forms of language (diglossia)

In many societies there are two (or more) varieties of the language. This often takes the form of a *high* (H) or official language, used on formal occasions, and a *low* (L) version, or a series of regional low versions, used on informal occasions. Examples are literary and colloquial Tamil, and the use of standard German and a local dialect in Luxembourg. The 'elaborated' and 'restricted' codes in Britain described by Bernstein (1971; and p. 298) and the different grammars in the USA described by Labov (1972*b*; and p. 303) are also cases of high and low forms of speech. The use of regional dialects may operate differently, in that the local form is used in both formal and informat settings (Dittman, 1976). The range of styles may be large, as has been found in Java and Indonesia, or relatively small, as has been found in the USA and Britain (Fishman, 1972).

The use of H and L forms of language in formal and informal situations is one of the most important ways in which language varies with situation. Brown and Fraser (1980) conclude

From acquaintance with a number of very different languages, we can speculate that such differentiation follows universal principles, so that 'high' forms of language share certain properties, such as elaboration of syntax, and lexicon, phonological precision, and rhythmicity, whereas 'low' forms share other properties, including ellipsis, repetition, speed and slurring. (p. 46)

We shall discuss some of these differences in more detail when we deal with grammar, vocabulary and accent.

The situations in which H and L speech are used are:

High	Low
formal	informal
planned, careful	unplanned, casual
education, work, religion	home, friends
interview, telephone	chat, face-to-face

What functions are performed by formal and informal speech? Formal speech appears to be directed mainly towards efficient communication of questions, information, etc., so that a lot of material is conveyed, with precision. Even more formal would be a legal document or a scientific paper. Informal speech contains questions, information, etc., but is concerned with keeping people happy and interested, or other interpersonal goals, in addition to pure task goals. H speech has more complex construction and a larger vocabulary so that more precision and more information are possible; L speech is simpler and takes grammatical short-cuts. While task–interpersonal is the main dimension of situations, formal–informal is the corresponding dimension of speech.

Other aspects of the difference between H and L forms are derived from class differences: more careful self-presentation is performed for many people by adopting more respectable forms of speech, especially in pronunciation. The class differences are in turn produced by historical factors, and especially by large movements of population, such as the Irish and Puerto Ricans emigrating to the USA.

The use of H and L forms is greatly affected by the relationship between speakers. Members of a family and close friends use L forms, while in work relationships and business transactions H forms are more common. H forms tend to be used between strangers and when there is a status difference, in much the same way that more formal modes of address are used (p. 301).

Elaborated and restricted codes

Bernstein (1959) suggested that lower-working class people in Britain use only a restricted code, whereas middle-class people can use both elaborated and restricted codes, where appropriate. The distinction between elaborated and restricted codes overlaps H and L forms, but also goes further. The restricted code is of a simpler grammatical construction, and has a smaller vocabulary. In addition there is more use of phrases that seem to need an immediate answer, such as 'didn't I?', and more sentences in which reason and conclusion are confounded to produce categorical assertions.

There has been a great deal of research into class differences in speech, in different countries, partly inspired by Bernstein's ideas. We do not propose to review this here, but it is fairly clear that there are class differences in speech style in Britain, the USA, France and Germany, and that they have some correspondence to Bernstein's hypotheses (Robinson, 1972; Dittmar, 1976).

Bernstein (1971) offered an explanation of these different speech codes. Working-class people spend their time in close face-to-face groups, and have developed a form of speech which has the functions of direct control of behaviour and role-definition in face-to-face situations; this code emphasises the communal, the concrete, the here-and-now, and positional rather than personalised forms of social control. Middle-class people, on the other hand, have developed a form of language which emphasises the unambiguous transmission of information, in a way that is not dependent on the immediate context for its meaning. Bernstein supposed that class differences in speech were derived from role-structure at work, and are passed on in the course of socialisation. An alternative view is that the main difference between the two codes is the extent to which an elaborate set of constructs is developed for understanding other people, with the result that middle-class people are more able to see the point of view of a variety of others, and can communicate with them accordingly (Applegate and Delia, 1980). Collett *et al.*, in experiment 11.1, found some of the usual Bernstein differences between children of different social classes, but found no significant differences in effectiveness of communication.

Criticism of the Bernstein doctrine has focused on possible situational differences in the use of his codes. Lawton (1968) found class differences as predicted by Bernstein, and found similar differences between the forms of writing in description and abstraction tasks – abstraction produced more elaborated writing. The amount of code-switching between tasks was greatest for middle-class boys; the class differences were greatest for the abstraction task. A number of studies have found that middle-class children can speak in a more abstract and complex manner, but that working-class children can speak in a similar way if the task or instructions require it (Cazden, 1970). In experiment 11.1, Collett *et al.* found that middle-class children, in the role of instructor, used more adjectives and conjunctions when the receiver was at a distance and could not see the instructor. However there was little evidence of working-class senders shifting to a middle-class speech style in this situation, which called for more explicit instructions. A number of studies have been carried out on class differences in socialisation, which also showed situational differences. These have consistently shown that working-class mothers control their children by direct commands without argument or persuasion, while middle-class mothers control their children by discussion of the consequences for the individuals concerned (e.g. Hess and Shipman, 1965; Newson and Newson, 1970).

What has been found so far is that people in Britain shift towards the elaborated code when the task is more abstract or involves communication with strangers. We saw earlier that H forms are produced by situations that encourage self-presentation. It seems very likely that elaborated speech is a strategy for self-presentation and is used on formal occasions.

Vocabulary (lexicon)

The H and L forms have a number of different words for the same things. Thus the words used by the police in their accounts as witnesses ('I was proceeding', etc.) simply replace those used by the same people on more informal occasions ('I was walking, strolling', etc.). However there is a difference in the size of the vocabularies used; the H version has a larger vocabulary, and there is less repetition of the same words (Robinson, 1972).

In order for two people to communicate in words, they must possess a common vocabulary, i.e. a number of words to which they attach similar meanings. In order to communicate in a particular situation they need common words for those features of the situation about which they need to communicate. This vocabulary may be quite small, as in the case of the words needed to order a drink when there is only tea or coffee; no verbs, indeed no grammar, need be involved in this case. Sometimes the vocabulary is very large; this is the case in some work settings, such as a botanical garden, where the people working there need to know the names of some thousands of plants.

A number of experiments have shown that the more two people share the same concepts, the better they can communicate, e.g. they need fewer messages (Moscovici, 1967). Rommetveit (1974) makes the point that every utterance takes a certain amount of shared information for granted, and adds something to it: 'the new is nested in the old'. This new material may include the introduction of new vocabulary. Mandelbrot (1954) found that when a time limit was imposed on a discussion about the influence of films on delinquency, the number of new words introduced declined over time – the common vocabulary was established faster.

Whorf (1956) maintained that in any culture language patterns and cultural norms develop together and are constantly influencing one another. The influence of culture on language can be illustrated by the number of different Eskimo words there are for snow. Experiments have shown how language influences memory: more verbally codable colours can later be recognised better from within a larger number of colours (Brown and Lenneberg, 1954). Our hypothesis is in effect that the vocabularies used in different situations are related to the nature of those situations.

A further hypothesis is provided by Zipf's law (1949), which states that the most frequently used words are the shortest. Krauss and Weinheimer (1964) found that terms commonly used in describing a series of pictures became shorter as the experiment proceeded. The establishment of a common vocabulary proceeded faster if the listener could provide feedback to show when he had understood.

It is hardly necessary to carry out research to show that the vocabularies used in cricket, surgery, golf and cooking are different: vocabularies used in connection with different tasks and activities are often quite distinctive. Gregory and Carroll (1978) cite some striking examples, for instance from dressmaking:

> Stitch armhole facing back to armhole facing front at
> shoulders and sides.
> Pin facing to armhole edge, RIGHT SIDES TOGETHER,
> matching notches and seams. Stitch.
> GRADE seam allowances. Clip curves.
> Turn facing to INSIDE. Press.
> Top stitch $\frac{3}{8}''$ (1 cm) from armhole edge. (p. 71)

They further point out that such vocabularies are 'embedded in situation' in the sense that there are words for all the important objects, events and activities in the situation.

Every technical field has to develop its own vocabulary to deal with all the distinctions that are needed – for example by surgeons:

It has taken hundreds of years and millions of dissections to build up the detailed and accurate picture of the structure of the human body that enables the surgeon to know where to cut. A highly specialized sublanguage has evolved for the sole purpose of describing this structure. The surgeon had to learn this jargon of anatomy before the anatomical facts could be effectively transmitted to him. Thus, underlying the 'effective action' of the surgeon is an 'effective language'. (Bross, 1973, p. 217)

There are interesting cross-cultural differences in the classification e.g. of illness, parts of the body, and plants. Some of these differences reflect features of life in those societies. For example, in Russia after the Revolution, extended kinship terms were abandoned since they were no longer important for determining a person's place in society (Fishman, 1972).

Terms of address vary with situation and relationship in all cultures that have been studied. In many languages there is a choice of personal pronoun, of the *tu* and *vous* kind, sometimes with a much larger set of alternatives. There is also the choice of addressing people by first name (FN), e.g. George, or by title and last name (TLN), e.g. Mr Smith, though again there are usually more alternatives – title (T), e.g. President, last name (LN), and affectionate and nicknames, e.g. Georgie, or Windbag. Some situations, for example court-rooms, Parliament, official committees, public occasions, emphasise status differences. In these situations the *vous* form and TLN are used, rather than FN (Ervin-Tripp, 1969).

Staples and Robinson (1974), in a study of a Southampton shop, found that formality of address varied with the situation. When speaking to one another in front of customers, employees used TLN or Sir; address was less formal in the staff canteen and least formal in the street, in a pub or at a staff dance.

The power or authority relations between two people affect the way they address each other. There is often asymmetrical use of *tu* and *vous*, FN and TLN (or T), as between parents and children, managers and workers, older and younger people. The other principle of relationship is that the symmetrical use of *tu* and FN indicates solidarity, intimacy, in-group feelings (Brown and Gilman, 1960; Brown and Ford, 1961). Staples and Robinson (1974) found that there was little asymmetry of address in front of customers (12 per cent), but much more in less formal settings (about 50 per cent); it was the superiors who switched to FN in informal settings, but this was not reciprocated by subordinates. Formality increased with the distance between ranks.

The development of a situational vocabulary is influenced by several further processes.

Avoiding emotional associations. Words often acquire undesirable additional meanings, such as emotional associations. There is then pressure to adopt new words. Thus 'negro' has been replaced by 'black' (USA); 'terrorist' or 'guerilla' may be replaced by 'freedom fighter', and so on. The titles of occupations are often upgraded in this way – 'lavatory man' to 'sanitary engineer', etc.

The same process has occurred in connection with medicine and nursing. Technical terms are used instead of common ones, e.g.

    stroke – cerebral thrombosis
    heart attack – coronary infarction
    cancer – carcinoma

In physiotherapy a whole new vocabulary has developed with the deliberate purpose of freeing various kinds of massage and manipulation from possible sexual overtones.

Preventing outsiders understanding. Several studies have shown that groups of criminals develop their own special vocabulary or 'argot', partly with the purpose of preventing outsiders from understanding. Such special vocabularies have been found for professional gamblers, pickpockets, smugglers, drug addicts, prisoners and others. These argots have been described as 'antilanguages', since they use an alternative vocabulary to that used by 'straight' society, and this has the function of creating and maintaining an alternative social reality. These antilanguages have special properties: they have a new vocabulary in certain areas, there are many words for the same thing (e.g. for prostitutes, policemen), and these terms have special emotional or attitudinal components (Halliday, 1978).

It is very clear that the vocabularies used in different situations are directly functional in providing the shared terms needed for communication, making the necessary distinctions, making common terms easy to use, and in certain situations avoiding emotional associations, preventing outsiders from understanding what is said, and providing an alternative view of society.

Grammar and sentence construction

A great deal of verbal communication uses minimal syntax. An utterance can ask questions ('red or white?'), give orders ('orange juice, porridge, toast and coffee'), convey information ('1974 Marina, 27 000 miles, red, good condition'), express emotions ('Disgusting') and attitudes to others ('darling'), enact social rituals ('good morning') and produce performative utterances ('guilty') without any evidence of grammatical construction.

During conversation, longer and more complete sentences are used. There are grammatical differences between H and L forms of language. H speech is more complex, has more subordinate clauses and more grammatical word categories. Joos (1962) distinguished five degrees of formality in American-English. Here are some examples of them:

intimate: 'Time?'

casual-personal: 'What's the time?'

social-consultative: 'Do you have the time on you, please?'

formal: 'I should like to know the time, please?'

frozen: 'I should be glad to be informed of the correct time'

Bernstein (1959) noted a number of grammatical differences between his restricted and elaborated codes, which we have seen vary between situations as well as between social classes. The restricted code included:

1. Short, grammatically simple, often unfinished sentences with a poor syntactical form stressing the active voice.
2. Simple and repetitive use of conjunctions ('so', 'then', 'because').
3. Little use of subordinate clauses to break down the initial categories of the dominant subject.
4. Infrequent use of impersonal pronouns as subjects of conditional clauses.

One of the key differences between the two codes is in complexity. Lindenfeld (1969) found that in France complexity was greater both for more formal situations and for middle-class as opposed to working-class people. The measures of complexity were sentence length, the use of subordinate clauses, the use of relative clauses ('the boy who . . .'), and nominalisation (use of clause as subject or object, e.g. 'I was glad he was away'). Some of the results are shown in Fig. 11.1.

H styles are closer to the official grammar of the language. However the L form can be regarded as having an alternative grammar whose rules can be written down. This has been done by Labov *et al.* (1968) and Wolfram (1969) for some aspects of the Black English Vernacular (BEV) as used in New York. Some of the rules found are:

1. Informal use of 'be', as in 'the answers always be wrong'.
2. Omission of the copula 'to be' after pronouns, as in 'She nice'.
3. Omission of -t and -d endings, especially if the next word starts with a consonant, as in 'he kick ball'.
4. Use of multiple negatives, as in 'I don't bother nobody'.

A further difference between H and L forms of language lies in the types of words used (Brown and Fraser 1980):

High has more	*Low has more*
nouns	verbs
adjectives	adverbs
prepositions	pronouns

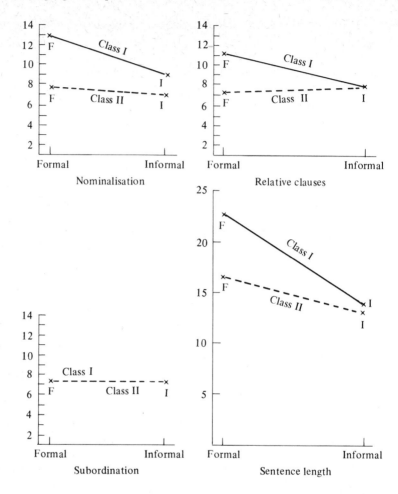

Fig. 11.1. Effect of social class and situation on speech. (After Lindenfeld, 1969.)

This reflects the different kinds of utterance used in formal and informal settings. Informal settings, where there is concern with the other people present, inevitably produces more pronouns, and hence more verbs. Formal speech is more impersonal, more about the task, and generates more nouns.

Grammar varies between situations in other ways as well. Scientific English uses passive verbs ('the mixture was heated'), and elaborate prefixes for nouns ('preganglionic, parasympathetic fibres'), in order to give a very precise account of events (Gregory and Carroll, 1978). This contrasts with the English of radio commentators, who speak in a distinctive style intended to arouse excitement and sustain interest rather than to make fine distinctions and considered statements.

There are a number of different types of utterance, which fulfil different communication functions. Some of these are as follows:

statement: conveys information
question: seeks information
order, instruction: influences another's behaviour
gossip, chat, jokes: sustains social relationships
promises, bets, names, etc.: creates a changed state of affairs

Since the main purpose of an interview is to obtain information, it consists mainly of questions and answers. The main purpose of teaching is instruction, so it consists mainly of statements, combined with questions to test how much has been learnt.

Complexity of utterance is affected by other situational factors – task and topic. A number of studies have found that children produce longer and more complex speech when talking about matters with which they are personally involved (Cazden, 1970). This may be because involvement leads to evaluation, which in turn may involve explanation, and explanation requires complex structures. Labov *et al*. (1968) give examples of embedded subordinated clauses in utterances giving explanations. The task may lead to complex structure in another way. Moffett (1968) found that elementary scientific observations required 'if – then' sentences, such as 'If I place a glass over the candle, the flame turns blue'. The sentence structure reflects the structure of a physical operation. Linde and Labov (1975) asked people 'Could you tell me the layout of your apartment?', to which the replies took the form either of maps or tours, in each case following a very definite order, reflecting a well-rehearsed strategy for talking about this topic.

Can we say that grammar reflects the nature of situations, or that it is functional in relation to situational goals? The main kind of variation seems to be between the simplified forms of grammar found in informal situations, and the more complex grammar used in formal situations and in writing. The reason is presumably that informal utterances are partly intended to have social consequences, and depend heavily on nonverbal accompaniments. Formal utterances are intended to convey more complex ideas, with precision. We have seen that the greater use of verbs and nouns in L and H speech respectively can be explained in a similar way. More complex utterances are used for explanations, and the complexity of utterances may reflect the structure of events in the physical world.

Accent, speed and volume

In Britain, the USA and elsewhere, accents vary with social class. They also vary with situation, the more upper-class version being used in more formal settings. The most detailed study of such accent shifts was carried out by Labov (1966), on 155 people in New York. Five phonological variables were studied: *oh, eh, r, th,* and *dh*. The greatest difference was for *th* (working-class pronunciation *t*), and there were very clear class differences for 'r' (as in 'bared', 'guard') at ends of words and before consonants (pronunciation silent). It was found that all five variables changed in pronunciation with both social class and situation. The results for *th* and *r* are shown in Figs. 11.2 and 11.3 respectively.

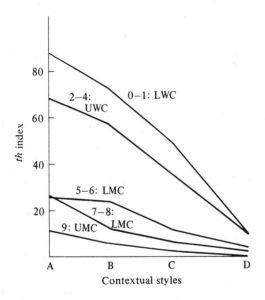

Fig. 11.2. Stratification of the variable *th* for adult speakers born in New York. A, casual speech; B, careful speech; C, reading style; D, word lists. (After Labov, 1966.)

The sound *r* is subject to 'hypercorrection' (Pygmalion effect) by lower-middle-class speakers, i.e. they go beyond upper-middle-class speech when speaking carefully. The H form of *r* is found much more among young people, showing that a historical change is taking place.

Evidently, what is happening is that since accent varies between social classes, it comes to be used as a social signal; when people are being careful, attending to their own speech, they become concerned with self-presentation and try to shift upwards.

Accent is functional for individuals, but accent systems do not have obvious functions – they are derived from historical movements of population with their speech styles. Under some conditions the reverse of accommodation takes place. Ethnic groups often try to maintain their dialects, or

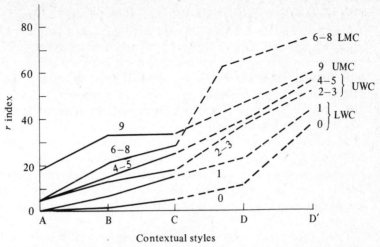

Fig. 11.3. Class distribution of the variable *r* (as in guard, car, etc.) for New York adults. Contextual styles as in Fig. 11.2. (After Labov, 1966.)

other aspects of speech style. This has happened with the Welsh, French-Canadians and American blacks. Individuals may diverge from one another in situations in which ethnic group differences are salient. Bourhis and Giles (1977) found that Welshmen shifted to a stronger Welsh accent in an experiment in which an English-sounding speaker challenged their reasons for learning the Welsh language, which he described as 'a dying language with a dismal future'. The individual's speech style is clearly functional for him in gaining acceptance as a member of a social group, or in expressing his rejection of it. On the other hand the speech systems as a whole do not appear to have any obvious functions; the differences in accent appear to be entirely arbitrary – there is no point or advantage in using one sound rather than another. In Britain working-class speakers may drop their *h*s, but upper-class speakers drop their *g*s, as when huntin', shootin' and fishin'.

Another important source of variation in voice quality is the speaker's attitude to those addressed and his emotional state. Anxiety, depression and other emotional states can be detected from tone of voice when a speaker is reading neutral passages. The information is carried by various aspects of voice; anxiety is conveyed by a breathy voice, rapid and irregular tempo and speech errors; depression is conveyed by slow speed and low pitch (Scherer, 1979). Attitudes to others affect voices in a similar way, and voice is only slightly less important than face in communicating friendly, hostile, superior and inferior attitudes (Mehrabian, 1972).

People speak louder if they are further apart, or of course if there is background noise. They speak loudly at certain kinds of social occasion

307

(e.g. parties and football matches) and softly in other settings (e.g. in church, even when there is no service in progress, and at concerts). They speak loudly when happy or angry, softly when depressed or bored. They speak loudly if trying to persuade or entertain; softly if they are conducting a meditation (Giles and Powesland, 1975; Harper, Wiens and Matarazzo, (1978). Extroverts speak with louder voices than introverts; they also speak first, talk more and succeed in being more persuasive than introverts (Carment, Miles and Cervin, 1965).

Speed and loudness lead us to some functions of language not so far discussed in this chapter. There is the need to communicate clearly, over distance, or against background noise. Speed and loudness are related to level of arousal – they reflect the levels of arousal at, e.g., parties or meditations, and they are used to control the state of other people on these occasions.

Crystal and Davy (1969) analysed the speech of radio broadcasters. They assumed that the goals of a commentator are to describe some activity, to provide background information, to produce an unbroken flow of talk, and to keep it interesting. Fluency is achieved by an absence of hesitation pauses, and the use of intonation to link sentences. Interest and excitement are generated by variety of pitch, volume and speed; high points are marked by staccato and crescendo; rhetorical questions are asked, and colourful words used.

Meaning (semantics)

Many linguists have recognised that the meaning of words and sentences depends on the context, i.e. the situation. There are several ways in which this occurs:

1. Pronouns: 'I', 'he', etc., are specified by the persons observed to be present in a situation.
2. Objects: 'this', 'that', etc., may be specified by glances or gestures, or by their prominence in the situation.
3. Abbreviations are often used, which are incomprehensible if one has no knowledge of the situation, e.g. 'butter', meaning 'Please pass it', or 'Can I buy some?' or 'Would you like some?'
4. Ambiguous sentences are made clear by the situation, e.g. 'They are shooting dogs', 'The bill is large', 'Put it on' (Lyons, 1977).
5. Some utterances, which sound like promises, threats, etc., make sense only in certain contexts. Labov (1969) gives examples of sentences such as 'If you eat any spinach I'll give you ten dollars', which only makes sense in a situation where the listener does want to eat spinach, and doesn't want to receive ten dollars – i.e. a

situation of a very definite and rather unusual goal structure. This utterance would be classified as a threat.

Speakers do not state the obvious; there is a principle of least effort whereby they tend to omit a lot of information (Leech, 1974). The situation provides much of the shared field of attention that utterances take for granted and to which they add something new (Rommetveit, 1974). However there are some sentences that make sense regardless of the context – e.g. 'It is raining' – though the full implications may well depend on the context (for example whether this was said during a long drought or during a cricket match). The principle of least effort works slightly differently in different codes: the elaborated code of middle-class speech utterances is much less situation-dependent than the restricted code of working-class speech.

Whether or not an utterance is received as a question, order, etc., depends on the situation. 'Would you be kind enough to pass the salt?' is not a question, but 'Would you be willing to lend me ten pounds?' is. 'What are you laughing at?', if asked by a teacher when children are not supposed to be laughing, is not a question but a sort of command. 'Can you play the piano?' may also be a command (Coulthard, 1977).

The effects of situation discussed so far do not relate meaning to the goals or the other basic features of situations. Is meaning related to goals? A sentence may be more or less comprehensible in itself, but its relations to the goal structure of the situation are very important, and will determine the utterances or other actions that follow from it. So the sentence 'Did you do it?' depends for its meaning on the situation in the sense that 'it' is defined by the situation. In addition the answer 'yes' might lead to reward or punishment. Scheflen (1973) describes an enigmatic event in which a man sat down in a restaurant, ignored the waiter, and ordered the head-waiter to bring him a 'seven and seven'. This depends on the situation in the sense that 'seven and seven' is the name for a special drink; more important, we need to know that the speaker owned the restaurant.

Individuals employ meaning systems to pursue their own goals. For example, a propagandist might use the language and concepts of a particular political or religious point of view, e.g. the level of unemployment, the proportion of the population that does not have enough to eat, the differences between rich and poor. Or a person might use words in order to mystify and to fail to communicate, as perhaps in schizophrenia.

Meaning depends in part on the relations between words. This may be because they are based on the same components, as 'father' consists of 'parent' and 'male'. One may be part of another, as 'finger' is part of 'hand'. One may be a subdivision of another, as 'dog' is a kind of 'animal'. Situational factors may affect meaning in this sphere. For example, in the game of cricket, a whole semantic field is activated, with a complete set of related terms such as 'ball', 'over', 'out', 'declare' (Clark and Clark, 1977).

Meaning also depends on the class of objects referred to and the classes with which it is contrasted – that is, on category size. In different settings 'dog' is contrasted with 'cat' (in the home), with 'bitch' (at the dog show), with 'lion', 'camel', etc. (at the zoo). There are finer distinctions, and more categories in certain spheres for particular situations. Thus we have 'tree', 'eucalyptus tree', and each of the 400-odd varieties of eucalyptus.

Meaning can also be looked at in terms of emotional and other reactions in multidimensional space, which can be studied by factor analysis or multidimensional scaling. Thus Rips, Shoben and Smith (1973) found that animals were classified in terms of two dimensions – size and ferocity. It seems very likely, however, that in different situations animals might be classified in terms of other dimensions, such as 'good to eat', 'good for skins', 'useful in agriculture', or other situational functions. In experiment 9.1 we described a study using multidimensional scaling, which found that in different situations different terms were used to describe the people present.

Meaning depends on situation in several ways. In order to save time and effort, abbreviations are used which only make sense if the context is known. The full meaning of an utterance can be grasped only in relation to the goals of the situation. The meaning systems used in zoos, dog shows and elsewhere are related to the goals of those events, and the same is true of the dimensions of emotional reaction.

Examples of language use in different situations

Informal conversation between middle-class adults. Speech here is relatively informal. There is 'normal non-fluency', with many speech errors, and odd noises like snorts and sniffs; sentences and utterances do not have clear boundaries; the basic construction is of short and simple sentences, loosely linked. The syntax contains considerable deviation from proper grammar, with grammatical errors, contractions such as 'I'll', use of words such as 'got', and expressions such as 'I mean' and 'sort of'. Vocabulary consists of common words and short words; simple adverbs such as 'very' are used, as opposed to 'considerably'. Meaning is implicit, and dependent on the context. Accent is middle-class received pronunciation. Discourse is rather rambling, with changes of topic, no evidence of planning, and interruptions (Crystal and Davy, 1969).

A university tutorial. Speech here is relatively formal, and elaborated; it may include some reading aloud, which produces careful speech. The syntax is correspondingly correct. The vocabulary is a fairly extensive technical one in the field of the tutorial, providing all the distinctions that are needed, and there is a lot of discussion of the meanings of particular terms, their definitions, and the relations between them. Accent will approximate to the usage of the tutor, to which the student will probably accommodate. The speed is fairly slow and the volume low, if the room is quiet. Discourse follows a very orderly pattern of alternating utterances, each of which is closely related to the one before.

A party. Speech here is decidely informal; the extent to which it is in the restricted code depends on the social class of the participants. A simple syntax is used, and sentences are often ungrammatical and unfinished. A fairly small vocabulary is used, reflecting the common interests of those present in sport, holidays, etc. Accent depends on the social class of those present, but is likely to shift upwards on such social occasions, even though they are informal, just as people will put on their best clothes. Speech is sometimes loud and fast (and sometimes slow and boring), reflecting the emotional atmosphere, and the effects of drink. Discourse tends to be erratic, with a lot of interruptions, and sudden changes of topic.

Conclusions

Can the variations in language between situations be explained in terms of the goals or other features of the situation? And can we explain why these functions are met by the particular dimensions of speech used for the purpose? Expressing group membership, and preventing others from understanding is done by accent, dialect and to some extent by vocabulary; this could not be done so well by volume or speed. Different grammars would be difficult to develop; and they would create communication barriers; this has happened with BEV, perhaps reflecting the extent of the cleavage in American society. More complex verbal tasks, such as explanations and descriptions of sequences of events, lead to more complex utterances with subordinate clauses.

Ease of communication, especially under difficult conditions, is met by louder, slower speech; the commonest words are shorter. Different tasks need different vocabularies, not different accents or grammar. Social situations produce informal speech, with simpler constructions, smaller vocabulary, more pronouns and verbs, fewer nouns. Some of these components are clearly useful in social as opposed to task situations; the explanation of others, such as the use of more verbs, is not so clear.

11.1. Social class and linguistic variation
P. COLLETT, R. LAMB, K. FENLAUGH AND P. MCPHAIL

The source of language variation that has been most thoroughly investigated in England is undoubtedly that of social class. In 1961 Bernstein labelled the speech styles of the middle class (MC) and the lower working class (LWC) the 'elaborated' and 'restricted' codes respectively, and in subsequent research he was able to point to several important differences between these two codes. He discovered, for instance, that there was far more use of subordinate clauses in the elaborated code, and that the restricted code was characterised by the use of fewer adjectives. Users of the restricted code also employed fewer uncommon adjectives, fewer adverbs and fewer conjunctions (Bernstein, 1962). This general picture of language divergence has been supported and extended by other investigators. Henderson (1970), for example, has shown that MC children employ a wider range of nouns than do LWC children, and Hawkins (1969) has demonstrated that the speech of MC children is more explicit than that of working-class (WC) children. In Hawkins' study five-year-olds were asked to describe a story depicted in a series of picture cards and paintings. He found that LWC children used more pronouns and fewer nouns than their MC counterparts, often simply relying on the listener to grasp their reference.

Bernstein has gone on to argue that the restricted code of the LWC has direct consequences, not only for the thinking of those who use the code, but also for their ability to communicate efficiently. Since the restricted code is manifestly coarser and less explicit, it may be regarded as making fewer and less fine distinctions, and that, according to Bernstein, is one of the reasons why the WC are open to political manipulation by the MC. The formulation of this argument is cast in a typical Whorfian mould, and as such it has not received any empirical support. The same can be said of Bernstein's argument about the relationship between speech codes and communication.

Bernstein has suggested that the restricted code 'does not facilitate the communication of ideas and relationships which require a precise formulation' (1959, p. 312). This is a clear case of a deficit argument which suggests that the nature of WC language predetermines and restricts the capacity of its users to communicate with each other. Here again no attempt has been made to test Bernstein's assertion. Instead he and his co-workers have merely relied on the assumption that an investigation of differences in the speech styles of the two classes will, in itself, be sufficient to indicate their cognitive and communicative abilities. But at no point have they offered any evidence which is independent of language to support their case. They have been content to rely on language measures as an index of language as well as cognition and/or communicative competence. Robinson has offered an unambiguous case for this procedure when he argues that 'differences in communicative efficiency can be exposed by linguistic analysis' (1972, p. 170).

Apart from the problems of inferring the limits of thought and communicative competence from the limits of language, there is also an additional question which surrounds the immutability of speech styles. Bernstein has suggested that ability to switch codes is an exclusive luxury of the MC; that while they can adopt a more restricted form of speech when the occasion arises, WC speakers have no choice in the matter and are confined to using the restricted code. Although Robinson (1965) has provided some evidence which suggests that WC children can alter their sociolinguistic register, at least in writing, the main argument against the immutability of speech styles has come from Labov. Labov (1972b) has provided a great deal of convincing argument, but unfortunately only anecdotal evidence, to support the notion that children select their speech style on the basis of situational requirements. 'The social situation', he says, 'is the most powerful determinant of verbal behaviour' (p. 191). Cazden (1970), who summarised the research on the impact of the situation, came to much the same conclusion. Labov also offered several examples to show that speech style is no guide to 'logical or . . . intelligent' use of the language (1972, p. 200).

The study reported below stemmed from two related ideas. Firstly there was the question of whether or not WC children might become more elaborate in their speech when the need for greater explicitness arises. Secondly there was the enduring issue of whether it was possible to demonstrate that differences in speech styles had communicative consequences, whether in effect differences in speech style were related to communicative efficiency. These two issues were examined concurrently through an experiment that was designed to test the following hypotheses:

1. Speech styles will not be related to communicative efficiency.
2. The speech styles of MC and LWC children will differ where the situational demands for explicitness are low but not where they are high.

Method

Subjects. Fifty-four children took part in the study; they were divided into groups of three so that within each group they were all of the same sex and social class. All the children were between the ages of ten and eleven.

Procedures. One of the three children was randomly assigned to the role of instructor (I), the other two to the role of receiver (R). While the Rs waited in an adjoining room, the I was shown, without verbal instruction,

313

how to manipulate and place a variety of objects in a small box. The objects included a red tin, corks, jars, a piece of card, a hot-water bottle, etc., each of which had its own place in the final arrangement.

Once the I had shown that he could place the objects into their correct positions in the right order, one of the Rs was brought into the room and it was explained that I would show R how to place the objects correctly in the box without I touching either the objects or the box. The Rs fell into two conditions, which were counterbalanced for order. In one, the together condition, I and R sat side by side in front of the table on which the objects and box had been placed, while in the other, the apart condition, R sat in front of the task materials while I stood some eight feet away, behind a screen which allowed him to see R but which prevented R from seeing him. The apart condition was designed to incorporate a greater need for explicitness. In the together condition I could use gestures, while R could observe I's line of sight, but because no such advantages were afforded in the apart condition the need for greater verbal clarity became more pressing. It was expected that the situational demands implicit in the design of the apart condition would force LWC children to adopt a more MC style of speech. Typically I might begin by instructing, say, R_1 while sitting beside him. R_1 would then leave the room, R_2 would enter and take up a position at the table and I would instruct him from behind the screen. All the instructions were tape-recorded, and the experimenters made notes on the number of mistakes made by R which I corrected.

Each trial (comprising both conditions) involved three different subjects, and all the subjects in a trial were of the same sex and social class (as defined by the Registrar-General's census). There were eighteen trials in all, nine with MC children, nine with WC children. Approximately half the trials in each class involved males, half females.

Results

The tape-recorded instructions of the Is, as well as the performance variables for each pair of subjects, were analysed under the categories listed in Table 11.2. Variables 1 to 18 are linguistic measures and variables 19 to 21 are performance measures. The titles of the linguistic measures are largely self-explanatory, with the possible exceptions of the terms 'range' and 'token'. The range of, say, words is simply the number of different words used by I. Token adjectives are demonstrative adjectives such as 'this' or 'that', while token adverbs are phrases such as 'like this' or 'like that', as opposed to explicit adverbial expressions, and token prepositions are words like 'here' or 'there', as against explicit locatives.

These categories were chosen because several of them had already been shown to distinguish between MC and LWC speech styles in terms of range of vocabulary and explicitness. Variables 17 and 18 were included because it was expected that they would distinguish complexity and completeness of sentences in speech. The last three variables are performance variables. They are as follows:

19. Time. The total time taken to complete the task (the experimenters did not indicate to the subjects that speed was necessary).
20. Number of errors. The number of errors which were corrected by *I*. Uncorrected errors were not counted since we were not testing *I*'s memory, but rather his ability to communicate his conception of how the objects should be arranged. This is a measure of the number of times an instruction had to be given before it was followed to *I*'s satisfaction.
21. Requests for repetition. This is the number of times *R* called for clarification of the instruction.

Each variable was analysed by a 2 (classes) × 2 (conditions) analysis of variance, with repeated measures on the second factor. The results of these analyses are summarised in Table 11.2, which shows the significant main effects for class and condition and the significant interactions between these two factors.

Significant main effects for class were found in relation to variables 5, 7, 8 and 18, showing that the instructions of MC children contained fewer prepositions, fewer pronouns, fewer token adjectives and fewer unfinished utterances than those of LWC children. With the exception of variable 5, none of these main effects was linked to interaction effects. In the case of this variable the main effect can be explained in terms of a greater use of prepositions by LWC children in the together condition. Otherwise, the three variables which showed a significant main effect for class can easily bear a Bernstein-type interpretation, as in each case LWC instructors employed more than their MC counterparts. Elsewhere in the data there are other differences which, although not significant, are nevertheless noteworthy because they are consistent with the picture outlined by Bernstein. For example MC instructors obtained slightly higher scores than LWC instructors on variables 2, 3, 12 and 13, and slightly lower scores than LWC instructors on variables 9 and 10. It is important to note that while there were significant class differences for several of the language variables (as well as trends in the expected direction on others), there were none for the performance variables, although there was a trend for LWC children to take longer, produce more corrected errors and make more requests for clarification. This notwithstanding, the results on the performance variables confirm the first hypothesis.

Table 11.2 also shows that there were six main effects for condition and that three of these were associated with significant interactions between class and condition. The three main effects for condition that were not linked to interaction effects occurred with variables 6, 10 and 14. Here we

TABLE 11.2. *Means and analyses of variance*

| | Mean scores | | | | Sources of variance | | |
| | Together | | Apart | | | | |
Variables	MC	LWC	MC	LWC	A (class)	B (condition)	A × B
Language variables							
1. No. of words	146.33	190.00	155.40	173.10	N.S.	N.S.	N.S.
2. No. of nouns	26.89	26.00	29.56	23.78	N.S.	N.S.	N.S.
3. No. of adjectives	6.67	7.67	14.22	8.44	N.S.	$P<0.01$	$P<0.05$
4. No. of adverbs	3.67	4.89	3.78	3.56	N.S.	N.S.	N.S.
5. No. of prepositions	14.33	18.22	15.67	13.67	$P<0.001$	N.S.	$P<0.01$
6. No. of conjunctions	6.56	9.56	5.67	6.89	N.S.	$P<0.05$	N.S.
7. No. of pronouns	11.67	18.22	10.56	16.89	$P<0.025$	N.S.	N.S.
8. No. of 'token' adjectives	2.67	4.11	1.33	4.22	$P<0.025$	N.S.	N.S.
9. No. of 'token' adverbs	1.00	2.44	0.78	1.33	N.S.	N.S.	N.S.
10. No. of 'token' prepositions	1.67	2.55	0.56	0.78	N.S.	$P<0.025$	N.S.
11. Range of words	50.67	51.11	55.00	53.67	N.S.	N.S.	N.S.
12. Range of nouns	13.88	13.56	16.00	13.22	N.S.	N.S.	N.S.
13. Range of adjectives	5.33	5.44	9.44	5.67	N.S.	$P<0.001$	$P<0.001$
14. Range of adverbs	2.89	3.33	2.00	1.78	N.S.	$P<0.05$	N.S.
15. Range of prepositions	5.78	5.89	6.00	6.00	N.S.	N.S.	N.S.
16. Range of conjunctions	1.67	2.67	1.89	1.78	N.S.	$P<0.05$	$P<0.001$
17. Range of subordinate clauses	0.78	1.56	1.33	1.44	N.S.	N.S.	N.S.
18. No. of unfinished utterances	0.33	1.78	0.33	1.11	$P<0.01$	N.S.	N.S.
Performance variables							
19. Time (seconds)	136.00	185.60	136.11	162.10	N.S.	N.S.	N.S.
20. No. of errors	3.11	4.78	3.11	4.22	N.S.	N.S.	N.S.
21. Requests for repetition	0.78	1.11	0.89	1.22	N.S.	N.S.	N.S.

316

find that, irrespective of class membership, instructors used more conjunctions, more token prepositions and a greater range of adverbs in the together condition than they did in the apart condition. In the case of variables 3, 13, and 16 there were significant main effects for condition as well as significant interaction effects for class × condition. In the case of variables 3 and 13 it is clear that the main effect for condition can be explained in terms of the interaction effect, specifically the use of more adjectives and a greater range of adjectives by MC instructors in the apart condition. Hypothesis 2 predicted an interaction between class and condition, but one in which LWC instructors become more like MC instructors in the apart condition. Inspection of the means for these two variables shows that there were no differences between MC and LWC instructors in the together condition, but that they were quite different in the apart condition. It is only in the case of variable 16 that we find anything that approximates to a confirmation of the second hypothesis. Here LWC instructors can be seen to use more conjunctions than MC instructors in the together condition, but the same number of conjunctions as their MC counterparts in the apart conditions. This provides a simple illustration of what we had expected might be a general pattern, namely that the situational requirements for greater explicitness in the apart condition would lead to LWC instructors becoming more MC in their speech style. As it happened, however, the results did not provide support for hypothesis 2, the 'adaptation to demand' hypothesis. With the exception of variable 16, the LWC children did not become more MC in their speech style when the demand arose to do so. Even variable 16 is not unproblematic, as Bernstein (1962) found that the MC use a greater range of conjunctions than the LWC. This turned out to be true for the apart condition but untrue overall, as the LWC used a markedly greater range in the together condition. Finally it is worth noting that no significant interaction effects occurred without corresponding main effects.

Discussion

In this study it was predicted that there would be an interaction between social class and condition for the language variables, that the speech of LWC children would become more MC in character when they were faced with the task of making themselves understood without the advantages of other communication channels. With the exception of one of the language variables this proved not to be the case, and we were therefore unable – at least with the manipulations used in this study – to discount Bernstein's suggestions concerning the immutability of WC speech. There were, however, several interactions between social class and condition which operated in the opposite direction to that predicted. Although these instances failed to confirm an hypothesis of adaptation on the part of WC children they do point to differential sensitivities to situational requirements of the children in the two social classes.

If we take the expedient of ignoring the class distinction altogether, we find that the instructors did adapt their speech style to the peculiar demands of each situation. Overall there was, for example, a greater use of adjectives in the apart condition, a finding which is consistent with the need to be more verbally explicit when hand and eye movements are not available for instruction. Similarly there was, overall, a more frequent use of token prepositions in the together condition. This again can be explained in terms of the inappropriateness of expressions like 'here' and 'there' when the instructor is hidden behind a screen.

The results of this study corroborate the general pattern of findings that has emerged in earlier work on social class and language. When the instructions of MC and LWC children were examined it was found that they differed in several important respects, but contrary to what is generally supposed, these linguistic differences were not reflected in the performance variables. This shows that WC speech cannot be regarded as an inferior mode of communication, and indicates that there is as yet no support for Robinson's contention that 'differences in communicative efficiency can be exposed by linguistic analysis'. The fact that there is no necessary relationship between the structure of speech and its communicative functions is not entirely surprising, especially when one considers that speech is always the property of one individual whereas communication is inevitably the property of at least two people. It is possible to describe the structure of speech according to some scheme or other, but a full understanding of its communicative properties must necessarily wait upon an analysis of what that speech does to or for the listener. As this study shows, the listener is by no means inactive. He builds upon the content of what he is given, filling in gaps and making explicit what is often implicit. Because communication is a joint activity it cannot, by definition, be exposed by an analysis of individual activity. Only by externalising the impact of speech, by requiring a listener, say, to follow instructions and then examining his performance, can we begin to explore the relationship between the characteristics of speech and the characteristics of communication.

12

Stressful situations

Introduction

Everyone finds some situations difficult or a source of anxiety. Most research relevant to stressful situations has been concerned with anxiety, for example in the form of fear of pain, of social embarrassment or other kinds of subjective distress. On the other hand it may be difficult to deal effectively with certain situations without necessarily experiencing high levels of anxiety. Marshall, Staian and Andrews (1977) found that social skills training improved social competence as rated by observers more than systematic desensitisation did, while systematic desensitisation had more effect on self-reports of anxiety. We shall see below that women report more social anxiety than men but fewer women complain of being socially inadequate. Social inadequacy has sometimes been equated with lack of assertiveness, but we have argued elsewhere that this is only one form of inadequacy (Argyle, 1980b).

Anxiety has been an active area of psychological research since the beginning of the century and has been studied by experimenters of various theoretical persuasions. Some have considered anxiety to be a stable, chronic state measurable in terms of a personality dimension (Cattell, 1950) while others have viewed it as a special reaction to situations in which a person has previously encountered pain (Miller and Dollard, 1945). Still others have viewed anxiety as a state of the person which varies across time and situations (Spielberger, 1966; Endler and Hunt, 1968). Anxiety has been investigated at different levels concentrating on specific processes – neurological, cognitive, interpersonal – and it has been studied as a dependent, intervening and independent variable.

It has not been until comparatively recently, with the popularity of the trait–state distinction, the $P \times S$ debate and the construction of S–R inventories of anxiety, as well as the work on social skills and social difficulty, that psychologists have turned their attention to the nature of the social situations that lead to stress and anxiety. They have attempted to determine the different effects of social stimuli on anxiety arousal, and how people cope with anxiety. A stressful situation is quite simply one that causes stress or anxiety in some sense to the person experiencing or perceiving it. Bryant and Trower (1974) defined it thus in their questionnaire survey of social difficulty in a student sample: 'The situation makes you feel anxious or uncomfortable, either because you don't know what to do, or because it makes you feel frightened, embarrassed or self-conscious' (p. 15). A considerable amount of work has been done by social and clinical psychologists in an effort to establish the types of stressful situations people experience, and dimensions underlying stressful situations, the specific elements in the situations that cause difficulty and the critical stages in a social situation, in order to help people deal with them more successfully.

In 1952 the American Psychiatric Association recognised the existence of conditions called 'transient situational personality disorders', which were defined as 'reactions which are more or less transient in character and which appear to be an acute symptom response to a situation without apparent underlying personal disturbance. The symptoms are the immediate means used by an individual in his struggle to adjust to an overwhelming situation'. Among the transient stress disorders are three major underlying conditions: (1) gross stress reactions, usually a severe response to natural disasters or military combat; (2) adult situational reactions, involving a variety of responses to situation crises centring on marriage, the family, work, sex and menopause, and physical health; (3) adjustment reactions of infancy and adolescence, involving situations of learning, adjusting, etc.

There are also a number of related areas in psychology concerned with situational anxiety. Two of these are the extensive work on life-events and illness by Rahe, Mahan and Arthur (1970), who have pointed out the relationship between changes in life patterns and psychiatric and physical illness, and the related research area on dying patients and grieving relatives (Hinton, 1975). However, both of these research areas are concerned with processes over time and are not strictly situational in approach.

The person–situation interaction model for anxiety and trait versus state anxiety

Over twenty years ago Cattell and Scheier (1958) made the distinction between trait and state in their attempt to redefine the nature of anxiety. Spielberger (1966) enlarged on this distinction: state anxiety is a transitory state or condition of the organism which fluctuates over time and varies in intensity; trait anxiety is a stable and relatively permanent personality characteristic which distinguishes between individuals in the way they perceive the world and experience certain emotional states. State anxiety is characterised by consciously perceived feelings of apprehension and tension, often associated with physiological arousal.

The trait–state distinction is similar to, but distinct from, the distinctions between chronic and acute anxiety and between fear and anxiety. Acute anxiety is characterised by episodic, unexpected, and seemingly not externally stimulated severe anxiety attacks. Chronic anxiety lasts over a period of months, even years, and conditions are marked by various psychological and physical symptoms associated with less severe states of anxiety. As regards the fear–anxiety distinction, experimenters have described fear as more temporal in nature and related to external events, while anxiety is a more chronic condition and usually produced by an internal system.

Spielberger (1972*a*) proposed the full trait–state anxiety theory, which has generated considerable research. He suggested (1978) that a comprehensive theory of anxiety must also differentiate between anxiety states, the stimulus conditions that evoke these states and the defences that serve to avoid or ameliorate them. As a final step the trait–state theory must describe and specify the characteristics of stressor stimuli that evoke differential levels of A-state in persons who differ in A-trait anxiety.

The principal assumptions of Trait-State Anxiety Theory may be briefly summarized as follows:

1. In situations that are appraised by an individual as threatening, an A-State reaction will be evoked. Through sensory and cognitive feedback mechanisms high levels of A-State will be experienced as unpleasant.
2. The intensity of an A-State reaction will be proportional to the amount of threat that the situation poses for the individual.
3. The duration of an A-State reaction will depend upon the persistence of the individual's interpretation of the situation as threatening.
4. High A-Trait individuals will perceive situations or circumstances that involve failure or threats to self-esteem as more threatening than persons who are low in A-Trait.
5. Elevations in A-State have stimulus (drive) properties that may be expressed directly in behavior, or that may serve to initiate psychological defenses that have been effective in reducing A-States in the past.
6. Stressful situations that are encountered frequently may cause an individual to develop specific coping responses or psychological defense mechanisms which are designed to reduce or minimize A-State.

(Spielberger, 1978, p. 44)

As a result of this work the State–Trait Anxiety Inventory (STAI) was devised by Spielberger, Gorsuch and Lushene (1970): subjects are asked to report how they generally feel (A-trait), and how they feel at the time of filling in the questionnaire (A-state), in order to obtain the two conceptually distinct measures of anxiety.

The trait–state research has thrown light on the relationship between A-trait and A-state anxiety and threatening situations. Spielberger and Smith (1966), Rappaport and Katkin (1972) and Hodges (1968) have demonstrated how situations that threaten failure or personal inadequacy cause high and low A-trait subjects to behave quite differently. Social situations that involve loss of self-esteem or are particularly ego-involving cause greater A-state arousal for high A-trait individuals than for low A-trait ones. However situations that pose a 'physical' rather than a 'psychological' threat do not discriminate between A-trait individuals. This latter finding, however, has been questioned by Endler and Shedletsky (1973) and McAdoo (1969), who pointed out that these findings depend on the strength of the stimulus. Further work (Shedletsky and Endler, 1974) revealed that the A-trait measure on the STAI in fact only measures anxiety associated with ego threat, ignoring anxiety associated with other threat situations such as physical danger, or ambiguous threat. Clearly anxiety has many dimensions, and any useful measure would have to consider all of them. The importance of this test is that the results may be extrapolated to other situations. Mellstrom, Zuckerman and Cicala (1978) found that A-trait measures were bad predictors of anxiety in three different situations and argued for more specificity in the definition of situations in tests. The results of the study indicated that the predictive validity of the specific measures was significantly greater than that of the general measure in seven out of thirty-two comparisons, whereas the reverse never occurred. Jurich and Jurich (1978), in a factor-analytic study of expressions of anxiety, found five factors; three of these were 'trait' variables, shown to be poor indicators of a subject's situational anxiety (activity level, degree of impulsiveness, time budgeting), and two were situational or state factors (level of excitement, orientation to the source of anxiety).

Zuckerman (1977) developed a situation-specific trait–state test for the prediction and measurement of affective responses. It is a development of the Spielberger State–Trait Scale and the Endler S–R Inventory in that this scale measures different dimensions of responses and situations – anxiety–fear arousal, positive affect, anger and aggression, attentive coping, sadness. Five classes of situations emerged from the factor analysis of the twenty stimulus situations which may possibly serve for the beginning of a taxonomy of affect-arousing situations: verbal attack, acceptance–success, fearful anticipation, ambiguous anticipation, physical threat and failure–rejection. Zuckerman also found that sex differences emerged on the trait but not the state tests, but that these were mainly in specific situations such as the threat of physical harm. The advantage of this scale is that it allows for prediction from either a general or a specific trait and allows one to examine the particular classes of situations in which particular affects are expressed.

Finally Lazarus and Laurier (1978) put forward a 'cognitive-phenomenological transactional' approach to stress and anxiety. They distinguished three conceptually distinct stress-relevant relationships between people and their environment – harm–loss, threat and challenge – maintaining these can only be understood in terms of the relationship between person and environment, and the balance of power between demands and resources. Environmental demands are external events that impose adaptive requirements which, in the event of failure of suitable action, will lead to negative consequences. Internal demands refer to desirable goals, values, commitments, programmes or tasks acquired by an individual or a social system, whose postponement and frustration would have negative consequences or implications. Adaptive resources consist of any properties of the system that have potential capacity to meet demands and hence to prevent the negative consequences. Thus transactions between persons and their immediate environments are either stressful or not, depending on the balance of power between the two specified opposing forces – demands and resources.

The behaviour therapy tradition developed by Lazarus (1963) and Eysenck (1976) has always focused on the specific situations that elicit anxiety. Traditionally various forms of anxiety are seen as the result of specific learning experiences which can be treated by such techniques as systematic desensitisation based on relaxation in the stressful situation or by using an anxiety-producing stimulus or by modelling the behaviour of another in a controlled role-play situation. Behaviour therapists report a fairly high success rate, especially for the treatment of specific phobias.

Endler, Hunt and Rosenstein (1962) concluded that in order to investigate adequately the trait of 'anxiousness' one must consider both the responses that characterise anxiousness and the situations likely to arouse it. They maintained that the expression of any behavioural trait is dependent on the type and the provocativeness of the situation and consists of responses of different types. An S–R (situation–response) Inventory of Anxiety was thus devised which sampled situations, responses and individual differences. This inventory has been fairly widely used with different populations. It has also stimulated researchers in other areas to draw up S–R inventories for other psychological processes, such as hostility (Endler and Hunt, 1968), dominance (Dworkin and Kihlstrom, 1978), leisure activity (Bishop and Witt, 1970) and self-disclosure (McCloskey, 1978).

In the original S–R inventory (Table 12.1) fourteen modes of response were presented for each of eleven situations, and subjects were required to report the intensity of responses (physiological reactions, feelings, direction of response, or effect on action in progress) for each situation. Endler *et al.* (1962) found that the percentage of variance attributable to situations and individual differences was small, but that interaction of person and situation contributed more of the total variation (10 per cent) and that a lot of variance was due to mode of response and interactions with it. They concluded: 'To fully understand trait anxiety (and also state anxiety) it is necessary to be cognisant of the evocative situations, and the person-by-situation interactions' (p. 152).

Endler and Hunt (1969) later administered six different forms of the S–R Inventory of Anxiety with different stimulus situations and modes of response to over twenty different subject groups that varied in age, class,

TABLE 12.1. *The S–R Inventory of Anxiety*

Situations	Mean score [a]
1. You are just starting off on a long automobile trip	22.5
2. You are going to meet a new date	26.2
3. You are going into a psychological experiment	24.9
4. You are crawling along a ledge high on a mountain-side	38.1
5. You are getting up to give a speech before a large group	34.6
6. You are going to a counselling bureau to seek help in solving a personal problem	30.5
7. You are starting out in a sail boat onto a rough sea	28.1
8. You are entering a competitive contest before spectators	30.5
9. You are alone in the woods at night	32.1
10. You are going into an interview for a very important job	30.1
11. You are entering a final examination in an important course	33.1

Modes of response	
1. Heart beats faster	32.7
2. Get an 'uneasy feeling'	31.1
3. Emotions disrupt action	21.2
4. Feel exhilarated and thrilled	33.2
5. Want to avoid situation	26.8
6. Perspire	24.1
7. Need to urinate frequently	17.8
8. Enjoy the challenge	29.9
9. Mouth gets dry	19.4
10. Become immobilised	15.8
11. Get full feeling in stomach	17.8
12. Seek experiences like this	33.1
13. Have loose bowels	13.1
14. Experience nausea	14.9

Each situation is presented with each mode of response, with a five-point scale of response. For example:

You are about to go on a roller coaster

Heart beats faster

1	2	3	4	5
not at all				much

The means for situations given above are summed across the fourteen modes of response, and the means for modes of response are summed across situations.

[a] For the Penn State Sample ($N = 169$).

sex and mental health, to obtain data on the generalisability of the proportions of total variance from their main factors and their interactions. Some age, sex and class differences emerged but they were not large. This new technique is seen to be an advance on 'omnibus inventories' for two reasons: firstly one gets a more differentiated picture of an individual's anxiety response pattern by making a profile of the anxiety intensity across types of situations, and secondly it provides a profile for each mode of response across situations. Thus the results led the experimenters to conclude that they would produce a better general personality description by categorising situations and response mode and then describing individuals in terms of the kinds of response they tend to manifest in various situations.

Others have devised their own S–R inventories, using different salient social and response modes and testing them on different populations. Furnham and Argyle (see experiment 12.1) constructed an S–R inventory to compare differences between four distinct groups in their reactions to stressful social situations. There are, however, a number of important criticisms to be made of the S–R format. Firstly, this inventory produces the very strange result that only 5 per cent of variance turns out to be due to persons, and a similar amount to situations. This is because the several modes of response and interactions with them take up so much variance. Olweus (1975) reanalysed Endler and Hunt's data, collapsing across modes of response, which was not used as a source of variance, with the result shown in Table 12.2. Cartwright (1975) carried out a similar analysis. In

TABLE 12.2 *Reanalysis of Endler and Hunt's (1966) three-way analysis as a two-way analysis*

	Anxiety inventory, 169 students: percentage of variance	
	Original three-way	Reanalysed two-way
Persons	5.8	26.5
Situations	5.3	22.9
P × S	10.0	50.7

From Olweus (1975).

addition he pointed out that a number of the eleven situations and fourteen modes of response are not really about anxiety at all, but refer to pleasurable excitement, as can be seen by inspecting Table 12.1. The removal of these items further increased the proportions of person and situation variance. Houston *et al.* (1978) demonstrated that subjects evaluated highly stressful situations more positively than less stressful situations, though they did not like the experience more.

Morelli and Friedman (1978) maintained that Endler *et al.*'s (1962) S–R inventory does not take into consideration cognitive factors that would correlate and interact with emotional responses to situations. Previous research demonstrated that emotional responses in a situation are related to cognitive labels available to the subject. Lastly, the inventory does not show the processes whereby aspects of person and situation interact to produce anxiety.

The dimensions of stressful situations

A considerable amount of work has gone into the analysis of the dimensions or factors of stressful situations. Using principal components analysis, factor analysis and multidimensional scaling, experimenters using different situations and different groups of subjects have come up with similar broad factors.

The method usually employed is to list and give a brief description of twenty to thirty salient situations that the subjects have experienced. The subjects are then asked to rate the situations according to a number of rating scales, and/or to compare them with one another. Statistical analysis usually reveals between two and five factors that are fairly easy to interpret. However there appear to be three major methodological problems surrounding this approach. Firstly subjects may never have experienced the situations they are asked to judge, and they may find the rating scales irrelevant to their own experience or cognitive constructs. Secondly when judging a 'stressful situation' such as a 'job interview', each subject may imagine and thus judge a quite different episode depending on the job, the interviewer, etc. Thirdly the technique can be laborious to the subjects.

All these studies have attempted to use well-known or new statistical tools to explore the subjective knowledge of subjects or the way in which they conceptualise situations. Useful though these dimensions are, however, they should be seen only as a first descriptive step in either creating a taxonomy of situations or understanding how they affect behaviour. We argued above (p. 4) that situations cannot wholly be classified in terms of dimensions but that they can also be discrete and discontinuous. That is, they cannot entirely be reduced to dimensions, but are more like chemical compounds, each with its own internal structure.

Endler and Okada (1975) found four main types of anxiety, corresponding to interpersonal threat, physical danger, new and strange situations and ambiguous situations. Rather similar results were found by Ekehammar, Magnusson and Ricklander (1974), who devised an S–R inventory of anxiety for a sample of 142 Swedish adolescents. As well as being a cross-cultural confirmation of earlier findings, multi-dimensional scaling revealed four factors, which the authors labelled 'ego threat', 'threat of pain', 'inanimate threat' and 'threat of punishment'.

Other studies have focused on anxiety in social situations. Bryant and Trower (1974) found that two major factors arose out of their principal-components analysis of thirty social situations experienced by a student population (Table 12.3). The first consisted of situations of initial

TABLE 12.3. *Percentages of a sample of Oxford students who reported moderate difficulty or worse in thirty situations*

Situations[a]	Present time	Year ago	P
21. Approaching others	36	51	0.001
14. Going to dances/discotheques	35	45	0.01
25. Taking initiative in conversation	26	44	0.001
5. Going to parties	25	42	0.001
19. Being with people you don't know well	22	37	0.001
8. Going out/opposite sex	21	38	0.001
11. Being in a group/opposite sex	21	35	0.001
24. Getting to know someone in depth	21	29	0.001
29. Talking about self and feelings	19	26	0.001
26. Looking at people in the eyes	18	26	0.001
22. Making decisions affecting others	17	31	0.001
17. Going into a room full of people	17	30	0.001
30. People looking at you	16	26	0.001
18. Meeting strangers	13	28	0.001
16. Being with younger people	13	19	0.01
7. Making friends of your own age	11	20	0.001
27. Disagreeing/putting forward views	9	23	0.001
4. Going into pubs	9	17	0.001
9. Being in a group/same sex	9	15	0.01
28. People standing/sitting very closely	9	14	0.001
10. Being in a group/men and women	8	18	0.001
6. Mixing with people at work	8	16	0.001
12. Entertaining in your own home	7	19	0.001
15. Being with older people	5	8	
23. Being with just one other person	4	9	0.01
13. Going into restaurants/cafés	3	10	0.001
2. Going into shops	1	5	0.05
1. Walking down the street	1	4	
3. Using public transport	1	3	
20. Being with friends	1	1	

From Bryant and Trower (1974).
Test of significance: χ^2, using McNemar's formula for correlated data. Yates's correction for continuity used where appropriate.
[a] Some situations are quoted here in abbreviated form.

contact with strangers, particularly of the opposite sex, while the second consisted of situations involving intimate social contact. Richardson and Tasto (1976) developed a social anxiety inventory of 166 items, which they factor-analysed. They found seven conceptually clear and non-orthogonal factors which accounted for 43 per cent of the variance. The factors were labelled as follows:

1. fear of disapproval or criticism by others
2. fear of social assertiveness and visibility
3. fear of confrontation and anger-expression
4. fear of heterosexual contact
5. fear of intimacy and interpersonal warmth
6. fear of conflict with or rejection by parents
7. fear of interpersonal loss

There are a number of other studies with essentially similar results (Hodges and Felling, 1970; Ekehammar, Schalling and Magnusson, 1975; Stratton and Moore, 1977; Zuckerman, 1977; Magnusson and Ekehammar, 1975).

Types of difficult social situation

The factor analyses discussed in the last two sections, and other work by clinical and social psychologists over the years, have established a number of situations commonly reported to be stressful and anxiety provoking. It is usually through work with people who report extreme anxiety avoidance reactions and inability to cope that the dynamics or underlying processes are revealed.

Situations characterised by the following psychological processes are often reported as threatening, stressful or unpleasant:

Intimacy. These include situations which involve actively seeking contact with relative strangers, particularly of the opposite sex. They often involve much self-disclosure, getting to know people in depth, and physical contact often with sexual overtones. Chaikin and Derlega (1976) reviewed the relationship between self-disclosure and mental health. There is also a large literature on minimal dating and heterosexual skill and anxiety (Twentyman and McFall, 1975; Hersen and Bellack, 1977).

Assertiveness. These include situations which involve standing up for one's rights, expressing active disagreement, being persistent and firm, and asking for clarification. Such situations as complaining about the service in shops, objecting to petty bureaucratic rules, refusing unreasonable social requests, queue jumping, dealing with aggression and interrupting in conversations, are often reported as difficult. These attitudes require high levels of social skill, dealing with the conflicting goals of refusing, perhaps hurting another while maintaining cordial tactful relations. Wolpe and Lazarus (1966) have devised well-validated situation-specific measures of interpersonal assertiveness.

Focus of attention. One of the most commonly expressed social difficulties is being the focus of attention of a group of observers. Giving a speech, being filmed or photographed, acting or performing in public, and being interviewed or closely questioned are commonly experienced as stressful. Other situations are answering questions from the audience (particularly if it is large), performing in a practical examination, and wearing clothes different from those of the people around one (e.g. being formally dressed at an informal party). Jeger and Goldfried (1976) have found how different sources of attention – live audience, camera, mirror – affect speech anxiety. Hollandsworth, Glazeski and Dressel (1978) devised ways of measuring anxiety in a job interview situation and of training people to cope better with these situations.

Complex social routines and etiquettes. These are situations that are formalised and ritualised, and found difficult primarily because people are not familiar with the sequence, meaning or purpose of the ritualised acts, or do not know how to present themselves or monitor their own behaviour. Marriages, funerals, dinner parties and committee meetings and certain social games, are examples of this type of situation. Also situations involving people from different cultural, national, ethnic or language groups are often found perplexing and bewildering to those who experience them.

Failure and rejection. Any situation in which there is a high chance of failure is potentially very stressful, as it affects one's self-esteem, confidence and self-image in front of others. Doing examinations, learning to perform certain skilled tasks, inviting people to dance, etc., are examples of these situations. Watson and Friend (1969) devised a 'fear of negative evaluation' scale which measured fear of failure and rebuttal in thirty situations.

Pain. Any situation that involves potential physical pain or injury is often experienced as stressful even if the chances of experiencing such pain are low. Examples of these may be visits to doctors and dentists, playing certain sports, such as boxing, wrestling, parachuting or rugby, donating blood, interacting with animals, certain jobs in industry, etc. Magnusson and Ekehammar (1975) found a clear somatic factor in adolescents' responses to situations of this kind.

Loss and bereavement. Any situation that involves the loss of a close friend, partner or family member, even if for a relatively short duration, can be very stressful, particularly to young children. It is also often very difficult helping or empathising with people who are in this state. The work of Hinton (1975) and Parkes (1975) has pointed to the stages and processes of grief and bereavement that are commonly encountered.

Other conditions or processes commonly experienced and found stressful are assessment (test anxiety, ergonomic appraisal), rapid social change, urban development, sensory deprivation and combat.

What makes situations difficult?

If we knew why some situations are difficult or stressful we should know how to train people to cope with them or possibly how to modify these situations.

Perhaps the main source of anxiety is the expectation and fear of physical pain or social rejection of some kind. This may be realistically based on past experience, or it may be quite unrealistic, as in the case of the phobias to be discussed later. There are two main therapeutic approaches here – to reduce the anxiety by means of behaviour therapy or to improve skills and the power to cope with situations by skills training. This would apply equally to fear of water and fear of public speaking. Situational analysis can explain some aspects of subjective stress in situations and can suggest how to improve skills of coping with them.

Motivation and goals. In difficult situations an individual may suffer from internal goal conflict if he is engaged in ingratiation, or conflict with other people (p. 76f.). The goal structure may be very complex, and people may not realise what the main goals of participants are, or how they are interrelated. What exactly are the main sources of conflict, internal and external, between parents and their teenage children? Or they may not know the goals (of parties, for example), or they may be pursuing goals which are inappropriate, such as seeking medical advice over dinner. Where situations involve conflict or possible conflict with others special skills of negotiation and persuasion are needed to manage them well.

Rules. The rules observed in stressful situations can be either too rigid and inhibiting, forcing a particular behavioural repertoire to be enacted, or else too vague, providing no guide to behaviour. The rules may also be very elaborate, requiring great skill to understand and obey them. Individuals often get the rules wrong – for example thinking that the candidate at an interview will ask the questions.

Repertoire and sequences. Some situations require performances that need self-confidence and skill but which may be difficult to perform, such as public speaking or being a master of ceremonies.

Concepts. Certain complex social situations require familiarity with concepts specific to those situations. Debates, auction sales, funerals, fights, have clear concepts that have to be understood if the episode is to be enacted successfully. Improved ways of seeing a situation can make it less stressful. Ellis (1957) drew attention to beliefs which can well be abandoned, such as thinking it is necessary to be loved and approved of by everyone.

Environmental constraints. There are numerous reasons associated with physical aspects of the situation that may lead to its becoming stressful. The actual setting may be strange or dangerous (a laboratory, a surgery); certain objects or props may elicit fear or anxiety responses (guns, knives, holy objects); environmental stressors such as light, heat, noise or smell may cause frustration, anger or pain; and the invasion of personal space, crowding or lack of manoeuvrability may be unpleasant.

Phobias in situations

By a phobia is meant an intense degree of anxiety produced by particular objects or situations. In some cases these appear to be completely irrational and may be based on the displacement of other feelings; in other cases the phobic person has once had a traumatic experience in this kind of situation so that the phobia is an extreme version of more normal situational anxieties. Often phobic people attempt to control their anxiety by totally avoiding the phobic object or situation. Although most phobic patients recognise that their fear is foolish and irrational they still respond immediately to the phobic situation with physical or psychological symptoms.

What distinguishes phobic from stressful situations is that phobic situations are not usually threatening, stressful or dangerous, whereas commonly experienced stressful situations are. Dixon, de Monchaux, and Sandler (1957) identified three dimensions of phobia from a factor-analytic study of twenty-six phobias – fear of separation, which often stems from anxiety about interpersonal relations; fear of rejection and authority; and fear of harm, which stems from intense fear reactions to situations associated with pain or unpleasant experiences. Some writers mention social phobia (Melville, 1977), which is really more akin to social inadequacy and is characterised by extreme anxiousness in specific social situations. Essentially there appear to be three broad categories of phobia: the fear of a specific object (e.g. snakes, sharp objects), fear of a specific situation or place (e.g. lifts, schools) and abstract fears (e.g. death, illness, dirt). Phobias are extremely common and are not found in any particular age, sex, social class or ethnic group. There are also competing theories about the origin and treatment of phobias.

Some of the more common situation phobias are:
1. Claustrophobia: fear of closed spaces such as aeroplanes, lifts, buses, trains, trenches. Some theorists have claimed that it is associated with death and birth fantasies, while others have seen it as a defence against the threat of sexual impulses.
2. Agoraphobia: fear of open or public places such as streets, squares,

public buildings. Psychoanalysts have claimed that this reaction means a fear of detachment from maternal dependence or a defence against an unconscious need to prostitute oneself.

3. Acrophobia: a morbid fear of high places, looking out of open windows or high ledges, said to be associated with self-destructive impulses.

Other situation phobias include being alone (autophobia), being in crowds (ochlophobia), empty rooms (kenophobia), home surroundings (ecophobia), strangers (xenophobia) and being touched (haptophobia).

The main techniques used to treat phobias are:

1. Desensitisation: after initially being relaxed the patient is introduced gradually to the object or situation that causes fear.

2. Flooding: with the patient's cooperation he is for some time confronted with the phobic object, from which it is difficult to escape.

3. Modelling: the patient is encouraged to imitate or model the therapist or another person's interaction in the feared situation or with the feared object.

4. Group therapy/social-skills training: a group of phobics discuss their fears with a therapist and then role-play and analyse elements or moves in a 'phobic' situation.

Difficulties reported by different groups of people

The situations that are found difficult vary somewhat between different groups of people, though within each group they fall into similar clusters and dimensions.

(a) *Students* have often been studied. The most difficult social situations for a sample of Oxford students were shown in Table 12.3. The equivalent situations and their factor loadings, for a sample of American students are shown in Table 12.4.

(b) *Medical students* are exposed to a special range of difficult situations. Bernstein (1975) used the series of situations, and obtained the anxiety scores, that are shown in Table 12.5.

(c) *Neurotic and psychotic patients* report more anxiety in social situations than do normals. Endler (1975) found only one anxiety factor, i.e. general anxiety, for neurotics, as opposed to the two to four factors found in samples of normals. Neurotics also show less situational variance in anxiety (Endler, 1973), and in other aspects of behaviour (Moos, 1968). Psychotics show even less situational variability. For each kind of patient, as they recover, situational variability increases.

On the other hand some neurotic patients, e.g. those with phobias, are anxious only in quite specific situations. Behaviour therapists have had most success with these patients; in cases of more pervasive and generalised anxiety they have focused desensitisation procedures on the main groups of

TABLE 12.4. *Scores on four stress factors for forty-four situations for American students*

Situations	Factor loadings			
	I	II	III	IV
3. Seeing someone bleed profusely from a cut arm	57	10	16	−01
7. Putting iodine on an open cut	53	10	04	04
10. Seeing a dog run over by a car	49	−05	30	−12
12. Walking in a slum alone at night	57	14	23	05
13. Giving blood at the blood bank	44	25	07	05
14. Riding an airplane in a storm	45	07	15	30
15. Being present at an operation or watching one in a movie	57	23	09	12
17. Having a tooth cavity filled	32	22	08	12
18. Climbing too steep a mountain	30	06	26	32
19. Paying respects at the open coffin of an acquaintance	41	06	30	04
29. Riding in a car going 95 miles per hour	46	−03	14	27
33. Passing a very bad traffic accident	56	15	28	03
42. Participating in a psychology experiment in which you receive electric shock	44	05	04	22
4. Asking a teacher to clarify an assignment in class	10	61	13	03
5. Giving a speech in front of class	17	56	25	09
21. Asking a question in class	08	70	12	05
23. Reciting a poem in class	11	62	20	13
25. Reciting in language class	09	50	12	18
30. Asking a teacher to explain the grading of your test	23	50	16	33
38. Volunteering an answer to a question in class	12	72	10	15
44. Asking a teacher to explain a question during a test	44	55	08	38
6. Introducing a friend and forgetting his name	14	23	47	02
9. Taking a test that you expect to fail	12	−02	56	17
11. Being in a difficult course for which you have inadequate background	22	10	45	15
16. Belching aloud in class	30	21	46	−17
20. Being refused membership in a social club	16	16	49	−01
22. Doing poorly in a course which seems easy to others	11	08	61	00
24. Having your date leave a dance with someone else	09	02	53	07
26. Finding the questions on a test extremely difficult	24	08	50	26

TABLE 12.4 (*cont.*)

28. Forgetting lines in a school play	17	10	*57*	10
34. Being the only person at a party not dressed up	10	29	*59*	11
36. Spilling your drink on yourself at a formal dinner party	05	22	*57*	16
39. Getting back a test you think you may have failed	26	12	*46*	20
1. Going on a blind date	−02	20	11	*57*
2. Asking someone for a date to a party	17	37	14	*45*
35. Introducing yourself to someone very attractive of the opposite sex	07	42	29	*47*
43. Kissing a date for the first time	07	20	02	*54*
31. Getting hurt in a fight	31	02	29	23
37. Having an interview for a job	32	35	21	37
40. Skiing out of control	35	06	22	40
Point-biserial correlation of sex with factor scores (high = females)	49[*]	01	02	−08
Correlation of trait-anxiety scale with factor scores	02	24[*]	24[*]	26[*]

From Hodges and Felling (1970).
Italicised numbers indicate high factor loadings for specific kinds of items.
[*] $P < 0.01$.

anxiety-provoking situations (Lazarus, 1963). The same has been found for patients suffering from social anxiety and distress; in a proportion of cases the anxiety is associated with a particular situation, or a definite group of situations (Argyle, 1980*b*).

Goldsmith and McFall (1975) interviewed in depth sixteen patients about problematic interpersonal situations, asking for detailed descriptions of the contexts, participants, purposes of the interaction and crucial moments. The difficult situational contexts most frequently reported were: dating, making friends, having job interviews, relating to authorities, relating to service personnel, interacting with highly intelligent or attractive people or people whose appearance was unusual. The most frequently mentioned critical moments in these problem situations were: initiating or terminating interactions, making personal disclosures, handling conversational silences, responding to rejection and being assertive.

(*d*) *Sex differences*. As stated above, females report more social anxiety and more anxiety in general than do males. Endler (1975) found that young

TABLE 12.5. *Mean levels of anxiety for American medical students in fifteen situations, at the beginning and end of medical school*

Situations	Pre-test (N=93) mean	Post-test (N=93) mean
1. Talking to a medical instructor about course subject matter	25.0	25.0
2. Talking to a medical instructor in a social situation	21.7	21.6
3. Interviewing a patient in the presence of an instructor	28.4	24.9
4. Examining a male patient	21.1	21.4
5. Examining a female patient	25.1	23.6
6. Having a nurse suggest a medication for your patient	19.0	18.5
7. Watching first surgical operation	28.2	26.6
8. Drawing blood on a patient	25.0	25.1
9. Discussing a fatal illness with a patient	25.5	24.4
10. Telling a relative that a patient died	24.8	23.0
11. Giving a rectal examination	21.5	20.5
12. Entering a final exam in an important course	33.9	32.3
13. Taking part in a psychological experiment	20.0	21.2
14. Seeking professional help in solving a personal problem	24.0	24.4
15. Questioning patients about their private lives	22.4	21.9

From Bernstein (1975).

females were most anxious in the face of physical danger and ambiguous situations. On the other hand far more males than females complain of, and are rated as, being socially incompetent in everyday situations (Bryant *et al.*, 1976).

(e) Cultural differences. There has been little research on cultural differences in the situations that people find difficult. However, it is interesting that most American social-skills training is concerned with assertiveness training, whereas in Britain the main problem appears to be making friends. The neglect of research into cultural differences has meant that tests and training are often culture-specific. Experiments 12.2 and 12.3 are concerned with cultural differences in the experience of social situations.

Experiment 12.3 looks at cross-cultural differences in the perception of social difficulty in certain social situations, while experiment 12.2 is concerned with the difficulty encountered when an individual changes cultures. Cross-cultural studies also provide unique insight into the implicit goals, rules and assumptions concerning everyday social situations within a culture.

12.1. Responses of four groups to difficult social situations
A. FURNHAM AND M. ARGYLE

Most of the experimental work on interactionism has been carried out in the area of anxiety. The reasons for this are two-fold: firstly, the original 'interactional' experiment using an S–R inventory and apportioning variance to person, situation and the interaction was carried out on anxiety (Endler *et al.*, 1962); and secondly, anxiety is very clearly determined by both internal (trait) and external (situation) cues.

Previous studies have not always piloted questionnaires to ensure that stimulus situations and responses were relevant and representative. No interactional study of anxiety has looked exclusively at social situations, most concentrating on situations of physical threat or danger. In addition most studies have included physiological, behavioural and emotional response modes without making any attempts to look at the difference between them. Fourthly, researchers have not considered what aspects of, or processes in, social situations are anxiety provoking, being content to demonstrate that anxiety is situation-specific.

Reviewers of person–situation studies have stated that for results to be meaningful and valid, they must be demonstrated to be both systematic and replicable. One method of achieving this would be to give the same questionnaire to subjects who differed demographically in terms of age, sex, education, etc.

This experiment had four objectives:

(*a*) To examine the differences in the social skills needed within and between social situations in order to determine what makes social situations difficult.

(*b*) To examine the stability of responses to difficult social situations across different samples of subjects.

(*c*) To explore the systematic patterns that underlie these effects.

(*d*) To examine the contributions of person, situation, response and interaction.

Method

Subjects. A total of 143 subjects were tested. They were from four quite distinct groups:

(*a*) Thirty-two adults, consisting of fifteen males and seventeen females (mean age 41.8 years, S.D. 9.6), most of whom had completed secondary education, and had full-time or part-time jobs.

(*b*) Forty post-graduate students, consisting of twenty-three males and seventeen females (mean age 26.7 years, S.D. 3.8), all of whom lived in a large post-graduate Oxford college, and were completing higher degrees, mostly in the sciences.

(*c*) Thirty-two occupational therapy students, all females (mean age 19.2 years, S.D. 4.1), in their second year of study in a school of occupational therapy.

(*d*) Thirty-nine schoolchildren consisting of nineteen females and twenty males (mean age 17.1 years, S.D. 1.05), completing their A-levels at a state school.

All the subjects were English speaking, of British extraction, and for the most part middle class.

Materials. A social anxiety questionnaire, in the S–R format (Endler *et al.*, 1962), was administered to each subject. There were fifteen situations and ten modes of response. Pilot work was carried out on both stimulus situations and responses; a total of thirty situations, commonly found to be difficult or anxiety provoking, was obtained from a number of scales (Endler *et al.*, 1962; Bryant and Trower, 1974; Janisse and Palys, 1976) and given to forty subjects who rated on numerous response scales their anticipated difficulty. The fifteen social situations with the highest scores were retained for the final questionnaire. The response scales were similarly selected from other questionnaires (Endler *et al.*, 1962; Colman and Halstead, 1973; Zuckerman, 1977) though a number of original responses were included. Those response scales that were most used were retained. In the final draft of the questionnaire the scales were randomised. Subjects were requested to indicate on a five-point scale the extent to which they were likely to respond in each of the ten ways to each situation. Each group of subjects, with the exception of the post-graduate group, was also asked to indicate their anticipated difficulty on six aspects of, or processes in, each situation. These processes were selected from the theoretical analysis of Harré and Secord (1972) on episode structure, and the empirical work of Goldsmith and McFall (1975) on critical moments in difficult situations.

Procedure. The two youngest subject groups were tested in a group in their classrooms, with the experimenter present to deal with any problems. The two older groups completed the questionnaire individually in their own time and returned it anonymously. The questionnaire took approximately twenty-five minutes to complete.

Results

The results were subjected to four different analyses.

1. A three-way analysis of variance was carried out on the ratings of difficulty for each of six processes, across each situation, for three groups (Table 12.6). All main effects were significant, demonstrating that there are

TABLE 12.6

(a) *Three-way analysis of variance results for the ratings of difficulty in social skills needs for each situation for three sample groups*

Source	F	P
Groups (3)	4.24	0.05
Process (6)	12.18	0.01
Situations (15)	12.65	0.01
Groups × processes	1.66	0.09
Groups × situations	1.91	0.05
Processes × situations	3.28	0.01
Error	1.15	0.10

(b) *The mean difficulty score for each stage averaged across all fifteen situations*

Process[a]	Mean	S.D.
Preparation: decisions to be made before entering the situation	2.59	0.25
Beginning: Introducing, approaching others, initiating contact	2.80	0.33
What to do: knowing the appropriate things to do and when (liturgy)	2.66	0.24
What to say: self-presentation, expressing feelings and ideas (dramaturgy)	2.83	0.32
Perception: other person, self and metaperception	2.60	0.19
Ending: how and when to leave	2.57	0.28

[a] Subjects were given each label and a full description of its meaning with examples.

different social skills or aspects of social competence involved in difficult social situations which lead them to be experienced as stressful, and further that there are group differences in relation to these effects. The skills that are overall most difficult are those relating to what to say (conversation, self-presentation, expression, etc.) and to beginning interactions (approaching others and initiating contact). One implication of these results, similar to those in other studies, is that difficult situations can be classified in terms of the social skills needed.

2. A three-mode factor analysis was performed to determine patterns of person, situation, response and interaction effects across the four samples. This technique was developed by Tucker (1966) and has been suggested as being potentially very useful in this area by Endler and Hunt (1969). The procedure has the advantage over more traditional factor-analytic methods in that it analyses all of the data to produce factors for each class of variable *and* also provides a 'core' matrix depicting the relationship between these factors.

Table 12.7 shows the situation and response factors for each group. There is a fairly high degree of similarity in the response factors across the four groups, the only exception being the schoolchildren group where the factors are reversed in comparison with other groups – that is, the major factor in the children seems to relate to anger and bewilderment whereas the other groups' major factor is anxiety. The factor structure for the situations differed quite considerably between the four groups, indicating a different pattern of situation perception. In all groups the first factor accounted for over a third of the variance. Thus it seems that whereas the perception of difficult situations is unstable across populations, the responses to these situations are fairly stable.

3. A cluster analysis was carried out on the situation and responses data for each population, in order to establish the similarity between dimensional and categorical representations. Although there were differences both within the same groups' dimensional and categorical results, and between group results within one statistical technique, certain patterns of similarity could be seen. Consider the cluster analysis results from one group – the occupational therapists. The situations appear to cluster into three groups (see Fig. 12.1): those dealing with assertiveness and counselling (1, 9, 11, 5, 6); those concerning intimacy and rituals (2, 4, 12, 3, 7, 10, 13, 14); and those concerning public speaking and apologising (8, 15). Similarly the responses (Fig. 12.2) cluster into three groups: anxiety/avoidance (1, 3, 4), anger/unhappiness (2, 7, 10) and unashamedness/confusion (5, 6, 9, 8).

Comparing Table 12.7 and Figs. 12.1 and 12.2 it is clear that the cluster and factor-analytic results are very similar for responses, but quite different for situations. This is because each test has different *a priori* assumptions and algorithms. The cluster analysis results for situations are more meaningful and interpretable than the factor analysis results.

4. A three-way analysis of variance was performed in order to determine the amount of variance accounted for by each factor, and the differences between the groups. The calculation followed the method of Endler (1966) and Golding (1975). Table 12.8 gives the percentages of variance accounted for by each factor, and the interactions. It shows that the percentages of variance accounted for by each component are fairly similar across the four

TABLE 12.7. *Factor-analytic results for situations and responses*

	Situations				Responses			
Subjects	Factor	Item[a]	Eigenvalue[b]	Variance	Factor	Items	Eigenvalue	Variance
Adults (32)	1. Intimacy, formal social occasion	2,4,5,7,10, 12,14	6.53	43.5	1. Upset, anxious	1,3,4,6,7,9, 20	4.2	42.9
	2. Assertiveness, focus of attention	1,3,9,8, 13,15,	1.0	7.0	2. Angry, frustrated	2,5,8	1.1	11.0
Post-graduate students (39)	1. Formal public behaviour	7,8,10,12 14	5.47	36.5	1. Upset, anxious	1,3,4,7,10	4.53	45.3
	2. Assertiveness, therapy	6,9,11,13	1.22	8.1	2. Angry, frustrated	2,6,8	1.04	10.4
	3. Complex ritualised formal occasion	3,4,5,13	1.04	6.9				
Occupational therapists (32)	1. Intimacy, initiation	2,6,10,11 12,13	5.33	35.6	1. Anxious	1,3,4,	4.04	40.4
	2. Complex ritualised formal occasion	3,4,5,14, 15	1.03	6.8	2. Angry, bewildered	2,5,6,8,9	1.30	13.0
School-children (40)	1. Unequal status interacting parties	4,7,11,13	5.44	36.2	1. Angry, bewildered, frustrated	2,6,7,8,9	3.91	39.1
	2. Focus of attention	3,8,12,15	1.11	7.4	2. Upset, anxious	1,3,4,8,10	1.18	11.8

[a] Items that loaded 0.40 and above were retained for inclusion on the scale.
[b] Only factors with an eigenvalue of 1.00 and above were considered.

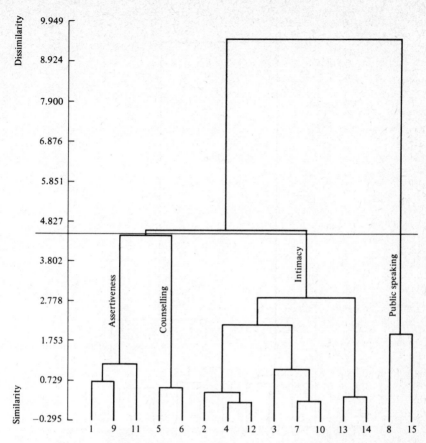

Fig. 12.1. Cluster analysis of situations: occupational therapy students.

TABLE 12.8. *Percentage of variance accounted for by each component derived from three-way analysis of variance results*

	Adults	Post-graduate students	Occupational therapists	Schoolchildren	Total
Person	20.22	13.15	12.58	17.00	15.68
Situation	2.32	4.19	5.91	2.42	2.85
Response	8.93	11.42	20.57	11.21	12.27
Person × situation	10.44	11.28	9.02	14.06	11.99
Person × response	10.44	6.08	10.98	7.98	6.38
Situation × response	3.57	6.08	10.98	7.98	6.38
Error	42.04	42.72	34.63	39.11	40.62

341

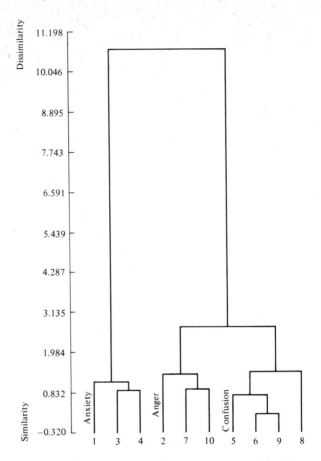

Fig. 12.2. Cluster analysis of responses: occupational therapy students.

groups, the occupational therapist group being most different in having a relatively low person and high response variance. These results are parallel to those derived from other S–R inventories of anxiety (Endler and Hunt, 1968, 1969; Ekehammar, Magnusson and Ricklander, 1974; Fisher, Horsfall and Morris, 1977). Table 12.9 presents the mean response score for each situation, for each of the four groups. This gives some idea of the overall discomfort of people in that situation.

Discussion

The results from this experiment are interesting for a number of reasons. The systematic patterns underlying the effects of persons, situations, responses and interaction were examined first by the use of three-mode factor analysis which analyses all of the data to produce the factors of each

342

TABLE 12.9. *Mean response scores for each situation across all four groups*

Situations	Mean response scores			
	Adults	Post-graduate students	Occupational therapists	Schoolchildren
1. Complaining to a neighbour who you know well about constant noisy disturbances	2.05	2.02	2.18	2.23
2. Taking a person of the opposite sex out for the first time for an evening	1.58	1.66	1.87	1.77
3. Going for a job interview	1.69	1.99	1.96	1.96
4. Visiting the doctor when unwell	1.85	1.68	1.78	1.84
5. Going to close relative's funeral	1.76	1.69	1.87	2.16
6. Going round to cheer up a depressed friend who asked you to call	1.93	1.93	1.67	2.07
7. Being a host or hostess at a large party (e.g. twenty-first birthday)	1.76	1.91	1.73	1.76
8. Give a short formal speech to a group of about fifty people that you don't know	2.20	2.24	2.46	2.54
9. Taking an unsatisfactory article back to a shop where you purchased it	2.12	2.11	2.18	2.01
10. Going across to introduce yourself to new neighbours	0.66	0.77	0.63	0.77
11. Dealing with a difficult and disobedient child	2.03	2.02	1.89	2.00
12. Going to a function with many people from a different culture	1.90	1.69	1.85	2.01
13. Playing a party game after dinner (charades, musical chairs)	2.15	2.12	1.91	1.67
14. Attending a distant relation's wedding ceremony when you know few people	1.80	1.86	2.04	1.95
15. Apologising to a superior for forgetting an important errand	2.16	2.34	2.06	2.60

class or mode of variable, as well as providing a core matrix depicting the interaction between these factors. Table 12.7 shows that there was more congruence between the response factors than between the situation factors. Considering the first situation factor alone, which in all cases accounts for over a third of the variance, it seems that the adults and post-graduate students have similar factors which differed from those for schoolchildren and occupational therapy students – indicating an age difference. This difference is also noticeable in the response mode, where the school-children's factors seem to be the inverse of the other groups – primarily bewildered, angry and frustrated and secondarily anxious. It seems, therefore, that though there is evidence of stability across samples of subjects, the factor analysis results and the analysis of variance results both highlight age differences. Given the nature of social anxiety and social difficulty this finding is not surprising.

Despite problems with the technique of apportioning variance to components derived from the three-way analysis of variance results, this produced two interesting points. Firstly the choice of specifically social situations as stimuli led to a higher person variation, indicating substantial individual differences in the reaction to these situations. Secondly, compared to other studies there was a relatively small response variation, due no doubt to the fact that responses were restricted to one type (i.e. emotional) rather than being of several types. Thus, as Argyle (1976) has pointed out, the variances obtained depend on how varied are the persons, situations or responses.

Finally the finding that situations differ considerably with regard to the difficulty of enacting certain social skills within them, points to a possible new direction for this research. Previous taxonomic work on difficult situations has relied on factor-analytic or multidimensional scaling techniques which show underlying dimensions between situations. As these results have not been particularly fruitful, it seems that by finding out what social skills are needed in a situation, and then building a taxonomy on the similarities and differences between these skills, a more useful and thorough taxonomy of stressful situations may be constructed.

12.2. Social difficulty in a foreign culture: the difficulties reported by foreign students in everyday social situations in England

A. FURNHAM AND S. BOCHNER
[A fuller version of this study is given in Bochner (in press).]

People who are new to a culture, or subculture – foreign students, tourists, immigrants, refugees, researchers – are at least for a period in the position of being unskilled in their new environment. Though usually socially skilled in their own culture, they are now forced into the frustrating and embarrassing role of being socially unskilled and inadequate in the new culture. They often do not know the language, they are bewildered by the different social routines of such things as eating, drinking, shopping and sexual contact; they are unaware of the implicit messages they give or receive by their own or others' nonverbal communication; they are astounded by different conventions of self-presentation, self-disclosure, assertiveness and friendship formation (Sue and Sue, 1977). In other words they suffer from what Oberg (1960) called 'culture shock'. The extent, the type and the duration of the difficulty foreigners may experience is dependent on a number of factors. These may be said to fall into three categories: the extent of the difference between the two cultures; individual differences and coping strategies; and sojourn experience, itself seen in terms of the treatment the sojourners receive from the host and the treatment given to nationals in the new culture.

This study aimed to do two things:

1. Firstly to map out empirically the types of social difficulty that students from a wide range of different cultures experience, by examining self-reported difficulty in specific everyday social situations that the students experience in England.
2. Secondly to determine whether there are any differences, or discernible patterns of cultural difference, in self-reported difficulty on the factors or dimensions arising from the above analysis.

The two aims of the study must be seen to be the necessary preliminary of pilot work for further empirical analysis, and hence the study is descriptive and exploratory.

Method

Subjects. Nearly 400 subjects from fifty-one countries were given the questionnaire. They were all in top classes from approved English language schools in London, Oxford and Cambridge. However, only 150 of these subjects were used for the major part of the analysis, as a number of potentially confounding variables were controlled. They were:

1. Age: only subjects between sixteen and thirty were used.
2. Marital status: only single subjects were used.
3. Education: only subjects who had completed secondary education were used, though most had begun or completed tertiary education.
4. Social class: Subjects in classes 1–4 on the Hall–Jones scale were used.
5. Length of stay in England: only subjects who had been in Britain for more than one month and less than nine months were used.
6. Previous visits to England: subjects who had been to Britain more than twice previously and/or had stayed for more than nine months in total were rejected.
7. Nationality: subjects were divided into three groups, labelled

'near', 'middle' and 'far' (indicating their geographical distance from Britain). The 'near' group consisted of North Europeans (mainly Swiss, Germans and French), the 'middle' group of South Europeans (mainly Greeks, Italians and Spaniards), and the 'far' group of Near and Far Easterners (mainly Iranians, Japanese and Iraqis). Cluster analysis supported this categorisation (see results section).

Materials. Each subject was given a questionnaire which consisted of a list of forty commonly occurring social situations in which they might experience difficulty. The list was derived from three sources: a scale devised by Trower *et al.* (1978); a scale devised by Colman and Halstead (1973); and finally pilot work consisting of interviews with about thirty foreign language students from different cultures where they were asked to report the situations they had found particularly difficult since coming to England. Subjects were then shown the complete list of situations and asked to indicate the amount of difficulty they had found in any they had personally experienced in England.

Procedure. All the students were tested during their classroom time by their teachers. The students' proficiency at English reading, writing and speaking was determined and the most competent students tested. Subjects were taken through the questionnaire line by line by the language teachers, who made sure that all the students understood the instructions, the questions and the responses required. As a result the questionnaire took about an hour to administer. In most of the schools either the subjects or the teachers were debriefed as to the purpose of the experiment.

Results

Three different analyses were carried out.

Factor analysis. Principal components and varimax analysis was carried out on the 150 subjects' test items. This also produced the mean 'difficulty' score for the forty items. Table 12.10 shows the ten situations that subjects had most difficulty with. A score of 1 represents no difficulty and 5 extreme difficulty. These results confirmed the pilot studies in which students had often complained of their difficulty in approaching host nationals, and in establishing a close, non-sexual relationship. The varimax results revealed six factors with an eigenvalue of above 1.50, which together accounted for 44 per cent of the variance (Table 12.11). Nearly all the factors were readily interpretable and descriptive labels were given to each. Similar factors commonly arise from studies on social-skills deficit (Trower *et al.*, 1978). It appears that these situations are experienced as difficult

TABLE 12.10. *The most difficult social situations for foreign students (N = 150)*

Situations	Mean[a]
5. Making British friends of your own age	2.66
33. Dealing with somebody who is cross, aggressive	2.44
15. Approaching others, starting up a friendship	2.43
25. Appearing in front of an audience (acting, speaking)	2.32
17. Getting to know people in depth, intimately	2.27
32. Understanding jokes, humour, sarcasm	2.23
21. Dealing with people staring at you	2.21
18. Taking the initiative in keeping the conversation going	2.20
14. Being with people that you don't know very well	2.16
23. Complaining in public, dealing with unsatisfactory service	2.10

[a] A score of 1 indicates no difficulty, 5 extreme difficulty.

because subjects do not possess, or do not know which are, the appropriate skills for dealing with them.

Factor 1 involved two themes: formal situations in which the student is dealing with others in terms of roles, and where there is often status difference, and situations in which the student is the focus of attention. To some extent both of these problems involve some understanding of the rules, conventions and etiquette in this culture.

Factor 2 involved managing or initiating friendships and understanding others. Many students in the pilot stage reported the coldness and stand-offishness of English people, and their loneliness at being deprived of close friends.

Factor 3 involved public rituals and is often anecdotally quoted as being a source of misunderstanding and difficulty. Curiously there were no significant sex or culture differences in this factor, implying that all the subjects were equally mildly disturbed by British queuing customs, and toiletry habits.

Factor 4 is clearly involved in initiating and maintaining contact. Possibly students had difficulty in the choice of suitable topics, self-presentation and self-disclosure, which might be different in their country of origin. Language itself of course is an important factor.

Factor 5 involved making public decisions. It is interesting to note the importance of shopping in this factor, as students often reported confusion as to where or how to purchase certain goods, especially food and medicines. A fairly high incidence of shoplifting among the population was reported by the teachers of the pupils.

Factor 6 is clearly one of negative assertiveness, commonly experienced. It is possible that the dress or racial characteristics of students occasion much public attention that the student is unable to cope with.

TABLE 12.11. *Factor-analytic results (varimax)*

Factor 1: Formal relations/focus of attention
Variance   17.9 per cent
Eigenvalue   7.16

Situations	Loading
25. Appearing in front of an audience	0.72
28. Dealing with people of higher status than you	0.70
27. Being the leader of a small group	0.68
24. Seeing a doctor	0.64
29. Reprimanding a subordinate	0.64
22. Attending a formal dinner	0.61
26. Being interviewed for something	0.60
17. Getting to know people in depth	0.45
23. Complaining in public	0.44

Factor 2: Managing intimate relationships
Variance   7.3 per cent
Eigenvalue   2.93

Situations	Loading
32. Understanding jokes, humour, sarcasm	0.72
18. Taking the initiative in keeping the conversation going	0.70
15. Approaching others, starting up a friendship	0.55
1. Making friends of your own age	0.43

Factor 3: Public rituals
Variance   5.6 per cent
Eigenvalue   2.25

Situations	Loading
36. Waiting in a queue	0.76
35. Using public and private toilet facilities	0.63

Factor 4: Initiating contact/introductions
Variance   4.8 per cent
Eigenvalue   1.92

Situations	Loading
11. Going into a room full of people	0.76
13. Meeting strangers and being introduced to new people	0.59
4. Going to discotheques or dances	0.54
14. Being with people that you don't know very well	0.51
38. Going into pubs	0.40

Factor 5: Public decision-making
Variance   4.6 per cent
Eigenvalue   1.85

Situations	Loading
2. Shopping in a large supermarket	0.79
3. Going on public transport (trains, buses, tubes)	0.57
16. Making ordinary decisions affecting others	0.52

TABLE 12.11 *(cont.)*

Factor 6: Assertiveness	
Variance 3.9 per cent	
Eigenvalue 1.56	
Situations	Loading
10. Going into restaurants or cafés	0.63
21. Dealing with people staring at you	0.62
33. Dealing with somebody who is cross and aggressive	0.57

Cluster analysis. Before further analysis of the data was attempted it was necessary to establish whether the crude division of subjects into three cultural groups was valid. A cluster analysis of subjects in terms of all their responses to the questionnaire was performed. Three clusters emerged and a χ^2 test was carried out comparing the 'predicted' clusters with the 'actual' clusters of subjects emerging from the analysis. The χ^2 of 59.67 was highly significant ($P < 0.0001$), as was the contingency coefficient C of 0.533, which is a measure of the extent of association (correlation) between two sets of attributes. We thus have support for our cultural categorisation.

Analysis of variance. A two-way analysis of variance was computed on the factor scores from each factor derived from the factor analysis. Thus six culture (3) by sex (2) analyses were done. It can be seen from Table 12.12 that whereas sex differences reached significance in one factor ('public decision-making'), cultural differences were significant on three factors and each time in the same direction. That is, North Europeans (the 'near' group) experienced less difficulty than the South Europeans (the 'middle' group), while those subjects from the Near and Far East (the 'far' group) experienced most difficulty. Factor 3, 'public rituals', and 6, 'assertiveness', revealed no significant effects, indicating that all foreign students experience similar amounts of difficulty in these situations.

Discussion

It has been widely documented that social skill is a multi-, not a unidimensional concept, involving many components and separate skills. Further, these skills are often situation-specific. It is thus to be expected that cultural and/or sex differences might occur for some skills but not for others. The results appear to indicate, firstly, that foreign students' difficulties concern mainly expressive and affiliative skills, as well as an understanding of specific norms and rules in this culture. Secondly, it seems that sex differences are relatively unimportant, a surprising finding given that many social-skills studies reveal consistent sex differences. It is possible that demographic and individual differences in social skills are small relative to

TABLE 12.12. *Two-way analysis of variance on the 'Difficult Situation Scale' factor scores*

Mean factor score				Source	F
Factor 1: Formal relations/focus of attention					
	'Near'	'Middle'	'Far'		
Male	−0.38	0.05	0.18	Culture	12.40***
Female	−0.60	0.10	0.66	Sex	0.46
				Interaction	1.79
Factor 2: Managing intimate relationships					
	'Near'	'Middle'	'Far'		
Male	−0.46	0.12	0.44	Culture	10.93***
Female	−0.49	0.06	0.32	Sex	0.20
				Interaction	0.02
Factor 3: Public rituals					
	'Near'	'Middle'	'Far'		
Male	−0.04	0.17	0.04	Culture	0.73
Female	−0.17	−0.15	0.07	Sex	0.36
				Interaction	0.42
Factor 4: Initiating contact/introductions					
	'Near'	'Middle'	'Far'		
Male	−0.38	0.27	0.33	Culture	5.88**
Female	−0.36	0.17	−0.06	Sex	1.04
				Interaction	0.69
Factor 5: Public decision-making					
	'Near'	'Middle'	'Far'		
Male	−0.05	−0.21	0.37	Culture	1.46
Female	−0.23	0.22	−0.07	Sex	0.21
				Interaction	3.52*
Factor 6: Assertiveness					
	'Near'	'Middle'	'Far'		
Male	−0.26	−0.12	0.04	Culture	0.77
Female	0.13	−0.07	0.20	Sex	1.68
				Interaction	0.41

*** $P < 0.001$; ** $P < 0.01$; * $P < 0.05$.

cultural and subcultural differences. Thirdly some situations are univer-sally found to be difficult or not difficult, suggesting transcultural effects.

The implications of these results are twofold. It seems important to establish the sorts of difficulty and the types of situation that people from different cultures are likely to experience in the host culture. These may be of both degree and type; that is, the culture difference determines the quality as well as the quantity of difficulty likely to be experienced. Thus it would be useful when counselling foreign students to understand the nature of the difficulties they are likely to encounter, explain the cultural differences, and offer some form of situation training. Secondly, it would be worthwhile for host nationals dealing with foreign students – teachers, landladies, cooks, local tradesmen – to be sensitised to the cultural traditions in social behaviour.

These results provide the start of what is potentially an important and neglected area of study. The limitations of this study could well be improved in others. We restricted ourselves to foreign students, who are by no means representative of other foreign groups such as immigrants and refugees. We also looked at broad cultural groups rather than specific cultures or nations, or within-cultural differences. Further, we restricted our study to an investigation of social, rather than work or specifically intergroup situations, which might well reveal different effects.

12.3. Cross-cultural differences in the experience of difficult social situations

A. FURNHAM

Trower *et al.* (1978) suggested that behaviour varies not only between situations, but also between cultures, social classes, racial groups and age groups in the same culture. They suggested that nonverbal signals, rules and rituals for particular situations, certain ideals, terms and concepts, and aspects of the social structure such as the relationship between men and women, young and old, supervisor and subordinate, vary between cultures.

One would therefore expect a different pattern of social difficulties to arise in different cultures and subcultures, both within cultures and between cultures. This study set out to examine the differences and similarities in social difficulty for everyday social situations in three distinct cultures, and the multidimensionality of the concept of social difficulty/ inadequacy in each culture. A careful effort was made to use equivalent samples of subjects in order to avoid invalid or artefactual results. Female South African nurses were used, as nursing is one of the few professions in South Africa in which people from three different cultures – European, African and Indian – have similar educational qualifications, job experience and competence in English, though the job status and role of the working woman is different in the three cultures. Also the discriminatory political system ensures that the cultures are kept physically distinct and separated.

Two hypotheses were formed:
1. There would be a significant difference in self-reported social difficulty in the three groups, Europeans expressing least difficulty

and Africans most. This difference was expected because of the socio-political structure of South Africa, where the minority white group is dominant in all aspects of social, economic and political life, and the Africans are usually below other black groups in terms of education, income and status.

2. That the concept of social difficulty is multi- not unidimensional, and that different factors would emerge for each group because of cultural differences.

Method

Subjects. A total of eighty-five subjects were tested. All subjects were female third-year nurses working in three (racially segregated) hospitals approximately fifty miles apart in Natal, South Africa. There were twenty-two Africans (mean age 21.59 years, S.D. 4.64), twenty-seven Indians (mean age 20.66 years, S.D. 4.54) and thirty-six Europeans (mean age 20.91 years, S.D. 4.57). They had equivalent educational qualifications, had received most of their education in English, and were at the same stage of their professional training. Most of them lived in institutionalised accommodation provided by the hospitals, and the subjects were a homogeneous group in terms of experience, interests, etc.

Materials. A modified version of the Bryant and Trower (1974) Social Situations Questionnaire was administered; this has been used in social-skills assessment (Trower *et al.*, 1978) and cross-cultural studies (Rim, 1976). The thirty items used in the original scale were included as well as ten others obtained from other sources (Argyle's (1978*b*) Social Situation Scale, pilot studies, and the work of Janisse and Palys (1976) and Magnusson and Ekehammar (1975)). Item 4 in the original scale ('Going into pubs') was omitted as women in South Africa are not legally allowed to go into pubs/bars. Other slight alterations to the original items were made mainly by the provision of synonyms for certain words or terms thought to be ambiguous or difficult to understand.

Procedure. All subjects were tested in small groups in their own racially segregated hospitals during their lecture time. A white member of the teaching staff and each group's own teacher were present while the questionnaire was being filled out in order to explain any language or meaning difficulties, should they arise. The questionnaire took about fifteen minutes to complete.

Results

Four analyses were performed on the data:

1. Analysis of variance between the total difficulty scores of the three

352

cultural groups, the error term being the variability between individuals. There was a highly significant difference between the three groups ($F = 15.48, P < 0.01$). The Europeans reported experiencing least social difficulty (mean 33.9), the Africans most (mean 61.2) and the Indians an intermediate amount (meant 46.6).

2. Analysis of variance between the questions, in order to check that difference in total scores was not simply due to one or two questions. There was a highly significant difference ($F = 14.14, P < 0.01$). Also the Student's t-test for each scale item between the three cultural groups was calculated. Two groups were tested at a time. In twenty-four out of forty scales Africans reported significantly more difficulty than Europeans, and in twelve of the forty scales Indians reported significantly more difficulty than Europeans (Table 12.13). Africans reported more difficulty (though not always significantly more) than Europeans in thirty-five out of forty situations.

3. Kendall's coefficient of concordance was performed on the difficulty scores to indicate to what extent different items are ranked in the same way by the three racial groups. The result was highly significant ($W = 0.44$, $P < 0.001$), revealing the similarity between the cultural groups in the situations they find difficult.

4. Factor analysis of each cultural group's data. A different factor structure emerged for each group, though certain similarities were apparent. The varimax rotation results are presented in Table 12.14; only factors with an eigenvalue of above 3.00 were considered. Items that loaded 0.4 and above on each factor were included. In the African group four factors emerged accounting for 52.2 per cent of the variance, in the Indian group three factors emerged which accounted for 42.1 per cent of the variance, while in the European group three factors emerged accounting for 44.1 per cent of the variance. The first factor in the African group consisted of situations in which public formal interaction took place, the subject being the focus of attention. The first factor in the Indian group consisted of situations involving making friends and interacting with peers, while the Europeans' first factor was similar to that of the Africans.

Discussion

The ANOVA results confirmed the first hypothesis, namely that there would be a significant difference in reported difficulty between the three groups, the Europeans reporting least difficulty and the Africans most. The Europeans in fact reported fairly minimal difficulty, the mean for fifteen items being under 2 (between slight and moderate difficulty), and only one item being over 2 (between moderate and great difficulty). Africans experienced slight to moderate difficulty in fifteen situations and moderate to great in sixteen situations. There was a significant difference in reported

TABLE 12.13. *Mean difficulty scores for three racial groups*

Situations[a]	Mean			Significant difference[b]		
	A	I	E	A/I	A/E	I/E
1. Walking down the street	0.54	0.29	0.11		*	
2. Going into shops	0.31	0.11	0.16			*
3. Going on public transport	1.00	0.70	0.30			*
4. Going to parties	1.77	1.40	0.77		*	*
5. Mixing with people at work	0.81	0.48	0.41	*		
6. Making friends of your own age	0.36	0.44	0.55			
7. Going out with an opposite-sex partner	1.31	1.25	0.69		*	*
8. Being with same age/sex group	0.95	0.22	0.47	*		
9. Being with same age/mixed sex group	1.04	0.66	0.30		*	*
10. Being with opposite sex group	2.54	1.77	0.63	*	*	*
11. Entertaining people in your own room	1.09	0.66	0.47		*	
12. Going into restaurants/cafés	1.36	0.96	0.22		*	*
13. Going to dances/discos	2.27	1.92	0.75		*	*
14. Being with older people	2.31	0.51	0.38	*	*	
15. Being with younger people	0.95	0.44	0.72			
16. Going into a room full of people	2.54	2.00	1.40		*	
17. Meeting strangers	2.09	1.48	1.27		*	
18. Being with people you don't know	2.18	1.81	1.33	*	*	
19. Being with friends	0.00	0.14	0.08			

No. Situation						
20. Approaching others	1.36	1.07	1.27		*	*
21. Making decisions affecting others	2.63	0.85	0.86			
22. Being with one person rather than group	0.50	0.44	0.25		*	*
23. Getting to know people in depth	2.31	1.51	0.77		*	
24. Taking initiative in conversation	1.63	1.14	1.25	*	*	
25. Looking at people in the eye	1.90	1.44	0.47		*	
26. Disagreeing and being assertive	2.13	0.81	0.66		*	*
27. People standing/sitting very close	1.72	1.22	0.77		*	
28. Talking about yourself/self-disclosure	2.45	1.55	1.25	*	*	*
29. People looking at you	2.63	1.85	1.19		*	*
30. Introducing two people	0.09	0.59	0.52			
31. Attending a formal dinner	1.31	1.25	1.08			
32. Complaining about unsatisfactory service	2.63	1.77	1.52	*	*	
33. Seeing a doctor/bank manager	1.04	1.03	1.19			
34. Appearing in front of an audience	2.09	2.55	2.30			
35. Being interviewed for something	1.63	1.88	1.66			
36. Being the leader of a small group	2.31	1.81	1.66		*	
37. Dealing with people of higher status	2.63	1.77	1.25	*	*	*
38. Reprimanding a subordinate	1.36	1.96	1.25			*
39. Mixing with people of another racial group	2.40	1.85	0.91	*	*	*
40. Apologising to a superior	1.13	1.07	1.05			

A, African; E, European; I, Indian.
[a] Situations are given in abbreviated form here.
[b] Student's t-test. P<0.05.

TABLE 12.14. *Factor analysis: varimax rotation*

Cultural group	Factors	Items[a]	Eigenvalue[b]	Variance
Africans (22)	1. Focus of attention, formal situations	7,34,35,36,37	6.9	17.9
	2. Peer group interaction, public appearance	2,8,12,13,21,27,28	5.4	13.6
	3. Intimate and problematic interaction	16,21,28,29,31,33,39,40	4.9	12.3
	4. Initiating contact, making friends	5,6,15,30,38	3.3	8.4
Indians (27)	1. Making friends, interacting with peers	6,8,11,17,38	8.9	22.2
	2. Focus of attention, assertiveness	21,23,24,26,32,34,35,36,38	4.4	11.2
	3. Focus of attention	1,22	3.4	8.7
Europeans (36)	1. Focus of attention, formal situations	11,15,26,29,30,34,35,36	9.9	24.8
	2. Public social situations	1,2,3,33	4.5	11.5
	3. Dealing with public social events	4,12,13,28,31	3.1	7.8

[a] Only items that loaded 0.40 and above were considered.
[b] Only factors with an eigenvalue of above 3.00 were considered.

difficulty between the Europeans and Africans in 60 per cent of the situations, and in 30 per cent of the situations between the Europeans and Indians.

White nurses report very little social difficulty – lower than that experienced by other populations (students and psychiatric patients) who have completed similar questionnaires (Janisse and Palys, 1976; Rim, 1976). They reported moderate to great difficulty in only one situation, 'appearing in front of an audience', a situation that is widely experienced as anxiety provoking. It is possible that the scale is not sensitive to the situations that are relevant to this population. On all but five scales the Africans expressed more difficulty than the Indians did, though Furnham (1979), using a similar population, found that Indians reported more difficulties in the field of assertiveness as measured by the Wolpe Assertiveness Inventory.

There seem to be two plausible explanations for these results. Firstly it is possible that the three cultural groups have had varying experiences of these social situations and the differences reflected lack of experience rather than inadequacy. Secondly, the varied roles of women in the three cultures may have accounted for some of the differences: even entering some of these situations may be prohibited, anticonformist or considered the domain of the male. There also may be differences in the groups' attitudes toward self-disclosure in questionnaires.

The factor analysis results support the second hypothesis, namely that social difficulty is multi- rather than unidimensional, and they show that a different factor structure emerged for each group. However, the stability of these factors is questionable given the relatively small size of the groups, and further work would have to be done to establish the nature of these different factors. The items that loaded on each factor were often fairly similar and a brief label has been given to each factor in each group. It is apparent from Table 12.14 that although each group has a unique factor structure there are certain similarities between the groups. Factor 1 in the African group, which accounts for 17.9 per cent of the variance, is similar to factor 2 in the Indian group, which accounts for 11.2 per cent of the variance, and similar to the European group's first factor, which accounts for 24.8 per cent of the variance; it involves assertiveness and being the focus of attention in informal and formal situations. Further the Africans' second factor appears to be similar to the Europeans' third factor, which involves dealing with conventional public social functions and occasions. It is clear that the scale is not unidimensional and that social difficulty takes several forms. It is possible that a clear factor structure would have emerged if certain difficult work situations had been included, a wider range of cross-culturally relevant social situations had been listed, and the description of the situations and responses had been fuller and more specific.

13

Applications of situational analysis

What use is the analysis of social situations? Many social problems, such as various kinds of law-breaking and mental disorder, have nearly always been tackled by attempts to modify the behaviour of individuals. We now know that situations and $P \times S$ interaction are at least as important as personality in explaining behaviour; it follows that we ought to be trying to modify situations as well as persons, or to match persons to situations better. With our new understanding of situations we are in a position to modify existing situations, and even to invent new ones. We are also in a better position to select people who are going to enter a situation (e.g. a job), and to train them to cope effectively in it.

Law-breaking

One of the earliest studies of the effect of the situation on behaviour, by Harteshorne and May (1928), showed that there was great situational variability and little individual consistency in twenty-four tests of cheating and stealing, in laboratory settings. There was, however, a minority of individuals who were unusually honest and another group who were exceptionally dishonest; for members of these two groups there was some consistency across situations. A later analysis of their data by Burton (1963) showed that a weak general factor was present. Nelsen, Grinder and Mutterer (1969), in a later study of honesty in temptation situations, found considerable person variance as well as situational variability. Farrington (1979) proposed a cost–benefit model to explain situational factors in honesty – more dishonesty when the anticipated rewards are greater, and the likelihood of punishment less. He found that 'lost letters' were less often returned if they contained more money, and if there was money as opposed to a postal order. Similar results have been obtained in studies of cheating in the classroom.

Crime is partly due to personality factors, although criminals choose suitable occasions to perform their crimes; their crimes are also prevented by situational factors – for example fitting a steering-wheel lock reduces the chances of a car being stolen (Mayhew et al., 1976), and the presence of policemen stops many offences being committed. Delinquency on the part of young people is much affected by temptations and other aspects of situations, since they are not yet committed to a life of crime (Glaser, 1974). There are certain forms of deviant behaviour found among the young that are greatly affected by situational factors.

Vandalism

This can be defined as wilful damage to property or amenities for no material gain. It consists mainly of damage to windows and lifts, putting up graffiti, leaving rubbish, and other damage to public housing, empty houses, parks, telephone kiosks, etc.

The Pruitt-Ingoes housing project in St Louis, Missouri, was opened in 1954 and consisted of 2762 apartments which were mainly occupied by black families, many without fathers. Vandalism was so extensive that in 1976 the entire building had to be demolished. Yancey (1971) showed that there were no semi-private spaces where neighbourly relations and informal networks could be established, and residents had few friends in the project. They could not supervise their own children, since play areas were out of sight, and attempts to supervise other people's children led to conflict with the parents; dangerous teenage gangs grew up that could only be restrained by police. Newman (1972) studies this and similar housing projects, and found a higher rate of mugging and other crimes in areas that were out of sight of the street or of residents, especially lobbies, halls, stairs and lifts. He put forward the concept of 'defensible space': an area will be defended against crime if there are (1) good surveillance, (2) perceived zones of territorial influence, (3) design which neutralises feelings of isolation, stigma and vulnerability, and (4) juxtaposition of difficult areas with safe zones.

It has been found in Britain that there is more vandalism in tower blocks and deck-access housing (i.e. with long internal corridors) than in accommodation with staircase access and balcony designs (Central Policy Review Staff, 1978). Most damage again occurs in semi-public areas.

It is now realised that the vandalism is not entirely due to design features, but also to the high density of children, delinquents and problem families. Part of the solution to such vandalism is to change the kind of people who live in these buildings. In deck-access buildings in Manchester, problem families were replaced by students; it is often possible to reduce the child density. However, more can be done by modifying the design of buildings. The following steps have been found to be successful: (1) avoid large areas of semi-public impersonal space, (2) avoid dark corners, and ensure that parents can see the children's play areas, (3) keep all property occupied, (4) use materials that are very strong, e.g. armour-plate glass or transparent plastics, and that are difficult to mark, e.g. glazed tiles, rough bricks, (5) provide all-night flood-lighting in certain areas, (6) install a resident caretaker or doorman (Clarke, 1978; Central Policy Review Staff, 1978).

There is also vandalism on buses. Mayhew *et al.* (1976) found that there was less damage when buses had conductors as well as drivers, and that there was most damage upstairs, and in the back seat. Again, lack of surveillance is an important situational factor.

Of course these situational changes are only suppressing vandalism without affecting the underlying causes – boredom, unemployment and alienation. It would be very desirable to tackle these too, for example through leisure centres, community projects and vocational guidance.

Shoplifting

There are undoubtedly personality factors here, in that shoplifting tends to be done by children, females, foreigners, and those who are mentally disturbed in various ways. There are also obvious personality–situation interactions: teenage girls steal tights, cosmetics, records, etc.; children steal sweets; students steal books; and women steal clothes. However, the problem can be dealt with by modification of the shop situation. An experiment in Bristol shops succeeded in reducing the losses from 6 per cent to 3 per cent by use of the methods described below (Home Office, 1973). The residual loss of 3 per cent was probably due to internal thefts by employees.

Better surveillance is probably the most important single factor. This can be carried out by store security officers, closed-circuit TV (perhaps combined with video-tape recordings, perhaps a dummy system), one-way screens, mirrors to improve observation of dark corners, and notices announcing that these devices are installed. Their value is more as deterrents than in actually making arrests, which may prove difficult in practice. Shops are helped to some extent by members of the public who report cases of shoplifting, though this too is affected by situational factors. The percentage of customers who report shoplifting has been assessed in a number of American field experiments; the range of figures obtained – from 8 per cent to 94 per cent – shows the importance of situational variables. Bystanders are more likely to report shoplifting by hippies, blacks, and other apparently low-status people. They are more likely to report those who have previously been rude to them. Bystanders will report more observed thefts if encouraged to do so, though notices have little effect; witnesses are more likely to report a theft if interviewed alone (Farrington, 1979).

Secondly, the goods can be locked up; for example typewriters and fur coats can be attached to chains, which may in turn be linked to an alarm bell, and locked showcases may also be used. Larger items can have electronic or magnetic devices attached which ring a bell if they are taken through the door; tickets can be issued for clothing taken into fitting rooms.

Chemists put medicines on shelves behind the counter so that customers have to ask for them, while many other goods are on open shelves.

Shoplifting has probably been increased by other situational changes, such as the attractive presentation of goods, so that people want to have them, and a reduction in the amount of interaction between customers and sales staff.

Thefts by employees are more difficult to prevent. The gambling casinos in Reno, Nevada, have great problems here: they have to prevent not only thefts (of money) by their very large staffs, but also collusion of the staff with the customers, for example to connive at winning the $25 000 prizes at Keno (a form of automated Bingo). Such theft and fraud is mostly prevented by very strict surveillance, both by roving floor supervisors and by observation windows over the gambling tables that have the higher stakes. An employee who infringes even a minor rule is dismissed at once.

Disorder at football grounds

The disorderly behaviour of fans at football grounds, and on the journey to and from the ground, was regarded as a major social problem in Britain during the years 1974–8. Many young people were arrested for violence to other fans and to property, e.g. buses and trains; fans would invade the pitch to chase each other, and surround and threaten policemen. It is now realised, from the research of social psychologists, that very few people were injured, very few of the large numbers attending were arrested or expelled, and that the 'violence' consisted mainly of ritualised insults and gestures, rather than actual bodily damage (Marsh *et al.*, 1978). Insofar as there was a problem it has now been largely controlled, through better understanding of the nature of the situation.

Those involved are almost entirely male, working class, and aged thirteen to twenty. The nature of the situation can be analysed in terms of the concepts we have been using.

Goals. These have not been studied directly, but it is thought that these young people are enjoying themselves, by noisy group activity, and enhancing their self-images by identifying with a group, denigrating other groups and demonstrating their toughness.

Rules. Marsh *et al.* (1978) have shown from interviews with fans that there are widely shared rules which restrain aggression and prevent bodily damage. A few disturbed personalities ignore these rules, and engage in real violence, but this is disapproved of (see p. 131).

Roles. There is a fairly clear structure of informal roles, such as 'chant leader', 'hooligan', 'nutter', 'town boys' and 'organiser'. Occupants of these roles occupy special spatial positions, and may wear special clothes, as well as having characteristic patterns of behaviour (see p. 176).

Repertoire. There are a number of special elements of behaviour, such as chanting, waving scarves, shouting insults, pushing and running.

Environmental setting. The two opposing groups of fans are now segregated in different parts of the ground, sometimes separated by wire-mesh fences.

Concepts. The definition of the situation has been elaborated by tradition and by the media; this definition has become accepted by the participants, who entertain the fantasy that they are dangerous hooligans engaged in bloody battles in which the other side are half-killed.

It should be added that this is a situation which is voluntarily chosen, indeed paid for, by those who enter it; it is one of the most popular leisure activities of football fans.

Violence at football grounds has been controlled in several ways. (1) The police, the media and the public have to some extent been persuaded to perceive the situation differently, as one of aggressive ritual and expression rather than true violence. (2) Environmental changes have been made at grounds, mainly in terms of better separation of opposing groups of fans and barriers to keep them off the pitch; efforts are also made to separate them before and after the match. (3) Other environmental changes include the provision of seating, and barriers within the terraces to prevent the crowd surging forward and to make the work of the police easier. (4) Policing is improved by the use of closed-circuit TV and two-way radios, by surveillance of trouble-spots outside the ground, by building up good relations with fans, and by acquiring skills for dealing with difficult crowd situations. (5) Restrictions are placed on the sale of alcohol, on the bringing of drink into the ground, and on the entry of drunken people (Sports Council and SSRC, 1978; Scottish Education Department, 1977). These methods of controlling violence are similar to those used in other examples of civil disturbance, such as on the American campuses in the 1960s.

Situational analysis can make another contribution to law-breaking – social skills training (SST) for offenders. Delinquents and prisoners are now receiving SST in a number of institutions. One approach concentrates on teaching the skills of applying for a job, being interviewed, and working under supervision (Sarason and Ganzer, 1971). Another approach could be to discover the situations in which an offender has got into trouble, and train him to deal with those situations better. There is evidence that violent attacks on other people, including rape, occur when the aggressor has been unable to get the other person to do something by the usual methods of persuasion. The solution might be training in persuasive, or even assertive, social skills for those situations where the trainee has been in trouble.

Mental disorder

It is now known that mental disorders are partly due to environmental stress (in combination with genetic factors and childhood experiences), and that these stresses are often due to particular situations which cause difficulty. These may be situations that everyone finds difficult – being exposed to great danger in wartime for prolonged periods, being a prisoner of war, stressful forms of work such as TV and air-traffic control, and social stresses such as dealing with very hostile or otherwise difficult people, tiring negotiations, long spells of public speaking. Some people find these situations more stressful than others – there is a clear personality component; and some people find particular forms of stress difficult, sometimes because they lack the social skills to deal with them. It depends partly on how they perceive the situation: Holmes and Houston (1974) found that subjects who were encouraged to think of electric shocks as an interesting new kind of physiological sensation produced a smaller physiological reaction to them.

Moos (1969) found that patients in a mental hospital were *more* consistent and less variable in their behaviour between situations than were members of the staff. As patients recovered, they became less consistent. Endler (1973) found that psychotics had the highest consistency across situations on an anxiety questionnaire, followed by neurotics and normals. Mariotto and Paul (1975) studied several disturbed psychiatric patients in a number of real-life settings; they found low variability, and that social behaviour was more variable than cognitive distortion. This low situational variability can be interpreted as a failure to respond appropriately and effectively to the demands of different situations. In a follow-up study two years later Mariotto (1978) found that situational and P×S variance had increased.

The contribution of situations to anxiety was discussed in Chapter 12 (p. 328f.). Many mental patients have phobias about particular situations – open spaces, public meetings, air travel – or about spiders, animals, and so on. Anxiety neurosis is now regarded by many psychiatrists as being in many cases a collection of specific phobias rather than generalised anxiety. Behaviour therapy for anxiety consists of desensitisation or flooding, based on the main situations causing anxiety. Cases of more generalised anxiety can be treated by focusing on the most anxiety-provoking classes of situations (Lazarus, 1963).

Schizophrenics, too, are affected by situations. They do not like being supervised at work, being criticised, or being questioned about their problems. Rutter (1976) found that schizophrenics did not avert gaze during discussion of impersonal topics, as compared with normals, though they did avert gaze during interviews. Braginsky, Braginsky and Ring (1969) found that schizophrenics (American definition) reported more symptoms when interviewed to see if they should go home than if interviewed to see if they should be put in a locked ward.

We discussed in Chapter 12 the kinds of social situations that are commonly found difficult. Bryant *et al.* (1976) found that about 27 per cent of out-patient neurotics were socially inadequate, and that this was one of their main problems. For many of these patients particular situations were the cause of the trouble, rather than social situations in general; they did not know the rules, understand the goals, or possess the necessary social skills (Trower *et al.*, 1978). It is possible to find the situations that are difficult for a patient by asking him to rate his anxiety or difficulty in different situations, or by other methods, described below.

SST is being increasingly used for various groups of clients. It is partly directed to universal skills which could apply to any situation – like sensitivity to nonverbal communication, rewardingness, and taking the role of the other. It also includes training for fairly specific situations, like asking someone for a date, and dealing with a difficult subordinate. The better understanding of situations can make an important contribution to these aspects of SST.

The assessment of social-skills deficits

Trower, Bryant and Argyle (1978) suggested a programme for assessment of difficulty in social situations and a method of training. In the assessment the subject is asked to perform in specific situations as well as to complete the Social Situations Questionnaire. This is to determine the nature of the situations and the particular skill deficit. Questions are asked about the goals and motivations in these situations, the subject's planning strategies, his perception of the situation and the nature of his performance. Social inadequates often seem unaware of the social rules and conventions in certain social situations; they do not know the range of social acts that are appropriate and meaningful; they are not aware of the contingency structure of a situation; they cannot start and stop encounters successfully, and they are unable to use nonverbal signals to negotiate mutually agreeable episodes.

Most techniques developed to assess social skills involve some form of assessment of behaviour in difficult social situations, either role-play or self-report. Rehm and Marston (1968) developed the Situation Test, which consists of ten situations requiring some form of heterosexual interaction. Male subjects are informed of the nature of the situation and have to reply to a line of dialogue, said by a female confederate, which is later rated. Twentyman and McFall (1975) devised a similar Social Behaviour Situations task which requires lengthy role-playing in six 'difficult situations'. Freedman *et al.* (1978) conceptualised delinquent behaviour as a manifestation of situation-specific social-behavioural skill deficits. They identified a number of adolescent problem situations which were validated by role-playing analysis and they were able to demonstrate that non-delinquents were rated as more competent in these situations than delinquents.

There is a host of self-report inventories used on student or psychiatric populations to assess difficulty in specific situations: Friedman (1968) Action Situation Inventory, Goldsmith and McFall (1975) Interpersonal Situation Inventory, and Wolpe and Lazarus (1966). Popular guides to learning social skills and assertiveness in particular also use situation training. Bower and Bower (1976) considered a set of standard 'problem' situations requiring assertive behaviour, and offered a sample solution script for each, as an example of how to behave.

As Hersen and Bellack (1976) in their review of social-skills assessment concluded: 'Rather than providing a single, global definition of social skill, we prefer a situation-specific conception of social skills. The overriding factor is effectiveness of behaviour in social interactions. However, determination of effectiveness depends on the context of the interaction, and, given any context, the parameters of the specific situation' (p. 512).

Social skills for mental patients

When it has been discovered which situations a patient finds most difficult, training can concentrate on these situations. Often these include making friends or assertiveness, and there are often idiosyncratic situational problems as well – e.g. reading the minutes, entering the staff room, making decisions in a group of friends. The training for a difficult situation consists first of a lengthy discussion of the situation, and an attempt to lay down the goal structure, rules, roles and repertoire. The difficulties are analysed and the possible skilled solutions discussed. This is then followed by the usual modelling and role-playing. In SST patients are trained in the hospital or clinic to deal with replicas of a number of social situations. There is sometimes difficulty in transferring the newly learnt skills to the real situations. The solution to this problem lies in 'homework': patients are encouraged, or required, to try out the new skills a number of times between the weekly sessions, and to report back, for further training if necessary. There is also the problem of whether training on one kind of assertiveness situation, for example, will generalise to other assertiveness situations. A number of studies have been carried out, and in a number of them there was little generalisation (Hersen and Bellack, 1976), perhaps suggesting that assertiveness requires rather different skills in different situations. On the other hand Goldsmith and McFall (1975) did obtain generalisation of social skills to new situations for psychiatric patients.

Capon (1977) used situation training as a way of integrating the social skills that had previously been learned in a social-skills programme. He analysed three social situations as specific examples: 'the wedding reception', 'the party' and 'the job interview'. Each situation involved role-play by a number of patients, which was carefully analysed and discussed by all the participants afterwards; they looked, for example, at assertiveness, self-disclosure and ability to sustain interaction. Various elements, or smaller sequences in each situation, such as introductions, were analysed and rehearsed, and the patients urged to 'break down' the entire situation into smaller elements that they could understand and deal with. Thereafter staff members (psychologists and nurses) demonstrated how they would perform the sequence and finally the patient and a staff member role-played the situation.

Marital therapy can also profit from situational analysis. The first step is to discover the situations in which trouble occurs. This might be the husband coming home from work and not speaking to his wife, disagreements over finance, or repeated rows of a standard pattern. The next step could be an analysis of the difficult situation, followed by suggestions of alternative ways of dealing with it. This could include treatment or SST for one partner; for example the 'sleeping husband syndrome' can be treated by a token reward system, in which he gets a token for each conversation, and three tokens can be exchanged for various physical rewards (Jacobson and Martin, 1976).

Other forms of situational therapy

It is common to make use of real-life situations in the treatment of phobias. Knapp, Crosby and O'Boyle (1978) treated a case of lift phobia first by imaginal desensitisation, then by exposure to a series of increasingly difficult lifts, ending with a 700-foot descent to the interior of the Hoover Dam in a crowded lift car. Similar use is often made of a variety of purely social situations. The psychiatric ward itself can be modified as a social situation, to have more therapeutic effect. Fairweather *et al.* (1969) designed a 'small group ward' in which the patients were responsible for getting jobs done, recommending patients for privileges, and other matters. Behaviour in the ward was greatly improved, patients left hospital sooner, and after leaving hospital more were employed and they spent more time with friends.

Similar methods have been developed for dealing with alcoholism. Sanchez-Craig (1979) has developed a form of treatment based on situational analysis. Patients keep a diary and fill in questionnaires to identify the problem situations in which they drink too much. They then rehearse self-statements designed to inhibit drinking, and they consider the consequences of drinking in these situations. They decide on rules, e.g. 'don't drink alone', 'don't go pub-crawling with friends', 'drink only in the company of people I enjoy'. They also decide on rules about the amount of drinking, e.g. a glass of sherry before a meal and one glass of wine with it. No follow-up results are available yet for this form of treatment.

Obesity can also be tackled by situational management; treatment consists of identifying and controlling the environmental stimuli that lead to overeating. This includes keeping food out of sight in the house, for example in opaque containers, and taking serving dishes off the table. A number of useful rules can be introduced, such as only eating at a designated eating place, not doing anything else while eating, such as watching TV, not buying 'junk food', and only shopping on a full stomach. Part of the aim is to break behaviour sequences that lead to overeating, such as: 'watching a long TV show – feeling bored – feeling sleepy – arguing with spouse – getting out of the easy chair – entering the kitchen – opening the refrigerator – eating cheesecake – feeling guilty – wanting more cheesecake' (Ferguson, 1975). An experimental study by Chapman and Jeffrey (1980) showed that situational management produced an average weight loss of 4 lb after eight weekly sessions; those who were in addition taught the setting of goals lost $7\frac{1}{2}$ lb.

Smoking too could probably be reduced by situational management, though the situational influences on smoking are rather complex. Best and Hakstian (1978) asked 331 subjects to rate their typical urge to smoke in sixty-six situations. Factor analysis produced twelve factors for males, eleven for females; these in turn produced four clusters of males with similar profiles, five clusters of females. The groups of heaviest smokers felt the urge to smoke in many situations; the lighter smokers had much more situational variability. These results suggest that situational analysis may not be so useful for heavy smokers as for lighter smokers. It would be worth studying the situations that different individuals associated with the urge to smoke, to see if the urge can be controlled in these situations and alternative behaviour substituted. If we look at some of the factors identified by Best and Hakstian we can see how this could be done. (1) Several of their factors are related to the desire to relax, as has been found by other investigators; other relaxation techniques could be used. (2) Another factor is projecting a mature and sophisticated image, which can certainly be done in other ways.

Other uses of social-skills training

SST is also widely used to help members of the public, including students and professional people, to deal with everyday encounters. Situation training involves role-playing specific episodes, with other clients in the prescribed roles and the trainee playing himself, though occasionally role-reversing with other participants is done to encourage the trainee to get a better idea of the consequence of his actions. The role-play session is video-taped and then played back. Firstly the client suggests alternative strategies and points for correction or improvement, and secondly other participants (staff and trainees) suggest or even act out alternative strategies. The situational role-playing is repeated until a satisfactory performance is achieved; then the interaction sequence is enacted, with a group or part of it, in a more realistic setting. Role-playing is also now used as a technique to measure the behavioural dimensions of social anxiety.

One of the commonest situations for which help is sought is making friends, with the same and opposite sex. The precise situation is specified (e.g. a party, a coffee break at work), goals, rules, repertoire, etc., are analysed, and sequences of skilled moves are demonstrated and role-played, with video play-back. When training people who have difficulties at parties, or making friends, we have found that they are sometimes mistaken about the goal structure of parties (people go to be sociable, and to meet new people), or about the rules (e.g. how to meet strangers at parties, how to get away from them) (Trower *et al.*, 1978).

We saw above that situational analysis can be used in the treatment of alcoholism and obesity. Situational analysis can be combined with traditional SST based on role-playing, with cognitive therapy, or behavioural self-control (Thoresen and Mahoney, 1974; Meichenbaum, 1977).

American practice in SST emphasises assertiveness, again in a number of specific situations – returning clothes which do not fit to a shop, being overcharged at a garage, etc. (Rich and Schroeder, 1976). Both clinical researchers and popular writers in the area of assertiveness training have pointed to the situational specificity of assertiveness. Bower and Bower (1976) suggested a four-step programme which enables unassertive people to understand and enact appropriate assertive behaviour in different situations. The four steps are:

> describe: explain the behaviour in need of change
> express: express the emotions that are felt
> specify: explicitly describe the desired behaviour change
> consequences: contracted agreement on the consequences of changing or not changing behaviour

This simple four-step method allows the client to unpick the problematic situation and to follow set scripts or models as to how to proceed.

Furnham (1979) also demonstrated that the concept of assertiveness was to some extent culture-bound and not required or perceived in the same way in different cultures. Assertiveness training might be improved if a full situational analysis were included. For example, we have provided the goal structure (p. 76f.); to this can be added the rules and repertoire of particular situations.

SST in schools has sometimes concentrated on seeing the point of view of other people, such as parents, teachers, the opposite sex or employers. The training may consist of role-playing of typical situations in which the children are able to experience the other roles (McPhail, Middleton and Ingram, 1978). This has also been used to reduce racial prejudice. One teacher divided the children in a class into brown-eyed and blue-eyed; for several days the brown-eyed children were given lower status – made to wear special collars, ridiculed by the teacher and denied privileges. The groups were later reversed. (Reported in a film *The Eye of the Storm*, cited by Baron and Byrne, 1977.) This was followed by an experiment by Weiner and Wright (1973) that assigned children at random to Orange or Green groups, identified by arm-bands. Afterwards the children were invited to a picnic with some black children from another school: 96 per cent accepted, compared with 62 per cent of those who had not had the discrimination experience.

Professional social skills

Professional people spend a great deal of time with people – clients, colleagues, subordinates – and a lot of their skill is social skill. Every kind of professional person has to deal with a number of situations, each requiring special skills. For example managers commonly have to deal with some or all of the following:

> selection interview
> appraisal interview
> personnel interview (counselling, grievance, etc.)
> committees, as member or chairman
> supervision of working groups
> dealing with subordinates
> negotiation, e.g. with unions
> selling
> cooperation and maintaining relationships with colleagues and superiors
> public speaking, presenting

Each of these situationally based skills has been studied, and training is regularly given for them (Sidney, Brown and Argyle, 1973; Argyle, 1978*b*). Such training is done much more effectively if there is a full awareness of the distinctive goal structure, rules, etc., of each situation. The optimum leadership skills vary considerably from one situation to another, and the appropriate training should vary accordingly. The evidence was discussed earlier on p. 61f.

Pendleton (experiment 13.1) has devised a method of training doctors in the skills of handling patients which is based on an analysis of the features of this situation. In particular he has studied the goals of doctors and patients and the implicit roles for this kind of encounter. Others have studied the repertoire of behaviour (p. 188f.), and the sequence of episodes (p. 220).

Cross-cultural training

An increasing number of people are visiting other countries, for longer or shorter periods. These visits are often a failure through the difficulties of coping with the other culture. The visitors suffer what Oberg (1960) called 'culture shock'. Furnham and Bochner (experiment 12.2) have attempted an empirical analysis of culture shock, outlining the areas of difficulty or confusion, because until one knows the nature of the difficulty training cannot take place. Various methods of training are now being given for those about to work abroad. One approach to such training produced the Illinois Culture Assimilator (Fiedler, Mitchell and Triandis, 1971). A critical-incident survey is carried out of some hundreds of occasions to find the main kinds of situation in which, for example, Americans have had difficulties in Greece. A tutor text is then constructed, so that people can be trained to deal with these situations. This approach emphasises knowledge of rules, and understanding of ideas and beliefs in the other culture. Situations in the Arab Middle East which cause difficulty include meals, bargaining, dealing with women and the conduct of business meetings. A Culture Assimilator for Australian aboriginals included difficulties for white nurses such as approaching an aboriginal house without infringing territorial rights. A number of books of training materials and exercises, designed for Americans, are now available (e.g. Nitsche and Green, 1977). In Britain the main training centre is at Farnham Castle, Surrey, where trainees meet nationals and returned expatriates from the area they are going to visit, as well as receiving detailed instruction about life in the culture they are going to.

Training centres for cross-cultural skills often depend on regular feedback from previous clients on the current difficulties in different areas, and the best ways of dealing with them. These may extend beyond the emphasis on rules and ideas of the Culture Assimilator, to include knowledge and use of the appropriate verbal and nonverbal skills. Training for other cultures may take the form of a tutor text, as in the Culture Assimilator, or role-playing, as in Collett's nonverbal communication training (1971). Role-playing would also be useful when unfamiliar social skills have to be learnt, such as barter, bribery or dealing with a different hierarchical structure. This could be improved by situational analysis of the difficult situations – bribery, negotiation, etc. (see Argyle, in press).

Intergroup situational differences

We described above methods of giving children the experience of being the object of prejudice – which had the effect of reducing their own racial prejudice. The members of one social group are often hostile towards the members of another group or groups, including racial and national groups, social classes and members of individual social groups of various kinds. This hostility is, however, only manifested in particular kinds of situation in which members of the two groups meet; the hostility is partly produced by the conflict in these situations.

Conflict of interest, competition

Sherif *et al.* (1961) showed experimentally that great hostility could be produced between two similar groups of boys by intergroup competition, and finally by situations in which one group ate the other group's food. This led to a degree of aggression, which required special steps to resolve. Racial conflict is often brought about, or increased, by competition for jobs, where the newcomers threaten the employment or promotion prospects of those who are there already. Problems also arise over housing: immigrants have difficulty in finding accommodation; when they do find somewhere to live, more immigrants join them; the neighbours are upset by the noise, overcrowding and unacceptable domestic habits of the newcomers, and they move out. Soon the whole area 'goes black' (or whatever colour is involved), threatening the peace and value of property round about.

Tajfel (1970) has argued that intergroup prejudice can occur without any conflict of interest: one group downgrades the other in order to sustain the belief in its own superiority in certain respects, and thus maintain the self-esteem of its members. The studies in this tradition suggest that this process is most likely to occur on the part of a low-status group, or when there is competition for status between two groups.

Situations with different rules

If one group has different rules from another, its members can be regarded as deviates from the rules of the first group, and will therefore be rejected. There are a large number of cultural rules that lead to such difficulties, both in mixed communities and for visitors to a culture. Examples are (*a*) food taboos, such as not eating certain kinds of meat, (*b*) not drinking alcohol, (*c*) elaborate rules about gifts, (*d*) ways of using the lavatory, (*e*) the amount of lateness that is acceptable, (*f*) the role of women, (*g*) bribery, which is a normal and essential part of business transactions in much of the world but illegal in Britain, (*h*) nepotism, which is a valued part of the social system in much of the world, and is regarded as repayment to relations who have contributed to the costs of education.

Noesjirwan (1978) found that rules of behaviour in Australia and Indonesia were very different, and could be grouped under three themes. (1) In Indonesia, in a waiting room, you should talk to others; in Australia you should do nothing or read. This is part of a general sociability theme, of maintaining friendly relationships with everyone. (2) In several situations in Indonesia if you disagree with someone you should just smile and agree; in

Australia you should express your disagreement or argue. This is part of a wider theme of emphasis on the community rather than the individual. (3) In Indonesia, when catching a bus which is about to go, you should walk at the usual pace; to pass another person in the library you should wait for him to move. These are part of a theme of maintaining a steady state, a life-style which is smooth, graceful and restrained, as contrasted with the Australian open and direct manner.

It is sometimes very difficult to deal with the problems created by different rules. For example, British businessmen doing business in Africa may deal with the bribery problem by paying a 'sales commission' to a local representative who negotiates the sale – keeping some of the fee and passing the rest on as a bribe; however this may be uncovered and questioned by accountants at head office. The wives of Europeans or Americans who go to work in Moslem countries often become very frustrated because they are not allowed to drive a car, or to work, while all the domestic work is done by servants. Part of the solution is to prepare them beforehand, giving them a chance to withdraw; and some jobs can be found in embassies, or in running nursery schools.

Some situations may be difficult to deal with because the behaviour of the other group is incomprehensible. For example some Australian aboriginals insist on keeping a smoky fire burning indoors, despite the heat and the risk to people with bronchitis or pneumonia; the explanation is that the fire is of special sacred significance (O'Brien and Plooij, 1977).

Different greetings, or other nonverbal signals

Methods of greeting vary widely between different cultures, from Japanese bowing to Indian *namesti* (Argyle, 1975), and the same is true of other nonverbal signals. The extent to which touch is used is quite different in contact and non-contact cultures, and easily produces misunderstandings. In Botswana there is no word for 'thank you'; instead the hands are held out in a special way.

Informal and intimate situations

A long history of research with the Bogardus social distance scale (1959) has shown that social distance from another group is felt more strongly for some situations than for others, in the following order:

     marriage
     regular friendship
     working side-by-side in an office
     as a neighbour
     as a speaking acquaintance

It is well established that there is less racial difficulty between people in work situations. Minard (1952) found that black and white American miners got on perfectly well when down the mine, but separated as soon as they left the mine. This phenomenon is usually explained in terms of the clear roles at work, which influence behaviour more strongly than do the intergroup roles (Secord and Backman, 1974). Integration at work may, however, depend on the ability of management to enforce such work roles (Banton, 1955). Members of different social classes similarly get on better at work than in more informal settings. Jones and Lambert (1967) found that religious settings were rated as the most favourable for interacting with immigrants, because of the pressures for solidarity; the next most favourable setting was work, followed by social-recreational, union, family and commercial.

Consumer psychology: taking account of the situation

In the study of consumer behaviour it has been repeatedly found that an individual's attitudes towards a product or brand do not give a very good prediction of his purchasing behaviour. Bearden and Woodside (1979), for example, found that attitudes towards brands of beer gave quite good predictions of intentions to buy, but rather poor predictions of behaviour. The situation in which beer was to be drunk – giving a party at home, going to a pub, watching TV, working at home, etc. – was a better predictor than general brand attitude. Belk (1975) studied ten situations in which it might occur to a person to buy snacks (e.g. 'you are shopping for a snack that you or your family can eat while watching television in the evenings'), and nine situations for buying meat (e.g. 'you are at the store to pick up some meat for a picnic and are trying to decide what to buy'). The 'situations' used in this and some other studies of consumer behaviour are a mixture of *buying* situations (e.g. shop, restaurant) and *consumption* situations (e.g. picnic, watching TV). Research in this area might be better if these two aspects of situations were more clearly distinguished.

Belk (1978*a*) studied the clothes people wore in different situations – the equivalent of 'consumption'. He analysed clusters of clothes and clusters of situations for individuals; for example 'Pete' wore old jeans or 'cut-offs', a T-shirt or sweatshirt, and sandals or tennis shoes, in outdoor situations like mowing the lawn and hiking.

In order to predict consumption or purchase of goods the separate contributions of personal preferences, type of situation and product can be analysed. Sandell (1968) studied variation in consumption of drinks as a function of persons and situations, i.e. water, tea, beer, wine, etc., in such situations as 'when alone', 'feeling sleepy in the afternoon', etc. Most variance was due to situation × drink interaction (e.g. drinking water when really thirsty). Belk (1974), in a three-way factor analysis, found that choice of snacks was mainly due to person × product interaction (e.g. person P prefers popcorn); next was product × situation (e.g. everyone eats ice-cream while watching TV). Choice of meat, on the other hand, was most due to product × situation (e.g. everyone has hot-dogs on picnics), and secondly to the main effect of product (e.g. everyone has hamburgers in all situations). There were factors of situations; for meat these were impromptu situations, dinner at home, weekend situations and relaxed situations. And there were factors of products; for meat these were fancy cuts, main course meats, and hot-dogs/hamburgers.

In another study Belk (1978*b*) studied some aspects of the purchase situation – how much effort the customer puts into buying. In this and other studies it was found that when something was bought as a gift, more time was spent, more stores visited and more money spent than when similar objects were bought for the purchaser himself. Generally speaking more effort was expended when more money was being spent. On the other hand a great deal of effort was put into buying clothes compared with buying other objects of similar price; clothes are more 'involving'.

This kind of analysis of consumption and purchasing situations could be very useful in the marketing of products, e.g. in designing advertisements or describing what products to offer in each setting. A more sophisticated analysis of situations, as developed in this book, could take it further.

Personnel selection

Individuals are selected for jobs at interviews, or in other assessment situations, which are totally different from the job situation. Or use is made of testimonials, which assess behaviour in some previous job, which may or may not be similar to the job being filled. When people are being assessed they are fully aware of this, and do their best to present themselves in a favourable light. Despite these difficulties, selection does have a modest success; final ratings by the selectors may correlate with later success on the job (among those selected) at 0.5 or 0.6. The new research on situations and P × S interaction does not appear to have penetrated yet to the world of personnel selection, and the implications of this research for selection have still to be worked out. In this section some initial thoughts about the problem are presented.

The assessment of success on the job
For many jobs, especially at higher levels of skill, there is no one index of success, since there are a number of different aspects of the job, often reflecting performance in a number of different situations. Sometimes this is accepted, and a series of different ratings are used. Sometimes it is found that there is little relation between success in different settings, and it is concluded that the criterion has 'low reliability' (e.g. OSS, 1948). A university

374

lecturer is appointed to teach, research and administer. Each of these three tasks can be further subdivided, e.g. teaching can be done in lectures, seminars, practical classes or tutorials. Assessment of a lecturer, for example for promotion or tenure purposes, would take account of all of these situations. In order to carry out personnel selection it is surely necessary to know the main situations of which the job consists, and to know which of these is most important, and how the weightings should be combined. Would a successful candidate be expected to perform adequately in all situations or would exceptional performance in one area compensate for mediocrity in others?

Kirchner and Dunnette (1957) asked a large sample of sales managers to describe critical incidents in selling; these were grouped into thirteen categories of behaviour (i.e. situational skills) which made a difference between successful and unsuccessful selling. Hemphill (1960) studied the jobs of ninety-three managers and found 575 job elements, such as 'deals with customers' complaints'. Statistical analysis showed that there were ten dimensions, such as 'technical aspects of products and markets', again corresponding to situational skills.

Prediction of behaviour from performance in similar situations

The most obvious implication of $P \times S$ research is that predictions should be made from very similar situations in the past. This is often done in practice: for internal promotion in firms the 'track record' is studied; for selecting research students third-year projects are inspected. Referees' reports are often useful here, though they suffer from problems of variable standards. Mosel and Cozan (1952) did a study in which supervisors and co-workers were interviewed about candidates' past performance; these predicted success at 0.33 to 0.79 for different jobs. Quite good predictions can be made about the future behaviour of law-breakers; prediction tables are regularly used to decide which prisoners to release on parole, indicators such as the number of past offences and use of drugs and drink being used (Mannheim and Wilkins, 1955).

However it is not always possible to find past situations that are sufficiently similar to the situation for which selection is being made. Students may not have been involved in situations like those at work; generally speaking work is more cooperative, though sometimes less friendly, more intense, and under greater direction, than the work of students. Students have sometimes done vacation jobs, though these tend to be low-grade manual jobs, and they may have had administrative and financial experience in running student organisations. Promotion may involve a change to quite different work, as in the promotion of a skilled worker to foreman, or an engineer to manager; the track record is less useful here.

Another approach is the use of tests that model situations on the job. One of the most widely used is leaderless group discussion (LGD), which has been used for the selection of civil servants, army officers, and others in supervisory positions. The test takes an hour and requires no equipment. The follow-up validity is quite good, 0.40 or above, and the ratings are fairly independent of what can be measured by other psychological tests. The LGD is predictive of job behaviour but does not measure personality traits. The main factor found in the ratings of behaviour in LGD is forceful leadership, initiative and capacity to influence others verbally. One problem with the LGD and other situational tests is that candidates have different amounts of prior experience of the situation in question (Vernon, 1964).

In the analysis of Office of Strategic Services' (OSS) assessments it was found impossible to express these in terms of general traits. There were three groups of measures corresponding to three kinds of test situation – pencil and paper tests, debate and discussion, and action situations like moving a log across a stream. As Sakoda (1952) points out, it is the situations in which a candidate has intelligence, initiative, emotional stability or other abilities which it is important to consider. We would expect that abilities in each area would predict performance in similar situations on the job.

Capacity to stand up to stress has also been measured by situational tests – for example by simulated cockpit experiences for pilots, and the OSS construction task in which two extremely unhelpful assistants were provided. However the validity of these stress tests appears to be very low (Anastasi, 1961). Other situational tests which have had more success are 'in-basket' routines, and asking prospective administrators to analyse complex dossiers. Tests of motor skills are of course based on simulation of industrial or other real-life situations.

The use of interviews

Interviews are used for nearly all selection, but interviewers are not always clear what they are doing. The situation of the interview is very different from nearly all job situations. It follows that behaviour during the interview itself should not be taken too seriously. If the candidate is very nervous, aggressive or silent, it does not follow that he will behave like this on the job. If he is very smartly dressed, it does not follow that he will always look like this. What can be done in the interview is to obtain reports from candidates on how they coped with a number of situations that are more similar to job situations.

Interviewers often ask questions about hobbies and leisure activities. Can anything be learnt from this line of questioning, and if so what? Usually leisure situations are very different from work situations, so that little useful information can be obtained. It is no use questioning potential civil servants about their taste in music, unless they have organised large concerts, or potential engineers about their mountaineering, except perhaps in terms of the strengths of ropes and similar technical matters.

The use of P × S equations

In principle this would be the best way of predicting behaviour in future job situations; the trouble is that we do not yet have enough knowledge of these equations. Some personality variables have considerable generality, in that they affect behaviour in a wide range of situations. IQ is one example, neuroticism is another. In both cases situational variables are fairly easy to allow for. For neuroticism the equation simply says that anxiety is greater for more neurotic people, and in more stressful situations. We can also take account of different forms of anxiety, in that some people are more affected by physical dangers, others by threatening social situations (p. 326). For variables like these, personality tests and questionnaires can be used.

Authoritarianism presents a very different prediction problem. If traditional theory is correct, certain people who are very submissive during an interview will be very dominant when they are in charge. Authoritarians tend to be invisible from above. They can be identified by certain lines of questioning in the interview; it is doubtful whether authoritarianism questionnaires are very suitable for selection purposes.

Predicting future P × S cycles

Predicting future behaviour in a new situation is only the first step in selection. When someone has spent some time in the new environment, his personality will change, in ways that are partly predictable. We expect that people will acquire new skills and knowledge, acquire new ambitions, perhaps become more self-confident. Some people are thought to be more trainable than others. This will produce a new P × S equation, and perhaps lead them to seek further situations, such as promotion. Personnel managers who specialise in manpower planning, or management development, have intuitive ideas on these subjects, but they could be pursued more rigorously, as they already have been in the fields of addiction and delinquency (Runyan, 1978).

The modification and invention of situations

One of the main possible applications of our greater understanding of how situations affect behaviour lies in the possibility of modifying those situations that are not working very well, and of inventing new situations which could satisfy various needs or resolve social problems. It is possible to modify or create situations by using the basic features of situations which we have been considering.

377

Goal structure

The most familiar kind of modification is the establishing of incentives for work. Workers can be paid by the time they put in, the amount they produce, the quality of their work, or for being cooperative, tidy, or anything else that can be rated on a rating scale. They can also be paid as a group, on a group bonus scheme, and this radically affects the relations between them, and the attitudes towards fast and slow workers (Argyle, 1972).

Another kind of imposed goal structure is the token economy, used in mental hospitals. Patients earn tokens for dressing themselves, washing, being cooperative, or anything else, and can exchange the tokens for food, sweets, cigarettes, etc. (Kazdin, 1977). Token economies can be used in the home to control difficult or disturbed children, and even spouses (p. 366).

We mentioned above the importance of avoiding a conflict of goals in intergroup relations. This can be done by setting up rules which do not discriminate between different groups, and which create cooperative situations. Sherif *et al*. (1961) resolved the conflict between their groups of boys by creating a superordinate goal – to restore the water supply. It is sometimes within the power of administrators, for example of large organisations or of cities, to reduce the extent of conflict between different groups over jobs, promotions, housing or other matters.

Experience of social interaction with members of another group results in reduced hostility if situations are basically cooperative. Cook (1970) reduced the anti-black feelings of prejudiced white girls by paying them to work two hours a day for a month with a black girl. Such cooperative contexts have more effect if they are also equal-status. Harding and Hoff-grefe (1952) found that white workers in a department store became less prejudiced towards black co-workers, but especially if they had been on equal-status terms.

Situations are sometimes confusing or difficult for socially unskilled or inexperienced people because the goal structure is not clear to them. They do not know what parties are for, or what exactly are the goals of candidates at selection interviews. They may not appreciate the nature of the conflicting goals, e.g. for a parent dealing with an adolescent child. It is possible to instruct individuals in these matters; the organisers of possibly ambiguous social events could make it perfectly clear to all what are the goals they can hope to attain and what are the difficulties. The invention of new situations can be based on goals. Are there some needs of individuals that are not being met, or some conflicts in society that need to be resolved, that could be helped by new situations? There are already examples of such invention of new situations in the various forms of non-violent protest, like the 'sit-in' and the 'teach-in', that have recently evolved. These situations appear to have a novel goal structure. An increasing need in society is for divorced or widowed people to find new mates; this has led to 'singles groups', 'singles bars' (in the USA) and to the proliferation of match-making organisations. There still appears to be a need for situations where people can make friends – a role once filled by pubs and churches. A new goal structure could be the exchange of friendship for money, or the exchange of introduction to other friends for money. Or the problem could be looked at the other way round – there are very many possible goal structures that have never given rise to situations, and these might be developed.

Repertoire

Psychologists have invented a number of new kinds of group meetings, mainly through quite minor modifications to the normal repertoire.

Brainstorming is a creative problem-session in which group members throw out ideas, and develop one another's suggestions, but there is no disagreement; one of the main obstacles to creative thinking is thus removed. (Unfortunately, follow-up studies show that individuals can do better at creative tasks than brainstorming groups: Taylor, Berry and Block, 1958.)

T-groups are like discussion groups except that conversation is restricted to what is happening here and now in the group, but there is no restriction on criticism of other members of the group.

Encounter groups realise another modification of the usual repertoire – bodily contact is permitted and encouraged between relative strangers. (Although this makes them very different from T-groups, there is no evidence that they are any more or less effective: Lieberman, Yalom and Miles, 1973.)

Are there any other changes in the repertoire that might usefully be explored? As we showed in Chapter 2, the nonverbal code is more or less universal, while verbal categories and verbal contents vary with the task. One possibility for therapeutic or friendship-forming groups might be to eliminate all negative nonverbal signals.

Rules

The changes in repertoire we have just discussed are also examples of new rules. Encounter groups have other rules, apart from repertoire changes, such as the rule that members should engage in a high degree of self-disclosure, and should establish intimate relationships with each other. In addition there are rules governing a number of specific activities like 'roll and rock', 'blind milling', and other exercises (Schutz, 1967).

Other examples of new rules are party games, like charades, clumps, and sardines, with their local variations, and board games, like Monopoly and Cluedo. Anyone who has tried to make up a new game will have found that the rules have to be adjusted very carefully in order to make the game 'work' satisfactorily; it is common to introduce local amendments to established games for the same reason. We traced recent modifications to the rules of rugby football (p. 128). Larger scale rules of society become modified in a similar way. One of the most striking changes in recent times has been the changes of rules governing pre-marital sex.

Changing the rules is one of the most familiar ways in which situations are changed in order to solve problems or improve things. Colleges establish and modify rules about visiting hours and noise at night; committees have rules about how long meetings may last, how often anyone may speak on one issue, and how large a majority is needed. If we wanted to invent a radically new kind of group or social situation, the drafting of the rules would be a central part of it. Another method may be to make social conventions more explicit, or in fact make them into rules, to encourage those not observing them to do so. We saw earlier that rules are created to help members to attain their goals, to guard against temptations and to prevent the disruption of the group.

Roles

Organisational problems can sometimes be solved by changes in roles and role relationships. Whyte (1948) tackled a common problem in restaurants of the friction that arises when waitresses have to give orders directly to cooks, who are of a higher status than themselves. His solution was to introduce an order spike on which the waitresses pinned the orders, for the cooks to deal with at their own pace. Trist *et al.* (1963) dealt with the problems of the Longwall method of coal-mining; three shifts did the separate tasks of cutting, filling and building up the walls, but they never met and they failed to cooperate, with the result that there was a high accident rate, low output and high absenteeism. The solution was to include some men doing each job on each shift, which led to considerable improvement.

Roles can be modified to solve a number of organisational problems: for example they can (1) improve communication or cooperation between individuals or groups, (2) create better working groups, which are smaller, cooperative, and complete a total task, (3) reduce status differences, (4) improve the style of leadership, (5) reduce role-conflicts, e.g. that result from one person being under the direction of two others (Argyle, 1972).

Environmental setting and equipment

Architects, decorators, and anyone who furnishes or even arranges a room, modify physical aspects of the environment in order to create some desired effect. We have seen that problems with football fans can be solved by keeping the two rival groups of fans well apart, preferably at opposite ends of the ground. We have seen that shoplifting can be greatly reduced by better surveillance, e.g. by closed-circuit TV and one-way mirrors. And we have seen that vandalism can be reduced, again by design for better surveillance, by less public space, and the use of strong materials and surfaces that are difficult to write on.

Environmental psychologists have produced numerous instances of how institutions can be redesigned to improve social interaction. As we reported earlier (p. 278), Sommer and Ross (1958) increased social interaction in a geriatric ward by placing chairs round coffee tables instead of along walls. Ittelson, Proshansky and Rivlin (1970) similarly increased social interaction between psychiatric patients by adding a sun-lounge, with comfortable chairs carefully arranged. Harold Cohen is reported to have reduced fights in a prison by environmental modification: he discovered that most fights took place at the corners of corridors, when inmates collided; he rounded off the corners and this prevented these collisions.

Furniture and equipment can also be changed: Victorian 'love-seats' encouraged love, S-shaped settees inhibited it. A desk that faces the room enables the person behind it to dominate the room and his visitors; if he faces out of the window a more equal relationship results (Joiner, 1976). Giving young children cooperative toys which it takes two to work (like see-saws) reduces quarrelling over toys. Isolates, who have no friends, can be placed in close proximity to each other, or to members of established groups, which will encourage friendship formation. Examples are putting children at the same desk, students in shared accommodation, and workers in the same room or work-place.

There is endless scope for further inventiveness in the design of physical space, especially if we include modification of visibility – who can see whom, closed-circuit TV, and other communication devices. The entire physical setting can be changed by a simple move to another meeting place, and new facilities can be made available.

Concepts

Patients undergoing psychoanalysis learn something of the technical vocabulary, and come to use some of the concepts. The same is true of most forms of therapy. It is found in therapeutic communities and in group therapies of all kinds. SST, which is usually done in groups, introduces trainees to the terminology of communication – social skills, rewardingness, mutual gaze and so on. Similar considerations apply to religious groups, not only different Christian groups, but Eastern religions, Transcendental Meditation, and so on. Much of the characteristic atmosphere of these groups derives from the special vocabulary and conceptual schemas. The conduct of political meetings depends on the theories of political activity held by those present, whether Marxist, liberal-democrat, or otherwise. However some schools of psychotherapy, oriental religion and politics have developed verbose and meaningless terminologies, 'psychobabble', which may create group cohesion but which must surely produce individual confusion as well.

Another conceptual change is a change in the perception of a situation – a boring rehearsal can be seen as a creative workshop, a dull committee as an exciting working party, an isolated group as a secret society, perhaps.

Sequences

Cross-cultural comparisons provide striking examples of variations on common sequences. The unwillingness to answer questions in some parts of Africa, and the Japanese unwillingness to give the answer 'no' are cases in point (p. 215). A number of new sequences have been generated in connection with various professional social skills. The social survey interview, with its rigid set of questions, including multiple-choice and follow-up questions, the various cycles of classroom behaviour used by teachers (p. 218f.), and the therapeutic style of non-directive therapists, are examples. It is perhaps in the construction of effective professional skills that most use could be made of further new sequences. New sequences can be introduced to a group – for example ceremonies for welcoming new members, saying goodbye to old ones or marking promotions, or periodic partly ritualised events aimed at promoting group solidarity.

A rather different approach to situational change is used by some social workers; there the aim is not to alter an institutionalised situation, but to modify situations that an individual client is finding difficult. This includes some forms of modification not possible for institutional situations, such as modifying the behaviour of individuals or of the whole group (e.g. a family), providing increased understanding of the goal structure and of self-defeating behaviour or other aspects of the situation, separating the individual from the group for a time, or disbanding the group (Siporin, 1972).

Friendship situations

We shall bring together some of the points discussed above, and consider how to design a situation in which people might make friends with others of the same or opposite sex. This is already done by organisers of lonely hearts clubs, dating agencies, and others. We might be able to improve on their situational design. The difficulties people have in establishing friendships can be gauged by the large number of dating agency and computer dating facilities available (Byrne, Ervin and Lamberth, 1970). Walster *et al.* (1966) arranged a computer dance after measuring people's attractiveness, intelligence and personality, yet the only factor which correlated with willingness to date again was attractiveness. They used situational factors to explain their failure to find any effects of liking and personality: the duration and context of the dance situation may have increased the import- ance of physical attractiveness and decreased the importance of other factors. It may therefore be equally important for dating agencies to choose appropriate situations for their clients to meet as to establish that people with similar hobbies, outlooks and personalities meet one another.

Research on friendship shows that people will like each other if they meet frequently, under rewarding circumstances, and are similar to one another in background, interests and values. They are more likely to have similar interests and values if the situation is linked to some shared activity, such as a hobby or political or religious activity. In that these situations have clear goals, and people share values and con- cepts, they are likely to lead to the formation of further acquaintance and thence perhaps friendship. There is a great advantage, there- fore, in basing friendship situations on a definite choice of activity, as well as keeping the group homogeneous in such variables as age and social class.

Encounter and T-groups attempt to short-circuit friendship and familiar- ity, usually by playing special games or doing tasks that create physical contact and self-disclosure. After the initial tension, people often begin to relax and to chat openly and make contact. Further, if they have had to introduce themselves and reveal certain information about themselves this provides the basis for further conversation or a sense of group feeling. This is particularly true if people are encouraged to divulge shameful personal information to a sympathetic audience, as in Alcoholics Anonymous and Gamblers Anonymous or Weight-Watchers.

Where there is difficulty in communication due to a deficit of some skill, as in the case of children or of cross-cultural contact, the organisation of relatively simple games or dances where there is physical contact often ensures later verbal contact and friendship formation. It is important to ensure that the games are neither embarrassing nor particularly compli- cated. It seems that where people are socially unskilled, for whatever reason, the more joint displacement activities organised for them, the better the chances of friendship formation (Cook, 1977).

Goal structure. The main goal is making friends, which makes a simple, positive and conflict-free goal structure. If there is some hobby or other activity, there is a double cooperative motivation.

Repertoire. The activity may be (*a*) conversation, though this is usually accompanied by (*b*) drinking and/or eating. There may be (*c*) social activities like dancing or games, and (*d*) hobby activities. For those who have difficulty in getting to know others, there should be a lot of activity besides conversation.

Rules. Presumably the usual party rules will apply, though not everyone will know them; people should keep to cheerful topics, dress smartly, be friendly, be polite, etc. (see p. 150f.). It would be very useful for this kind of situation to introduce some further rules, such as 'don't disagree with people' and 'don't express nonverbal disapproval'. It should also be clear that everyone is free to talk to anyone else without further introduction.

Roles. It is useful to have one or more people who can play the role of host, and introduce or otherwise look after people.

Physical environment. This should be attractive, warm, with soft lights; if there is music it should not drown conversation (as it does at discos). Furniture should be comfortable, with sofas or chairs grouped to make conversation easy.

13.1. A situational analysis of general practice consultations

D. PENDLETON

In the field of medical practice and training, a situational analysis cannot be said to exist *per se*. The elements of such an analysis can, however, be shown to be present. This report will discuss some of these elements under the headings of rules, expectations and goals, and will review their implications for general practice medicine and medical training.

Rules

In Chapter 5 it was demonstrated that visits to the doctor are generally seen as intimate, goal-directed and highly rule-governed. They are situations in which the doctor is seen as being in charge and in which expression of mutual affect should not occur. These rules are, however, only implicit in the encounter and are also quite general. Many more specific rules do exist but these are rarely made explicit. However, any deliberate or unintentional breaking of a rule creates a social difficulty and also makes the participants conscious of the rule's existence. Thus an analysis of problems experienced by participants in medical interviews helps to throw light on some of the rules that are operating.

In a study of 920 general practice consultations, Pendleton and Jaspars demonstrated that communication difficulties are experienced by the doctors in approximately one in five consultations. By an examination of the nature of the difficulties reported by the doctors it is possible to infer some of the rules seen by the doctors to be implicit in this situation.

From Table 13.1 the following implicit rules could be said to exist:

1. Problems should be presented one at a time.

384

2. Patients should believe what the doctor tells them.
3. Patients should have confidence in the doctor.
4. Patients should tell the doctor all the relevant information they know.
5. Patients should cooperate with the doctor.
6. Patients should do what the doctor tells them to do.
7. Patients should give the doctor lots of feedback about whether or not they understand what is being said.
8. Patients should not talk too much.
9. Doctors should not contradict colleagues.
10. Doctors should come to a clear diagnosis.
11. Doctors should not drink too much!

Since these rules have been derived from communication difficulties reported by doctors it is to be expected that most of the implicit rules will have consequences for the patients' behaviour. We tend not to blame ourselves for difficulties we experience. This is a recurrent finding of workers in attribution theory (Brickman, Ryan and Wortman, 1975). It is also to be expected since the training received by most medical practitioners can be described as doctor-centred. Most medical training takes place in hospitals, where patients are expected to be passive, though cooperative, recipients of medical treatment. When newly qualified doctors enter general practice, however, they soon become aware of the differences between general practice medicine and that practised in hospital. Their difficulties are considerable and arise, in part, because the rules they have been trained to use are now largely inappropriate.

Patients in general practice are rarely as passive as in hospital and, increasingly, they present problems which clinically are not serious, so the demands of general practice are for a different kind of medicine: one which is other than a curative service for sick people. Difficulties are encountered, therefore, when doctor and patient are working with different assumptions about the requirements for their behaviour. Indeed, doctors report that their patients are the greatest source of both enjoyment and frustration in their work (Cartwright and Anderson, 1979).

Expectations

Korsch and her colleagues (Korsch, Freeman and Negrete, 1971) presented considerable evidence that, for a variety of reasons, patients communicate only a minority of their expectations to their doctors. The worrying aspect of this is, however, that patients whose expectations were in no way dealt with were much less likely to be satisfied with their consultations. Moreover dissatisfied patients were much less likely to comply with their doctor's instructions and advice. This was such a clear tendency that Korsch and her colleagues strongly recommended that doctors should always discover and

TABLE 13.1. *Difficulties reported by doctors in 920 general practice consultations*

Difficulties	Frequency	Percentage
(A) *Consultation variables*		
(i) The interaction process		
1. Sex difference: doctor–patient	4	
2. Patient is extremely young child	10	
3. Another person presents problem:	24	
mother (19)		
other (5)		
4. More than one problem presented:	33	
simultaneously (30)		
'by the way' (3)		
5. Clash of purpose: doctor–patient	5	
6. Loss of confidence in doctor	8	
7. Patient does not believe doctor	11	
8. Patient does not understand what		
doctor says to him	7	
9. Patient withholds information	14	
10. Patient does not know something	6	
11. Patient is deliberately obstructive		
(includes lying)	5	
12. Difficult or impossible to influence the		
patient (behaviour)	3	
13. Difficult or impossible to persuade the		
patient:	15	
there *is* a problem (3)		
there is *not* a problem (12)		
14. Difficult to establish reason for the		
patient's attendance	2	
15. Doctor experiences adverse reaction to		
patient (e.g. bored, irritated)	22	
16. Feedback problem	10	
Total: interaction process	179	57.6
(ii) Constraints of the situation		
17. Insufficient time for consultation	5	
18. Difficult topic:	9	
seriousness (e.g. cancer) (5)		
taboo (e.g. sex, VD) (4)		
Total: situation constraints	14	4.5
(iii) The nature of the medical problem		
19. No diagnosis	6	
20. Professional dilemma (e.g. doctor		
wants to reverse a colleague's decision)	8	
Total: medical problem	14	4.5
Total: consultation variables	207	66.6

TABLE 13.1 (*cont.*)

Difficulties	Frequency	Percentage
(B) *Patient variables*		
(i) Traits (more or less enduring attributes)		
21. Culture difference: doctor–patient (language, dialect, class)	19	
22. Physical defect (e.g. blind, deaf)	6	
23. Patient of low intelligence	10	
24. Patient is shy	14	
25. Patient is overtalkative (garrulous)	6	
26. Patient has mental problem	2	
Total: patient traits	57	18.3
(ii) States (more or less temporary attributes)		
27. Patient is confused	12	
28. Patient is anxious	22	
29. Patient is depressed	6	
30. Patient is angry	2	
31. Patient is nervous	3	
Total: patient states	45	14.5
Total: patient variables	102	32.8
(C) *Doctor variables*		
(i) Traits		
None		
(ii) States		
32. Doctor's physical state (e.g. hangover)	2	
Total: doctor variables	2	0.6

$N = 311$.

deal with a patient's expectations in every consultation. This pattern was also true for a patient's worries and concerns.

Goals and outcomes

The overall goals of general practice are quite complex (Byrne and Long, 1976; Freeman and Byrne, 1976), but there appears to be broad agreement that a thorough knowledge of clinical medicine, although necessary, is insufficient to achieve those goals. Long-term goals must include the creation of sound human relationships, within which the doctor can practise his or her unique form of medicine; to do this will require the learning of behavioural skills (Byrne and Long, 1976). Goals for the general practitioner must be both long-term and short-term. Long-term goals will often be formulated in terms of rapport and trust, while short-term goals will more often include clinical goals for the management and control of illness.

But even the long-term goals will usually only be achieved by repeated successful encounters with the patient. Thus, for any consultation, the general practitioner will hold long-term and short-term goals of both a clinical and a psychological nature. The patient's goals, however, are usually formulated in terms of treatment.

Support for these assertions comes from the data from a study of general practice consultations in the Oxford region reported in Table 13.2. The study involved interviewing doctors and patients separately immediately before they saw one another, video-tape recording the consultations, and then interviewing each party again immediately after the consultation had taken place. In all, data have been collected from 120 consultations in this way, but information on the parties' goals is available from a group of four doctors and seventy-one patients. Before each consultation the doctors were asked about both their long-term and their short-term goals for the patient, and patients were asked what they wanted from the consultation. The replies to these open questions were then independently categorised. After the consultation, each party was reminded what their declared goals had been and asked whether or not they felt their goals had been achieved.

The doctors' long-term goals can be seen to be primarily psychological in nature, although there are considerable differences between the doctors in these scores. Doctors' short-term goals are, in contrast, primarily physical or organic in nature, as are the patients' goals, although often the patients reported a desire to be reassured by the doctor, and frequently held goals concerning medication. Patients, not surprisingly, held explicit goals for nearly all consultations whereas doctors, sometimes having no prior knowledge of the reasons for a patient's attendance, had clearly stated goals in just two out of three consultations. Doctors' short-term goals for consultations are, proportionately, the most frequently achieved. It is striking, however, that in no consultation were conflicting goals expressed, although in approximately 25 per cent of all consultations doctor and patient held unrelated goals. From Table 13.1 it can be seen that clash of purpose was shown to be an infrequent occurrence.

The significance of each party's goals for the consultation and their knowledge of the rules and conventions that operate in it can best be understood in terms of how they affect the structure of the consultation. Each party's goals and rules form what can be called a hidden agenda; if these goals and rules are complementary, or at least compatible, the structure of the consultation should be mutually satisfactory. When, however, the doctor's and patient's goals are unrelated it is often the doctor's agenda that is dealt with most completely, as can be seen from Table 13.2. Indeed, it is not uncommon for the doctor to begin a consultation in which he has explicitly stated short-term goals by dealing with those matters first. The consequence of this is that certain patients forget some of the matters they

388

TABLE 13.2. Doctor's and patient's goals

	Doctor's goals: long-term[a]				Doctor's goals: short-term[a]				Patient's goals[a]			
	Phys.	Psych.	Med.	Other	Phys.	Psych.	Med.	Other	Phys.	Psych.	Med.	Other
Total expressed	18	34	1	–	39	16	3	3	59	20	27	5
Total achieved	11	22	1	–	37	16	3	3	51	17	24	5
Percentage consultations in which goals were clearly expressed ($N = 71$)	63				69				99			
Percentage consultations in which expressed goals were achieved	64[b]				96				87			

[a] Phys., physical; Psych., psychological; Med., medicinal.
[b] This figure represents the percentage of consultations in which the doctors felt they made a *contribution towards* their long-term goals.

wanted to raise. Occasionally, to aid their memory, patients produce a written list of matters to be dealt with.

Implications

Byrne and Long showed that the consultation can be seen in terms of specific phases (p. 220), and implicit in these phases are rules for appropriate behaviour. The first part of the consultation is most appropriately the time for the doctor to discover the reasons for the patient's attendance, which would require that the patient should be allowed to express himself fully and that the doctor should listen. Once the doctor feels that he knows why a particular patient has come, it is appropriate for the doctor to clarify the story presented and to explore hypotheses. This will usually require an interrogative phase. Finally the doctor will need to inform the patient what he has discovered and what needs to be done about it. In this phase it is appropriate for the doctor to do most of the talking and for him to check that the patient understands and accepts what has been said.

This is the description of an idealised consultation which may rarely take place in every detail as stated, but the requisite skills of patient management can be learned, primarily with the aid of video-recordings of naturally occurring consultations. This can be achieved quite unobtrusively, even in small consultation rooms, by the use of the recording set-up illustrated in Fig. 13.1 In the Oxford research, the camera has also been modified to correct the left–right reversal brought about by the use of the mirror.

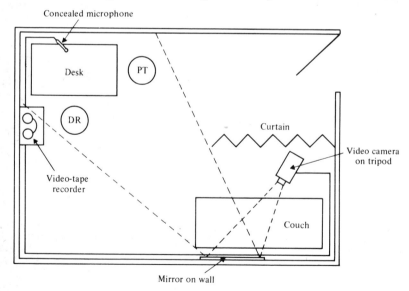

Fig. 13.1. Video-recording equipment in the consulting room. DR, doctor; PT, patient.

13.1. A situational analysis of GP consultations

There is now ample evidence that training of this kind can produce demonstrable and marked improvements in the behavioural skills of both clinical medical students (Pendleton and Wakeford, 1980) and general practitioners alike (Verby, Holden and Davis, 1979). Thus, a situational analysis provides a framework within which to understand communication difficulties in medical consultations, while training in interpersonal skills helps doctors to improve their level of competence in dealing with their patients.

14

Conclusions

We shall not attempt to summarise the results of research carried out by ourselves and others into situations, but rather we shall address ourselves to a number of general issues.

The classification and analysis of situations

Although we initially expressed some scepticism about the value of dimensional analysis of situations, two of the dimensions that have arisen from these studies have appeared in the form of main divisions in our cluster analyses, based on various features. These are task–social, and casual–intimate or involved. When we have analysed situations into types, using cluster analysis, only a limited number of basic types have appeared. Some of these are as follows, though the list could be extended further:

1. formal social events
2. intimate encounters with close friends or relations
3. casual encounters with acquaintances
4. formal encounters in shops and offices
5. asymmetrical social-skills occasions (e.g. teaching, interviewing, supervision)
6. negotiation and conflict
7. group discussion

Are the features which we initially proposed sufficient, and are they all necessary? There is one more feature which might be added to some situations, and this is emotional atmosphere, for we have found that emotional expression is part of the rules in situations such as weddings and parties. When using our set of features in situational social-skills training we have found that certain features are most useful: *goal structure*, *rules*, *skills to overcome difficulties*. It is these features that the socially unskilled most often get wrong. For purposes of modifying situations, *environmental setting* is, however, the easiest to change.

Our earlier writings on this subject (e.g. Argyle, 1980a) have attracted the criticism that we give 'insufficient attention to the capacity of participants to create, modify and transform the situation, through individual action or negotiation' (Ginsburg, 1980). As we said in Chapter 1, it has been our intention to study common situations, with which people are familiar, and within which we believe most social behaviour takes place. Rommetveit and Blakar (1979) have made the point that verbal communication requires the establishment of common meanings, and of a body of information which can be taken for granted. In fact it is only in Chapter 11, on language and speech, that we have found clear evidence for such a negotiated consensus, but this was found in encounters between strangers in unfamiliar laboratory settings. In our own research, on rules and concepts in particular, we have found a high level of agreement about the properties of everyday situations among members of a subculture.

The explanation of situations and their features

We have seen that situations are social constructions by members of a culture or subculture. It is possible to play football because of the rules, the limits of the pitch, the restricted repertoire, etc., which confine within narrow limits what players may do; the rules and other features, however, also make the game possible by generating a pattern of cooperative interaction in which certain moves are endowed with shared meaning.

We have used the functional model to explain many of the features of situations. In some cases this is perfectly straightforward, as the following example shows. One of the goals of patients in visiting their doctor turns out to be 'seeking reassurance that their illness is not serious'. One of the repertoire of elements is 'asking for reassurance' and one of the common sequences is asking for it and getting it. Slightly less obvious, but still within the domain of manifest needs which can be traced to individual goals, is the development of criminal argots and similar specialised vocabularies, whose purpose is to prevent outsiders from understanding. Another example is the development of concepts and categories needed for the task in hand.

The more interesting side of functionalism is explanation in terms of latent needs. We showed that there are universal rules, applying to all situations, that exist to facilitate communication and to prevent disruption and withdrawal. Other rules, applying to one or two situations, have the function of helping people to avoid common temptations in those situations, and helping participants to cope with common sources of difficulty. Role-systems develop in situations, and have functions such as providing division of labour and a pattern of authority, where needed.

Another kind of latent function is the modification of needs in a displaced form. Ritualised forms of aggression, e.g. at football grounds, are a means of expressing aggression indirectly, just as other kinds of ritual are known to relieve anxiety. It seems very likely that a number of situations provide for status needs and self-presentation, though we have not tested this directly.

The functional theory is also useful in connection with the modification and invention of situations. When the modification of an unsatisfactory situation is being considered, it is important to keep in mind both the manifest and the latent needs that are met in that situation and to ensure that they can still be satisfied.

We have also looked at situations as integrated systems in which all the parts are interdependent. If one feature is changed, other features have to change too. We have come across a number of examples of this interdependence. (*a*) We have just seen that goals affect repertoire, sequence and rules. (*b*) Role structure and environment are interdependent: the design of court-rooms, churches and council chambers, for example, shows how a role structure leads to certain seating arrangements, which in turn reinforce the role structure. (*c*) The rules bring about a coordinated pattern of behaviour with its repertoire, sequences and roles, as in games. (*d*) Concepts are reflected in language, and both reflect the central activities in a situation. There is almost no systematic research in this area however. It would be possible to take any feature as an independent variable, and to study the effect of varying it on other features of a situation. This would enable us to study the ways in which features are interrelated.

It might be helpful to compare the social-situation model to a 'system' or even a 'mobile'. If one is to understand the dynamic structure of a mobile one has to know not only the weight and shape of each piece but also the way in which the pieces are connected together – the length of the cotton that attaches each piece to the rod, the number of rods, etc. Only when we understand the structure of the end state (resting position) of the mobile can we begin to understand how external factors (wind, heat) could change the shape to some new configuration.

The model proposed here is called in mathematics a step-wise function model, and is akin in some respect to Anderson's (1974) Averaging model of person perception and Argyle and Dean's (1965) Affiliative balance model. Essentially it proposes that there are three essential regions (Fig. 14.1) in which the elements can vary, each having different effects on the situation:

1. There is a region within which any one variable can change without any noticeable effect (e.g. room temperature between certain ranges), though this region might be different for each variable.
2. Beyond this region there is a second 'equilibrium region' where alteration in one or more variables leads to a compensation in other variables to maintain the structural stability of the situation (e.g. changing the social role from supervisor to counsellor might lead to a change in social goals from academic criticism to personal matters).
3. Finally there is a third stage beyond which no compensation/equilibration will take place and the structure and definition of the situation changes.

As yet no mathematical equation has been worked out for this model and

Conclusions

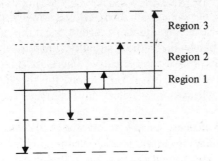

Fig. 14.1. Graphical representation of the equilibrium mobile model.

there are clearly many difficulties to overcome before this could be done, but this might serve as the basis for model-building in this area.

Variability between situations

Psychologists have been undecided about whether or not there are universal principles of sequence, for example, or whether social behaviour is basically different in different kinds of situations. In each area that we have examined there is evidence for generality in some respects but not in others. In *repertoire*, for example, categories of nonverbal communication are much the same in all situations; speech acts are similar, though different subdivisions are needed in different settings, especially in task areas; but verbal contents and activity categories vary greatly. For *concepts*, the evaluative dimension is used for other persons in all situations, though its contents vary. On the other hand constructs for abilities and other task-related dimensions vary considerably between situations. It may be possible to formulate principles of social behaviour in a more abstract way, which is universal. Our functional analysis suggests one way of doing this: situations develop repertoires and concepts that are needed to reach situational goals. The analysis of *sequences of interaction* provides another example of a universal abstract principle: the four-step social-skill sequence is found universally, though its contents vary.

Implications for the study of personality

This book is about situations, not about personality, but one of our original aims was to contribute to the study of P × S interaction. We should now redress the balance and point out that, although there are the uniformities of behaviour which we have described within situations, there is a lot of individual variation as well. To use our game analogy, there is a great deal of varied individual play within the rules at football – variations due to different degrees of skill and motivation, and in style of play.

From the point of view of situational analysis, personality can be described in terms of the choice and avoidance of certain situations, and the adopting of certain styles of behaviour in those situations that are entered. But why do we want to study or assess personality? There are three main purposes: for selection and other forms of prediction, for therapy, and simply to understand those with whom we come into contact.

Selection and other predictions. We saw in Chapter 13 that situational analysis has a number of implications for personnel selection. This includes selecting people for jobs, for educational courses, and for release on parole. We argued that there should be more detailed study of the situations that those under study will enter, and their relative importance. Future performance can best be predicted from performance in similar situations in the past. When selection tests are used, these should be situationally relevant rather than claiming to measure general traits. So testers should assess social skills, intellectual competence, and anxiety in the kinds of situations which the candidate will face on the job.

Therapy. In order to treat patients it is necessary first to assess them clinically. This is a matter of individual diagnosis, which is quite different from the comparison with others needed for selection purposes. We maintain that the diagnosis should include situational analysis, to find out the range of situations that the patient finds difficult, or that upset him. The next stage is to find out exactly what it is about these situations that the patient finds difficult. In the case of social-skills training these difficulties can be stated in terms of the conceptual scheme used in this book: ignorance of rules or concepts, deviant motivations, ignorance of repertoire, inability to produce socially skilled social acts or sequences of acts. We have applied situational analysis to various kinds of SST and found it extremely useful. Meanwhile other therapists have independently been using some form of situational analysis for patients with alcoholism and obesity problems. We believe that situational analysis would be useful with many kinds of patients, and that the use of our methods would make this approach more effective.

But what can we say about 'personality dynamics', i.e. those more general, or more central processes whose conflicts give rise to behaviour in many situations? It is possible to do more than list a person's behaviour in a lot of situations if a general pattern can be discerned – for example if he avoids all situations of a certain type, or gives a similar performance in a wide range of situations. Again, when someone experiences an important 'life-event' like death of spouse, losing a job, or emigrating, this can be described in terms of the changes of situations he experiences – often the loss of a number of rewarding situations. The most helpful treatment might consist of helping him to find alternative, substitute situations, or training him to cope better with the new situations to which he is exposed.

There are also second-order personality characteristics, which describe in general terms how people react to situations. One of the best-known properties of this kind is internal–external control (Phares, 1976).

Understanding people. It is normal to want to understand those with whom we come into contact, partly in order to deal with them more effectively, but partly perhaps as an end in itself, out of curiosity. We have seen that certain constructs are widely used for this purpose, 'friendly evaluation/extroversion' being the most popular. Other constructs are used differentially in different situations and for different kinds of persons (e.g. children versus doctors). In other words people are aware of the limited range of relevance of most constructs. Terms like 'neurotic' and 'anxious' should be used more carefully, since there are several kinds of anxiety (e.g. in social situations versus in physical danger).

In forming impressions of our friends and colleagues we usually see them only in a restricted range of situations – for example we do not see friends at work or see work colleagues at play. We are rarely able to form an overall impression but then we do not really need to. However if we are sufficiently interested in someone to want to form a fuller picture of his personality, then we need to know how he behaves in a much wider range of situations. We also need to know the range of situations he prefers and enters most often, and the situations he avoids. It is also interesting to know how he groups situations, since he will behave in a similar way in situations in each group (Argyle and Little, 1972).

Situational analysis and the crisis in social psychology

During recent years there has been extensive criticism of the conduct of research in social psychology. We and our colleagues at Oxford have voiced such criticisms ourselves (e.g. Argyle, 1969), and have been deeply involved in the development of new research methods and ways of thinking which are not open to these objections (e.g. Ginsburg, 1980). How far can situational analysis help to resolve the crisis or crises in social psychology?

The most widely voiced attack on traditional social psychology has been the objection to laboratory experiments, which are thought to be artificial, open to experimenter effects and demand characteristics, and capable of producing misleading results. The deception often involved is regarded as unethical. Situational analysis can make several contributions to this problem. Firstly, it shows how the experimental situation can itself be studied, to see what the implicit rules are, the roles of subject and experimenter, the goal structure for subjects, and so on. Very likely some laboratory situations are entirely acceptable, while others will produce misleading results. It is only possible to generalise to situations with similar features. Secondly situational analysis shows that experimental manipulations should be made with great care, so that it is clear exactly which feature is being altered, and preferably only one feature should be altered at a time. Thirdly, situational factors may be of importance, in that an effect might occur only in certain kinds of situation. For example when do people actually make attributions of the behaviour of themselves or others?

Another line of criticism has been that social psychology has been too behaviouristic, treating people like animals which respond passively and unthinkingly to stimuli, whereas they should be treated like human beings who are capable of thinking and planning, following rules and using language. The appropriate method of understanding another person's behaviours is to ask him for his account of what he was doing and why he did it (Harré and Secord, 1972). We have discussed this doctrine in detail elsewhere (Argyle, 1978*a*) and we accept much of it. We particularly welcome the emphasis on rule-following, concepts and language, and the motivation of behaviour; there are chapters in this book on each of these topics. The most useful new research to be produced by members of the 'new paradigm' group has perhaps been into the rules of disorderly situations (Marsh *et al.*, 1978; see above, p. 130f.).

However we feel that the methods advocated by this group are too loose, and need to be replaced by more rigorous ones, such as those we have described here, for the analysis of rules, goals, etc. There is also the serious and now familiar problem that individuals are simply not aware of some of the causes of their behaviour – as in cases of unconscious motivation, small nonverbal signals from others and concept formation, for example (Nisbett and Wilson, 1977). We too have relied heavily on self-reports, and have found that with suitable measuring instruments people can report a great deal of the rules, goals, etc., of situations. But there are some aspects of situations that cannot be reported, such as system needs and other latent functions, which have to be investigated via their consequences.

A third level of criticism of social psychology comes from a group of European social psychologists (Israel and Tajfel, 1972; Tajfel and Fraser, 1978). They argue that laboratory situations leave out the relationships between people as members of a group, such as social class, which normally influence social behaviour. Group relationships are explicitly included in our way of analysing situations, as part of the role-system. Our method also has a contribution to make to the study of intergroup relations, by analysing in detail the set of situations in which trouble between two groups takes place. Another point made in Israel and Tajfel (1972) is that American social psychologists have not paid enough attention to ideological factors in social behaviour. They are thinking primarily of Marxist ideology, but the point is a more general one. This too we have explicitly included in our analysis, as part of the concepts used in situations.

A fourth line of criticism, from the other side of the Atlantic, is Gergen's (1973) persuasive argument that social psychological findings are different at different historical periods, so that the findings can have no permanent validity. We have shown that the features of situations change over time, and that situations themselves come and go, in a process of natural selection. Tracing such developments, and the cultural initiation and diffusion of situations, would be a valuable historical study. For example, the English pub can now be found in many parts of the world. However, we believe that the underlying principles, for example of functional relationships, are of greater stability.

To conclude this section, we should say that a variety of research methods in social psychology are acceptable and valuable – including certain kinds of laboratory experiment, role-played experiments, statistical field studies and ethological methods (Ginsburg, 1980) – but we think it is most important that investigators should be clear about the nature of the situation studied, and that generalisation from it can only be to situations with similar features.

Further applications of situational analysis

We have discussed two of the main applications of situational analysis – its use in social-skills training and other therapy, and its implications for personnel selection. The other main area of practical application is where it is possible to alter situations that are causing difficulty. If behaviour is just as much due to situations and to personality–situation interaction as to personality, it follows that social problems might be solved by changing situations rather than people, or by matching people to situations better.

It is possible to alter the situations when trouble occurs, in vandalism and some other kinds of delinquency. Situational modification is already being done by environmental psychologists and others, but is mainly confined to changing the physical environment. We suggest that altering other features of the environment may be more appropriate in some cases – e.g. altering the rules (as has happened with rugby football), the repertoire (as in the invention of T-groups, encounter groups and brainstorming groups) or roles (as in some new industrial work-flow systems).

Situational analysis, 'the psychology of situated action' (Ginsburg, 1980), also has important implications for several branches of psychology and the social sciences. For social psychology it offers an analysis of one of its most important variables, hitherto neglected, or manipulated in an uncoordinated way in different experiments. We now have some idea of the real components of this variable, and we have a new way of looking at and evaluating laboratory studies. For clinical psychology and psychiatry we have a new approach to therapy which is already being used in social-skills training, and in the treatment of obesity and alcoholism. For sociology we have evidence for the amount of consensus in the perception of situations, which goes strongly against approaches such as symbolic interactionism that emphasise individual definitions of the situation and on-the-spot construction of shared definitions. For linguistics we have shown the extent of situational variability in language, suggesting a new field of linguistic research, which could go far in explaining linguistic phenomena in general.

References

Journal abbreviations

Acta Psychol.	Acta Psychologica
Admin. Sci. Quart.	Administrative Science Quarterly
Adv. exp. soc. Psychol.	Advances in Experimental Social Psychology
Amer. Anthrop.	American Anthropologist
Amer. educ. Res. J.	American Educational Research Journal
Amer. J. Dis. Child.	American Journal of Diseases of Children
Amer. J. Psychiat.	American Journal of Psychiatry
Amer. J. Psychol.	American Journal of Psychology
Amer. Psychol.	American Psychologist
Amer. sociol. Rev.	American Sociological Review
Ann. N.Y. Acad. Sci.	Annals of the New York Academy of Sciences
Ann. Rev. Psychol.	Annual Review of Psychology
Anthrop. Ling.	Anthropological Linguistics
Arch. gen. Psychiat.	Archives of General Psychiatry
Austral. J. Psychol.	Australian Journal of Psychology
Behav. Res. Ther.	Behaviour Research and Therapy
Behav. Sci.	Behavioral Science
Behav. Ther.	Behavioral Therapy
Brit. J. educ. Psychol.	British Journal of Educational Psychology
Brit. J. med Psychol.	British Journal of Medical Psychology
Brit. J. Psychol.	British Journal of Psychology
Brit. J. soc. clin. Psychol.	British Journal of Social and Clinical Psychology
Brit. J. Sociol.	British Journal of Sociology
Brit. med. J.	British Medical Journal
Bull. CERP	Bulletin du CERP
Bull. Psychol.	Bulletin de Psychologie
Bull. Psychonom. soc.	Bulletin of the Psychonomic Society
Canad. J. behav. Sci.	Canadian Journal of Behavioural Science
Canad. psychol. Rev.	Canadian Psychological Review
Child Developm.	Child Development
Counsel. Psychol.	Counseling Psychologist
Develpm. Psychol.	Developmental Psychology
Diss. Abstr. Int.	Dissertation Abstracts International
Educ. psychol. Meas.	Educational and Psychological Measurement
Envir. Behav.	Environment and Behavior
Eur. J. soc. Psychol.	European Journal of Social Psychology

Genet. Psychol. Monogr.	Genetic Psychology Monographs
Hum. Ecol.	Human Ecology
Hum. Org.	Human Organization
Hum. Relat.	Human Relations
Int. J. Amer. Ling.	International Journal of American Linguistics
Int. J. Psychol.	International Journal of Psychology
Int. J. soc. Psychiat.	International Journal of Social Psychiatry
Int. J. sport Psychol.	International Journal of Sport Psychology
IPAR Res. Bull.	Institute for Personality Assessment and Research Bulletin
J. abnorm. Psychol.	Journal of Abnormal Psychology
J. abnorm. soc. Psychol.	Journal of Abnormal and Social Psychology
J. appl. Behav. Anal.	Journal of Applied Behavior Analysis
J. appl. Psychol.	Journal of Applied Psychology
J. appl. soc. Psychol.	Journal of Applied Social Psychology
J. behav. Ther. exp. Psychiat.	Journal of Behavior Therapy and Experimental Psychiatry
J. child Lang.	Journal of Child Language
J. child Psychol. Psychiat.	Journal of Child Psychology and Psychiatry and Allied Disciplines
J. clin. Psychol.	Journal of Clinical Psychology
J. consult. Psychol.	Journal of Consulting Psychology
J. consult. clin. Psychol.	Journal of Consulting and Clinical Psychology
J. consumer Res.	Journal of Consumer Research
J. counsel. Psychol.	Journal of Counseling Psychology
J. environ. Psych. nonverb. Behav.	Journal of Environmental Psychology and Nonverbal Behavior
J. exp. child Psychol.	Journal of Experimental Child Psychology
J. exp. Educ.	Journal of Experimental Education
J. exp. Psychol.	Journal of Experimental Psychology
J. exp. soc. Psychol.	Journal of Experimental Social Psychology
J. gen. Psychol.	Journal of General Psychology
J. indiv. Psychol.	Journal of Individual Psychology
J. leisure Res.	Journal of Leisure Research
J. market. Res.	Journal of Marketing Research
J. nerv. ment. Dis.	Journal of Nervous and Mental Diseases
J. Pers.	Journal of Personality
J. pers. Assess.	Journal of Personality Assessment
J. pers. soc. Psychol.	Journal of Personality and Social Psychology
J. pers. soc. Psychol. Monogr.	Journal of Personality and Social Psychology Monographs
J. Psychol.	Journal of Psychology
J. Psychosom. Res.	Journal of Psychosomatic Research
J. Res. Pers.	Journal of Research in Personality
J. Roy. Coll. gen. Pract.	Journal of the Royal College of General Practitioners
J. soc. Issues	Journal of Social Issues
J. soc. Psychol.	Journal of Social Psychology
J. soc. Ther.	Journal of Social Therapy

References

J. Speech Hear. Res.	Journal of Speech and Hearing Research
J. Theory soc. Behav.	Journal for the Theory of Social Behaviour
J. verb. Learn. verb. Behav.	Journal of Verbal Learning and Verbal Behavior
Lang. Speech	Language and Speech
Manag. Sci.	Management Science
Multi. Behav. Res.	Multivariate Behavior Research
N.Z. Psychol.	New Zealand Psychologist
Org. Behav. Hum. Perf.	Organisational Behavior and Human Performance
Pacif. sociol. Rev.	Pacific Sociological Review
Pediat. Res.	Pediatric Research
Percept. mot. Skills	Perceptual and Motor Skills
Pers. soc. Psychol. Bull.	Personality and Social Psychology Bulletin
Personnel Psychol.	Personnel Psychology
Pract. Anthrop.	Practical Anthropology
Prog. exp. Pers. Res.	Progress in Experimental Personality Research
Psychol. Bull.	Psychological Bulletin
Psychol. Med.	Psychological Medicine
Psychol. Monogr.	Psychological Monographs
Psychol. Rep.	Psychological Reports
Psychol. Rev.	Psychological Review
Psychonom. Sci.	Psychonomic Science
Psychosom. Med.	Psychosomatic Medicine
Rep. Res. soc. Psychol.	Representative Research in Social Psychology
Res. Psychother.	Research in Psychotherapy
Scand. J. Psychol.	Scandinavian Journal of Psychology
Sci. Amer.	Scientific American
Soc. Prob.	Social Problems
Soc. Sci. Forum	Social Science Forum
Sociol. Soc. Res.	Sociology and Social Research

Ainsworth, M. D. S., Bell, S. M. and Stayton, D. J. (1974). Infant–mother attachment and social development: socialisation as a product of reciprocal responsiveness to signals. In M. P. M. Richards (ed.) *The Integration of a Child into a Social World*. London: Cambridge University Press.

Alker, H. (1972). Is personality situationally specific or intrapsychically consistent? *J. Pers.*, **40**, 1–16.

Allen, V. L. (1965). Situational factors in conformity. *Adv. exp. soc. Psychol.*, **2**, 133–76.

Allen, V. L. and Crutchfield, R. S. (1963). Generalisation of experimentally reinforced conformity. *J. abnorm. soc. Psychol.*, **67**, 326–33.

Allport, G. W. (1961). *Pattern and Growth in Personality*. New York: Holt, Rinehart and Winston.

Altman, I. (1972). 'Reciprocity of interpersonal exchange'. Paper presented at 80th Annual Meeting of the American Psychological Association.

Altman, I. (1975). *The Environment and Social Behavior*. Monterey, Calif.: Brooks/Cole.

References

Altman, I. (1976). Environmental psychology and social psychology. *Pers. soc. Psychol. Bull.*, **2**, 96–113.

Anastasi, A. (1961). *Psychological Testing*. New York: Macmillan.

Anderson, N. (1974). Cognitive algebra: integration theory applied to social attribution. *Adv. exp. soc. Psychol.*, **7**, 1–101.

Applegate, J. L. and Delia, J. G. (1980). Person-centred speech, psychological development and the contexts of language usage. In R. N. St Clair and H. Giles (eds.) *The Social and Psychological Contexts of Language*. Hillsdale, NJ: Erlbaum.

Argyle, M. (1969). *Social Interaction*. London: Methuen.

Argyle, M. (1972). *The Social Psychology of Work*. London/Harmondsworth: Allen Lane/Penguin.

Argyle, M. (1975). *Bodily Communication*. London: Methuen.

Argyle, M. (1976). Personality and social behaviour. In R. Harré (ed.) *Personality*. Oxford: Blackwell.

Argyle, M. (1978a). Discussion chapter: an appraisal of the new approach to the study of social behaviour. In M. Brenner, P. Marsh and M. Brenner (eds.) *The Social Contexts of Method*. London: Croom Helm.

Argyle, M. (1978b). *The Psychology of Interpersonal Behaviour*, 3rd edn. Harmondsworth: Penguin.

Argyle, M. (1980a). The analysis of social situations. In M. Brenner (ed.) *The Structure of Action*. Oxford: Blackwell.

Argyle, M. (1980b). Interaction skills and social competence. In M. P. Feldman and J. Orford (eds.) *The Social Psychology of Psychological Problems*. New York: Wiley.

Argyle, M. (in press). Intercultural communication. In M. Argyle (ed.) *Handbook of Social Skills*. London: Methuen.

Argyle, M. and Beit-Hallahmi, B. (1975). *The Social Psychology of Religion*. London: Routledge and Kegan Paul.

Argyle, M. and Cook, M. (1976). *Gaze and Mutual Gaze*. London: Cambridge University Press.

Argyle, M. and Dean, J. (1965). Eye-contact, distance and affiliation. *Sociometry*, **28**, 289–304.

Argyle, M. and Graham, J. A. (1976). The Central Europe experiment – looking at persons and looking at objects. *J. environ. Psychol. nonverb. Behav.*, **1**, 6–16.

Argyle, M., Graham, J. A., Campbell, A. and White, P. (1979). The rules of different situations. *N.Z. Psychol.*, **8**, 13–22.

Argyle, M. and Kendon, A. (1967). The experimental analysis of social performance. *Adv. exp. soc. Psychol.*, **3**, 55–98.

Argyle, M. and Little, B. R. (1972). Do personality traits apply to social behaviour? *J. Theory soc. Behav.*, **2**, 1–35.

Argyle, M. and McHenry, R. (1971). Do spectacles really affect judgments of intelligence? *Brit. J. soc. clin. Psychol.*, **10**, 27–9.

Asch, S. E. (1952). *Social Psychology*. Englewood Cliffs, NJ: Prentice-Hall.

Atkinson, J. W. (ed.) (1958). *Motives in Fantasy, Action and Society*. Princeton, NJ: Van Nostrand.

Atkinson, J. W. (1977). Motivation for achievement. In T. Blass (ed.) *Personality Variables in Social Behavior*. Hillsdale, NJ: Erlbaum.

Austin, J. (1962). *How to do Things with Words*. Oxford University Press.

Avedon, E. M. (1971). The structural elements of games. In E. M. Avedon and B. Sutton-Smith (eds.) *The Study of Games*. New York: Wiley.

Avigdor, R. (1953). Etude expérimentale de la genèse des stéréotypes. *Cahiers internationaux de sociologie*, 14, 154–68.

Bach, K. (1975). Analytical social philosophy – basic concepts. *J. Theory soc. Behav.*, 5, 189–214.

Bales, R. F. (1950). *Interaction Process Analysis*. Cambridge, Mass.: Addison-Wesley.

Bales, R. F. and Slater, P. E. (1955). Role differentiation in small decision-making groups. In T. Parsons, R. F. Bales *et al*. (eds.) *The Family, Socialization and Interaction Processes*. New York: Free Press.

Bales, R. F. and Strodtbeck, F. L. (1951). Phases in group problem-solving. *J. abnorm. soc. Psychol.*, 46, 485–95.

Bales, R. F., Strodtbeck, F. L., Mills, T. and Roseborough, M. E. (1951). Channels of communication in small groups. *Amer. sociol. Rev.*, 16, 461–8.

Ball, D. W. (1970a). The definition of the situation: some theoretical and methodological consequences of taking W. I. Thomas seriously. In J. Douglas (ed.) *Existential Sociology*. New York: Appleton-Century-Crofts.

Ball, D. W. (1970b). An abortion clinic ethnography. *Soc. Prob.*, 14, 293–301.

Bandura, A. and Walters, R. (1963). *Social Learning and Personality Development*. New York: Holt, Rinehart and Winston.

Bannister, D. and Mair, J. M. M. (1968). *The Evaluation of Personal Constructs*. New York and London: Academic Press.

Banton, M. (1955). *The Coloured Quarter: Negro Immigrants in an English City*. London: Cape.

Barbu, Z. (1964). Definition of the situation. In J. Gould and W. Kolb (eds.) *A Dictionary of the Social Sciences*. London: Tavistock.

Barker, R. (1960). Ecology and Maturation. In M. Jones (ed.) *Nebraska Symposium on Motivation 8*. Lincoln: University of Nebraska Press.

Barker, R. G. (1963). On the nature of the environment. *J. soc. Issues*, 19, 17–38.

Barker, R. G. (1968). *Ecological Psychology: Concepts and Methods for Studying the Environment of Human Behavior*. Stanford, Calif.: Stanford University.

Barker, R. G. and Gump, P. (1964). *Big School, Small School*. Stanford, Calif.: Stanford University Press.

Barker, R. G. and Wright, H. F. (1949). Psychological ecology and the problem of psychosocial development. *Child Develpm.*, 40, 131–43.

Barker, R. G. and Wright, H. F. (1951). *One Boy's Day*. New York: Harper and Row.

Barker, R. G. and Wright, H. F. (1954). *Midwest and its Children: the Psychological Ecology of an American Town*. Evanston, Ill.: Row, Peterson.

Barker, R. G. and Wright, H. F. (1955). *Midwest and its Children*. New York: Harper and Row.

Barnes, R. M. (1958). *Motion and Time Study*. New York: Wiley.

Baron, R. A. (1972). Reducing the influence of an aggressive model: the restraining effects of peer censure. *J. exp. soc. Psychol.*, 8, 266–75.

Baron, R. A. and Ball, R. L. (1974). The aggression-inhibiting influence of non-hostile humor. *J. exp. soc. Psychol.*, 10, 23–33.

Baron, R. A. and Bell, P. (1975). Aggression and heat: mediating effects of prior provocation and exposure to an aggressive model. *J. pers. soc. Psychol.*, 31, 825–32.

Baron, R. A. and Bell, P. (1977). Sexual arousal and aggression by males: effects of type of erotic stimuli and prior provocation. *J. pers. soc. Psychol.*, **35**, 79–87.

Baron, R. A. and Byrne, D. (1977). *Social Psychology*. Boston, Mass.: Allyn and Bacon.

Baron, R. A. and Ransberger, V. (1978). Ambient temperature and the occurrence of collective violence: the 'long hot summer' revisited. *J. pers. soc. Psychol.*, **36**, 351–60.

Barry, H., Child, I. and Bacon, M. (1959). Relation of child training to subsistence economy. *Amer. Anthrop.*, **61**, 51–63.

Bates, E. (1976). *Language and Context: the Acquisition of Pragmatics*. New York and London: Academic Press.

Baum, A. and Roman, S. (1974). 'Differential response to anticipated crowding: psychological effects of social and spatial density'. Unpublished manuscript, Trinity College (Cited in Baron and Byrne, 1977.).

Bearden, W. O. and Woodside, A. G. (1979). Consumption occasion influence on consumer brand choice. *Decision Sciences*, **9**, 273–83.

Beattie, G. W. (1979). The skilled art of conversation interaction: verbal and nonverbal signals in its regulation and management. In W. T. Singleton, P. Spurgeon and R. B. Stammers (eds.) *The Analysis of Social Skill*. New York: Plenum.

Becker, S., Lerner, M. and Carroll, J. (1966). Conformity as a function of birth order and type of group pressure: a verification. *J. pers. soc. Psychol.*, **3**, 242–4.

Belk, R. W. (1974). An exploratory assessment of situational effects in buyer behavior. *J. market. Res.*, **11**, 156–63.

Belk, R. W. (1975). Situational variables and consumer behavior. *J. consumer Res.*, **2**, 157–64.

Belk, R. W. (1978a). Developing product-specific taxonomies of consumption situations. College of Commerce and Business Administration, University of Illinois at Urbana-Champaign. (Roneoed.)

Belk, R. W. (1978b). The effects of product involvement and task definition on anticipated consumer effort. College of Commerce and Business Administration, University of Illinois at Urbana-Champaign. (Roneoed.)

Bell, R. T. (1976). *Sociolinguistics*. London: Batsford.

Bellack, A. A., Kliebard, H. M., Hyman, R. T. and Smith, F. L. (1966). *The Language of the Classroom*. New York: Teachers College Press, Columbia University.

Bem, D. J. (1972). Constructing cross-situational consistencies in behaviour: some thoughts on Alker's critique of Mischel. *J. Pers.*, **40**, 17–26.

Bem, D. J. and Allen, A. (1974). On predicting some of the people some of the time: the search for cross-situational consistency in behaviour. *Psychol. Rev.*, **81**, 506–20.

Bennett, D. and Bennett, J. (1970). Making the scene. In G. Stone and H. Farberman (eds.) *Social Psychology through Symbolic Interaction*. Lexington, Mass.: Ginn-Blaisdell.

Bennis, W. G. and Shepard, H. A. (1956). A theory of group development. *Hum. Relat.*, **9**, 415–37.

Berger, P. L. and Luckman, T. (1966). *The Social Construction of Reality*. Garden City, NJ: Doubleday.

Berkowitz, L. (1974). Some determinants of impulsive aggression: role of mediated association with reinforcement for aggression. *Psychol. Rev.*, **81**, 165–76.

Berkowitz, L. and Le Page, A. (1967). Weapons as aggression-eliciting stimuli. *J. pers. soc. Psychol.*, **7**, 202–7.

Berne, E. (1966). *Games People Play*. London: Deutsch.

Bernstein, B. (1959). A public language: some sociological implications of a linguistic form. *Brit. J. Sociol.*, **10**, 311–26.

Bernstein, B. (1961). Aspects of language and learning in the genesis of the social process. *J. child Psychol. Psychiat.*, **1**, 313–24.

Bernstein, B. (1962). Social class, linguistic codes and grammatical elements. *Lang. Speech*, **5**, 221–40.

Bernstein, B. (1971, 1973 and 1975). *Class, Codes and Control*, vols. 1, 2 and 3. London: Routledge.

Bernstein, L. (1975). Situational anxiety reduction in medical students. *Journal of Thanatology*, **3**, 187–90.

Berry, J. W. and Annis, R. C. (1974). Ecology, culture and psychological differentiation. *Int. J. Psychol.*, **9**, 173–93.

Best, J. A. and Hakstian, A. R. (1978). A situation-specific model for smoking behavior. *Addiction Behaviors*, **3**, 79–92.

Biddle, B. J. and Thomas, E. J. (eds.) (1966). *Role Theory: Concepts and Research*. New York: Wiley.

Bierhof, H. W. and Bierhof-Alferman, D. (1976). The use of psychological theories by 'naive' judges: a study of implicit personality theory. *Eur. J. soc. Psychol.*, **6**, 429–45.

Billig, M. (1977). The new social psychology and 'facism'. *Eur. J. soc. Psychol.*, **7**, 393–432.

Birdwhistell, R. (1970). *Kinesics and Context*. Philadelphia: University of Pennsylvania Press.

Bishop, D. W. and Witt, P. A. (1970). Sources of behavioural variance during leisure time. *J. pers. soc. Psychol.*, **16**, 352–60.

Blauner, R. (1964). *Alienation and Freedom*. Chicago: University of Chicago Press.

Block, J. (1971). *Lives Through Time*. Berkeley: Bancroft.

Blood, R. O. and Wolfe, D. N. (1960). *Husbands and Wives*. New York: Free Press.

Blurton-Jones, N. (1972). Categories of child–child interaction. In N. Blurton-Jones (ed.) *Ethological Studies of Child Behaviour*. London: Cambridge University Press.

Bochner, S. (ed.) (in press). *Cross-Cultural Interaction*. Oxford: Pergamon Press.

Bogardus, E. S. (1959). 'Social distance'. Los Angeles (privately published paper).

Bonacich, P. and Lewis, G. H. (1973). Function specialization and sociometric judgment. *Sociometry*, **36**, 31–41.

Boomer, D. S. (1978). The phonemic clause: a speech unit in human communication. In A. Siegman and S. Feldstein (eds.) *Nonverbal Behavior and Communication*. Hillsdale, NJ: Erlbaum.

Borden, R., Bowen, R. and Taylor, S. (1971). Shock setting behavior as a function of physical attack and extrinsic reward. *Percept. mot. Skills*, **33**, 563–8.

Borgatta, E. F. (1962). A systematic study of interaction process scores, peer and self-assessments, personality and other variables. *Genet. Psychol. Monogr.*, **65**, 219–91.

Bossard, J. H. S. and Boll, E. S. (1956). *The Large Family System*. Philadelphia: University of Pennsylvania Press.

Bourhis, R. Y. and Giles, H. (1977). The language of intergroup distinctiveness. In H. Giles (ed.) *Language, Ethnicity and Intergroup Relations*. New York and London: Academic Press.

Bower, S. A. and Bower, G. H. (1976). *Asserting Yourself*. Reading, Mass.: Addison-Wesley.

Brackman, J. (1967). The put-on. *New Yorker*, 24 June, 34–73.

Braginsky, B. M., Braginsky, D. D. and Ring, K. (1969). *Methods of Madness: the Mental Hospital as a Last Resort*. New York: Holt, Rinehart and Winston.

Brannigan, C. R. and Humphries, D. A. (1972). Human non-verbal behaviour, a means of communication. In N. Blurton-Jones (ed.) *Ethological Studies of Child Behaviour*. London: Cambridge University Press.

Breer, P. E. (1960). 'Predicting interpersonal behavior from personality and role'. Ph.D. thesis, Harvard University.

Brenner, M. (1980). *The Social Structure of the Research Interview*. New York and London: Academic Press.

Brickman, P., Ryan, K. and Wortman, C. (1975). Causal chains: attribution of responsibility as a function of immediate and prior causes. *J. pers. soc. Psychol.*, **32**, 1060–7.

Bromley, D. B. (1977). *Personality Descriptions in Ordinary Language*. New York: Wiley.

Brookes, M. and Kaplan, A. (1972). The office environment; space planning and affective behaviour. *Human Factors*, **14**, 373–91.

Bross, I. D. J. (1973). Languages in cancer research. In G. P. Murphy *et al.* (eds.) *Perspectives in Cancer Research and Treatment*. New York: A. R. Liss.

Brown, R. and Ford, M. (1961). Address in American English. *J. abnorm. soc. Psychol.*, **62**, 375–85.

Brown, P. and Fraser, C. (1980). Speech as a marker of situation. In K. Scherer and H. Giles (eds.) *Social Markers in Speech*. Cambridge: Cambridge University Press.

Brown, R. and Gilman, A. (1960). The pronouns of solidarity and power. In T. A. Sebeok (ed.) *Style in Language*. New York: Wiley.

Brown, R. and Lenneberg, E. H. (1954). A study in language and cognition. *J. abnorm. soc. Psychol.*, **49**, 454–62.

Bruner, J. S. (1975). The ontogenesis of speech acts. *J. child Lang.*, 2, 1–19.

Bryan, J. H. and Test, M. A. (1967). Models and helping: naturalistic studies in aiding behaviour. *J. pers. soc. Psychol.*, **6**, 400–7.

Bryant, B. and Trower, P. (1974). Social difficulty in a student population. *Brit. J. educ. Psychol.*, **44**, 13–21.

Bryant, B., Trower, P., Yardley, K., Urbieta, H. and Letemendia, F. (1976). A survey of social inadequacy among psychiatric outpatients. *Psychol. Med.*, **6**, 101–12.

Burgess, R. (1968). Communication networks: an experimental re-evaluation. *J. exp. soc. Psychol.*, **4**, 324–37.

Burke, P. J. (1967). The development of task and social-emotional role differentiation. *Sociometry*, **30**, 379–92.

Burns, T. (1955). The reference of conduct in small groups: cliques and cabals in occupational milieux. *Hum. Relat.*, **8**, 467–86.

Burron, D. and Bucher, B. (1978). Self-instructions as discriminative cues for rule-breaking or rule-following. *J. exp. child Psychol.*, **26**, 46–57.

Burroughs, W., Schultz, W. and Aubrey, S. (1973). Quality of argument, leadership votes, and eye contact in three-person leaderless groups. *J. soc. Psychol.*, **90**, 89–93.

Burton, R. V. (1963). Generality of honesty reconsidered. *Psychol. Rev.*, **70**, 481–99.

Buss, A. (1977). The trait–situation controversy and the concept of interaction. *Pers. soc. Psychol. Bull.*, **3**, 196–201.

Byrne, D. and Buehler, J. (1955). A note on the influence of propinquity upon acquaintanceships. *J. abnorm. soc. Psychol.*, **51**, 147–8.

Byrne, D., Ervin, C. H. and Lamberth, J. (1970). Continuity between the experimental study of attraction and real life computer dating. *J. pers. soc. Psychol.*, **16**, 157–65.

Byrne, P. S. and Long, B. E. L. (1976). *Doctors Talking to Patients*. London: HMSO.

Calhoun, L. G., Selby, J. W. and Wroten, J. D. (1977). Situation constraint and type of causal explanation: the effects of perceived 'mental illness' and social rejection. *J. Res. Pers.*, **11**, 95–100.

Campbell, A. (1980). *Female Delinquency in Social Context*. Oxford: Blackwell.

Canter, D. (1972). Royal Hospital for Sick Children. *Architects' Journal*, 6 Sept., 525–64.

Canter, D. (1977). *The Psychology of Place*. London: Architectural Press.

Canter, S. and Canter, D. (eds.) (1979). *Designing for Therapeutic Environments: A Review of Research*. New York: Wiley.

Canter, D. and Lee, K. H. (1974). A non-reactive study of room usage in modern Japanese apartments. In D. Canter and T. Lee (eds.) *Psychology and the Built Environment*. London, Architectural Press.

Canter, D., Stringer, P., Griffiths, I., Boyce, P., Walters, D. and Kenny, C. (1975). *Environmental Interaction: Psychological Approaches to our Physical Surroundings*. New York: International University Press.

Canter, D. and Wools, R. (1970). A technique for the subjective appraisal of buildings. *Building Science*, **5**, 187–98.

Capon, M. (1977). 'Basic course in social skills training'. Unpublished Manual, St Crispin's Hospital, Northampton.

Carlson, R. (1971). Where is the person in personality research? *Psychol. Bull.*, **75**, 203–19.

Carment, D. W., Miles, C. S. and Cervin, V. B. (1965), Persuasiveness and persuasibility as related to intelligence and extraversion. *Brit. J. soc. clin. Psychol.*, **4**, 1–7.

Carney, R. (1966). The effect of situational variables on the measurement of achievement motivation. *Educ. psychol. Meas.*, **26**, 675–90.

Carroll, J. D. and Chang, J. (1970). Analysis of individual differences in multidimensional scaling via an N-way generalisation of 'Eckart-Young' decomposition. *Psychometrika*, **35**, 238–42.

Carter, L. F. and Nixon, M. (1949). An investigation of the relationship between four criteria of leadership ability for three different tasks. *J. Psychol.*, **27**, 245–61.

Cartwright, A. and Anderson, R. (1979). Patients and their doctors 1977. Occasional paper 8. *J. Royal. Coll. gen. Pract.*, March.

Cartwright, D. (1975). Trait and other sources of variance in the S–R Inventory of Anxiousness. *J. pers. soc. Psychol.*, **32**, 408–14.

Cattell, R. B. (1950). *Personality: a Systematic Theoretical and Factual Study*. New York: McGraw-Hill.

Cattell, R. B. (1965). *The Scientific Analysis of Personality*. Harmondsworth: Penguin.

Cattell, R. B. and Scheier, I. (1958). The nature of anxiety: a review of thirteen multivariate analyses comprising 814 variables. *Psychol. Rep.*, **4**, 351–88.

Cazden, C. B. (1970). The situation: a neglected source of social class differences in language use. *J. soc. Issues*, **26**(2), 35–60.

Central Policy Review Staff (1978). *Vandalism*. London: HMSO.

Certier, B. (1970). 'The exchange of self-disclosures in same sexed and heterosexual groups of strangers'. Unpublished PhD thesis, University of Cincinnati.

Chadwick-Jones, J. K. (1976). *Social Exchange Theory*. New York and London: Academic Press.

Chaikin, A. and Derlega, V. (1976). Self disclosure. In J. W. Thibaut, J. Spence and R. Carson (eds.) *Contemporary Topics in Social Psychology*. Morristown, NJ: General Learning Press.

Chandler, R., Cook, B. and Dugovics, D. (1978). Sex differences in self-reported assertiveness. *Psychol. Rep.*, **43**, 395–402.

Chapman, S. L. and Jeffrey, D. B. (1980). Situational management, standard setting, and self-reward in a behavior modification weight loss program. *J. consult. clin. Psychol.*, **46**, 1588–9.

Chemers, M. M., Rice, R. W., Sundstrom, E. and Butler, W. M. (1975). Leader esteem for the least preferred co-worker score, training and effectiveness: an experimental evaluation. *J. pers. soc. Psychol.*, **31**, 401–9.

Cherry, F. and Deaux, K. (1975). 'Fear of success vs. fear of gender-inconsistent behaviour: a sex similarity'. Paper given to Midwestern Psychological Association, Chicago. (Cited by Wrightsman (1977).)

Chomsky, N. (1957). *Syntactic Structures*. The Hague: Mouton.

Ciolek, M. (1979). 'Zones of co-presence in face-to-face interaction: some observational data'. Unpublished paper, Dept of Experimental Psychology, University of Oxford.

Clark, H. H. and Clark, E. (1977). *Psychology and Language*. New York: Harcourt Brace.

Clark, R. and Word, L. (1974). Why don't bystanders help? Because of ambiguity? *J. pers. soc. Psychol.*, **24**, 392–400.

Clarke, D. D. (1975). The use and recognition of sequential structure in dialogue. *Brit. J. soc. clin. Psychol.*, **14**, 333–9.

Clarke, D. D. (in press). *The Structural Analysis of Verbal Interaction*. Oxford: Pergamon Press.

Clarke, R. V. G. (ed.) (1978). *Tackling Vandalism*. London: HMSO.

Cliff, N. and Young, F. W. (1968). On the relation between unidimensional judgments and multidimensional scaling. *Org. Behav. Hum. Perf.*, **3**, 269–85.

Cofer, C. N. and Appley, M. H. (1964). *Motivation: Theory and Research*. New York: Wiley.

Cohen, A. R. (1961). Cognitive tuning as a factor affecting impression formation. *J. Pers.*, **29**, 235–45.

References

Cohen, A. R., Stotland, E. and Wolfe, D. M. (1955). An experimental investigation of need for cognition. *J. abnorm. soc. Psychol.*, **51**, 291–4.

Cohen, J., Sladen, B. and Bennett, B. (1975). The effects of situational variables on judgments of crowding. *Sociometry*, **38**, 273–81.

Cohen, P. S. (1968). *Modern Social Theory*. London: Heinemann.

Cohen, R. (1971). An investigation of the diagnostic processing of contradictory information. *Eur. J. soc. Psychol.*, **1**, 475–92.

Collett, P. (1971). On training Englishmen in the non-verbal behaviour of Arabs: an experiment in intercultural communication. *Int. J. Psychol.*, **6**, 209–15.

Collett, P. (1977). (ed.) *Social Rules and Social Behaviour*. Oxford: Blackwell.

Collett, P. (1980). Mossi salutations. Report to Harry Frank Guggenheim Foundation.

Collett, P. and Marsh, P. (1974). Patterns of public behaviour: collision avoidance on a pedestrian crossing. *Semiotica*, **12**, 281–99.

Collins, B. E. and Raven, B. H. (1969). Group structure: attraction, coalition, communication and power. In G. Lindzey and E. Aronson (eds.) *The Handbook of Social Psychology*, vol. 4. Reading, Mass.: Addison-Wesley.

Colman, S. and Halstead, H. (1973). A questionnaire study of situations and response styles in anxiety: a pilot study. *Brit. J. soc. clin. Psychol.*, **12**, 393–401.

Cook, M. (1977). The social skill model and interpersonal attraction. In S. Duck (ed.) *Theory and Practice in Interpersonal Attraction*. New York and London: Academic Press.

Cook, S. W. (1970). Motives in a conceptual analysis of attitude-related behavior. *Nebraska Symposium on Motivation 18*. Lincoln: University of Nebraska Press.

Coser, L. A. (1964). *The Functions of Conflict*. New York: Free Press.

Cottrell, L. (1942). The analysis of situational fields. *Amer. sociol. Rev.*, **7**, 370–82.

Coulthard, M. (1977). *An Introduction to Discourse Analysis*. Harlow: Longman.

Coutts, L. and Schneider, F. (1975). Visual behavior in an unfocussed interaction as a function of sex and distance. *J. exp. soc. Psychol.*, **11**, 64–77.

Cozby, P. (1973). Self disclosure: a literature review. *Psychol. Bull.*, **79**, 73–91.

Craik, K. (1966). The prospects for an environmental psychology. *IPAR Res. Bull.*, University of California.

Craik, K. (1970). Environmental psychology. In K. Craik *et al.* (eds.) *New Directions in Psychology*, vol. 4. New York: Holt, Rinehart and Winston.

Craik, K. (in press). Environmental assessment and situational analysis. In D. Magnusson (ed.) *Toward a Psychology of Situations: An Interactional Perspective*. New York: Erlbaum.

Craik, K. and McKechnie, G. (1978). *Personality and the Environment*. Beverly Hills: Sage Publications.

Crassini, B., Law, H. and Wilson, E. (1979). Sex differences in assertive behaviour? *Austral. J. Psychol.*, **31**, 15–19.

Crockett, W. (1955). Emergent leadership in small, decision-making groups. *J. abnorm. soc. Psychol.*, **51**, 378–83.

Crutchfield, R. (1955). Conformity and character. *Amer. Psychol.*, **10**, 191–8.

Crutchfield, R. (1959). Personal and situational factors in conformity to group pressure. *Acta Psychol.*, **15**, 386–8.

Crystal, D. and Davy, D. (1969). *Investigating English Style*. Harlow: Longman.

Cumming, L. L. and El Salmi, A. M. (1968). Empirical research on the bases and correlates of managerial motivation: a review of the literature. *Psychol. Bull.*, **70**, 127–44.

D'Andrade, R. G. (1967). Sex differences and cultural institutions. In E. E. Maccoby (ed.) *The Development of Sex Differences*. London: Tavistock.

Darley, J. and Batson, D. (1973). From Jerusalem to Jericho: a study of situational and dispositional variables in helping behavior. *J. pers. soc. Psychol.*, **27**, 100–8.

Davison, M. L. and Jones, L. E. (1976). A similarity attraction model for predicting sociometric choice from perceived group structure. *J. pers. soc. Psychol.*, **33**, 601–12.

Dawkins, R. (1976). Hierarchical organisation: a candidate principle for ethology. In P. P. G. Bateson and R. A. Hinde (eds.) *Growing Points in Ethology*. Cambridge: Cambridge University Press.

Denzin, N. (1974). Symbolic interactionism and ethnomethodology. In J. Douglas (ed.) *Understanding Everyday Life*. London: Routledge and Kegan Paul.

Derlega, V., Harris, M. and Chaikin, A. (1973). Self disclosure, reciprocity, liking and the deviant. *J. exp. soc. Psychol.*, **9**, 277–84.

Deutsch, M. (1949). An experimental study of cooperation and competition. *Hum. Relat.*, **2**, 199–231.

Deutsch, M. (1968). Field theory in social psychology. In G. Lindzey and E. Aronson (eds.) *Handbook of Social Psychology*, vol. 1. Reading, Mass.: Addison-Wesley.

Deutsch, M. and Gerard, H. B. (1955). A study of normative and informational social influences upon individual judgment. *J. abnorm. soc. Psychol.*, **51**, 629–36.

DeVore, I. (ed.) (1965). *Primate Behavior*. New York: Holt, Rinehart and Winston.

De Waele, J.-P. and Harré, R. (1976). The personality of individuals. In R. Harré (ed.) *Personality*. Oxford: Blackwell.

Dickman, H. R. (1963). The perception of behavioral units. In R. G. Barker (ed.) *The Stream of Behavior*. New York: Appleton-Century-Crofts.

Dittmar, N. (1976). *Sociolinguistics*. London: Arnold.

Dixon, J., de Monchaux, C. and Sandler, J. (1957). Patterns of anxiety: the phobias. *Brit. J. med. Psychol.*, **30**, 34–40.

Doise, W. (1969). Stratégies de jeu à l'intérieur et entre des groupes de nationalités différents. *Bull. CERP*, **18**, 13–26.

Doise, W. (1979). *Groups and Individuals*. Cambridge: Cambridge University Press.

Doise, W. and Weinberger, M. (1972–3). Répresentation masculines dans différentes situations de rencontres mixtes. *Bull. Psychol.*, **26**, 649–57.

Dollard, J. and Auld, F. (1959). *Scoring Human Motives: a Manual*. New Haven, Conn.: Yale University Press.

Dollard, J. and Miller, N. (1950). *Personality and Psychotherapy*. New York: McGraw-Hill.

Donnerstein, E. and Wilson, P. (1976). Effects of noise and perceived control on ongoing and subsequent aggressive behavior. *J. pers. soc. Psychol.*, **34**, 774–81.

Douglas, M. (1972). Deciphering a meal. *Daedalus*, Winter.

Drag, R. (1971). 'The bus-rider phenomenon and its generalizability: a study of self-disclosure in student–stranger vs. college or roommate dyads'. Unpublished paper, University of Florida. (Cited in Goodstein and Reinecker, 1974.)

Duck, S. (ed.) (1977). *Theory and Practice in Interpersonal Attraction*. New York and London: Academic Press.

Duncan, S. (1969). Nonverbal communication. *Psychol. Bull.*, **72**, 118–37.

References

Duncan, S. and Fiske, D. W. (1977). *Face-to-Face Interaction*. Hillsdale, NJ: Erlbaum.

Dunkin, M. J. and Biddle, B. J. (1974). *The Study of Teaching*. New York: Holt, Rinehart and Winston.

Durkheim, E. (1895). *The Rules of Sociological Meaning* (1938 ed), trans. S. A. Solomay and J. H. Mueller. Chicago: Chicago University Press.

Durlak, J. and Lehmen, J. (1974). User awareness and sensitivity to open space: a study of traditional and open plan schools. In D. Canter and T. Lee (eds.) *Psychology and the Built Environment*. London: Architectural Press.

Duval, S. and Wicklund, R. A. (1972). *A Theory of Objective Self-awareness*. New York and London: Academic Press.

Dworkin, R. and Kihlstrom, J. (1978). An S–R inventory of dominance for research on the nature of person–situation interactions. *J. Pers.*, **46**, 43–56.

Eddy, G. and Sinnett, E. (1973). Behavior setting utilization by emotionally disturbed college students. *J. consult. clin. Psychol.*, **40**, 210–16.

Efran, J. S. (1968). Looking for approval: effect on visual behavior of approbation from persons differing in importance. *J. pers. soc. Psychol.*, **10**, 21–5.

Efran, M. S. and Cheyne, J. (1974). Affective concomitants of the invasion of shared space: behavioral, physiological and verbal indications. *J. pers. soc. Psychol.*, **29**, 219–26.

Eiser, J. R. and Stroebe, W. (1972). *Categorization and Social Judgement*. New York and London: Academic Press.

Eisler, R., Hersen, M., Miller, P. M. and Blanchard, E. B. (1975). Situational determinants of assertive behaviors. *J. consult. clin. Psychol.*, **43**, 330–40.

Ekehammar, B. (1974). Interactionism in personality from a historical perspective. *Psychol. Bull.*, **81**, 1026–48.

Ekehammar, B. and Magnusson, D. (1973). A method to study stressful situations. *J. pers. soc. Psychol.*, **27**, 176–9.

Ekehammar, B., Magnusson, D. and Ricklander, L. (1974). An interactionist approach to the study of anxiety. *Scand. J. Psychol.*, **15**, 4–14.

Ekehammar, B., Schalling, D. and Magnusson, D. (1975). Dimensions of stressful situations. *Multi. Behav. Res.*, **10**, 155–64.

Ekman, P., Friesen, W. V. and Ellsworth, P. (1972). *Emotion in the Human Face: Guidelines for Research and a Review of Findings*. New York: Pergamon Press.

Elder, G. H. (1962). Structural variations in the child rearing relationship. *Sociometry*, **35**, 241–62.

Ellis, A. (1957). Rational psychotherapy and individual psychology. *J. indiv. Psychol.*, **13**, 38–44.

Ellsworth, P. C. (1975). Direct gaze as a social stimulus: the example of aggression. In P. Pliner *et al.* (eds.) *Nonverbal Communication of Aggression*. New York: Plenum.

Ellsworth, P. C. and Langer, E. (1976). Staring and approach: an interpretation of the stare as a nonspecific activator. *J. pers. soc. Psychol.*, **33**, 117–22.

Emswiller, T., Deaux, K. and Willits, J. (1971). Similarity, sex, and requests for small favors. *J. appl. soc. Psychol.*, **1**, 284–91.

Endler, N. (1966). Estimating variance components from mean squares for random and mixed effects analysis of variance models. *Percept. mot. Skills*, **22**, 559–70.

Endler, N. (1973). The person versus the situation – a pseudo issue? A response to Alker. *J. Pers.*, **41**, 287–303.

References

Endler, N. (1975). The case for person–situation interactions. *Canad. psychol. Rev.*, **16**, 1–6.

Endler, N. and Edwards, J. (1978). Person by treatment interactions in personality research. In L. Pervin and M. Lewis (eds.) *Perspectives in International Psychology*. New York: Plenum.

Endler, N. and Hunt. J. (1968). S–R inventories of hostility and comparisons of the proportions of variance from persons, responses, and situations for hostility and anxiousness. *J. pers. soc. Psychol.*, **9**, 309–15.

Endler, N. and Hunt, J. (1969). Generalizability of contributions from sources of variance in the S–R Inventory of Anxiousness. *J. Pers.*, **37**, 1–24.

Endler, N., Hunt, J. and Rosenstein, A. (1962). An S–R inventory of anxiousness. *Psychol. Monogr.* **76**, 17.

Endler, N. and Magnusson, D. (1976a). Toward an interactional psychology of personality. *Psychol. Bull.*, **83**, 956–74.

Endler, N. and Magnusson, D. (eds.)(1976b). *Interactional Psychology and Personality*. Washington, DC: Hemisphere Publishing Corp.

Endler, N. and Okada, M. (1975). A multidimensional measure of trait anxiety: the S–R inventory of general trait anxiousness. *J. consult. clin. Psychol.*, **43**, 319–29.

Endler, N. and Shedletsky, R. (1973). Trait vs. state anxiety, authoritarianism and ego threat vs. physical threat. *Canad. J. behav. Sci.*, **5**, 347–61.

Epstein, S. (1979). The stability of behavior: on predicting most of the people much of the time. *J. pers. soc. Psychol.*, **37**, 1097–127.

Epstein, S. and Fenz, W. D. (1965). Steepness of approach and avoidance gradients in humans as a function of experience. *J. exp. Psychol.*, **70**, 1–25.

Ervin-Tripp, S. M. (1969). Sociolinguistics. *Adv. exp. soc. Psychol.*, **4**, 91–165.

Exline, R. (1971). Explorations in the process of person perception: visual interaction in relation to competition, sex, and need for affiliation. *J. Pers.*, **31**, 1–20.

Exline, R., Gray, D. and Schuette, D. (1965). Visual behavior in a dyad as affected by interview context and sex of respondent. *J. pers. soc. Psychol.*, **1**, 201–9.

Exline, R. and Winters, L. (1965). Affective relations and mutual glances in dyads. In S. Tomkins and C. Izard (eds.) *Affect, Cognition and Personality*. London: Tavistock.

Eysenck, H. J. (ed.) (1973). *Handbook of Abnormal Psychology*. London: Pitman Medical.

Eysenck, H. J. (1975). *The Eysenck Personality Questionnaire Manual*. London: Hodder and Stoughton.

Eysenck, H. J. (1976). *The Measurement of Personality*. Lancaster: MTP Press.

Eysenck, H. J., Arnold, W. and Meili, R. (1972). *Encyclopedia of Psychology*, vol. 1. Herder, West Germany: Search Press.

Eysenck, H. J. and Nias, D. (1978). *Sex, Violence and the Media*. London: Morris Temple Smith.

Eysenck, S. and Zuckerman, M. (1978). The relationship between sensation-seeking and Eysenck's dimensions of personality. *Brit. J. Psychol.*, **69**, 483–7.

Fairweather, G. W., Sanders, D. H., Maynard, H., Cressler, D. L. and Black, D. S. (1969). *Community Life for the Mentally Ill*. Chicago: Aldine.

Farrington, D. P. (1979). Experiments on deviance with special reference to dishonesty. *Adv. exp. soc. Psychol.*, **12**, 207–52.

Faucheux, C. and Moscovici, S. (1960). Etudes sur le créativité des groupes. II. Tache, structure des communications et réussite. *Bull. CERP*, **9**, 11–22.

414

Fenz, W. D. and Epstein, S. (1967). Gradients of physiological arousal as a function of an approaching jump. *Psychosom. Med.*, **29**, 33–51.

Ferguson, J. M. (1975). *Learning to Eat: Behavior Modification for Weight Control.* New York: Hawthorn Books.

Ferguson, N. (1977). Simultaneous speech, interruptions, and dominance. *Brit. J. soc. clin. Psychol.*, **16**, 295–302.

Festinger, L. (1957). *A Theory of Cognitive Dissonance.* Evanston, Ill.: Row, Peterson.

Festinger, L., Schachter, S. and Back, K. (1950). *Social Pressures in Informal Groups.* New York: Harper.

Fiedler, F. (1964). A contingency model of leadership effectiveness. *Adv. exp. soc. Psychol.*, *1*, 149–90.

Fiedler, F. (1967). *A Theory of Leadership Effectiveness.* New York: McGraw-Hill.

Fiedler, F. (1971). Validation and extension of the contingency model of leadership effectiveness: a review of empirical findings. *Psychol. Bull.*, **76**, 128–48.

Fiedler, F. (1977). What triggers the Person–Situation interaction in leadership? In D. Magnusson and N. Endler (eds.) *Personality at the Crossroads.* Hillsdale, NJ: Erlbaum.

Fiedler, F., Mitchell, R. and Triandis, H. C. (1971). The culture assimilator: an approach to cross-cultural training. *J. appl. Psychol.*, **55**, 95–102.

Firth, J. R. (1957). *Papers in Linguistics, 1934–1951.* London: Oxford University Press.

Fisek, M. A. and Ofshe, R. (1970). The process of status evolution. *Sociometry*, **33**, 327–46.

Fisher, A., Horsfall, J. and Morris, H. (1977). Sport personality assessment: a methodological re-examination. *Int. J. sport. Psychol.*, **8**, 92–102.

Fisher, J. and Nadler, A. (1976). Effect of donor resources on recipient self-esteem and self-help. *J. exp. soc. Psychol.*, **12**, 139–50.

Fishman, J. A. (1972). *The Sociology of Language.* Rowley, Mass.: Newbury House.

Fishman, J. A. and Greenfield, L. (1970). Situational measures of normative language views in relation to person, place and topic among Puerto Rican bilinguals. *Anthropos*, **65**, 602–18. (Reprinted in J. A. Fishman (ed.) *Advances in the Sociology of Language*, vol. 2. The Hague: Mouton (1972).)

Flanders, N. A. (1970). *Analyzing Teaching Behavior.* Reading, Mass.: Addison-Wesley.

Fleishman, E. A. and Harris, E. F. (1962). Patterns of leadership behavior related to employee grievances and turnover. *Personnel Psychol.*, **15**, 43–56.

Foa, U. G. (1961). Convergences in the analysis of the structure of interpersonal behavior. *Psychol. Rev.*, **68**, 341–53.

Fonagy, I. (1971). Double coding in speech. *Semiotica*, **3**, 189–222.

Forgas, J. P. (1976). The perception of social episodes: categorical and dimensional representations in two different social milieux. *J. pers. soc. Psychol.*, **34**, 199–209.

Forgas, J. P. (1978). Social episodes and social structure in an academic setting: the social environment of an intact group. *J. exp. soc. Psychol.*, **14**, 434–48.

Forgas, J. P. (1979). *Social Episodes: the Study of Interaction Routines.* New York and London: Academic Press.

Forgas, J. P., Argyle, M. and Ginsburg, G. J. (1980). Person perception as a function of the interaction episode: the fluctuating structure of an academic group. *J. soc. Psychol.*, **109**, 207–22.

415

References

Forgas, J. P. and Brown, L. (1977). Environmental and behavioral cues in the perception of social encounters: an exploratory study. *Amer. J. Psychol.*, **90**, 635–44.

Fox, R. (1977). The inherent rules of violence. In P. Collett (ed.) *Social Rules and Social Behaviour*. Oxford: Blackwell.

Fraisse, P. (1968). The experimental method. In J. Piaget, P. Fraisse and M. Reuchler (eds.) *Experimental Psychology: its Scope and Method*. London: Routledge and Kegan Paul.

Frederickson, N. (1972). Toward a taxonomy of situations. *Amer. Psychol.*, **27**, 114–23.

Freedman, B., Rosenthal, L., Donahoe, C., Schlundt, D. and McFall, R. (1978). A social-behavioral analysis of skill deficits in delinquent and nondelinquent adolescent boys. *J. consult. clin. Psychol.*, **46**, 1448–62.

Freeman, J. and Byrne, P. S. (1976). The assessment of vocational training for general practice. Reports from General Practice, No. 17. *J. Roy. Coll. gen. Pract.*

Freemon, B., Negrete, V. F., Davis, M. and Korsch, B. M. (1971). Gaps in doctor–patient communication: doctor–patient interaction analysis. *Pediat. Res.*, **5**, 298–311.

Friedman, P. (1968). 'The effects of modelling and role-playing on assertive behaviour'. Unpublished PhD thesis, University of Wisconsin.

Fries, C. C. (1952). *The Structure of English*. New York: Harcourt, Brace.

Frodi, A. (1977). Sexual arousal, situational restrictiveness and aggressive behavior. *J. res. Pers.*, **11**, 48–58.

Furnham, A. (1978). Conformity behaviour and persuasibility: a bibliography. *Percept. mot. Skills*, **47**, 1281–2.

Furnham, A. (1979). Assertiveness in three cultures: multidimensionality and cultural differences. *J. clin. Psychol.*, **35**, 522–7.

Furnham, A. (in press). Personality and activity preference. *Brit. J. soc. clin. Psychol.*

Furnham, A. and Bochner, S. (in press). Social difficulty in a foreign culture: An empirical analysis of culture shock. In S. Bochrer (ed.) *Cross-Cultural Interaction*. Oxford: Pergamon Press.

Furnham, A., Trevethan, R. and Gaskell, G. (in press). The relative contribution of verbal, vocal and visual channels to person perception: experiment and critique. *Semiotica*.

Gaertner, S. and Bickman, L. (1971). Effects of race on the elicitation of helping behavior: the wrong number technique. *J. pers. soc. Psychol.*, **20**, 218–22.

Galassi, J., Delo, J., Galassi, M. and Bastien, S. (1974). The college self-expression scale: a measure of assertiveness. *Behav. Ther.*, **5**, 165–71.

Galassi, J. and Galassi, M. (1979). A comparison of the factor structure of an assertion scale across sex and population. *Behav. Ther.*, **10**, 117–28.

Gambrill, E. (1977). *Behavior Modification*. San Francisco: Jossey-Bass.

Gambrill, E. and Richey, C. (1975). An assertion inventory for use in assessment and research. *Behav. Ther.*, **6**, 550–61.

Gans, H. (1961). *The Urban Villagers*. New York: Free Press.

Garfinkel, H. (1963). Trust and stable actions. In O. J. Harvey (ed.) *Motivation and Social Interaction*. New York: Ronald Press.

Garfinkel, H. (1967). *Studies in Ethnomethodology*, Englewood Cliffs, NJ: Prentice-Hall.

References

Garvey, C. (1977). *Play*. London: Fontana and Open Books.

Geen, R. S. (1968). Effects of frustration, attack and prior training in aggressiveness upon aggressive behavior. *J. pers. soc. Psychol.*, **9**, 316–21.

Geen, R. S. and O'Neal, E. (1969). Activation of cue-elicited aggression by general arousal. *J. pers. soc. Psychol.*, **11**, 289–92.

Gergen, K. (1973). Social psychology as history. *J. pers. soc. Psychol.*, **26**, 309–20.

Gilbert, A. (1972). Observation and recent correctional architecture. *New Environments for the encarcerated*. Washington: National Institute for Law Enforcement and Criminal Justice.

Giles, H. and Powesland, P. F. (1975). *Speech Style and Social Evaluation*. New York and London: Academic Press.

Giles, H., Taylor, D. M. and Bourhis, R. Y. (1973). Towards a theory of interpersonal accommodation through language: some Canadian data. *Language in Society*, **2**, 177–92.

Ginsburg, G. J. (1980). Epilogue. In M. Brenner (ed.) *The Structure of Action*. Oxford: Blackwell.

Glaser, B. G. and Strauss, A. L. (1967). Awareness contexts and social interaction. *Amer. sociol. Rev.*, **29**, 669–79.

Glaser, D. (1974). The classification of offenses and offenders. In D. Glaser (ed.) *Handbook of Criminology*. Chicago: Rand McNally.

Glass, D. and Singer, J. (1972). *Urban Stress*. New York and London: Academic Press.

Goffman, E. (1956). *The Presentation of Self in Everyday Life*. Edinburgh: Edinburgh University Press.

Goffman, E. (1959). *The Presentation of Self in Everyday Life*. New York: Anchor Books.

Goffman, E. (1961a). *Encounters*. Indianapolis: Bobbs-Merrill.

Goffman, E. (1961b). *Asylums*. New York: Arrow Books.

Goffman, E. (1961c). The neglected situation. *Amer. Anthrop.*, **66**, 133–6.

Goffman, E. (1963). *Behavior in Public Places*. Glencoe, Ill.: Free Press.

Goffman, E. (1967). *Interaction Ritual*. New York: Anchor/Doubleday.

Goffman, E. (1969). *Strategic Interaction*. Philadelphia: University of Pennsylvania Press.

Goffman, E. (1971). *Relations in Public*. London: Allen Lane, the Penguin Press.

Golding, S. (1975). Flies in the ointment: methodological problems in the analysis of variance due to persons and situations. *Psychol. Bull.*, **82**, 278–88.

Goldsmith, J. B. and McFall, R. M. (1975). Development and evaluation of an interpersonal skill-training program for psychiatric inpatients. *J. abnorm. Psychol.*, **84**, 51–8.

Goodstein, L. D. and Reinecker, V. M. (1974). Factors affecting self disclosure: a review of the literature. *Prog. exp. Pers. Res.*, **7**, 49–74.

Goody, E. N. (1978). Towards a theory of questions. In E. N. Goody (ed.) *Questions and Politeness*. Cambridge: Cambridge University Press.

Goranson, R. and King, D. (1970). 'Rioting and daily temperature: analysis of the US riots in 1967'. Unpublished paper, York University, Toronto. (Cited in Baron and Byrne (1977).)

Gordon, R. (1952). Interaction between attitudes and the definition of the situation in the expression of opinion. *Amer. sociol. Rev.*, **17**, 50–8.

417

Gorer, G. (1968). Man has no 'killer' instinct. In M. Montagu (ed.) *Man and Aggression*. London: Oxford University Press.

Gouaux, C. (1971). Induced affective states and interpersonal attraction. *J. pers. soc. Psychol.*, **20**, 37–43.

Gould, P. and White, R. (1974). *Mental Maps*. Harmondsworth: Penguin.

Gouldner, A. (1950). *Studies in Leadership*. New York: Harper.

Graham, J. A., Argyle, M., Clarke, D. D. and Maxwell, G. (in press). The salience, equivalence and sequential structure of behavioural elements in different social situations. *Semiotica*.

Graham, J. A., Argyle, M. and Furnham, A. (in press). The goal structure of situations. *Eur. J. soc. Psychol.*

Granownsky, S. and Krossner, W. J. (1970). Kindergarten teachers as models for children's speech. *J. exp. Educ.*, **38**, 23–8.

Greenwell, J. and Dengerink, H. (1973). The role of perceived versus actual attack in human physical aggression. *J. pers. soc. Psychol.*, **26**, 66–71.

Gregory, M. and Carroll, S. (1978). *Language and Situation*. London: Routledge and Kegan Paul.

Grice, H. P. (1975). Logic and conversation. In P. Cole and J. L. Morgan (eds.) *Syntax and Semantics, vol. 3, Speech Acts*. New York and London: Academic Press.

Griffitt, W. (1970). Environmental effects on interpersonal affective behavior: ambient effective temperature and attraction. *J. pers. soc. Psychol.*, **15**, 240–4.

Griffitt, W. and Veitch, R. (1971). Hot and crowded: influence of population density and temperature on interpersonal affective behavior. *J. pers. soc. Psychol.*, **17**, 92–8.

Gross, N., Mason, W. S. and McEachern, A. W. (1958). *Explorations in Role Analysis*. New York: Wiley.

Grusec, J. (1972). Demand characteristics of the modeling experiment: altruism as a function of gaze and aggression. *J. pers. soc. Psychol.*, **22**, 139–48.

Guetzkow, H. and Simon, H. A. (1955). The impact of certain communication nets upon organization and performance in task-oriented groups. *Manag. Sci.*, **1**, 233–50.

Gullahorn, J. (1952). Distance and friendship as factors in the gross interaction matrix. *Sociometry*, **15**, 123–34.

Hall, D. T. and Nougaim, K. E. (1968). An examination of Maslow's need hierarchy in an organizational setting. *Org. Behav. Hum. Perf.*, **3**, 1–11.

Hall, E. T. (1966). *The Hidden Dimension*. New York: Doubleday.

Hall, J. and Beil-Warner, D. (1978). Assertiveness of male Anglo- and Mexican-American college students. *J. soc. Psychol.*, **105**, 175–8.

Halliday, M. A. K. (1978). *Language as Social Semiotics*. London: Arnold.

Halliday, M. A. K., McIntosh, A. and Strevens, P. (1964). *The Linguistic Sciences and Language Teaching*. Harlow: Longman.

Hamblin, R. L. (1958). Leadership and crisis. *Sociometry*, **20**, 322–35.

Hamilton, P. and Copeman, A. (1970). The effect of alcohol and noise on components of a tracking and monitoring task. *Brit. J. Psychol.*, **61**, 149–56.

Hardin, G. (1956). Meaninglessness of the word protoplasm. *Scientific Monthly*, **82**, 112–20.

Harding, J. and Hoffgrefe, R. (1952). Attitudes of white department store employees towards Negro co-workers. *J. soc. Issues*, **8**(1), 18–28.

Hare, A. P. (1952). Interaction and consensus in different sized groups. *Amer. sociol. Rev.*, **17**, 261–7.

Harper, R. G., Wiens, A. N. and Matarazzo, J. D. (1978). *Nonverbal Communication: the State of the Art.* New York: Wiley.

Harré, R. (1972). The analysis of episodes. In J. Israel and H. Tajfel (eds.) *The Context of Social Psychology: a Critical Assessment.* New York and London: Academic Press.

Harré, R. (1976). Disclosing oneself in one's possessions. In R. Harré (ed.) *Life Sentences.* New York: Wiley.

Harré, R. (1977). Friendship as an accomplishment: an ethogenic approach to social relationships. In S. Duck (ed.) *Theory and Practice in Interpersonal Attraction.* New York and London: Academic Press.

Harré, R. and Secord, P. (1972). *The Explanation of Social Behaviour.* Oxford: Blackwell.

Harris, M. (1968). *The Rise of Anthropological Theory.* London: Routledge and Kegan Paul.

Harris, M. (1975). *Cows, Pigs, Wars and Witches.* London: Hutchinson.

Harteshorne, H. and May, M. A. (1928). *Studies in the Nature of Character.* New York: Macmillan.

Harteshorne, H. and May, M. A. (1932). *Studies in the Organization of Character.* New York: Macmillan.

Harvey, O. J., Hunt, D. E. and Schroder, H. M. (1961). *Conceptual Systems and Personality Organization.* Stanford: Stanford University Press.

Hawkins, P. (1969). Social class, the nominal group and reference. *Lang. Speech*, **12**, 125–35.

Haythorn, W., Couch, A., Haefner, D., Langham, P. and Carter, L. (1956). The effects of varying combinations of authoritarian and equalitarian leaders and followers. *J. abnorm. soc. Psychol.*, **53**, 210–19.

Heider, F. (1958). *The Psychology of Interpersonal Relations.* New York: Wiley.

Hemphill, J. K. (1950). Relations between the size of the group and the behavior of 'superior' leaders. *J. soc. Psychol.*, **32**, 11–22.

Hemphill, J. K. (1960). *Dimensions of Executive Positions.* Bureau of Business Research Monograph 98. Columbo: Ohio State University.

Henderson, D. (1970). Social class differences in form class usage among 5-year-old children. In W. Brandes and D. Henderson (eds.) *Social Class, Language and Communication.* London: Routledge and Kegan Paul.

Hendrick, C. and Brown, S. (1971). Introversion, extroversion and interpersonal attraction. *J. pers. soc. Psychol.*, **20**, 31–6.

Henley, N. (1973). Status and sex: some touching observations. *Bull. Psychonom. Soc.*, **2**, 91–3.

Herbst, P. G. (1952). The measurement of family relationships. *Hum. Relat.*, **5**, 3–35.

Hersen, M. and Bellack, A. S. (1976). Social skills training for chronic psychiatric patients: rationale, research findings, and future directions. *Comprehensive Psychiatry*, **17**, 559–80.

Hersen, M. and Bellack, A. S. (1977). Assessment of social skills. In A. Ciminero, K. Calhoun and H. Adams (eds.) *Handbook of Behavioral Assessment.* New York: Wiley.

Hersen, M., Eisler, R. and Miller, P. (1973). Development of assertive responses:

clinical measurement and research considerations. *Behav. Res. Ther.*, 11, 505–21.

Hess, R. D. and Shipman, V. C. (1965). Early experience and the socialization of cognitive modes in children. *Child Develpm.*, 36, 800–86.

Highlen, P. (1976). Effects of social modeling and cognitive structuring strategies on affective self-disclosure of single, undergraduate males. *Diss. Abstr. Int.*, 36, 5823A.

Highlen, P. and Gillis, S. (1978). Effects of situational factors, sex and attitude on affective self-disclosure and anxiety. *J. counsel. Psychol.*, 25, 270–6.

Himelstein, P. and Kimbrough, W., Jr (1963). A study of self disclosure in the classroom. *J. Psychol.*, 55, 437–40.

Hinton, J. (1975). *Dying*. Harmondsworth: Penguin.

Hodges, W. (1968). Effects of ego threat and threat of pain on state anxiety. *J. pers. soc. Psychol.*, 8, 364–72.

Hodges, W. and Felling, J. (1970). Types of stressful situations and their relation to trait anxiety and sex. *J. consult. clin. Psychol.*, 34, 333–7.

Hoffman, L. R. (1965). Group problem-solving. *Adv. exp. soc. Psychol.*, 2, 99–132.

Holahan, C. and Saegert, S. (1973). Behavioral and attitudinal effects of large scale variation in the physical environment of psychiatric wards. *J. abnorm. Psychol.*, 82, 454–62.

Holland, J. (1966) *The Psychology of Occupational Choice: A Theory of Personality Types and Model Environments*. Waltham, Mass.: Blaisdell.

Hollander, E. (1964). *Leaders, Groups and Influence*. London: Oxford University Press.

Hollander, E. (1978). *Leadership Dynamics*. New York: Free Press.

Hollandsworth, J., Glazeski, R. and Dressel, M. (1978). Use of social skills training in the treatment of extreme anxiety and deficient verbal skills in the job interview setting. *J. appl. Behav. Anal.*, 11, 259–69.

Holmes, D. S. and Houston, B. K. (1974). Effectiveness of situation redefinition and affective isolation in coping with stress. *J. pers. soc. Psychol.*, 29, 212–18.

Holzman, M. and Forman, V. P. (1966). A multidimensional content-analysis of therapeutic technique in psychotherapy with schizophrenic patients. *Psychol. Bull.*, 66, 263–81.

Homans, G. C. (1951). *The Human Group*. London and New York: Routledge and Kegan Paul, Harcourt Brace Jovanovich.

Homans, G. C. (1961). *Social Behavior: its Elementary Forms*. New York: Harcourt, Brace and World.

Homans, G. C. and Schneider, D. (1955). *Marriage, Authority and Final Causes*. Glencoe, Ill.: Free Press.

Home Office (1973). *Shoplifting, and Thefts by Shop Staff*. London: HMSO.

Horner, M. (1970). Femininity and successful achievement: a basic inconsistency. In J. Bardwick *et al.* (eds.) *Feminine Personality and Conflict*. Monterey, Calif.: Brooks/Cole.

Horowitz, M., Duff, D. and Stratton, L. (1969). Personal space and the body-buffer zone. *Arch. gen. Psychiat.*, 11, 651–6.

Houston, B., Bloom, L., Burish, T. and Cummings. E. (1978). Positive evaluation of stressful experiences. *J. Pers.*, 46, 205–14.

Hovland, C. I. and Sherif, M. (1952). Judgmental phenomena and scales of attitude measurement: item displacement in Thurstone scales. *J. abnorm. soc. Psychol.*, **47**, 822–32.

Hudson, L. (1968). *Frames of Mind*. London/Harmondsworth: Methuen/Penguin.

Huesmann, L. R. and Levinger, G. (1976). Incremental exchange theory: a formal model for progression in dyadic social interaction. *Adv. exp. soc. Psychol.*, **9**, 191–229.

Humphreys, M. (1974). Relating wind, rain and temperature to teachers' reports of young children's behaviour. In D. Canter and T. Lee (eds.) *Psychology and the Built Environment*. London: Architectural Press.

Hurwitz, J., Zander, A. and Hymovitch, B. (1960). Some effects of power on the relation among group members. In D. Cartwright and A. Zander (eds.) *Group Dynamics: Research and Theory*, 2nd edn. New York: Harper and Row.

Hutt, C. and Vaizey, M. (1966). Differential effects of group density on social behaviour. *Nature*, **209**, 1371–2.

Hymes, D. (1972). Models of the interaction of language and social life. In J. J. Gumperz and D. Hymes (eds.). *Directions in Sociolinguistics: the Ethnography of Communication*. New York: Holt, Rinehart and Winston.

Hymes, D. (1977). *Foundations in Sociolinguistics*. London: Tavistock.

Ickes, W. J. and Kidd, R. F. (1976). An attributional analysis of helping behavior. In J. H. Harvey, W. J. Ickes and R. F. Kidd (eds.) *New Directions in Attribution Theory*. Hillsdale, NJ: Erlbaum.

Israel, J. and Tajfel, H. (eds.) (1972). *The Context of Social Psychology*. New York and London: Academic Press.

Ittelson, W. H., Proshansky, H. M. and Rivlin, L. G. (1970). The environmental psychology of the psychiatric ward. In H. M. Proshansky *et al.* (eds.) *Environmental Psychology*. New York: Holt, Rinehart and Winston.

Ittelson, W., Proshansky, H. M., Rivlin, L. and Winkel, G. (1974). *An Introduction to Environmental Psychology*. New York: Holt, Rinehart and Winston.

Jackson, J. (1966). A conceptual and measurement model for norms and roles. *Pacif. sociol. Rev.*, **6**(9), 35–47.

Jacobson, N. S. and Martin, B. (1976). Behavioral marriage therapy: current status. *Psychol. Bull.*, **83**, 540–56.

Janisse, M. and Palys, T. (1976). Frequency and intensity of anxiety in university students. *J. pers. Assess.*, **40**, 502–15.

Jaspars, J. M. F. (1966). *On Social Perception*. Leiden: University of Leiden Press.

Jeger, A. and Goldfried, M. (1976). A comparison of situation tests of speech anxiety. *Behav. Ther.*, **7**, 252–5.

Johnson, H. M. (1961). *Sociology: a Systematic Introduction*. London: Routledge and Kegan Paul.

Joiner, D. (1976). Social ritual and architectural space. In H. M. Proshansky, W. H. Ittelson and L. G. Rivlin (eds.) *Environmental Psychology*, 2nd edn. New York: Holt, Rinehart and Winston.

Jones, E. E. and Davis, K. (1965). From acts to dispositions: the attribution process in person perception. *Adv. exp. soc. Psychol.*, **2**, 219–66.

Jones, E. E. and Gerard, H. B. (1967). *Foundations of Social Psychology*. New York: Wiley.

Jones, E. E. and Gordon, E. (1972). Timing of self disclosure and its effects on personal attraction. *J. pers. soc. Psychol.*, **24**, 358–65.

Jones, E. E. and Nisbett, R. E. (1972). The actor and the observer: divergent perceptions of the causes of behavior. In E. E. Jones, D. E. Kanouse, H. H. Kelley, R. E. Nisbett, S. Valins and B. Weiner (eds.) *Attribution: Perceiving the Causes of Behavior*. Morristown, NJ: General Learning Press.

Jones, F. E. and Lambert, W. E. (1967). Some situational influences on attitudes towards immigrants. *Brit. J. Sociol.*, **8**, 408–24.

Jones, L. E. and Young, F. W. (1973). Structure as a social environment–longitudinal individual differences scaling of an intact group. *J. pers. soc. Psychol.*, **24**, 108–21.

Joos, M. (1962). The five clocks. *Int. J. Amer. Ling.*, **28**(2), part V.

Jourard, S. (1964). *The Transparent Self*. New York: Van Nostrand.

Jourard, S. (1971). *Self Disclosure: an Experimental Analysis of the Transparent Self*. New York: Wiley.

Jourard, S. and Friedman, R. (1970). Experimenter–subject 'distance' and self disclosure. *J. pers. soc. Psychol.*, **15**, 278–82.

Jurich, A. and Jurich, J. (1978). Factor analysis of expressions of anxiety. *Psychol. Rep.*, **42**, 1203–10.

Kahn, R. L., Wolfe, D. M., Quinn, R. P. and Snoek, H. D. (1964). *Organizational Stress*. New York: Wiley.

Kasmar, J. (1970). The development of a usable lexicon of environmental descriptors. *Envir. Behav.*, **2**, 153–69.

Kazdin, A. E. (1977). *The Token Economy*. New York: Plenum.

Kelley, H. H. (1969). Attribution theory in social psychology. In D. Levine (ed.) *Nebraska Symposium of Motivation*, vol. 15. Lincoln: University of Nebraska Press.

Kelley, H. H. (1972). Attributions in social interaction. In E. E. Jones *et al.* (eds.) *Attribution: Perceiving the causes of behavior*. Morristown, NJ: General Learning Press.

Kelley, H. H. and Thibaut, J. W. (1969). Group problem-solving. In G. Lindzey and E. Aronson (eds.) *The Handbook of Social Psychology*, vol. 4. Reading, Mass.: Addison-Wesley.

Kelly, G. A. (1955). *The Psychology of Personal Constructs*, 2 vols. New York: Norton.

Kelvin, P. (1969). *The Bases of Social Behaviour*. New York: Holt, Rinehart and Winston.

Kelvin, P. (1973). A social-psychological examination of privacy. *Brit. J. soc. clin. Psychol.*, **12**, 248–61.

Kendon, A. (1967). Some functions of gaze direction in social interaction. *Acta Psychol.*, **26**, 22–63.

Kendon, A. (1976). Some functions of the face in a kissing round. *Semiotica*, **15**, 299–334.

Kendon, A. and Ferber, A. (1973). A description of some human greetings. In R. P. Michael and J. H. Crook (eds.) *Comparative Ethology and Behaviour of Primates*. New York and London: Academic Press.

Kennedy, D. and Highlands, D. (1964). 'Buildings and organizational effectiveness'. Unpublished paper given at 63rd meeting of American Anthropological Association, Detroit, Michigan. (Cited in Ittelson *et al.*, 1970.)

Kent, G. G., Davis, J. D. and Shapiro, D. A. (1978). Resources required in the construction and reconstruction of conversation. *J. pers. soc. Psychol.*, **36**, 13–22.

Kerckhoff, A. (1974). The social context of interpersonal attraction. In T. Huston (ed.). *Foundations of Interpersonal Attraction*. New York and London: Academic Press.

Kinzel, A. (1970). Body-buffer zones in violent prisoners. *Amer. J. Psychiat.*, **127**, 59–64.

Kirchner, W. K. and Dunnette, M. D. (1957). Identifying the critical factors in successful salesmanship. *Personnel*, **34**, 54–9.

Kleck, R. and Rubenstein, C. (1975). Physical attractiveness, perceived attitude similarity and interpersonal attraction in an opposite-sex encounter. *J. pers. soc. Psychol.*, **31**, 107–14.

Klein, J. (1965). *Samples from English Cultures* (2 vols.). London: Routledge and Kegan Paul.

Kluckholm, C. (1944). *Navaho Witchcraft*. Papers of the Peabody Museum of American Archeology and Ethnology, Harvard University, vol. 22 no. 2.

Knapp, T. J., Crosby, H. W. and O'Boyle, M. W. (1978). Using the natural environment in counseling for therapeutic change: a case study. *Psychol. Rep.*, **42**, 1048–50.

Konečni, V. (1975). The mediation of aggressive behaviour: arousal level versus anger and cognitive labelling. *J. pers. soc. Psychol.*, **32**, 706–12.

Korsch, B. M., Freeman, D. and Negrete, V. F. (1971). Practical implications of doctor–patient interaction: analysis for paediatric practice. *Amer. J. Dis. Child.*, **121**, 110–14.

Korsch, B. M. and Nygrete, V. F. (1972). Doctor–patient communication. *Sci. Amer.*, Aug., 66–73.

Krause, M. (1970). Use of social situations for research purposes. *Amer. Psychol.*, **25**, 748–53.

Krauskopf, C. (1978). Comments on Endler and Magnusson's attempt to redefine personality. *Psychol. Bull.*, **85**, 280–3.

Krauss, R. M. and Weinheimer, S. (1964). Changes in reference phrases as a function of frequency of use in social interaction: a preliminary study. *Psychonom. Sci.*, **1**, 113–14.

Kroger, R. O. (1967). The effects of role demands and test-cue properties upon personality test performance. *J. consult, Psychol.*, **31**, 304–12.

Labov, W. (1966). *The Social Stratification of New York City*. Washington, DC: Center for Applied Linguistics.

Labov, W. (1972a). *Sociolinguistic Patterns, vol. 4*, Conduct and Communication. Philadelphia: University of Pennsylvania Press.

Labov, W. (1972b) The logic of nonstandard English. In P. Giglioli (ed.) *Language and Social Context*. Harmondsworth: Penguin.

Labov, W., Cohen, P., Robins, C. and Lewis, J. (1968). *A Study of the Non-Standard English of Negro and Puerto Rican speakers in New York City*, vols. 1 and 2. Final Report, Cooperative Research Project 3288. Washington DC: Office of Health, Education and Welfare.

La Gaipa, J. (1977). Testing a multidimensional approach to friendship. In S. Duck (ed.) *Theory and Practice in Interpersonal Attraction*. New York and London: Academic Press.

Lakoff, R. (1972). Language in context. *Language*, **48**, 907–27.

Landfield, A. W. and Nawas, M. M. (1964). Psychotherapeutic improvement as a function of communication and adoption of therapist's values. *J. counsel. Psychol.*, **11**, 336–41.

Langer, E. J. (1975). The illusion of control. *J. pers. soc. Psychol.*, **32**, 311–28.

Latané, B. and Dabbs, J. (1975). Sex, group size and helping in three cities. *Sociometry*, **38**, 180–94.

Latané, B. and Darley, J. (1968). Group inhibition of bystander intervention in emergencies. *J. pers. soc. Psychol.*, **10**, 215–21.

Latané, B. and Darley, J. (1970). *The Unresponsive Bystander: Why Doesn't he Help?* New York: Meredith Corporation.

Latané, B. and Rodin, J. (1969). A lady in distress: inhibiting effects of friends and strangers on bystander intervention. *J. exp. soc. Psychol.*, **5**, 189–202.

Lauer, R. and Handel, W. (1977). *Social Psychology: the Theory and Application of Symbolic Interactionism*. Boston, Mass.: Houghton Mifflin.

Laumann, F. and House, J. (1970). Living room style and social attributes: the patterning of material artifacts in a modern urban community. *Sociol. Soc. Res.*, **54**, 321–42.

Lawton, D. (1968). *Social Class, Language and Education*. London: Routledge and Kegan Paul.

Lazarus, A. (1963). The results of behavior therapy in 126 cases of severe neurosis. *Behav. Ther. Res.*, **1**, 65–78.

Lazarus, A. (1971*a*). *Behavior Therapy and Beyond*. New York: McGraw-Hill.

Lazarus, R. (1971*b*). *Personality*. Englewood Cliffs, NJ: Prentice-Hall.

Lazarus, R. and Laurier, R. (1978). Stress-related transactions between person and environment. In L. Pervin and M. Lewis (eds.) *Perspectives in Interactional Psychology*. New York: Plenum.

Leach, E. (1966). Anthropological aspects of language: animal categories and verbal abuse. In E. H. Lenneberg (ed.) *New Directions in the Study of Language*. Cambridge, Mass.: MIT Press.

Lee, T. (1957). On the relation between the school journey and social and emotional adjustment in rural infant children. *Brit. J. educ. Psychol.*, **27**, 101–14.

Lee, T. (1976). *Psychology and the Environment*. London: Methuen.

Leech, G. (1974). *Semantics*. Harmondsworth: Penguin.

Lefebvre, L. (1975). Encoding and decoding of ingratiation in modes of smiling and gaze. *Brit. J. soc. clin. Psychol.*, **14**, 33–42.

Lemaine, G. (1966). Inégalité, comparison, et incomparabilité: esquisse d'une théorié de l'originalité sociale. *Bull. Psychol.*, **20**, 1–9.

Lévi-Strauss, C. (1969). *The Elementary Structures of Kinship*, trans. J. H. Bell *et al.* Boston, Mass.: Beacon Press. (Originally published in 1949.)

Levine, M. and Sutton-Smith, B. (1973). Effects of age, sex and task on visual behavior during dyadic interaction. *Developm. Psychol.*, **9**, 400–5.

Levinger, G. (1974). A three-level approach to attraction: toward an understanding of pair relatedness. In T. Huston (ed.) *Foundations of Interpersonal Attraction*. New York and London: Academic Press.

Lewin, K. (1935). *A Dynamic Theory of Personality*. New York: McGraw-Hill.

Lewis, J., Baddeley, A., Bonham, K. and Lovett, D. (1970). Traffic pollution and mental efficiency. *Nature*, **225**, 95–7.

Ley, P. (1977). Psychological studies of doctor–patient communication. In S. Rachman (ed.) *Contributions to Medical Psychology*, vol. 1. Oxford: Pergamon Press.

Lieberman, M. A., Yalom, I. D. and Miles, M. B. (1973). *Encounter Groups: First Facts*. New York: Basic Books.

References

Liebman, M. (1970). The effects of sex and role norms on personal space. *Envir. Behav.*, **2**, 208–46.

Linde, C. and Labov, W. (1975). Spatial networks as a site for the study of language and thought. *Language*, **51**, 924–39.

Lindenfeld, J. (1969). The social conditions of syntactic variation in French. *Amer. Anthrop.*, **71**, 890–8.

Llewellyn, K. (1962). *Jurisprudence.* Chicago: Chicago University Press.

Lockhart, K. L., Abrahams, B. and Oskerson, D. N. (1977). Children's understanding of uniformity in the environment. *Child Developm.*, **48**, 1521–31.

Lundberg, U., Bratfisch, O. and Ekman, G. (1972). Emotional involvement and subjective distance: a summary of investigations. *J. soc. Psychol.*, **87**, 169–77.

Lyman, S. M. and Scott, M. B. (1970). *A Sociology of the Absurd.* New York: Appleton-Century-Crofts.

Lynch, K. (1960). *The Image of the City.* Cambridge, Mass.: MIT Press.

Lyons, J. (1969). *Introduction to Theoretical Linguistics.* Cambridge: Cambridge University Press.

Lyons, J. (1977). *Semantics* (2 vols.). Cambridge: Cambridge University Press.

McAdoo, W. (1969). 'The effects of success, mild failure on A-state subjects who differ in A-trait.' Unpublished PhD, Florida State University.

McAdoo, W. (1972). 'Effects of psychological stress on state anxiety for subjects who differ in trait anxiety'. Paper given at Southeastern Psychological Association, Atlanta.

Macaulay, R. (1970). A skill for charity. In J. Macaulay and L. Berkowitz (eds.). *Altruism and Helping Behavior: Social Psychological Studies of some Antecedents and Consequences.* New York and London: Academic Press.

McClelland, D. C., Atkinson, J. W. Clark, R. A. and Lowell, E. L. (1953). *The Achievement Motive.* New York: Appleton-Century-Crofts.

McCloskey, J. (1978). 'The interactional approach to self disclosure'. Unpublished paper given at British Psychological Society Conference, Cardiff.

McDavid, J. (1959). Personality vs. situational determinants of conformity. *J. abnorm. soc. Psychol.*, **58**, 241–6.

McFall, R. and Twentyman, C. (1973). Four experiments on the relative contributions of rehearsal, modeling and coaching to assertion training. *J. abnorm. Psychol.*, **81**, 199–218.

McGovern, R., Tinsley, D., Liss-Levinson, N., Laventive, R. and Britton, G. (1975). Assertion training for job interviews. *Counsel. Psychol.*, **5**, 65–8.

McGrew, P. (1970). Social and spatial density effects on spacing behaviour in preschool children. *J. child Psychol. Psychiat.*, **11**, 197–205.

McGrew, W. C. (1972). *An Ethological Study of Children's Behaviour.* New York and London: Academic Press.

McGuire, W. (1968). Personality and susceptibility to social influence. In E. Borgatta and W. Lambert (eds.) *Handbook of Personality Theory and Research.* Chicago: Rand McNally.

McHugh, P. (1968). *Defining the Situation.* Indianapolis: Bobbs-Merrill.

McPhail, P. (1967). The development of social skill in adolescents. Unpublished paper given to British Psychological Society (Cited in Argyle (1969).)

McPhail, P., Middleton, D. and Ingram, D. (1978). *Moral Education in the Middle Years.* Harlow: Longman.

Magnusson, D. (1971). An analysis of situational dimensions. *Percept. mot. Skills*, **32**, 851–67.

Magnusson, D. and Ekehammar, B. (1973). An analysis of situational dimensions: a replication. *Multi. Behav. Res.*, **8**, 331–9.

Magnusson, D. and Ekehammar, B. (1975). Anxiety profiles based on both situational and response factors. *Multi. Behav. Res.*, **10**, 27–43.

Mahl, G. F. (1968). Gestures and body movements in interviews. *Res. Psychother.*, **3**, 295–346.

Malinowski, B. (1944). *A Scientific Theory of Culture*. Chapel Hill, NC: University of Carolina Press.

Mandelbrot, B. (1954). Structure formelle des textes et communication. *Word*, **10**, 1–27.

Mann, J. W. (1963). Rivals of different rank. *J. soc. Psychol.*, **61**, 11–28.

Mann, L. (1969). Queue culture: the waiting line as a social system. *Amer. J. Sociol.*, **75**, 340–54.

Mann, R. D. (1959). A review of the relationships between personality and performance in small groups. *Psychol. Bull.*, **56**, 241–70.

Mann, R. D., Gibbard, G. S. and Hartman, J. J. (1967). *Interpersonal Styles and Group Development*. New York: Wiley.

Mannheim, H. and Wilkins, L. T. (1955). *Prediction Methods in Relation to Borstal Training*. London: HMSO.

Mariotto, M. J. (1978). Interaction of person and situation effects for chronic mental patients: a two-year follow-up. *J. abnorm. Psychol.*, **87**, 676–9.

Mariotto, M. J. and Paul, G. L. (1975). Persons versus situations in the real-life functioning of chronically institutionalised mental patients. *J. abnorm. Psychol.*, **84**, 483–93.

Marsden, G. (1971). Content-analysis studies of psychotherapy: 1954 through 1968. In A. E. Bergin and S. L. Garfield (eds.) *Psychotherapy and Behavior Change: an Empirical Analysis*. New York: Wiley.

Marsh, P., Rosser, E. and Harré, R. (1978). *The Rules of Disorder*. London: Routledge and Kegan Paul.

Marshall, W. C., Stoian, M. and Andrews, W. R. (1977). Social skills training and self-administered desensitization in the reduction of public speaking anxiety. *Behav. Res. Ther.*, **15**, 115–17.

Maslow, A. H. (1954). *Motivation and Work*. New York: Harper.

Maslow, A. H. and Mintz, N. (1956). Effects of esthetic surroundings: I. Initial effects of three esthetic conditions upon perceiving 'energy' and 'well-being' in faces. *J. Psychol.*, **41**, 247–54.

Mayhew, P., Clarke, R. V. G., Sturman, A. and Hough, J. M. (1976). Crime as opportunity. Home Office Research Study No. 34. London: HMSO.

Mead, G. H. (1934). *Mind, Self and Society*. Chicago: Chicago University Press.

Mehrabian, A. (1972). *Nonverbal Communication*. Chicago: Aldine-Atherton.

Mehrabian, A. (1978). Characteristic individual reactions to preferred and unpreferred environments. *J. Pers.*, **46**, 717–31.

Mehrabian, A. and Diamond, S. (1971). Effects of furniture arrangement, props and personality in social interaction. *J. pers. soc. Psychol.*, **20**, 18–30.

Mehrabian, A. and Russell, J. A. (1974). *An Approach to Environmental Psychology*. Cambridge, Mass.: MIT Press.

Meichenbaum, D. (1977). *Cognitive-Behavior Modification*. New York: Plenum.

Meier, R. (1962). *A Communications Theory of Urban Growth*. Cambridge, Mass.: MIT Press.

Mellstrom, M., Zuckerman, M. and Cicala, G. (1978). General versus specific traits in the assessment of anxiety. *J. consult. clin. Psychol.*, **46**, 423–31.

Melville, J. (1977). *Phobias and Obsessions: their Understanding and Treatment*. London: Allen and Unwin.

Mendeleev, D. F. (1879). *La loi périodique des éléments chimiques*. Paris: Renau, Maulde and Cock.

Merton, R. K. (1949). *Social Theory and Social Structure*. Glencoe, Ill.: Free Press.

Milgram, S. (1970). The experience of living in cities. *Science*, **167**, 1461–8.

Milgram, S. (1974). *Obedience to Authority*. New York: Harper and Row.

Miller, N. E. (1944). Experimental studies of conflict. In J. McV. Hunt (ed.) *Personality and the Behavior Disorders*, 2 vols. New York: Ronald Press.

Miller, N. E. and Dollard, J. (1945). *Social Learning and Imitation*. London: Kegan, Paul, Trench and Trubner.

Miller, G. H., Galanter, E. and Pribram, K. H. (1960). *Plans and the Structure of Behavior*. New York: Holt.

Minard, R. D. (1952). Race relationships in the Pocahontas coal field. *J. soc. Issues*, **8**(1), 29–44.

Mintz, J., Luborsky, L. and Auerbach, A. H. (1971). Dimensions of psychotherapy: a factor-analytic study of ratings of psychotherapy sessions. *J. consult. Psychol.*, **36**, 106–20.

Mintz, N. (1956). Effects of esthetic surroundings. *J. Psychol.*, **41**, 459–66.

Mischel, W. (1968). *Personality and Assessment*. New York: Wiley.

Mitchell, J. (1957). Cons, square Johns, and rehabilitation. In B. J. Biddle and E. J. Thomas (eds.) *Role Theory: Concepts and Research*. New York: Wiley.

Mitchell, T. R., Larson, J. R. and Green, S. G. (1977). Leader behavior, situational moderators, and group performance: an attributional analysis. *Org. Behav. Hum. Perf.*, **18**, 254–68.

Mixon, D. (1972). Instead of deception. *J. Theory soc. Behav.*, **2**, 145–77.

Moerk, E. L. (1977). *Pragmatic and Semantic Aspects of Early Language Development*. Baltimore: University Park Press.

Moffett, J. (1968). *Teaching the Universe of Discourse*. Boston, Mass.: Houghton Mifflin.

Mohanna, A. I. and Argyle, M. (1960). A cross-cultural study of structured groups with unpopular central members. *J. abnorm. soc. Psychol.*, **60**, 139–40.

Moos, R. H. (1968). Situational analysis of a therapeutic community milieu. *J. abnorm. Psychol.*, **73**, 49–61.

Moos, R. H. (1969). Sources of variance in response to questionnaires and in behavior. *J. abnorm. Psychol.*, **74**, 405–12.

Moos, R. H. (1970). Differential effects of psychiatric ward settings on patient change. *J. nerv. ment. Dis.*, **151**, 316–21.

Moos, R. H. (1973a). Conceptualizations of human environments. *Amer. Psychol.*, **28**, 652–65.

Moos, R. H. (1973b). *Military Company Environment Scale Manual*. Palo Alto, Calif.: Stanford University Press.

Moos, R. H. (1974). *Ward Atmosphere Scale Manual*. Palo Alto, Calif.: Consulting Psychologists Press.

Moos, R. (1976). *The Human Context: Environmental Determinants of Behavior*. New York: Wiley.

Moos, R. H. (1979). 'The social climate scales: an overview'. Unpublished paper, Dept of Psychiatry, Stanford University.

Moos, R. H. and Schwartz, J. (1972). Treatment environment and treatment outcome. *J. nerv. ment. Dis.*, **154**, 264–75.

Morelli, G. and Friedman, B. (1978). Cognitive correlates of multidimensional trait anxiety. *Psychol. Rep.*, **42**, 611–14.

Morley, I. E. and Stephenson, G. M. (1977). *The Social Psychology of Bargaining*. London: Allen and Unwin.

Morris, D., Collett, P., Marsh, P. and O'Shaugnessy, M. (1979). *Gestures: their Origins and Distribution*. London: Cape.

Morsbach, H. (1973). 'Non-verbal communication in Japan'. Unpublished paper, Dept of Psychology, Glasgow University.

Morsbach, H. (1977). The psychological importance of ritualised gift exchange in modern Japan. *Ann. N.Y. Acad. Sci.*, **293**, 98–113.

Moscovici, S. (1967). Communication processes and the properties of language. *Adv. exp. soc. Psychol.*, **3**, 226–70.

Moscovici, S. (1976). *Social Influence and Social Change*. New York and London: Academic Press.

Moscovici, S. and Lage, E. (1976). Studies in social influence. III. Majority vs. minority influence in a group. *Eur. J. soc. Psychol.*, **6**, 149–74.

Mosel, J. N. and Cozan, L. W. (1952). The accuracy of application blank work histories. *J. appl. Psychol.*, **36**, 365–9.

Moss, M. and Page, R. (1972). Reinforcement and helping behavior. *J. appl. soc. Psychol.*, **2**, 360–71.

Mulder, M. (1960). Communication structure, decision structure and group performance. *Sociometry*, **23**, 1–14.

Murray, H. A. (1938). *Explorations in Personality*. London: Oxford University Press.

Nahemow, L. and Lawton, M. (1975). Similarity and propinquity in friendship formation. *J. pers. soc. Psychol.*, **32**, 205–13.

Nelsen, E. A., Grinder, R. E. and Mutterer, M. L. (1969). Sources of variance in behavioral measures of honesty in temptation situations. *Develpm. Psychol.*, **1**, 265–79.

Neulinger, J. (1978). *The Psychology of Leisure*, 3rd edn. Springfield, Ill.: Thomas.

Neulinger, J. and Raps, C. (1972). Leisure attitudes of an intellectual elite. *J. Leisure Res.*, **4**, 196–207.

Newman, O. (1972). *Defensible Space*. London: Architectural Press.

Newson, J. and Newson, E. (1970). *Four Years Old in an Urban Community*. Harmondsworth: Penguin.

Newtson, D. (1973). Attribution and the unit of perception of ongoing behavior. *J. pers. soc. Psychol.*, **28**, 28–38.

Newtson, D. and Engquist, G. (1976). The perceptual organisation of ongoing behavior. *J. exp. soc. Psychol.*, **12**, 436–50.

Newtson, D., Engquist, G. and Bois, J. (1977). The objective basis of behavior units. *J. pers. soc. Psychol.*, **35**, 847–62.

Ninio, A. and Bruner, J. (1978). The achievement and antecedents of labelling. *J. child Lang.*, **5**, 1–15.

Nisbett, R. E., Caputo, C., Legart, P. and Marecel, J. (1973). Behavior as seen by the actor and as seen by the observer. *J. pers. soc. Psychol.*, **27**, 154–64.

Nisbett, R. E. and Wilson, T. D. (1977). Telling more than we know: verbal reports on mental processes. *Psychol. Rev.*, **84**, 231–59.

Nitsche, R. and Green, A. (1977). *Situational Exercises in Cross-cultural Awareness.* Columbus, Ohio: C. Merrill.

Noesjirwan, J. (1978). A rule-based analysis of cultural differences in social behaviour: Indonesia and Australia. *Int. J. Psychol.*, **13**, 305–16.

Norman, R. and Scott, W. (1952). Colour and affect: a review and semantic evaluation. *J. gen. Psychol.*, **46**, 185–223.

Norman, W. T. (1963). Toward an adequate taxonomy of personality attributes: replicated factor structure in peer nomination personality ratings. *J. abnorm. soc. Psychol.*, **66**, 574–83.

Nuthall, G. A. (1968). An experimental comparison of alternative strategies for teaching concepts. *Amer. educ. Res. J.*, **5**, 561–84.

Oberg, K. (1960). Culture shock: adjustment to new cultural environments. *Pract. Anthrop.*, **7**, 177–82.

O'Brien, G. E. and Plooij, D. (1977). Comparison of programmed and prose culture training upon attitudes and knowledge. *J. appl. Psychol.*, **62**, 499–505.

Olberz, P. and Steiner, I. (1969). Order of disclosure and the attribution of dispositional characteristics. *J. soc. Psychol.*, **79**, 287–8.

Olweus, D. (1975). ' "Modern" interactionism in personality psychology and the analysis of variance components approach, a critical examination'. Unpublished paper given at Symposium on Interactional Psychology, Stockholm.

Olweus, D. (1977). 'Modern' interactionism in personality psychology and the analysis of variance components approach. In D. Magnusson and N. Endler (eds.) *Personality at the Crossroads.* Hillsdale, NJ: Erlbaum.

Opinion Research Corporation Study (1962). In J. Neulinger (ed.) *The Psychology of Leisure.* Springfield, Ill.: Thomas.

Orne, M. T. (1962). On the social psychology of the psychological experiment: with particular reference to demand characteristics and their implications. *Amer. Psychol.*, **17**, 776–83.

Orvis, B. R., Kelley, H. H. and Butler, D. (1976). Attributional conflict in young couples. In J. H. Harvey, W. J. Ickes and R. F. Kidd (eds.) *New Directions in Attribution Theory*, vol. 1. Hillsdale, NJ: Erlbaum.

Osgood, C. E., Suci, G. J. and Tannenbaum, P. H. (1957). *The Measurement of Meaning.* Urbana: University of Illinois.

OSS (Office of Strategic Services) (1948). *Assessment of Men.* New York: Rinehart.

Paivio, A. (1965). Personality and audience influence. *Prog. exp. Pers. Res.*, **2**, 127–73.

Parkes, C. (1975). *Bereavement: Studies of Grief in Adult Life.* Harmondsworth: Penguin.

Parsons, T. (1942). Age and sex in the social structure of the United States. *Amer. sociol. Rev.*, **7**, 604–16.

Parsons, T. (1951). *The Social System.* Glencoe, Ill.: Free Press.

Parsons, T. (1961). An outline of the social system. In T. Parsons *et al.* (eds.) *Theories in Society: Foundations of Modern Sociological Theory.* New York: Free Press.

References

Parsons, T., Bales, R. F. and Shils, E. A. (1953). *Family, Socialization and Interaction Process*. New York: Free Press.

Patterson, G. R., McNeal, S., Hawkins, N. and Phelps, R. (1967). Reprogramming the social environment. *J. child. Psychol. Psychiat.*, **8**, 181–95.

Patterson, M. (1973). Compensation in nonverbal immediacy behaviors: a review. *Sociometry*, **36**, 237–352.

Patterson, M. (1976). An arousal model of interpersonal intimacy. *Psychol. Rev.*, **83**, 235–45.

Peabody, D. (1967). Trait inferences: evaluative and descriptive aspects. *J. pers. soc. Psychol. Monogr.*, **7**.

Pearce, P. (1977). 'The social and environmental perceptions of overseas tourists'. Unpublished D. Phil. thesis, University of Oxford.

Pendleton, D. A. and Jaspars, J. M. F. (1979). 'Assessment and theory of communication difficulties in general practice consultations: the doctor's perspective'. Unpublished paper, Dept. of Experimental Psychology, University of Oxford.

Pendleton, D. A. and Wakeford, R. (1980). Training in interpersonal skills for medical students: an evaluation study. Unpublished Paper, University of Oxford.

Pervin, L. A. (1968). Performance and satisfaction as a function of individual–environment fit. *Psychol. Bull.*, **69**, 56–68.

Pervin, L. A. (1976). A free response description approach of person–situation interaction. *J. pers. soc. Psychol.*, **34**, 465–74.

Pervin, L. A. (1978*a*). *Current Controversies and Issues in Personality*. New York: Wiley.

Pervin, L. A. (1978*b*). Definitions, measurements and classifications of stimuli, situations and environments. *Hum. Ecol.*, **6**, 71–105.

Pervin, L. A. and Lewis, M. (eds.) (1978). *Perspectives in Interactional Psychology*. New York: Plenum.

Phares, E. J. (1976). *Locus of Control in Personality*. Morristown, NJ: General Learning Press.

Piaget, J. (1932). *The Moral Judgement of the Child*. London: Kegan Paul.

Pike, K. (1967). *Language in Relation to a Unified Theory of Human Behavior*. The Hague: Mouton.

Piliavin, I., Piliavin, J. and Rodin, J. (1975). Costs, diffusion and the stigmatized victim. *J. pers. soc. Psychol*, **32**, 429–38.

Piliavin, J. and Piliavin, I. (1972). Effect of blood on reactions to a victim. *J. pers. soc. Psychol.*, **23**, 353–61.

Pomazal, R. and Clore, G. (1973). Helping on the highway: the effects of dependency and sex. *J. appl. soc. Psychol.*, **3**, 150–64.

Price, R. H. and Blashfield, R. (1975). Explorations in the taxonomy of behavior settings. *Amer. J. Comm. Psychol.*, **3**, 335–52.

Price, R. H. and Bouffard, D. L. (1974). Behavioral appropriateness and situational constraint as dimensions of social behavior. *J. pers. soc. Psychol.*, **30**, 579–86.

Psathas, G. and Arp, D. J. (1966). A thematic analysis of interviewer's statements in therapy-analogue interviews. In P. J. Stone, D. C. Dunphy, M. S. Smith and D. M. Ogilvie (eds.) *The General Inquirer: a Computer Approach to Content Analysis*. Cambridge, Mass.: MIT Press.

Psychological Corporation (1957). *Wechsler Adult Intelligence Scale*. New York: Psychological Corporation.

References

Rackham, N., Honey, P. and Colbert, M. J. (1971). *Developing Interactive Skills.* Northampton: Wellens.

Rahe, R., Mahan, J. and Arthur, R. (1970). Prediction of near-future health change from subjects' preceding life changes. *J. Psychosom. Res.*, **14**, 401–6.

Rapaport, A. (1969). *House, Form and Culture.* Englewood Cliffs, NJ: Prentice-Hall.

Rapaport, A. (1977). *Human Aspects of Urban Form: Towards a Man–Environment Approach to Urban Form and Design.* Oxford: Pergamon Press.

Rappaport, H. and Katkin, E. (1972). Relationships among manifest anxiety, response to stress, and the perception of autonomic activity. *J. consult. clin. Psychol.*, **38**, 219–24.

Rehm, L. P. and Marston, A. R. (1968). Reduction of social anxiety through modification of self-reinforcement: an instigation therapy technique. *J. consult. clin. Psychol.*, **32**, 565–74.

Reynolds, V. (1976). *The Biology of Human Action.* Reading and San Francisco: W. H. Freeman.

Rich, A. R. and Schroeder, H. E. (1976). Research issues in assertiveness training. *Psychol. Bull.*, **83**, 1081–96.

Richardson, E. (1967). *The Environment of Learning.* London: Nelson.

Richardson, F. and Tasto, D. (1976). Development and factor analysis of a social anxiety inventory. *Behav. Ther.*, **7**, 453–62.

Rim, Y. (1976). A note on personality, psychological disturbance and difficulties in social groups in two cultures. *Interpersonal Develpm.*, **6**, 91–5.

Rips, L. J., Shoben, E. J. and Smith, E. E. (1973). Semantic distance and the verification of semantic relations. *J. verb. Learn. verb. Behav.*, **12**, 1–20.

Robbins, R. (1965). 'The effects of cohesiveness and anxiety on self disclosure under threatening conditions'. Unpublished Ph.D. thesis, University of Missouri.

Robinson, W. P. (1965). The elaborated code in working class language. *Lang. Speech*, **8**, 243–52.

Robinson, W. P. (1972). *Language and Social Behaviour.* Harmondsworth: Penguin.

Robson, R. A. H. (1967). 'The effects of different group sex compositions on support and coalition formation'. Paper given to the Canadian Sociology and Anthropology Association, University of British Columbia.

Rogers, C. (1961). *On Becoming a Person.* Boston, Mass.: Houghton Mifflin.

Rohe, W. and Patterson, A. (1974). 'The effects of varied levels of resources and density on behavior in a day care center'. Environmental Design Research Association Paper, Milwaukee. (Cited in Wrightsman, 1977.)

Rommetveit, R. (1974). *On Message Structure: a conceptual Framework for the Study of Language and Communication.* New York: Wiley.

Rommetveit, R. and Blakar, R. M. (eds.) (1979). *Studies of Language, Thought and Verbal Communication.* New York and London: Academic Press.

Rosenberg, L. (1961). Group size, prior experience and conformity. *J. abnorm. soc. Psychol.*, **63**, 436–7.

Rosenberg, M. (1957). *Occupations and Values.* Glencoe, Ill.: Free Press.

Rosengren, W. and de Vault, S. (1963). The sociology of time and space in an obstetrical hospital. In H. M. Proshansky *et al.* (eds.) *Environmental Psychology.* New York: Holt, Rinehart and Winston.

References

Rosenshine, B. (1971). *Teaching Behaviours and Student Achievement*. Slough: National Foundation for Educational Research.

Rosenthal, R. (1966). *Experimenter Effects in Behavior Research*. New York: Appleton-Century-Crofts.

Rosenthal, R. and Rosnow, R. (eds.) (1969). *Artifacts in Behavioral Research*. New York and London: Academic Press.

Ross, A. (1971). Effect of increased responsibility on bystander intervention: the presence of children. *J. pers. soc. Psychol.*, **19**, 306–10.

Ross, J. R. (1970). On declarative sentences. In R. A. Jacobs and P. S. Rosenbaum (eds.) *Readings in English Transformational Grammar*. Waltham, Mass.: Ginn-Blaisdell.

Rotter, J. (1954). *Social Learning and Clinical Psychology*. Englewood Cliffs, NJ: Prentice-Hall.

Rotter, J. (1955). The role of the psychological situation in determining the direction of human behavior. *Nebraska Symposium on Motivation*, **3**, 245–68.

Rotton, J., Barry, T., Frey, J. and Soler, E. (1976). 'Air pollution and interpersonal attraction'. Unpublished paper, University of Dayton. (Cited in Baron and Byrne (1977).)

Rubin, J. (1962). Bilingualism in Paraguay. *Anthrop. Ling.*, **4**(1), 52–8.

Ruesch, J. and Kees, W. (1972). *Nonverbal Communication*. Berkeley: University of California Press.

Runkel, P. J. (1956). Cognitive similarity in facilitating communication. *Sociometry*, **19**, 178–91.

Runyan, W. M. (1978). The life-course as a theoretical orientation: sequences of person-situation interaction. *J. Pers.*, **46**, 569–91.

Rushton, J. P. (1976). Socialization and the altruistic behavior of children. *Psychol. Bull.*, **83**, 898–913.

Rutter, D. R. (1976). Visual interaction in recently admitted and chronic long-stay schizophrenic patients. *Brit. J. soc. clin. Psychol.*, **15**, 295–303.

Ryan, A. (1970). *The Philosophy of the Social Sciences*. New York: Pantheon Books.

Sacks, H. (1972). Notes on police assessment of moral character. In D. Sudnow (ed.) *Studies in Social Interaction*. London: Collier-Macmillan.

Sakoda, J. M. (1952). Factor analysis of OSS situational tests. *J. abnorm. soc. Psychol.*, **47**, 843–52.

Sanchez-Craig, M. (1979). 'Reappraisal therapy: a self-control strategy for abstinence and controlled drinking'. Unpublished paper, Addiction Research Foundation, Toronto.

Sandell, R. G. (1968). Effects of attitudinal and situational factors on reported choice behavior. *J. market. Res.*, **5**, 405–8.

Sarason, I. G. and Ganzer, V. J. (1971). *Modeling: an Approach to the Rehabilitation of Juvenile Offenders*. Washington DC: US Dept. of Health, Education and Welfare.

Sarbin, T. R. and Allen, V. L. (1968). Role theory. In G. Lindzey and E. Aronson (eds.) *The Handbook of Social Psychology*, vol. 1. Reading, Mass.: Addison-Wesley.

Saskatchewan Newstart (1972). *Socanic Coaching Manual*. Prince Albert, Sask.: Dept of Manpower and Immigration.

Saussure, F. de (1916). *Cours de linguistique générale*. Paris: Payot. (English trans. by

W. Baskin as *Course in General Linguistics*. New York: Philosophical Library (1955).)

Schachter, S. (1959). *The Psychology of Affiliation: Experimental Studies of the Sources of Gregariousness*. Stanford: Stanford University Press.

Schachter, S. and Singer, J. E. (1962). Cognitive, social and physiological determinants of emotional state. *Psychol. Rev.*, **69**, 379–99.

Schank, R. E. and Abelson, R. P. (1977). *Scripts, Plans, Goals and Understanding*. Hillsdale, NJ: Erlbaum.

Scheff, T. (1966). *Being Mentally Ill*. Chicago: Aldine.

Scheflen, A. E. (1973). *How Behavior Means*. New York: Gordon and Breach.

Scheflen, A. E. and Scheflen, A. (1972). *Body Language and the Social Order*. Englewood Cliffs, NJ: Prentice-Hall.

Schegloff, E. and Sacks, H. (1973). Opening up closings. *Semiotica*, **8**, 289–327.

Scherer, K. R. (1979). Nonlinguistic indicators of emotion and psychopathology. In C. E. Izard (ed.) *Emotions in Personality and Psychopathology*. New York: Plenum.

Schneider, D. (1973). Implicit personality theory: a review. *Psychol. Bull.*, **79**, 294–309.

Schultz, L. (1960). The wife assaulter. *J. soc. Ther.*, **6**, 103–11.

Schulz, R. and Barefoot, J. (1974). Nonverbal responses and affiliative conflict theory. *Brit. J. soc. clin. Psychol.*, **13**, 237–43.

Schutz, W. C. (1967). *Joy*. New York: Grove Press.

Scott, M. B. and Lyman, S. (1968). Accounts. *Amer. sociol. Rev.*, **33**, 46–62.

Scottish Education Department (1977). *Report of the Working Group on Football Crowd Behaviour*. Edinburgh: HMSO.

Searle, J. (1969). *Speech Acts: an Essay in the Philosophy of Language*. London: Cambridge University Press.

Sears, R. R., Maccoby, E. E. and Levin, H. (1957). *Patterns of Child Rearing*. New York: Row, Peterson.

Secord, P. F. and Backman, C. W. (1974). *Social Psychology*, 2nd edn. New York: McGraw-Hill.

Secord, P. F., Bevan, W. and Katz, B. (1956). The Negro stereotype and perceptual accentuation. *J. abnorm. soc. Psychol.*, **53**, 78–83.

Segal, M. (1974). Alphabet and attraction: an unobtrusive measure of the effect of propinquity in a field setting. *J. pers. soc. Psychol.*, **30**, 654–7.

Sells, S. (1963). *Stimulus Determinants of Behavior*. New York: Ronald Press.

Sewell, W. R. D. (1971). Environmental perception and attitudes of engineers and public health officials. *Envir. Behav.*, **3**, 23–56.

Sewell, W. R. D. and Little, B. R. (1973). Specialists, laymen and the process of environmental appraisal. *Regional Studies*, **7**, 161–71.

Sharp, L. (1952). Steel axes for stone-age Australians. *Hum. Org.*, **11**(2), 17–22.

Shaw, M. E. (1964). Communication networks. *Adv. exp. soc. Psychol.*, **1**, 111–47.

Shaw, M. E. and Gilchrist, J. C. (1956). Intra-group communication and leader choice. *J. soc. Psychol.*, **43**, 133–8.

Shedletsky, R. and Endler, N. (1974). Anxiety: the state–trait model and the interaction model. *J. Pers.*, **42**, 511–27.

Sherif, C. W. (1976). *Orientation in Social Psychology*. New York: Harper and Row.

Sherif, M., Harvey, O. J., White, B. J., Hood, W. R. and Sherif, C. W. (1961). *Intergroup Conflict and Cooperation: the Robber's Cave Experiment*. Norman, Okla.: University Books Exchange.

Sherif, M. and Sherif, C. W. (1953). *Groups in Harmony and Tension*. New York: Harper and Row.

Sherrod, D. and Downs, R. (1974). Environmental determinants of altruism: the effects of stimulus overload and perceived control on helping. *J. exp. soc. Psychol.*, **10**, 468–79.

Sherrod, D., Hage, J., Halpern, P. and Moore, D. (1977). Effects of personal causation and perceived control on responses to an aversive environment: the more control, the better. *J. exp. soc. Psychol.*, **13**, 14–27.

Short, J., Williams, E. and Christie, B. (1976). *The Social Psychology of Telecommunication*. New York: Wiley.

Shure, G. H., Rogers, M. S., Larsen, I. M. and Tassone, J. (1962). Group planning and task effectiveness. *Sociometry*, **25**, 263–82.

Sidney, E., Brown, M. and Argyle, M. (1973). *Skills with People*. London: Hutchinson.

Silverman, I. (1977). *The Human Subject in the Psychological Laboratory*. New York: Pergamon Press.

Simmel, G. (1950). 'The stranger'. In K. Wolff, *The Sociology of Georg Simmel*. New York: Free Press.

Simon, A. and Boyer, E. G. (eds.) (1974). *Mirrors for Behavior*, 3rd edn. *Classroom Interaction Newsletter*.

Simonson, N. (1973). 'Self disclosure and psychotherapy'. Unpublished paper, University of Massachusetts. Cited in Chaikin, A. and Derlega, V. (1976).

Sinclair, J. McH. and Coulthard, R. M. (1975). *Towards an Analysis of Discourse*. London: Oxford University Press.

Siporin, M. (1972). Situational assessment and intervention. *Social Casework*, **68**, 91–109.

Sissons, M. (1971). The psychology of social class. In *Money, Wealth and Class*. Bletchley, Bucks.: Open University Press.

Sistrunk, D. and McDavid, J. (1971). Sex variables in conforming behavior. *J. pers. soc. Psychol.*, **17**, 200–7.

Sivadon, P. (1970). Space as experienced: therapeutic implications. In W. Proshansky, W. Ittelson and L. Rivlin. (eds.) *Environmental Psychology: Man and his Physical Setting*. New York: Holt, Rinehart and Winston.

Slater, P. J. B. (1973). Describing sequences of behaviour. In P. P. G. Bateson and P. H. Klopfer (eds.) *Perspectives in Ethology*. New York and London: Plenum.

Slater, P. J. B. (1977). *The Measurement of Intrapersonal Space by Grid Technique*. New York: Wiley.

Slobin, D., Miller, S. and Porter, L. (1968). Forms of address and social relations in a business organization. *J. pers. soc. Psychol.*, **8**, 289–93.

Smith, B. O., Meux, M. O., Coombs, J., Nuthall, G. A. and Precians, R. (1967). *Studies in the Strategies of Teaching*. Urbana, Ill.: Bureau of Educational Research, University of Illinois.

Smith, M. B., Bruner, J. S. and White, R. W. (1956). *Opinions and Personality*. New York: Wiley.

Smith, P. (1974). Aspects of the playgroup environment. In D. Canter and T. Lee (eds.) *Psychology and the Built Environment*. London: Architectural Press.

Smith, P. and Curnow, R. (1966). 'Arousal hypothesis' and the effect of music on purchasing behavior. *J. appl. Psychol.*, **50**, 255–6.

Sommer, R. (1969). *Personal Space*. Englewood Cliffs, NJ: Prentice-Hall.

Sommer, R. and Becker, F. (1969). Territorial defense and the good neighbor. *J. pers. soc. Psychol.*, **11**, 85–92.

Sommer, R. and Osmond, H. (1961). Symptoms of institutional care. *Soc. Prob.*, **8**, 254–63.

Sommer, R. and Peterson, P. (1967). Study of careers re-examined. *College and Research Libraries News*, July, 263–72.

Sommer, R. and Ross, H. (1958). Social interaction on a geriatrics ward. *Int. J. soc. Psychiat.*, **4**, 128–33.

Spielberger, C. (1966). Theory and research on anxiety. In C. Spielberger (ed.) *Anxiety and Behavior*. New York and London: Academic Press.

Spielberger, C. (ed.) (1972a). *Anxiety: Current Trends in Theory and Research*, vol. 2. New York and London: Academic Press.

Spielberger, C. (1972b). Conceptual and methodological issues in research on anxiety. In C. Spielberger (ed.) *Anxiety: Current Trends in Theory and Research*, vol. 1. New York and London: Academic Press.

Spielberger, C. (1978). *Stress and Anxiety*, vol. 5. New York: Wiley.

Spielberger, C., Gorsuch, R. and Lushene, R. (1970). *Manual for the State–Trait Anxiety Inventory*. Palo Alto, Calif.: Consulting Psychologists Press.

Spielberger, C. and Smith, L. (1966). Anxiety (drive), stress and serial position effects in serial-verbal learning. *J. exp. Psychol.*, **72**, 589–95.

Sports Council and SSRC (1978). *Public Disorder and Sporting Events*. London: Sports Council and SSRC.

Staples, L. M. and Robinson, W. P. (1974). Address forms used by members of a departmental store. *Brit. J. soc. clin. Psychol.*, **13**, 131–42.

Staub, E. (1970). A child in distress: the influence of age and number of witnesses on children's attempts to help. *J. pers. soc. Psychol.*, **14**, 130–40.

Staub, E. (1971). Helping a person in distress: the influence of implicit and explicit 'rules' of conduct of children and adults. *J. pers. soc. Psychol.*, **17**, 137–44.

Steer, A. B. (1972). 'Transition points in social encounters'. Paper given to British Psychological Society. (Dept of Psychology, Birkbeck College, London.)

Steer, A. B. and Lake, J. (1972). 'Nonverbal cues in the termination of encounters: an example of a transition point in social interaction'. Unpublished paper given at British Psychological Society Conference, Oxford.

Steinzor, B. (1950). The spatial factor in face to face discussion groups. *J. abnorm. soc. Psychol.*, **45**, 522–55.

Stern, G. G. (1969). *People in Context: the Measurement of Environmental Interaction in School and Society*. New York: Wiley.

Stern, G. G., Stein, M. I. and Bloom, B. S. (1956). *Methods in Personality Assessment of Human Behavior in Complex Social Settings*. New York: Free Press.

Stokols, D. (1972). On the distinction between density and crowding: some implications for future research. *Psychol. Rev.*, **79**, 275–7.

Stokols, D. (1978). Environmental psychology. *Ann. Rev. Psychol.*, **29**, 253–95.

Stokols, D. Group × place transactions: some neglected issues in psychological research on settings. In D. Magnusson (eds.) *Toward a Psychology of Situations: An Interactional Perspective*. New York: Erlbaum (in press).

Stone, G. P. and Farberman, H. A. (eds.) (1970). *Social Psychology through Symbolic Interaction*. Waltham, Mass.: Ginn-Blaisdell.

Stone, P. J., Dunphy, D. C., Smith, M. S. and Ogilvie, D. M. (1966). *The General Inquirer: a Computer Approach to Content Analysis*. Cambridge, Mass.: MIT Press.

Storms, M. D. (1973). Videotape and the attribution process: reversing actors' and observers' points of view. *J. pers. soc. Psychol.*, **27**, 165–75.

Storms, M. D. and Nisbett, R. E. (1970). Insomnia and the attribution process. *J. pers. soc. Psychol.*, **16**, 319–28.

Stratton, T. T. and Moore, C. L. (1977). Application of the robust factor concept to the fear survey schedule. *J. behav. Ther. exp. Psychiat.*, **8**, 229–35.

Stringer, P. H. (1973). Do dimensions have face validity? In M. von Cranach and I. Vine (eds.) *Social Communication and Movement.* New York and London: Academic Press.

Stringer, P. H. (1974). Individual differences in repertory grid measures for a cross section of the female population. In D. Canter and T. Lee (eds.) *Psychology and the Built Environment.* London: Architectural Press.

Stroebe, W., Thompson, V. D., Insko, C. A. and Reisman, S. R. (1970). Balance and differentiation in the evaluation of linked attitude objects. *J. pers. soc. Psychol.*, **16**, 38–47.

Strupp, H. H. and Wallach, M. S. (1965). A further study of psychiatrists' responses in quasi-therapy situations. *Behav. Sci.*, **10**, 113–34.

Sue, W. and Sue, D. (1977). Barriers to effective cross-cultural counseling. *J. counsel. Psychol.*, **24**, 420–9.

Sutton-Smith, B. and Rosenberg, B. G. (1970). *The Sibling.* New York: Holt, Rinehart and Winston.

Swart, C. and Berkowitz, L. (1976). Effects of a stimulus associated with a victim's pain on later aggression. *J. pers. soc. Psychol.*, **33**, 623–31.

Sykes, G. M. and Matza, D. (1957). Techniques of neutralization: a theory of delinquency. *Amer. sociol. Rev.*, **22**, 664–70.

Taba, H. (1966). *Teaching Strategies and Cognitive Functioning in Elementary School Children.* USOE Cooperative Research Project No. 2404. San Francisco: San Francisco State College.

Tagiuri, R. (1958). Social preference and its perception. In R. Tagiuri and L. Petrullo (eds.) *Person Perception and Interpersonal Behavior.* Stanford: Stanford University Press.

Tajfel, H. (1957). Value and the perceptual judgment of magnitude. *Psychol. Rev.*, **64**, 192–204.

Tajfel, H. (1970). Experiments in intergroup discrimination. *Sci. Amer.*, **223**, 96–102.

Tajfel, H. (1978). The structure of our views about society. In H. Tajfel and C. Fraser (eds.) *Introducing Social Psychology.* Harmondsworth: Penguin Books.

Tajfel, H. and Fraser, C. (1978). *Introducing Social Psychology.* Harmondsworth: Penguin Books.

Tajfel, H. and Wilkes, A. L. (1963). Classification and quantitative judgement. *Brit. J. Psychol.*, **54**, 101–14.

Talland, G. A. (1957). Role and status structure in therapy groups. *J. clin. Psychol.*, **13**, 27–33.

Taylor, D. W., Berry, P. C. and Block, C. H. (1958). Does group participation when brainstorming facilitate or inhibit thinking? *Admin. Sci. Quart.*, **3**, 23–47.

Taylor, S., Gammon, C. and Capasso, D. (1976). Aggression as a function of the interaction of alcohol and threat. *J. pers. soc. Psychol.*, **34**, 938–41.

Thibaut, J. W. and Faucheux, C. (1965). The development of contractual norms in a bargaining situation under two types of stress. *J. exp. soc. Psychol.*, **1**, 89–102.

Thibaut, J. W. and Kelley, H. H. (1959). *The Social Psychology of Groups.* New York: Wiley.

Thomas, E. J. (1957). Effects of facilitative role interdependence on group functioning. *Hum. Relat.*, **10**, 347–66.

Thomas, E. J. and Fink, C. F. (1963). Effects of group size. *Psychol. Bull.*, **60**, 371–84.

Thomas, W. and Thomas, D. S. (1928). *The Child in America.* New York: Knopf.

Thompson, G. G. (1962). *Child Psychology.* Boston, Mass.: Houghton Mifflin.

Thoresen, C. E. and Mahoney, M. J. (1974). *Behavioral Self-control.* New York: Holt, Rinehart and Winston.

Thurley, J. and Wirdenius, H. (1973). *Supervision: a Reappraisal.* London: Heinemann.

Toch, H. (1969). *Violent Men: an Inquiry into the Psychology of Violence.* Harmondsworth: Penguin.

Tomkins, S. (1963). Shame-humiliation and the taboo on looking. In S. Tomkins (ed.) *Affect, Imagery and Consciousness*, vol. 2. New York: Springer.

Triandis, H. C. (1960). Cognitive similarity and communication in a dyad. *Hum. Relat.*, **13**, 175–83.

Trist, E. L., Higgin, G. W., Murray, H. and Pollock, A. B. (1963). *Organizational Choice.* London: Tavistock.

Trites, D., Galbraith, F., Sturdevant, M. and Leckwary, J. (1970). Influence of nursing-unit design on the activities and subjective feelings of nursing personnel. *Envir. Behav.*, **11**, 303–34.

Trower, P., Bryant, B. and Argyle, M. (1978). *Social Skills and Mental Health.* London: Methuen.

Truax, C. B. and Mitchell, K. M. (1971). Research on certain therapist interpersonal skills in relation to process and outcome. In A. E. Bergin and S. L. Garfield (eds.) *Handbook of Psychotherapy and Behavior Change.* New York: Wiley.

Tucker, L. (1966). Some mathematical notes on three-mode factor analysis, *Psychometrika*, **31**, 279–311.

Tuckman, B. W. (1965). Developmental sequence in small groups. *Psychol. Bull.*, **63**, 384–99.

Turner, J. (1973). 'Competition and category-conflict: self versus group for social value versus economic gain'. PhD thesis, University of Bristol.

Twentyman, C. and McFall, R. (1975). Behavioral training in social skills in shy males. *J. consult. clin. Psychol.*, **43**, 384–95.

Twining, W. and Miers, D. (1976). *How to do Things with Rules.* London: Weidenfeld and Nicolson.

Van Hooff, J. A. R. A. M. (1973). Structural analysis of the social behaviour of a semi-captive group of chimpanzees. In M. von Cranach and I. Vine (eds.) *Social Communication and Movement.* New York and London: Academic Press.

Vaughan, G. (1964). The trans-situational aspect of conforming behavior. *J. Pers.*, **32**, 335–54.

Veitch, R. and Griffitt, W. (1976). Good news, bad news: affective and interpersonal effects. *J. appl. soc. Psychol.*, **6**, 69–75.

Verby, J. E., Holden, P. and Davis, R. H. (1979). Peer review of consultations in primary care: the use of audiovisual recordings. *Brit. med. J.*, i, 1686–8.

Vernon, P. E. (1964). *Personality Assessment.* London: Methuen.

Vroom, V. H. (1964). *Work and Motivation*. New York: Wiley.

Walster, E., Aronson, V., Abrahams, D. and Rottman, L. (1966). Importance of physical attractiveness in dating behavior. *J. pers. soc. Psychol.*, **4**, 508–16.

Walster, E. and Piliavin, J. (1972). Equity and the innocent bystander. *J. soc. Issues*, **28**, 165–89.

Walters, R. H. and Parkes, R. D. (1964). Social motivation, dependency and susceptibility to social influence. *Adv. exp. soc. Psychol.*, **1**, 232–76.

Warr, P. B. (1965). Proximity as a determinant of positive and negative sociometric choice. *Brit. J. soc. clin. Psychol.*, **4**, 104–9.

Warr, P. B. (ed.) (1971). *Psychology at work*. Harmondsworth: Penguin.

Warr, P. B., and Knapper, C. (1968). *The Perception of People and Events*. New York: Wiley.

Watson, O. (1972). *Proxemic Behaviour: Cross-Cultural Study*. The Hague: Mouton.

Watson, O. and Friend, R. (1969). Measurement of social-evaluative anxiety. *J. consult. clin. Psychol.*, **33**, 448–57.

Watson, O. and Graves, T. (1966). Quantitative research in proxemic behavior. *Amer. Anthrop.*, **68**, 971–85.

Watzlawick, P., Beavin, J. H. and Jackson, D. D. (1967). *Pragmatics of Human Communication*. New York: Norton.

Webb, E., Campbell, D., Schwartz, R. and Sechrest, L. (1966). *Unobtrusive Measures: Nonreactive Research in the Social Sciences*. Chicago: Rand McNally.

Weiner, B. (1980). *Human Motivation*. New York: Holt, Rinehart and Winston.

Weiner, M. J. and Wright, F. E. (1973). Effects of undergoing arbitrary discrimination upon subsequent attitudes toward a minority group. *J. appl. soc. Psychol.*, **3**, 94–102.

Wells, B. (1965). The psycho-social influence of building environments: sociometric findings in large and small office spaces. *Build. Sci.*, **1**, 153–65.

Westin, A., (1967). *Privacy and Freedom*. New York: Atheneum.

Whorf, B. L. (1956). *Language, Thought and Reality*. (ed. J. B. Carroll). Cambridge, Mass.: Technology Press.

Whyte, W. F. (1943). *Street Corner Society: the Social Structure of an Italian Slum*. Chicago: Chicago University Press.

Whyte, W. F. (1948). *Human Relations in the Restaurant Industry*. New York: McGraw-Hill.

Wicker, A. (1969). Size of church membership and members' support of church behavior settings. *J. pers. soc. Psychol.*, **13**, 278–88.

Wicker, A. (1971). An examination of the 'other variables' explanation of attitude–behaviour inconsistency. *J. pers. soc. Psychol.*, **19**, 18–30.

Wicker, A. (1973). Undermanning theory and research. *Rep. Res. soc. Psychol.*, **4**, 185–206.

Wicker, A., McGrath, J. and Armstrong, G. (1972). Organisation size and behavior setting capacity as determinants of member participation. *Behav. Sci.*, **17**, 499–513.

Wiesenthal, D., Koza, P., Edwards, J., Walton, A., Endler, N. and Emmott, S. (1978). Trends in conformity research. *Canad. psychol. Rev.*, **19**, 41–58.

Williams, F. and Naremore, R. (1969). Social class differences in children's syntactic performance: a quantitative analysis of field study data. *J. Speech Hear. Res.*, **12**, 778–93.

Wilson, L. and Rogers, R. W. (1975). The fire this time: effects of race of target, insult, and potential retaliation on black aggression. *J. pers. soc. Psychol.*, **32**, 857–64.

Wilson, W., Chun, N. and Kayatani, M. (1965). Projection, attraction and strategy choices in intergroup competition. *J. pers. soc. Psychol.*, **2**, 432–35.

Winch, P. (1958). *The Idea of a Social Science*. London: Routledge and Kegan Paul.

Winter, W. D. and Ferreira, A. J. (1967). Interaction process analysis of family decision-making. *Family Process*, **6**, 155–72.

Wish, M., Deutsch, M. and Kaplan, S. J. (1976). Perceived dimensions of interpersonal relations. *J. pers. soc. Psychol.*, **33**, 409–20.

Wish, M. and Kaplan, S. J. (1977). Toward an implicit theory of interpersonal communication. *Sociometry*, **40**, 234–46.

Wittgenstein, L. (1953). *Philosophical Investigations*. Oxford: Blackwell.

Wohlwill, J. and Heft, H. (1978). Environments fit for the developing child. In H. McGurk (ed.) *Ecological Factors in Human Development*. Amsterdam: North-Holland.

Wolff, K. (1964). Definition of the situation. In J. Gould and W. Kolb (eds.) *A Dictionary of the Social Sciences*. London: Tavistock.

Wolfram, W. A. (1969). *A Sociolinguistic Description of Detroit Negro Speech*. Washington, DC: Center for Applied Linguistics.

Wolpe, J. and Lazarus, A. (1966). *Behavior Therapy Techniques*. New York: Pergamon Press.

Woodward, J. (1960). *The Saleswoman*. London: Pitman.

Woodward, J. (1965). *Industrial Organization: Theory and Practice*. London: Oxford University Press.

Wortman, C. B. (1975). Some determinants of perceived control. *J. pers. soc. Psychol.*, **31**, 282–94.

Wright, B. and Rainwater, L. (1962). The meanings of color. *J. gen. Psychol.*, **67**, 89–99.

Wright, C. J. and Nuthall, G. (1970). Relationships between teacher behavior and pupil achievement in three experimental elementary science lessons. *Amer. educ. Res. J.*, **7**, 477–91.

Wrightsman, L. S. (1977). *Social Psychology*. Monterey, Calif.: Brooks/Cole.

Yakimovich, D. and Saltz, E. (1971). Helping behavior: the cry for help. *Psychonom. Sci.*, **23**, 427–8.

Yancey, W. L. (1971). Architecture, interaction, and social control: the case of a large-scale public housing project. *Envir. Behav.*, **3**(1), 3–18.

Young, B. (1969). The effects of sex, assigned therapist or peer role, topic intimacy and expectations of partner compatibility on dyadic communication patterns. *Diss. Abstr.*, **30**, 857B.

Young, E., Rimm, D. and Kennedy, T. (1973). An experimental investigation of modeling and verbal reinforcement in the modification of assertive behavior. *Behav. Res. Ther.*, **11**, 317–19.

Zajonc, R. (1968). Attitudinal effects of mere exposure. *J. pers. soc. Psychol. Monogr. Suppl.*, **9**, 1–27.

Zanna, M. P. and Cooper, J. (1976). Dissonance and the attribution process. In J. H. Harvey, W. J. Ickes and R. F. Kidd (eds.) *New Directions in Attribution Theory*. Hillsdale, NJ: Erlbaum.

Zeichner, A., Wright, J. and Herman, S. (1977). Effects of situation on dating and assertive behavior. *Psychol. Rep.*, **40**, 375–81.

Zigler, E. and Child, I. L. (1969). Socialization. In G. Lindzey and E. Aronson (eds.) *The Handbook of Social Psychology*. Reading, Mass.: Addison-Wesley.

Zimbardo, P. G. (1973). A Pirandellian prison. *New York Times Sunday Magazine*, 8 Apr., 38–60.

Zipf, G. K. (1949). *Human Behavior and the Principle of Least Effort*. Cambridge, Mass.: Addison-Wesley.

Zuckerman, M. (1974). The sensation seeking motive. In B. A. Maher (ed.) *Progress in Experimental Personality Research*, vol. 7. New York and London: Academic Press.

Zuckerman, M. (1977). Development of a situation specific trait state test for the prediction and measurement of affective responses. *J. consult. clin. Psychol.*, **45**, 512–23.

Zuckerman, M. (1978). Sensation seeking and psychopathy. In R. Hare and D. Schalling (eds.) *Psychopathic Behavior*. New York: Wiley.

Names index

Abelson, R. P. 5, 70, 222, 242
Abrahams, B. 241
Abrahams, D. 382
Ainsworth, M. D. S. 185
Alker, H. 36
Allen, A. 14
Allen, V. L. 169, 177
Allport, G. W. 14
Altman, I. 66, 267, 275, 285
Anastasi, A. 376
Anderson, N. 394
Anderson, R. 385
Andrews, W. R. 319
Annis, R. C. 26
Applegate, J. L. 299
Appley, M. H. 73
Argyle, M. 1, 2, 10, 12, 15, 28, 32, 36,
    37, 59, 60, 61, 74, 75, 77, 82, 104, 134,
    149, 168, 169, 173, 174, 175, 194, 210,
    216, 223, 226, 232, 235, 236, 265, 294,
    319, 325, 334, 344, 352, 364, 369, 370,
    372, 378, 380, 392, 394, 397, 398
Arnold, W. 3
Aronson, V. 382
Arp, D. J. 192
Arthur, R. 320
Asch, S. E. 26, 55
Atkinson, J. W. 68, 79, 83, 86
Aubrey, S. 61
Auerbach, A. H. 192
Auld, F. 192
Austin, J. 181, 194, 294
Avedon, E. M. 6, 31
Avigdor, R. 237

Back, K. 53
Backman, C. W. 373
Bacon, M. 26
Baddely, A. 281
Bales, R. F. 72, 167, 174, 175, 180, 183,
    184, 185, 187, 188, 189, 191, 193, 197,
    201, 202, 220; in Parsons *et al.* 27,
    166, 171, 175
Ball, D. W. 17, 244
Bandura, A. 44

Bannister, D. 233
Banton, M. 373
Barefoot, J. 60
Barker, R. G. 5, 22, 23, 34, 37, 270,
    286, 289
Barnes, R. M. 195
Baron, R. A. 44, 45, 83, 280, 369
Barry, H. 26
Barry, T. 281
Bastien, S. 49
Bates, E. 224
Batson, C. 46
Baum, A. 43
Bearden, W. O. 373
Beattie, G. W. 61
Becker, F. 275
Becker, S. 55
Beil-Warner, D. 51
Beit-Hallahmi, B. 1, 28
Belk, R. W. 41, 373, 374
Bell, P. 44, 280
Bell, R. T. 296
Bell, S. M. 185
Bellack, A. A. 218
Bellack, A. S. 328, 365
Bem, D. J. 14, 36
Bennett, B. 277
Bennett, D. 268
Bennett, J. 268
Bennis, W. G. 166
Berger, P. L. 17, 128, 243
Berkowitz, L. 45
Berne, E. 217
Bernstein, B. 297, 298, 299, 312, 313,
    315, 317, 332, 335
Berry, J. W. 26
Berry, P. C. 379
Best, J. A. 367
Bevan, W. 238
Bickman, L. 49
Biddle, B. J. 165, 189
Bierhof, H. W. 240
Bierhof-Alferman, D. 240
Billig, M. 18
Birdwhistell, R. 180, 211

441

Names index

Subject index